BEHIND THE SCENES IN

American Government

Peter Woll BRANDEIS UNIVERSITY

BEHIND THE SCENES IN
American Government

Personalities and Politics

Fourth Edition

LITTLE, BROWN AND COMPANY
Boston   Toronto

Library of Congress Cataloging in Publication Data

Main entry under title:

Behind the scenes in American government.

    Includes bibliographical references.
    1. Politicians—United States—Addresses, essays,
lectures.   2. Statesmen—United States—Addresses,
essays, lectures.   3. United States—Politics and
government—20th century—Addresses, essays, lectures.
I. Woll, Peter, 1933–
JK271.B533   1983   320.973   82-20389
ISBN 0-316-95152-8

Library of Congress Catalog Card No. 82-20389

ISBN 0-316-95152-8

9   8   7   6   5   4   3   2   1

MU
Published simultaneously in Canada
by Little, Brown & Company (Canada) Limited

Printed in the United States of America

For Rochelle Jones

PREFACE

This book is designed as a supplementary text for introductory American government courses. It is also an exciting complement to a wide range of courses that analyze parties and political campaigning, interest groups and lobbyists, the media and political consultants, the presidency, Congress, the courts, and the bureaucracy.

Politics is, by any measure, fascinating. But this fascination is not often conveyed to students because many books and courses concentrate on structures and processes at the expense of the individuals who constitute the life-blood of politics. And it is, after all, the people in politics who shape its character, just as they themselves are shaped by it. This book illustrates how character and personality affect the political process, and the way in which political institutions such as the presidency may remold the personalities of those who are directly, and sometimes those who are indirectly, involved. The book consists of vignettes of famous politicians, pressure group leaders, journalists and political consultants, members of Congress, White House staffers and presidential advisers, Supreme Court justices, and top-level bureaucrats. By introducing students to the colorful and powerful personalities who are to be found in politics, I hope to make American government the lively subject that it should be.

The fourth edition strengthens the book in several ways. A new chapter has been added to give students a behind-the-scenes glimpse of the world of political reporters and consultants. David Halberstam describes how the *Los Angeles Times* and its star political correspondent launched the career of Richard M. Nixon. The media is always vital to political communications, but direct mail has also become an important means of swaying financial contributors and voters. Richard Viguerie, the undisputed master of the direct mail consultants and the force behind the National Conservative Political Action Committee (NCPAC), is portrayed. The author of the selection, Sidney Blumenthal, rightly calls Viguerie the Postmaster General of the Right. Finally, John Ehrlichman gives a riveting account of the way in which presidents and their aides tend to view the press, and describes how the Nixon White House attempted to manage the news.

The new edition continues to present fresh profiles of important contemporary political figures. Garry Wills provocatively examines how

Edward Kennedy has become the "prisoner of power." *Washington Post* reporter Lou Cannon, Reagan-watcher for well over a decade, gives a fresh perspective on how Reagan's personality and style helped him to win the presidency.

Chapter Two, on pressure groups and lobbyists, is entirely new. A lively *Newsweek* story depicts the entry of the Reverend Jerry Falwell into politics as the leader of the Moral Majority. A portrait of Phyllis Schlafly adds another dimension to the examination of conservative political leaders. The next selections are analyses of prominent Washington power brokers by *Wall Street Journal* reporter Albert Hunt and journalist Steven Emerson. They respectively focus upon the meteoric political careers of Washington attorneys Thomas Boggs, Jr., and Fred Dutton, who are among the most influential lobbyists in the nation's capital.

Chapter Four, "The Presidency" retains James Fallows's penetrating analysis of how the style of President Jimmy Carter hampered strong leadership. George Reedy and John Dean continue to give insider accounts of the environment of the White House and the important role of the presidential staff. A new selection by Henry Kissinger depicts the hard-ball politics of the Nixon White House as the Watergate revelations began to break. David Wise examines "Why the President's Men Stumble" in a new piece that reveals how the character and style of presidents set the ethical tone for the White House and the boundaries of power for presidential subordinates.

New York Times reporter Martin Tolchin adds a new selection to Chapter Five, on the Congress, in his portrayal of Tennessee Republican Howard Baker, who happily found himself in the position of Senate majority leader after the 1980 elections. Roland Evans and Robert Novak provide a historical perspective on Congress in their masterly analysis of how Lyndon B. Johnson ruled the Senate when he was its majority leader. The chapter continues its in-depth depictions of prominent contemporary Capitol Hill figures: Massachusetts Senator Edward Kennedy; West Virginia Senator Robert Byrd, who went from majority to minority leader in the 97th Congress; and Russell Long of Louisiana, who dominated Capitol Hill when he was the chairman of the Finance Committee and continued to play an important role even after he lost the chairmanship to Kansas Senator Robert Dole when the Senate became Republican in 1981. No picture of Congress would be complete without Massachusettes Congressman and House Speaker Thomas P. (Tip) O'Neill, the subject of Jimmy Breslin's lively vignette.

In Chapter Six, the popular selection by Bob Woodard and Scott Armstrong that gives a behind-the-scenes account of the Supreme Court's abortion decision has been retained in this edition, along with Earl Warren's firsthand description of the interplay of personalities in the Court when it confronted the desegregation cases.

The book's concluding chapter on the bureaucracy retains Sanford Unger's classic piece on J. Edgar Hoover ("The King"), and adds a new selection by Jonathan Alter that portrays prominent political entrepreneurs in the bureaucracy, including Admiral Hyman Rickover.

An underlying theme of this book is that the personalities and styles of people in high positions in politics do shape the political process. However, many political scientists, including our first — the framers of the Constitution — believe that structural arrangements can shape and determine human behavior. The framers of our system of government were not particularly concerned with the deeper psychological variants in human beings; they delved into psychopolitics only to the extent of accepting the premise that persons, particularly those entering the political process, are likely to be motivated by self-interest rather than by the national interest.

Thus the framers carefully constructed our system of separation of powers and of checks and balances for the purpose of controlling the baser side of human nature. The safeguards they established offered protection against unbridled political ambition, the pursuit of self-interest in the political process, and the possibility of tyranny. The map of our political system, devised by men such as Alexander Hamilton and James Madison, resembled a military map, with defensive and offensive positions being taken by the armies — the branches of government — and with differing weapons being provided to the combatants. Balancing the forces would ensure that victory would not be certain on any one side, and that after the forces grew exhausted by their perpetual and often futile combat they would seek not unconditional surrender but a negotiated peace settlement. By carefully controlling the conditions of political warfare, the framers hoped to limit governmental power and to shape policy in the people's interest.

James Madison in *Federalist 51* succinctly stated the framers' views on human nature and how it should be controlled within government:

> But the greatest security against a gradual concentration of the several powers in the same department, consists in giving to those who administer each department, the necessary constitutional means, and personal motives, to resist encroachments of the others. The provision for de-

fense must in this, as in all other cases, be made commensurate to the danger of attack. Ambition must be made to counteract ambition. The interest of the man must be connected with the constitutional rights of the place. It may be a reflection on human nature, that such devices should be necessary to control the abuses of government. But what is government itself, but the greatest of all reflections on human nature? If men were angels, no government would be necessary. If angels were to govern men, neither external nor internal controls on government would be necessary. In framing a government, which is to be administered by men over men, the great difficulty lies in this: you must first enable the government to control the governed; and in the next place oblige it to control itself. A dependence on the people is, no doubt, the primary control on the government; but experience has taught mankind the necessity of auxiliary precautions.

The relatively simple governmental model established by the framers to control political evil and at the same time to provide effective government has undergone many changes over the more than a century and a half since the Constitution was ratified. Before the end of the nineteenth century the presidency had developed imperial powers, due not only to historical circumstances but also to the character of the men who had occupied the office from the beginning. Thomas Jefferson, who opposed a strong presidency while he was in Paris at the time the Constitution was framed, ironically changed his mind after his election to the presidency in 1800. The forceful and determined character of Abraham Lincoln helped not only to save the Union but also to establish precedents for the growth of presidential power. The personalities of presidents Theodore Roosevelt, Woodrow Wilson, Franklin D. Roosevelt, Harry S. Truman, John F. Kennedy, Lyndon B. Johnson, Richard M. Nixon, Jimmy Carter, and Ronald Reagan all had a profound effect on the institution of the presidency. Just as presidential character helped to build up the office, it also was responsible for bringing it into temporary disrepute after Watergate. No one would deny that the personality of Richard Nixon played a significant role in the Watergate affair, particularly in the way it was handled in the White House, nor that the personality of Gerald Ford helped to restore dignity to the White House.

Just as the transformations in the presidency have been shaped by the personalities of the men who have held the office, so have changes in other political institutions. The characters of the persons who operate behind the scenes in our political parties, particularly of the political bosses, affect not only grassroots politics and policies, but also the politics adopted by the national parties. Who can deny that many differences in government among cities such as Boston, Philadelphia, New York, and Chicago are due to the contrasting characters of the individuals who have shaped the politics of those cities? States, too, have their political bosses and powerful political leaders who help to determine their political character.

At the national level the personalities of presidential candidates help to shape party policies and the nature of the people drawn to the party. Although the Democratic party was in part responsible for the shaping of Franklin D. Roosevelt, his character and style had a profound effect on the nature of the party as well. The same is true of other forceful presidential candidates. The grueling primary process for selecting delegates to national party conventions, which expanded to thirty-four primaries in 1980, tests certain dimensions of a candidate's character, although not necessarily those attributes that make for a successful president.

As the personalities of party leaders help to shape the nature and role of parties and government, the character of pressure group elites affects the management of those groups, the policies they sponsor, and their style of operation in government. One need only recall such famous labor leaders as John L. Lewis, president of the United Mine Workers during the Roosevelt era; Walter Reuther, who led the United Automobile Workers for so many years; and George Meany, once head of the AFL-CIO, to see how a few men have molded the labor union movement and the policies that the unions have pushed onto government. A personality profile of Ralph Nader would go a long way toward explaining his policies and his success. How Common Cause operates, its belief in democratic government and the possibilities of bringing about change through the electoral process, reflects in large part the character and beliefs of its first leader, John Gardner. The leaders of the New Right and the Moral Majority, such as Richard Viguerie, Phyllis Schlafly, and Jerry Falwell, portrayed in the text, have all had a profound impact upon their political causes. One of the most important and ubiquitous of all pressure groups — the press — is shaped by the personal beliefs and personalities of those who run it and write for it. What one reads in newspapers, magazines, and journals often reflects the beliefs of the writers and editors. Lastly, those who sell their services to influence government, particularly the Washington lawyers, also have their own styles of operation, which frequently derive from their personalities.

Congress is a venerable and highly structured institution, but it too has an important personal dimension, found in the personalities of its leaders and the chairmen of its committees. Legislative styles and policies frequently depend on the characters of congressmen. Congress is composed of men and women who are not simply conduits for the few electoral demands that exist, but who act as they are motivated by their consciences and by their psychological needs for power and status within the institution.

The courts and the bureaucracy were designed to be more nearly neutral politically than were the president and the Congress and such obvious political advocates as parties and pressure groups. The judiciary was to dispense justice impartially and independently of the political arms of government, and the bureaucracy was to administer the laws. But here, too, the characters and personalities of judges and bureaucrats influence how justice is carried out and how laws are implemented.

I would like to thank William Ethridge, whose perceptive and timely editorial judgments and recommendations creatively shaped both the third and fourth editions of this book, and Donald Palm, whose guidance is reflected in this fourth edition. Cynthia Chapin once again skillfully and efficiently guided the manuscript through the production process. Rochelle Jones, to whom the book is dedicated, continues to help keep the author abreast of the Washington political scene. Her suggestions for this as for previous editions have been invaluable and reflect her enthusiasm and originality in many ways. Finally, no acknowledgments would be complete for any of my books without thanks to Barbara Nagy, who for years has made enjoyable what would otherwise be a burdensome writing task.

CONTENTS

*brokers in Washington. In the 1980s his time and political skills are
devoted to the representation of Saudi Arabia, whose interests he
assiduously protects and advances as he plays the Washington
power game.*

*The casual style of the former minority leader and presidential
contender belied an underlying toughness and political virtuosity
that forged a united Republican majority in the Senate behind
President Reagan's program. Martin Tolchin, who covers Congress
for the* New York Times, *portrays a man who became the chief
Republican on Capitol Hill.*

CHAPTER SIX
THE COURTS

CHAPTER SEVEN
THE BUREAUCRACY

BEHIND THE SCENES IN
American Government

POLITICAL PARTIES AND POLITICIANS

Chapter One

In classical democractic theory, political parties are supposed to bridge the gap between people and government. They are to be the principal policymakers, presenting contrasting choices to the electorate so that, by voting, people can participate in the choice of government programs. It is important that a political party have control over its candidates and office-holders, because a party that has a majority in the legislature and controls the executive will then be able to carry out its platform.

Although political parties in an ideal situation are suited to presenting meaningful and realistic policy choices for the electorate, they also serve the personal goals of their active members, which may have nothing at all to do with implementing one public policy instead of another. Roberto Michels, the great European political sociologist of the early twentieth century, draws from German sociologist Max Weber to define the political party as:

> A spontaneous society of propaganda and of agitation seeking to acquire power, in order to procure thereby for its active militant adherents chances, ideal and material, for the realization of either objective aims or of *personal advantages,* or of both. Consequently, the general orientation of the political party, whether in its personal or impersonal aspect, is that of *machtstreben* (striving to power).[1]

In this chapter we will be concerned with the personal motives of active party members. These motives affect the organization and orientation of political parties at national, state, and local levels. The drive for power may completely overshadow party policy. American party leaders are more interested in power than in ideology, and therefore will often shape their policy promises in accordance with the wishes of the majority of the electorate. And, in the absence of any clear electoral desires, which is a common situation, party leaders themselves must determine their actions, which are usually directed toward expanding their power and status in both the party and the government.

[1] Alfred De Grazia, Roberto Michels' *First Lectures in Political Sociology* (Minneapolis: University of Minnesota Press, 1949), p. 134. Italics added.

Their personalities often determine the kinds of decisions they will make, and the way in which they conduct their offices. At the lower levels of parties, particularly in city party machines, the orientation of adherents is often economic security as much as a drive for power. Policy is almost completely irrelevant at these lower echelons.

THE FOLLOWING SELECTION DE-scribes the kinds of people and personalities that controlled the political machine in Chicago, from its powerful leader, Mayor Richard J. Daley, to the men who helped to keep him in office, including precinct workers and captains and city bureau-crats appointed by the mayor to serve the party. Chicago politics clearly revealed a cult of personality in operation. The organization, operations, and policies of the Democratic party in Chicago were a perfect reflection of the personality of Mayor Richard J. Daley.

1 Mike Royko
THE BOSS

KUNSTLER: Mayor Daley, do you hold a position in the Cook County Democratic Committee?

WITNESS: I surely do, and I am very proud of it. I am the leader of my party.

KUNSTLER: What was that?

WITNESS: I surely do, and I am very proud of it. I am the leader of the Democratic party in Cook County.

KUNSTLER: Your honor, I would like to strike from that answer anything about being very proud of it. I only asked whether he had a position in the Cook County Democratic party.

HOFFMAN: I will let the words "I surely do" stand. The words after those may go out and the jury may disregard the expression of the witness that he is very proud of his position.

The Hawk got his nickname because in his younger days he was the outside lookout man at a bookie joint. Then his eyes got weak, and he had to wear thick glasses, so he entered politics as a precinct worker.

He was a hustling precinct worker and brought out the vote, so he was rewarded with a patronage job. The Hawk, who had always loved uniforms but had never worn one, asked his ward committeeman if he could become a member of the county sheriff's police department. They gave him a uniform, badge, and gun, and declared him to be a policeman.

But the Hawk was afraid of firearms, so he asked if he could have a job that didn't require carrying a loaded gun. They put him inside the

From *Boss: Richard J. Daley of Chicago* by Mike Royko. Copyright © 1971 by Mike Royko. Reprinted by permission of the publishers, E. P. Dutton & Co., Inc.

County Building, supervising the man who operated the freight elevator. He liked the job and did such a good job supervising the man who operated the freight elevator that the Hawk was promoted to sergeant.

When a Republican won the sheriff's office, the Hawk was out of work for one day before he turned up in the office of the county treasurer, wearing the uniform of a treasurer's guard. His new job was to sit at a table near the main entrance, beneath the big sign that said "County Treasurer," and when people came in and asked if they were in the county treasurer's office, the Hawk said that indeed they were. It was a good job, and he did it well, but it wasn't what he wanted because he really wasn't a policeman. Finally his committeeman arranged for him to become a member of the secretary of state's special force of highway inspectors, and he got to wear a uniform that had three colors and gold braid.

The Hawk is a tiny piece of the Machine. He is not necessarily a typical patronage worker, but he is not unusual. With about twenty-five thousand people owing their government job to political activity or influence, nothing is typical or unusual.

The Hawk keeps his job by getting out the Democratic vote in his precinct, paying monthly dues to the ward's coffers, buying and pushing tickets to his ward boss's golf outing and $25-a-plate dinners. His reward is a job that isn't difficult, hours that aren't demanding, and as long as he brings out the vote and the party keeps winning elections, he will remain employed. If he doesn't stay in the job he has, they will find something else for him.

Some precinct captains have had more jobs than they can remember. Take Sam, who worked his first precinct forty-five years ago on the West Side.

"My first job was as a clerk over at the election board. In those days to succeed in politics you sometimes had to bash in a few heads. The Republicans in another ward heard about me and they brought me into one of their precincts where they were having trouble. I was brought in as a heavy, and I took care of the problem, so they got me a job in the state Department of Labor. The job was . . . uh . . . to tell the truth, I didn't do anything. I was a payroller. Then later I went to another ward as a Democratic precinct captain, where they were having a tough election. I did my job and I moved over to a job as a state policeman. Then later I was a city gas meter inspector, and a pipe fitter where they had to get me a union card, and an investigator for the attorney general, and when I retired I was an inspector in the Department of Weights and Measures."

The Hawk and Sam, as precinct captains, are basic parts of the Machine. There are some thirty-five hundred precincts in Chicago, and every one of them has a Democratic captain and most captains have assistant captains. They all have, or can have, jobs in government. The better the captain, the better the job. Many make upwards of fifteen thousand dollars a year as supervisors, inspectors, or minor department heads.

They aren't the lowest ranking members of the Machine. Below them are the people who swing mops in the public buildings, dump bedpans in the County Hospital, dig ditches, and perform other menial work. They don't work precincts regularly, although they help out at election time, but they do have to vote themselves and make sure their families vote, buy the usual tickets to political dinners and in many wards, contribute about two percent of their salaries to the ward organization.

Above the precinct captain is that lordly figure the ward committeeman, known in local parlance as "the clout," "the Chinaman," "the guy," and "our beloved leader."

Vito Marzullo is a ward committeeman and an alderman. He was born in Italy and has an elementary school education, but for years when he arrived at political functions, a judge walked a few steps behind him, moving ahead when there was a door to be opened. Marzullo had put him on the bench. His ward, on the near Southwest Side, is a pleasant stew of working class Italians, Poles, Mexicans, and blacks. A short, erect, tough, and likable man, he has had a Republican opponent only once in four elections to the City Council. Marzullo has about four hundred patronage jobs given to him by the Democratic Central Committee to fill. He has more jobs than some ward bosses because he has a stronger ward, with an average turnout of something like 14,500 Democrats to 1,200 Republicans. But he has fewer jobs than some other wards that are even stronger. Marzullo can tick off the jobs he fills:

"I got an assistant state's attorney, and I got an assistant attorney general, I got an electrical inspector at twelve thousand dollars a year, and I got street inspectors and surveyors, and a county highway inspector. I got an administrative assistant to the zoning board and some people in the secretary of state's office. I got fifty-nine precinct captains and they all got assistants, and they all got good jobs. The lawyers I got in jobs don't have to work precincts, but they have to come to my ward office and give free legal advice to the people in the ward."

Service and favors, the staples of the precinct captain and his ward boss. The service may be nothing more than the ordinary municipal functions the citizen is paying taxes for. But there is always the feeling that they could slip if the precinct captain wants them to, that the garbage pickup might not be as good, that the dead tree might not be cut down.

Service and favors. In earlier days, the captain could do much more. The immigrant family looked to him as more than a link with a new and strange government: he was the government. He could tell them how to fill out their papers, how to pay their taxes, how to get a license. He was the welfare agency, with a basket of food and some coal when things got tough, an entree to the crowded charity hospital. He could take care of it when one of the kids got in trouble with the police. Social welfare agencies and better times took away many of his functions, but later there were still the traffic tickets to fix, the real estate tax assessments he might lower. When a downtown office didn't provide service, he was a direct link to government, somebody to cut through the bureaucracy.

In poor parts of the city, he has the added role of a threat. Don't vote, and you might lose your public housing apartment. Don't vote, and you might be cut off welfare. Don't vote, and you might have building inspectors poking around the house.

In the affluent areas, he is, sometimes, merely an errand boy, dropping off a tax bill on the way downtown, buying a vehicle sticker at City Hall, making sure that the streets are cleaned regularly, sounding out public opinion.

The payoff is on election day, when the votes are counted. If he produced, he is safe until the next election. If he didn't, that's it. "He has to go," Marzullo says. "If a company has a man who can't deliver, who can't sell the product, wouldn't he put somebody else in who can?"

Nobody except Chairman Daley knows precisely how many jobs the Machine controls. Some patronage jobs require special skills, so the jobholder doesn't have to do political work. Some are under civil service. And when the Republicans occasionally win a county office, the jobs change hands. There were more patronage jobs under the old Kelly-Nash Machine of the thirties and forties, but civil service reform efforts hurt the Machine. Some of the damage has been undone by Daley, however, who let civil service jobs slip back into patronage by giving tests infrequently or making them so difficult that few can pass, thus making it necessary to hire "temporary" employees, who stay "temporary" for the rest of their lives. Even civil service employees are subject to political pressures in the form of unwanted transfers, withheld promotions.

On certain special occasions, it is possible to see much of the Machine's patronage army assembled and marching. The annual St. Patrick's Day parade down State Street, with Daley leading the way, is a display of might that knots the stomachs of Republicans. An even more remarkable display of patronage power is seen at the State Fair, when on "Democrat Day" thousands of city workers are loaded into buses, trains, and cars which converge on the fairgrounds outside Springfield. The highlight of the fair is when Daley proudly hoofs down the middle of the grounds' dusty racetrack in ninety-degree heat with thousands of his sweating but devoted workers tramping behind him, wearing old-fashioned straw hats and derbies. The Illinois attorney general's staff of lawyers once thrilled the rustics with a crack manual of arms performance, using Daley placards instead of rifles.

Another reason the size of the patronage army is impossible to measure is that it extends beyond the twenty to twenty-five thousand government jobs. The Machine has jobs at racetracks, public utilities, private industry, and the Chicago Transit Authority, which is the bus and subway system, and will help arrange easy union cards.

Out of the ranks of the patronage workers rise the Marzullos, fifty ward committeemen who, with thirty suburban township committeemen, sit as the Central Committee. For them the reward is more than a comfortable payroll job. If they don't prosper, it is because they are ignoring the advice of their Tammany cousin George Washington Plunkett, who said, "I seen my opportunities and I took 'em." Chicago's ward bosses take 'em, too.

Most of them hold an elective office. Many of the Daley aldermen are ward bosses. Several are county commissioners. Others hold office as county clerk, assessor, or recorder of deeds and a few are congressmen and state legislators. Those who don't hold office are given top jobs running city departments, whether they know anything about the work or not. A ward boss who was given a $28,000-a-year job as head of the city's huge sewer system was asked what his experience was. "About twenty years ago I was a house drain inspector." "Did you ever work in the sewers?" "No, but many a time I lifted a lid to see if they were flowing." "Do you have an engineering background?" "Sort of. I took some independent courses at a school I forget the name of, and in 1932 I was a plumber's helper." His background was adequate: his ward usually carries by fifteen thousand to three thousand votes.

The elective offices and jobs provide the status, identity, and retinue of coat holders and door openers, but financially only the household money. About a third of them are lawyers, and the clients leap at them. Most of the judges came up through the Machine; many are former ward bosses themselves. This doesn't mean cases are always rigged, but one cannot underestimate the power of sentimentality. The political lawyers are greatly in demand for zoning disputes, big real estate ventures, and anything else that brings a company into contact with city agencies. When a New York corporation decided to bid for a lucrative Chicago cable TV franchise, they promptly tried to retain the former head of the city's legal department to represent them.

Those who don't have the advantage of a law degree turn to the old reliable, insurance. To be a success in the insurance field, a ward boss needs only two things: an office with his name on it and somebody in the office who knows how to write policies. All stores and businesses need insurance. Why not force the premium on the friendly ward boss? As Marzullo says, everybody needs favors.

One of the most successful political insurance firms is operated by party ancient Joe Gill. Gill gets a big slice of the city's insurance on public properties, like the Civic Center and O'Hare Airport. There are no negotiations or competitive bidding. The policies are given to him because he is Joe Gill. How many votes does Prudential Life deliver? The city's premiums are about $500,000 a year, giving Gill's firm a yearly profit of as much as $100,000.

Another firm, founded by the late Al Horan, and later operated by his heirs and County Assessor P. J. Cullerton gets $100,000 a year in premiums from the city's park district. Since Cullerton is the man who sets the taxable value of all property in Cook County, it is likely that some big property owners would feel more secure being protected by his insurance.

When the city's sprawling lake front convention hall was built, the insurance business was tossed at the insurance firm founded by George Dunne, a ward boss and County Board president.

Another old-line firm is operated by John D'Arco, the crime syndicate's man in the Central Committee. He represents the First Ward, which includes the Loop, a goldmine of insurable property. D'Arco has never bothered to deny that he is a political appendage of the Mafia, probably because he knows that nobody would believe him. A denial would sound strained in light of his bad habit of being seen with Mafia bosses in public. Besides, the First Ward was controlled by the Mafia long before D'Arco became alderman and ward committeeman.

D'Arco's presence in the Central Committee has sometimes been an embarrassment to Chairman Daley. Despite D'Arco's understandable efforts to be discreet, he can't avoid personal publicity because the FBI is always following the people with whom he associates. When D'Arco announced that he was leaving the City Council because of poor health, while remaining ward committeeman, the FBI leaked the fact that Mafia chief Sam Giancana had ordered him out of the council in a pique over something or other. Giancana could do that, because it is his ward; D'Arco only watches it for him. One of Giancana's relatives has turned up as an aide to a First Ward congressman. Another Giancana relative was elected to the state Senate. At Daley's urging, the First Ward organization made an effort to improve its image by running a young banker for alderman. But the banker finally resigned from the council, saying that being the First Ward's alderman was ruining his reputation.

When he is asked about the First Ward, Daley retreats to the democratic position that the people elect D'Arco and their other representatives, and who is he to argue with the people? He has the authority, as party chairman, to strip the First Ward, or any ward, of its patronage, and there are times when he surely must want to do so. Raids on Syndicate gambling houses sometimes turn up city workers, usually sponsored by the First Ward organization. While he has the authority to take away the jobs, it would cause delight in the press and put him in the position of confirming the Mafia's participation in the Machine. He prefers to suffer quietly through the periodic flaps.

The question is often raised whether he actually has the power, in addition to the authority, to politically disable the Mafia. It has been in city government longer than he has, and has graduated its political lackeys to judgeships, the various legislative bodies, and positions throughout government. While it no longer is the controlling force it was in Thompson's administration, or as arrogantly obvious as it was under Kelly-Nash, it remains a part of the Machine, and so long as it doesn't challenge him but is satisfied with its limited share, Daley can live with it, just as he lives with the rascals in Springfield.

Ward bosses are men of ambition, so when they aren't busy with politics or their outside professions, they are on the alert for "deals." At any given moment, a group of them, and their followers, are either planning a deal, hatching a deal, or looking for a deal.

Assessor Cullerton and a circle of his friends have gone in for buying up stretches of exurban land for golf courses, resorts, and the like. Others hold interests in racetracks, which depend on political goodwill for additional racing dates.

The city's dramatic physical redevelopment has been a boon to the political world as well as the private investors. There are so many deals involving ranking members of the Machine that it has been suggested that the city slogan be changed from *Urbs In Horto*, which means "City in a Garden," to *Ubi Est Mea*, which means "Where's mine?"

From where Daley sits, alone atop the Machine, he sees all the parts, and his job is to keep them functioning properly. One part that has been brought into perfect synchronization is organized labor — perhaps the single biggest factor in the unique survival of the big city organization in Chicago. Labor provides Daley with his strongest personal support and contributes great sums to his campaigns. Daley's roots are deep in organized labor. His father was an organizer of his sheet-metal workers' local, and Bridgeport was always a union neighborhood. With politics and the priesthood, union activity was one of the more heavily traveled roads to success. Daley grew up with Steve Bailey, who became head of the Plumbers' Union, and as Daley developed politically, Bailey brought him into contact with other labor leaders.

Thousands of trade union men are employed by local government. Unlike the federal government and many other cities, Chicago always pays the top construction rate, rather than the lower maintenance scale, although most of the work is maintenance. Daley's massive public works projects, gilded with overtime pay in his rush to cut ribbons before elections, are another major source of union jobs.

His policy is that a labor leader be appointed to every policymaking city board or committee. In recent years, it has worked out this way: the head of the Janitors' Union was on the police board, the park board, the Public Buildings Commission, and several others. The head of the Plumbers' Union was on the Board of Health and ran the St. Patrick's Day parade. The head of the Electricians' Union was vice-president of the Board of Education. The Clothing Workers' Union had a man on the library board. The Municipal Employees' Union boss was on the Chicago Housing Authority, which runs the city's public housing projects. The head of the Chicago Federation of Labor and somebody from the Teamsters' Union were helping run the poverty program. And the sons of union officials find the door to City Hall open if they decide on a career in politics.

The third major part of the Machine is money. Once again, only Daley knows how much it has and how it is spent. As party chairman, he controls its treasury. The spending is lavish. Even when running against a listless nobody, Daley may spend a million dollars. The amount used for "precinct money," which is handed out to the precinct captains and used in any way that helps bring out the Democratic vote, can exceed the entire Republican campaign outlay. This can mean paying out a couple of dollars or a couple of chickens to voters in poor neighborhoods, or bottles of cheap wine in the Skid Row areas. Republicans claim that the Democrats will spend as much as $300,000 in precinct money alone for a city election. To retain a crucial office, such as that of county assessor, hundreds of thousands have been spent on billboard advertising alone. Add to that the TV and radio saturation, and the spending for local campaigning exceeds by far the cost-per-vote level of national campaigning.

The money comes from countless sources. From the patronage army, it goes into the ward offices as dues, and part of it is turned over to party headquarters. Every ward leader throws his annual $25-a-head golf days, corned beef dinners, and picnics. The ticket books are thrust at the patronage workers and they either sell them or, as they say, "eat them," bearing the cost themselves.

There are "ward books," with page after page of advertising, sold by precinct workers to local businesses and other favor-seekers. Alderman Marzullo puts out a 350-page ad book every year, at one hundred dollars a page. There are no blank pages in his book. The ward organizations keep what they need to function, and the rest is funneled to party headquarters.

Contractors may be the biggest of all contributors. Daley's public works program has poured billions into their pockets, and they in turn have given millions back to the party in contributions. Much of it comes from contractors who are favored, despite the seemingly fair system of competitive bidding. In some fields, only a handful of contractors ever bid, and they manage to arrange things so that at the end of the year each has received about the same amount of work and the same profit. A contractor who is not part of this "brotherhood" refrains from bidding on governmental work. If he tries to push his way in by submitting a reasonable bid, which would assure him of being the successful low bidder, he may suddenly find that the unions are unable to supply him with the workers he needs.

Even Republican businessmen contribute money to the Machine, more than they give to Republican candidates. Republicans can't do anything for them, but Daley can.

The Machine's vast resources have made it nearly impossible for Republicans to offer more than a fluttering fight in city elections. Daley, to flaunt his strength and to keep his organization in trim, will crank out four hundred thousand primary votes for himself running unopposed. His opponent will be lucky to get seventy thousand Republicans interested enough to cast a primary vote.

Unlike New York, Los Angeles, and other major cities, Chicago has no independent parties or candidates jumping in to threaten, or at least pull votes away from the leaders. It is no accident. Illinois election laws are stacked against an independent's ever getting his name on a voting machine.

In New York, a regular party candidate needs five thousand signatures on his nominating petitions, and an independent must have seventy-five hundred. With any kind of volunteer organization, an independent can get the names, which is why New York will have half a dozen candidates for mayor.

The requirements are even less demanding in L.A., where a candidate needs a seven-hundred-dollar filing fee and petitions bearing five hundred names. L.A. voters have a dozen or so candidates from which to choose.

But Chicago has never, in this century, had more than two candidates for the office of mayor. The state legislature took care of the threat from troublesome independents years ago.

When Daley files his nominating petitions, he needs about thirty-nine hundred names, a figure based on one-half of one percent of his party's vote in the previous election. Daley usually gets so many names that the petitions have to be brought in by truck. Using the same formula his Republican opponent needs about twenty-five hundred signatures, which isn't difficult, even for a Chicago Republican.

But an independent would have to bring in about sixty to seventy thousand signatures. He needs five percent of the previous total vote cast. And not just anybody's signature: only legally defined independents, those who have not voted in the recent partisan primaries.

That's why there are only two candidates for mayor and the other offices in Chicago — a Republican and a Democrat. And sometimes there aren't even that many, Mayor Kelly having once handpicked his Republican opponent.

The only alternative for an independent is to run as a write-in candidate, a waste of time.

It has never happened, but if an independent somehow managed to build an organization big and enthusiastic enough to find seventy thousand independent voters who would sign his petition, he would probably need an extra thirty thousand signatures to be sure of getting past the Chicago Election Board, which runs the city's elections and rules on the validity of nominating petitions. Names can be ruled invalid for anything short of failing to dot an "i." An illiterate's "X" might be acceptable on a Machine candidate's petition, but the Election Board is meticulous about those of anybody else.

The board used to be run by a frank old rogue, Sidney Holzman, who summed up its attitude toward the aspirations of independents, Republicans, and other foreigners:

"We throw their petitions up to the ceiling, and those that stick are good."

Despite all these safeguards and its lopsided superiority over local opposition, the Machine never fails to run scared. For this reason, or maybe out of habit, it never misses a chance to steal a certain number of votes and trample all over the voting laws. Most of it goes on in the wards where the voters are lower middle class, black, poor white, or on the bottle. To assure party loyalty, the precinct captains merely accompany the voter into the voting machine. They aren't supposed to be sticking their heads in, but that's the only way they can be sure the person votes Democratic. They get away with it because the election judges, who are citizens hired to supervise each polling place, don't protest. The Democratic election judges don't mind, and the Republican election judges are probably Democrats. The Republicans assign poll watchers to combat fraud but they never have enough people to cover all of the precincts. If they prevented the common practices, imaginative precinct captains would merely turn to others. In some wards, politically obligated doctors sign stacks of blank affidavits, attesting to the illness of people they have never seen, thus permitting the precinct captain to vote the people in their homes as absentee voters for reasons of illness. And several investigations have established that death does not always keep a person's vote from being cast.

The aforementioned Holzman was always philosophical about vote fraud, conceding that it occurred, and even saying that "a good precinct captain will always find a way to steal votes," but asserting: "In city elections, we don't have to steal to win. And in state-wide elections, the

Republicans are stealing so much downstate, that all we do is balance it out."

Out of this vast amalgam of patronage, money, special interests, restrictive election laws, and organizational discipline emerge a handful of candidates, and they are what it is supposed to be all about.

Most of them come up through the system, as Daley did, beginning as doorbell ringers, working in the jobs their sponsors got for them, pushing the ward book, buying the tickets, doing the favors, holding the coats, opening the doors, putting in the fix, and inching their way up the organizational ladder, waiting for somebody to die and the chance to go to the legislature, into the City Council, and maybe someday something even bigger.

As hard as a party member may try, and as bright and presentable as he may be, he probably won't make it if he isn't from a strong ward with an influential ward boss. A loyal, hard-working City Hall lawyer can become a judge, if his ward brings in the vote and his sponsor pushes him, while in another ward, where the Republicans dominate and the ward boss just hangs on, the City Hall lawyer can only dream of his black robe.

Judge Wexler, Daley's night school classmate, lived with this problem. Wexler had worked feverishly as the city's chief prosecutor of slum cases, dragging landlords into court, reaping publicity for the mayor's administration, while deftly avoiding the toes of slum landlords who had political connections. For years he trotted into Daley's office with his news clippings. But when slate-making time came around, other people got to be judges.

"My ward committeeman was so weak, he couldn't do anything. I used to ask him for a letter to the Central Committee sponsoring me for a judgeship. You have to have a sponsoring letter. And he'd say: 'A letter for you? I want to be a judge myself, and I'm not getting anywhere.' I would have never made it if it hadn't been for Daley and knowing him from night school. He did it for me personally."

Wexler was fortunate. For the others with ambitions, it is either a strong committeeman and advancement, or an obscure job with nothing to put in the scrap book.

Only one other shortcut exists, and it is part of the system of the Machine: nepotism. A Chicago Rip Van Winkle could awaken to the political news columns and, reading the names, think that time had stood still.

There was Otto Kerner, Cermak's confidante and a federal judge, and he begat Otto Kerner, governor, federal judge, and husband of Cermak's daughter; John Clark, ward boss and assessor, begat William Clark, attorney general and 1968 U.S. Senate candidate; Adlai Stevenson, governor and presidential candidate, begat Adlai Stevenson, U.S.

Senator; Dan Ryan, ward boss and County Board president, begat Dan Ryan, ward boss and County Board president; Edward Dunne, mayor, begat Robert Jerome Dunne, judge; John J. Touhy, ward boss and holder of many offices, begat John M. Touhy, Illinois House Speaker; Joe Rostenkowski, ward boss, begat Daniel Rostenkowski, congressman; Arthur Elrod, ward boss and county commissioner, begat Richard Elrod, Sheriff; John Toman, ward boss and sheriff, begat Andrew Toman, county coroner; Thomas Keane, ward boss and alderman, begat Thomas Keane, ward boss and alderman; Joe Burke, ward boss and alderman, begat Edward Burke, ward boss and alderman; Paul Sheridan, ward boss and alderman, begat Paul Sheridan, alderman; Theodore Swinarski, ward boss, begat Donald Swinarski, alderman; Ald. David Hartigan begat Neil Hartigan, ward boss and chief park district attorney; Louis Garippo, ward boss, begat Louis Garippo, judge; Michael Igoe, federal judge, begat Michael Igoe, County Board secretary; Daniel McNamara, union leader, begat Daniel McNamara, judge; Thomas Murray, union leader and school board member, begat James Murray, congressman and alderman; Peter Shannon, businessman and friend of Daley, begat Dan Shannon, Park District president; Morgan Murphy, Sr., business executive and friend of Daley, begat Morgan Murphy, Jr., congressman; William Downes, real estate expert and friend of Daley, begat a daughter, who married a young man named David Stahl, who became deputy mayor; James Conlisk, police captain and City Hall favorite, begat James Conlisk, police superintendent; Daniel Coman, ward boss and city forestry chief, begat Daniel Coman, head of the state's attorney's civil division.

They are their brothers' keepers, too.

Alderman Keane keeps his brother on the powerful board of real estate tax appeals; Assessor Cullerton keeps his brother in the City Council and his brother-in-law as his chief deputy assessor; Ald. Harry Sain kept his brother as city jail warden when sheriff; and County Board President Dunne keeps his brother as boss of O'Hare and Midway airports, and Cong. John Kluczynski keeps his brother on the state Supreme Court.

Nobody in the Machine is more family conscious than Chairman Daley. Cousin John Daley became a ward committeeman and served several terms in the state legislature, where his remarkable resemblance to the mayor sometimes unnerved his associates. Uncle Martin Daley had a well paying job in county government that he did so skillfully he seldom had to leave his home. Cousin Richard Curry heads the city's legal department. Daley's four sons are just finishing law school, so their public careers have not yet been launched, but the eldest, Richard, at twenty-seven, was a candidate for delegate from his district to the state constitutional convention. He piled up the biggest vote in the state. The people in Bridgeport recognize talent. And the sons have been judge's clerks while going through school. When one of the mayor's daughters married, Daley promptly found a city executive job for the father of his new son-in-law.

Daley didn't come from a big family but he married into one, and so Eleanor Guilfoyle's parents might well have said that they did not lose a daughter, they gained an employment agency. Mrs. Daley's nephew has been in several key jobs. Her sister's husband became a police captain. A brother is an engineer in the school system. Stories about the number of Guilfoyles, and cousins and in-laws of Guilfoyles, in the patronage army have taken on legendary tones.

There are exceptions to the rules of party apprenticeship and nepotism. A few independent Democrats have been dogged enough to defeat weak Machine candidates in primaries for alderman, or, as happened once in the Daley years, for a seat in Congress. But it is never easy, and the strain leaves most independents so exhausted that most of them eventually embrace the Machine, at least gently, to avoid recurring primary struggles.

In theory, anybody can walk right into party headquarters at slate-making time, go before the ward bosses who make up the committee, and present themselves as prospective candidates. One political hanger-on, a disc jockey, even caught them in a mirthful mood, and when he actually got down on his knees and begged, they let him run for a minor office. But even the slate-makers do not kid themselves into thinking they are deciding who the candidates will be. They listen to the applicants, push their favorites, the men from their wards, and wait for Chairman Daley to make up his mind. Some of the men on the slate-making committee have been surprised to find that they themselves were slated to run for offices they hadn't even sought. It is a one-man show, and they know it. This vignette illustrates it:

In 1968, slate-makers were putting together their county ticket. They listened to the applicants, talked it over, then Daley and a couple of the party ancients came out of another room with the list.

Daley had decided that the strongest candidate for the crucial office of state's attorney, the county's prosecutor, would be Edward Hanrahan, a former federal prosecutor. It is a "must" office because a Republican would use it to investigate City Hall. Hanrahan was the strongest candidate because his Republican opponent also had an Irish name.

But slating Hanrahan required that the incumbent, John Stamos, who had been appointed to fill a vacancy, be shifted to something else. Stamos, a diligent and skilled young prosecutor, was Greek; Greeks were a small voting bloc, and Stamos was just professional and aloof enough to make some party elders nervous. Daley had decided to let

Stamos run for the office of Illinois attorney general, which has prestige but less power and challenge. That completed the ticket.

Their decision made for them, the slate-makers filed out of the conference room to go downstairs and meet the news media. As they came out, one of them saw Stamos and said, "Congratulations, John, you're going for attorney general."

"Bullshit," Stamos said, adding, "I won't go for it." Daley reasoned, but Stamos repeated, "Bullshit." And left the hotel.

While the slate-makers stood around looking confused, Daley told a secretary to call Frank Lorenz, an obedient party regular who was between elective offices. She got him on the phone and Daley said, "Come on over, Frank, you're the candidate for attorney general."

One of the slate-makers later said: "If Lorenz had stepped out to take a piss, he would have missed out, and the next guy Daley thought of would have got it, if he answered his phone. That's the way things are run sometimes, and everybody says we're so goddamn well organized."

A minute or two later, it was all resolved. Normally, Stamos would have been punished. But for party unity and to avoid alienating big Greek financial contributors, he was elevated to the state appellate court.

"You never know what in the hell is going to happen in there," a ward boss said. "He moves us around like a bunch of chess pieces. He knows why he's doing it because he's like a Russian with a ten-year plan, but we never know. I think his idea is to slate people who aren't going to try to rival him or add to someone else's strength. Look at how Cullerton got to be assessor. First he was a nothing alderman. He was a real nothing. But Daley put him in as finance chairman so he could have somebody who wouldn't get out of line. Then he put him in as assessor. Keane wanted assessor for his brother George. George would have loved it. Funny how people love to be assessor, haw! But Daley wasn't about to give Tom Keane the assessor's office, so he looked around and there was faithful Parky Cullerton.

"When he had to pick a chief judge, who were the logical guys? Neil Harrington, but he couldn't give it to Neil because he used to be part of the old South Side faction, and Daley wouldn't trust him. Harold Ward? He is independent, he might tell Daley to go screw himself or something.

"So he gave it to John Boyle, because he knew he'd have Boyle's complete loyalty. Why? Because Boyle had that scandal when he was state's attorney years ago and after that he couldn't get elected dogcatcher. He was a whipped dog, so he was perfect for Daley.

"And there's this thing he has with old people. Jesus, we've reslated people who were so senile they didn't even know what office they were running for. When it gets to that point, you know it has got to be something more than him being soft-hearted. There were some we could have just told them they were being reslated, and they would never have known the difference. He does it because then he doesn't have to worry about them. They'll sit there on the County Board or wherever they are and do just what they're told.

"It's one-man rule, absolutely. It used to be that if Kelly got mad at you, there were seven or eight guys you could go to and get it squared. The same thing with Nash, and when Arvey was chairman. But there's only one Daley. You're dead if he doesn't like you. There's no point in going to someone to try to get it squared because they can't, and they won't even try because they're afraid it'll get him mad at them. He's a friend of mine, but he can be a mean prick."

Just how mean, and how subtle, was discovered by Arnold Maremont, a millionaire industrialist and art collector who decided he wanted to go into politics and to start at the top.

Daley does not dislike millionaires. He lets them contribute to the party, serve on advisory boards, take on time-consuming appointments and help elect Machine Democrats to office.

Maremont had done it all. He contributed money, worked in Governor Kerner's campaign, led a campaign to pass a $150,000,000 bond issue that revitalized the state's mental health program, and pitched in on numerous liberal causes and mental health and welfare programs.

His dream was to be a U.S. senator, and in early 1961 he went to Daley's office and told him that he'd like to run against Sen. Everett Dirksen. He made it clear that he wanted to do it properly and not jump into the primary as a maverick. The party's blessing was what he was after.

Daley showed interest, but said he had certain reservations: mainly he wasn't sure if downstate county chairmen would support a Jew. He suggested that Maremont tour the state, talk to the county chairmen, and he indicated strongly that if Maremont made a good showing, he'd be Daley's man.

Maremont pushed aside his business and civic work and spent most of the early summer barnstorming through Illinois. A spunky, brash man, he'd walk into a bar in a tiny Southern Illinois town — grits and gravy country — and announce: "My name's Arnold Maremont. I want to run for the Senate and I'm a Jew." People seemed to like him, as he wolfed down chicken and peas dinners at the county meetings, charming little old ladies and picking up support from the chairmen.

All the while, he sent back regular reports to Daley: they will go for a Jew! Elated, he headed back to Chicago, ready to give Daley his final report and the good news. He got back to town just in time to pick up that day's papers and read that Daley had, indeed, decided to slate a Jewish senatorial candidate: Cong. Sidney Yates, a party regular.

That ended Maremont's political ambitions. Furious, he was convinced that Daley had merely used him to conduct a free one-man survey of downstate Illinois. He wouldn't have even tried had he ever heard Daley explain why he is so dedicated a party man: "The party permits ordinary people to get ahead. Without the party, I couldn't be mayor. The rich guys can get elected on their money, but somebody like me, an ordinary person, needs the party. Without the party, only the rich would be elected to office."

If Daley's one-man rule bothers the men who sit on the Central Committee, they are careful to keep it to themselves. The meetings take on the mood of a religious service, with the committeemen chanting their praise of his leadership. "It has been . . . my pleasure and honor . . . to give him my advice. . . . The greatest mayor . . . in the country . . . the world . . . the history of the world . . ."

Only once in recent years has anybody stood up and talked back, and he was one of the suburban committeemen, generally referred to around party headquarters as "a bunch of meatheads."

The suburban committeeman, Lynn Williams, a wealthy manufacturer and probably the most liberal member of the Central Committee, had been angered by Daley's attacks on liberals after the 1968 Democratic Convention. Daley had been making speeches lambasting pseudoliberals, liberal-intellectuals, suburban liberals, suburban liberal-intellectuals, and pseudoliberal-intellectual suburbanites. He had been shouting: "Who in the hell do those people think they are? Who are they to tell us how to run our party?"

Williams, a strong supporter of young Adlai Stevenson, who had angered Daley with an attack on "feudal" politics, stood up, finally, at a Central Committee meeting and delivered a scathing rebuttal to Daley, saying that without liberal participation the party would be nothing but a skeleton, its only goal, power.

As he talked, the committeemen's heads swiveled as if they were watching a tennis game, wonder and fear on their faces. They had never heard such talk, and wondered what Chairman Daley would do. Strike him with lightning. Throw the bum out?

When Williams finished, Daley, in a surprisingly soft voice, said, "I've always been a liberal myself."

Other committeemen joined in his defense, recalling countless liberal acts by Daley. One man shouted at Williams, "Perhaps you didn't know, but this happens to be a very liberal outfit."

The shock of the committeemen at the sound of somebody criticizing Daley didn't surprise Williams. He has said: "Most of them are mediocrities at best, and not very intelligent. The more successful demon-

strate cunning. Most are in need of slavery — their own — and they
want to follow a strong leader."

In March 1970, the committeemen met for the purpose of reelecting
Daley chairman. Alderman Keane nominated him and eighteen other
committeemen made lengthy speeches seconding the nomination. One
of them recited, "R, you're rare; I, you're important; C, you're courageous; H, you're heavenly; A, you're able; R, you're renowned; D, you're
Democratic; J, is for your being a joy to know; D, you're diligent; A,
you're adorable; L, you're loyal; E, you're energetic; and Y, you're
youthful."

Once again Lynn Williams stood, but not to criticize. He, too, joined
in the praise and made one of the seconding speeches. Daley had since
slated young Adlai Stevenson III, whom Williams had supported, for
the U.S. Senate. Daley and Williams even exchanged handshakes. In a
way, Williams seemed to emphasize his own point about the committee's need to follow a strong leader.

EACH POLITICAL PARTY DETER-
mines for itself the procedures
for the selection of candidates.
Since 1968 both major parties have
undergone a democratization process
that has resulted in expanding grass-
roots participation in party affairs
through various new procedures,
the most important of which is the
increase in the number of national
convention delegates selected
through state primaries. In 1980 the
number of states adopting the primary method for the selection of delegates and for the determination of
presidential preferences of the electorate expanded to thirty-five, a remarkable number by any past standards. The Democratic party in particular pushed the primary selection
method after the debacle of the 1968
convention, which numerous party
members believed to have been boss-
controlled.

The dissatisfaction of party leaders
with the delegate rules of the Democratic party led to a rules change for
1984, providing that party officials, including two-thirds of the Democrats
in Congress, will be seated and control 14 percent of the delegate votes.
Primaries will continue to be important, but grass-roots control will be
less emphasized than in the 1970s.

Party procedures for delegate selection to national conventions are, of
course, institutional. What effect do
these rules have on the personalities
of the candidates? Do they help to determine what types of people will run
for the nomination? What other effects do they have on individuals during the preconvention campaign, and
later, after they have run for nomination? The comments of those who
have run, or who have been involved
in nominating campaigns, are not encouraging. All observers seem to
agree that the campaigns have a deep
and adverse impact on the psyche
and physical condition of those who
are running, and often on campaign
staffs. The primary campaigns breed
paranoia, uncertainty, physical fatigue and sleeplessness, and unnerving tensions due to tight scheduling.
Participants in the nominating process universally describe it as "grueling," "inhuman," and "crazy." The
conditions of campaigning make the
large number of aspirants for the
presidency all the more remarkable.

The following selection tells what
it means to run for the presidential
nomination, and describes the effect
of the selection procedures on the
candidates as well as the effects of the
candidates' personalities on the process.

2 Elizabeth Drew
RUNNING

In selecting those who might occupy the most important office in this country — the Presidency — we put our potential leaders through a process that is both strange and brutal. The people who might make crucial decisions about war and peace, about our taxes, who will have enormous effect on the quality of our lives, our social order, the civility of our public discourse, undergo an experience from which few human beings could emerge whole. Some do not. The evidence of the damaging nature of modern political campaigns — the scarred veterans, the burnt-out cases, the bitterness — is all about. "They never come out of it the same," one senator said of colleagues of his who had run for the Presidential nomination or the Presidency. Moreover, the pressures on those who undertake Presidential campaigns are growing. In 1960, John F. Kennedy ran in only seven primaries. Now, as a result of subsequent political reforms, there are twenty-nine Democratic primaries. In addition, the Democrats' reform rules have led to more open processes for choosing delegates by convention or caucus in the other states. As politics has become more open, the growth in participation has led to growth in demands on candidates. Other developments have added to the strains a campaign imposes on the candidate. One is the growth in the variety and skill of pressure groups. Another is the education of the populace — which is increasingly well informed about politics. Intensified coverage by the press intensifies the stress. One mistake and a candidate can be destroyed. Those relatively modern inventions — television and the jet plane — have added not to the politicians' ease but to the demands that are put upon them or that they put upon themselves. One gets the impression that the entire Presidential selection process is about to snap, and that new forms and styles must emerge.

Curiously, the questions of why people run and why the race often leaves such deep scars may have common answers. Running for the Presidency appears to have an impact on the ego that is unlike that of any other endeavor. *Homo candidatus* might be said to undergo a unique human experience. There are some exceptions, but many candidates for the Presidency seem to react with strikingly similar emotions — even those who enter the race with the best of motives, who are thoughtful people, who care deeply about their country. They feel an extraordinary exhilaration in making the race — a great lift, an unparalleled expansion of self-esteem. It is as if the limits on ambition and ego were removed. All this is reinforced by aides and backers who are themselves susceptible to expansion of ego and fantasies of power. They are investors in power, who stand to gain if the candidate wins. The aides and other investors fuel a candidate's ambition and flog him on. After a while, the candidate, caught in a web of ambition (his own and others'), begins to believe that he can win — has to believe it in order to go through what he does — and begins to picture himself in the Oval Office. In the deepest fatigue, he continues to function on an unnatural flow of energy — a kind of high. It is the only way to get through it. Set against this is the devastation of losing — the deflated self-esteem, the bitterness, the sheer physical difficulty of adjusting to the sudden cessation of activity. Two years after his unsuccessful race for the Presidency was over, one former candidate told a Senate colleague, "I still wake up nights campaigning."

Almost every campaign eventually generates uncommon stress: there is infighting among the staff and the reaction of an exhausted candidate to that infighting; failures in staff work (often caused by rivalries); unfair attacks by opponents; the necessity of appealing for money and other forms of help from people whom one holds in low esteem or people who may exact an exorbitant price — not just in commitments to policies but also in promises of federal appointment or demands on a candidate's time. There are constant pressures to take various positions on issues — to win one constituency but do it in a way that does not lose another. There are pressures to be something one is not — to change everything from one's haircut to one's personality. There is pressure to be shallow, sensational, so as to get press attention. Aides grow quarrelsome and suspicious. And all the while the candidate is being asked to undertake more than human flesh can endure. Understandably, the self-pity that is endemic among politicians — who feel overworked, underappreciated, and misunderstood — reaches great intensity in the candidate for national office. As a result of the pressures, candidates get derailed from their strategies — if they ever had them. Concentration on substance — even for those who wish to engage in it — becomes increasingly difficult. Planning for what one would actually do if one should win the Presidency becomes almost out of the question.

A losing campaign as often as not leaves an atmosphere of bitter recrimination. Political defeat really is an orphan. Former aides and advisers go about telling how it could have been otherwise if this or that piece of advice had been followed. Participants in campaigns write whole score-settling books. Candidates go through self-doubt, rationalization, and examination of the "but for"s that stood between them and victory. The "but for" exercises prompt them, often successfully, to run again; having experienced the stratosphere of a Presidential campaign, many — most, it seems — find it difficult to readjust to previous routines. Of course, good things also happen to people who run in Presidential campaigns. They can receive a political education that is unequalled. They can learn unforgettable lessons about their country — about issues, about constituencies. They can learn about the mood of the people and the subtleties of that mood. They can gain a better understanding of where they can lead people — if they choose to — of how to lead them by gaining their trust and unlocking their higher aspirations and motivations. And they are given some preparation for the pressures involved in trying to govern a complicated nation. But — in the very nature of contemporary campaigning — the costs seem to outweigh the benefits. Good people can get through campaigns and survive, but at a heavy price — for them and for us. And some good people — after a close look — count themselves out. Campaigns have become a screening process that does not always screen out, or in, the right qualities.

Conversations with former candidates for the Presidential nomination and for the Presidency and with several former campaign aides give one a striking picture of what can happen to a candidate who seeks the highest office. "It leaves scar tissue," one former campaign manager said. "There's no way it can't have a deep impact on the candidate's psyche and physical condition. For a person in public life, it is the aspiration to the ultimate. There is no way a losing candidate can pick himself up and pretend nothing has happened to him. Even though you haven't lost your public position, you feel you're a loser. It hurts. You wonder what you did wrong. There are all the self-doubts. The system rewards success. There is no second place."

Another man who has participated in several campaigns said, "Everyone at the end of a campaign has blown off at his staff every night — thinks his mother is going to vote against him and his wife is trying to subvert him."

"It's the way they lay their egos on the line," said Mark Shields, a heavyset, thirty-eight-year-old man who has worked in several campaigns. "It's a terribly vulnerabilizing experience."

I asked Shields at lunch one day to tell me something about how campaigns work.

"Most of them don't work," he replied. "Everybody in the business is an amateur. Everybody looks at the last campaign. Most people have only one good campaign in them or maybe, if they're lucky, two. It's a total absorption of emotional, psychic, physical energy. It's not like being in the Senate. The Senate is bad preparation for a presidential campaign. A senator can say 'Let's have hearings on tire safety' or something else and issue a press release and in three months hold hearings and issue another press release. In a Presidential campaign, issues are thrust upon you — a Middle East crisis, a public employees' strike. The press wants to know what you would do. That's more like the Presidency. You get too many easy answers as a senator. A senator can make statements, offer testimony, send a letter to the Internal Revenue Service. He can be for housing, but he doesn't have to say where it's going to be built. He can't do that in a Presidential campaign." Shields continued, "The toughest thing in running for President is to understand the fact that there are millions of people who are going to make a judgment about you who don't know you. And then you have to ask people you don't like for their help — that's tough. How many fools can you suffer in one day? And how many speeches can you give? How many days can you take away from home and still feel good? Can you resist trying to be your own campaign manager? All day, you'll get complaints about those dopes who did this and that. How good are you at raising money? How many people can you be nice to? Can you convince other people that you are worth their time and money?"

Another former campaign manager told me, "The physical, emotional, and energy strain is so staggering that you end up with a person whose emotional and physical level has to be beyond human — it has to be animal. Look at the candidate as a person. Quite often, he's a husband; he's a father; there are problems at home. There are financial problems, if he's honest. Quite often, there are arguments with the family, or there is a distance from the family — an emotional acceptance of a dreadful circumstance. There is a terrible emotional drain on the candidates. They are like an automobile whose lights have been left on overnight — and just maybe you can start it. The whole thing is excruciating. I wish to Christ you could spend just one whole day on the inside of a difficult campaign. At the end of the day, the candidate used to look at me with red eyes and say, 'For what? How much more do I have to do?'"

"A lot of them go into a Presidential campaign with the idea that the United States might be one big congressional district or state," said a man who was active in the 1972 campaign. "They begin by thinking they can wander around the country the way they wandered around the state. Then the shock sets in. Frankly, what it takes out of them is a great deal. Most normal people can concentrate on only one thing at a time. The candidate has to realize that the only thing he can handle is being an articulate, good candidate. He can't think about whether the mail is going out or the money is coming in. The biggest thing is fatigue. The staff sits around and says, 'Can the candidate do this?' or 'Can the candidate do that?' The candidate can hardly walk."

An aide to one of the current candidates, when I asked him what candidates have to go through, replied, "They have to go through a whole lot of — a lot of running around. You really have to want to be President. We run our guy; we really run him. You just have to come to grips with the fact that your life is not your own for some period of time. We run him a lot harder than we should. He's good about it, but every once in a while it has an adverse impact on his performance. He begins to answer questions too long; his speeches become too long; he becomes less precise."

"Here is a truism about politics," said one former campaign manager. "Candidates' wives hate schedulers and advance men. They always think their husband is being overscheduled."

One day in October, I asked George McGovern to give me some of his impressions of what it was like to go through a campaign. We talked during lunch in the senators' dining room in the Capitol. McGovern began by talking about his experience in 1972. Understandably, he said he thinks that the system of primaries and state caucuses is "pretty good," but he feels that the general election gives all the advantages to the incumbent. "I suppose I reflect the bias of someone who won in the selection process and lost so disastrously in the general election," he said. Still, McGovern has some things to say about running for the Presidency that illuminate what a candidate goes through.

"I think running for the Presidency is different from anything else," McGovern said. "Maybe it isn't that it's so different but that the stakes are so much higher. You always know when you're in a Presidential campaign that a slip of the tongue or an ill-advised statement can be devastating. In a statewide race, you have time to make up for such a thing. But in a Presidential campaign it's as if you were always in the seventh game of the World Series — one error and it could all be over. The sense of excitement and tension is always there — day and night. It's physically exhausting on the one hand and exhilarating on the other. You literally live for months on the flow of adrenalin. I was tired, but I went at a pace that couldn't be sustained at any other time. It couldn't be sustained by the staff, by the press — they had to be rotated. The great weakness is that there is seldom any opportunity for reflection. Even when there is a rest time scheduled, your mind and your emotions are racing ahead, and you're anxious for some scheduler to give you something to do, so you don't have to go through the pain of thinking about what you're doing. And there's always some scheduler with extra things for you to do."

McGovern continued, "One of the cruellest things that go on in Presidential politics is the struggle for the candidate's body. It goes on from the county chairman to the campaign manager. The handshaking tours have to be drastically curtailed. They're really a lot of baloney. They don't add very much to the process in terms of the candidate's security and the candidate's dignity, and they really don't make sense. The candidate arrives at the airport and sometimes spends half an hour shaking hands with the first three rows of people. Candidates do it for two reasons: one, to show how democratic they are; two, to inflate their egos. It's pretty heady stuff to have dozens of people waving their hands in the air to touch you. It makes you feel you're some sort of gift to them. But it really doesn't contribute to the education of the public or the candidate." Candidates also go through the handshaking routine because it gives them a chance to show their popularity to television audiences.

McGovern offered an example of the kind of incident that can cause havoc in a campaign and irritate a candidate's already raw nerves. Toward the end of his election campaign, he decided to interrupt his scheduled appearances in various towns and "media markets" to do some nationwide telecasts. (This decision itself was much disputed within the McGovern campaign. One former McGovern campaign official still talks of it as "disastrous," causing as it did the unmaking of so many commitments, and he blames other McGovern advisers for the decision.) "The first television address was highly successful," McGovern recalls. "It was on the Vietnam war. The second was on economic problems. I had numerous meetings with economists and staff members who were travelling with me, and I cleared it at one o'clock in the afternoon, and we dispatched it back here to be put on the TelePrompTer at the Capitol, in time for the taping at nine o'clock. Well, when we landed and I was all made up and ready to go at seven o'clock, there was nothing on the TelePrompTer. The staff back here had decided they didn't like the speech and were fighting about it. So, after fuming for an hour, I said, 'I want that speech I cleared this afternoon.' But there was no time to rehearse or go over it. I was mad; I was exhausted; I was unnerved. That kind of thing happened a dozen times; it draws every ounce of energy out of you."

Edmund Muskie now has sufficient seniority in the Senate to have an elegant hideaway office in the Capitol — actually, Sam Ervin's former hideaway. As we sat there — in a high-ceilinged room with chandeliers, brown leather furniture, and a spectacular view of the Mall leading to the Washington Monument — Muskie, relaxed, sometimes with one of his long legs slung over an arm of his chair, talked about his 1972 campaign for the Democratic nomination. He offered a number of insights into the experiences of a candidate.

"The most difficult problem — and I wish I'd seen it in advance as well as I do in retrospect — is for the candidate to control his campaign and be himself and be sure the campaign reflects that," Muskie said. "People don't buy an organization — they buy a candidate, his philosophy, his character, his goals. But the campaign starts to overwhelm the candidate." Referring to his role as Vice-Presidential candidate on Hubert Humphrey's ticket, Muskie continued, "In 1968, I went in at the top. It was a new experience, a liberating experience, and the organization responded to me pretty well. It was a pretty good start. Odd as it may seem, the bad start for 1972 was the Election Eve speech" — the televised speech he gave on the eve of the 1970 congressional elections, which was in sharp contrast to a poorly delivered speech on law and order by Richard Nixon, and increased the talk of Muskie as the probable candidate in 1972. "All of a sudden, I was the front-runner — without the resources, without the organization. There was a tidal wave of people wanting to respond, to be involved, and we didn't have the physical capacity to handle it. Being front-runner made me defensive, overprotective, and too damn structured. I suddenly got up there on a high wire and wasn't sure enough of myself to take it and handle it naturally. People have reported that my staff acted as if I were already President." In a characteristically different perception, or assessment of blame, some members of Muskie's campaign staff say that it was Muskie who acted as if he were already President. Muskie remarked, "People in Maine say, 'You weren't the Ed Muskie we knew.' I suspect that's still some of my problem in Maine." Muskie is up for reelection to the Senate in 1976. This is seen as a reason for him to remain out of at least the early primaries next year, even if, as many people believe, he would like another chance at the Presidency. If he does not face substantial opposition in seeking reelection to the Senate seat and if the situation seems opportune, he could still enter some of the later Presidential primaries. In the meantime, he can stand apart from the melee and win national attention as chairman of the Senate Budget Committee while other candidates battle it out.

I asked Muskie what his major problem was in 1972.

"The pressures on your time and energy," he replied. "That's always the problem — so many people seeking access to the candidate. And then there is the physical need to get around the country and get exposure. Those are the pressures that the staff sees and responds to. They have a very useful tool — the white space on the calendar. When the white space is full, they've done their job. The candidate has his own priorities in regard to where he should go and whom he should see and finding time to think through a program for the country. The staff doesn't consider this. Their candidate is a mechanical man who can find the time to think through his positions on abortion and the gay movement, on the economy. These are the things the candidate doesn't get time to think through. I look at these guys who are running now, and wonder how they can do it. The press wants instant responses to everything, and if you don't give them instant responses they believe that you haven't thought it through, that you don't have any answer. Those are the kinds of things that frustrated me. Unless you've got the time to think, to formulate your own policy, you've missed the essence of it, the excitement of it, and you've become a frenetic thing moving around the landscape proving you've got more energy, more charisma, more instant answers than anyone else."

Muskie paused, and then continued, "The exposure to crowds is exhilarating, and is useful if you don't overdo it. I can understand why President Ford likes it; he probably didn't have much as a congressman from Michigan. It gives you some feeling that people respond to you, they think they need you, they can believe in you. There's nothing like that to give a man the adrenalin flow that permits him to believe in himself. But we do overdo it. We need to change the balance, to get more of a dialogue. Think back to Franklin D. Roosevelt and Al Smith. We didn't have the jet plane. There wasn't this constant rush to get around the country and get near the people. It was so much more leisurely and there was so much more communication. F.D.R. and Truman travelled on trains; they didn't plunge through crowds. Television is supposed to reduce the expenditure of energy. It seems to have done the opposite. I wonder whether, if the candidates could get together and agree on a pace and a style, it wouldn't work just as well. Or if one candidate did it — reduced the running around — I'm not sure it wouldn't take."

I asked Muskie about the problem of raising money.

"That's going to continue to be a problem," he answered. Like several politicians, Muskie has misgivings about the new law to reform financing of campaigns, which limits individual contributions to a thousand dollars and requires Presidential candidates, in order to get federal matching funds, to raise at least five thousand dollars, in contributions of no more than two hundred and fifty dollars, in each of twenty states. (The new law, which is under review by the Supreme Court, also sets limits on how much may be spent in each state.) It was far easier for some politicians to go to fewer contributors for larger sums — which is precisely what the new law is designed to prevent. Therefore, while from some politicians' point of view the old money-raising system had its difficulties, some of them don't like the new one much better. "It costs a lot of money to raise money from the grass roots," Muskie said. "The methods, such as mass mailing, can be overused and lose their productiveness. You'll have every candidate in the land sending letters." Muskie laughed, and added, "We'll have to raise the postal rates." Of his own experience in raising money in 1972, Muskie said, "I'd spend days and days going to see one individual — travelling to New York, travelling to Chicago, to see one guy who was a potential contributor. Being the front-runner was very costly. We had to keep it going for two years. You have a tremendous organization to keep going, and at the first signs of stumbling the money starts drying up. That's what brought us down eventually. The New Hampshire and Florida primaries were tremendously expensive and didn't raise much money. We had to spend money we'd raised in New York and California. Wisconsin was pretty tough. In Illinois you can raise the money, but Pennsylvania — when the outcome of that primary was disappointing we had to fold. It was a classic case of too much too soon, of peaking too soon. Adlai Stevenson" — the Democratic senator from Illinois and son of the former Presidential candidate — "used to say, 'Cut off and run from the Senate floor.' That would be easier to do this year than then."

I asked Muskie why, given the strains he had described, people run for the Presidency — especially more than once.

"It's a very heady business, really, to suddenly find yourself near the top, and to breathe constantly the atmosphere of those who simply take it for granted that you're going to be the next President of the United States — not just the staff but also the press and your foes," Muskie replied. "It does things to you. You begin subconsciously to believe it yourself. You begin to consider the heavy responsibilities you have before you announce your position on something. It was the source of a lot of my difficulty, I fear, but at the same time it was a rather wonderful feeling. It would be nice if you could go through an experience like that on a trial-run basis — psychologically, mentally, physically — before you actually do it. In so many ways, I could do it much better now. But that's true of so much of life — you can't live it twice. The really invigorating parts of a campaign are the exposure to crowds and the all too scarce opportunities that you have to actually sit down with people and thrash out policies for the country — the chance to get into it and get good brains you can bounce off of. And so much of what we did of that ended up in the Democratic platform in 1972. I know I was perceived as not being issue-oriented, but I think the problem was that we tried to cover too much. We weren't identified with *an* issue, and people want to associate you with one issue or stand. George McGovern created that; George Wallace created that. What I was trying to do apparently isn't doable. I was trying to project the image of someone who could reach out to all segments of the Democratic Party and establish a common cause with them. I managed to come out second with all of them."

Muskie laughed, and continued, "I came out fourth in the Florida primary. A Yankelovich survey a couple of days later showed I was the only one who could get more Democratic votes than Nixon there. And I'll tell you a historical footnote about New Hampshire. There was this game about the percentage by which I had to win New Hampshire.

After starting out with sixty per cent, the press settled on fifty per cent. I got forty-six per cent, and it was decided I'd lost. Later, it was found that I actually got forty-nine and nine-tenths per cent of the vote. I just found that out this spring. I got some satisfaction out of that, but it wasn't of any practical use."

Muskie continued, "Right after the Manchester *Union Leader* incident, I was not aware that it bore the seeds of disaster." His public display of emotion when, shortly before the New Hampshire primary, he attacked the *Union Leader* for printing a story taken to be critical of Mrs. Muskie and broke down and, according to some press reports, cried, was considered nearly fatal to his election chances. "As a matter of fact, my understanding as I went through New Hampshire was that it made a very favorable impression," Muskie told me. "I thought it was a bit of a triumph. That shows you how the candidate's perception can be off. I also found out later that the press had a different perception of what happened from mine. The press thought I cried. I didn't. I was madder than hell, and I choked. Up to that point, I was perceived as able, controlled, disciplined, stable, strong, and the image of that incident undermined what had been my basic strength. Which comes back to my basic point — you have to be yourself and have to be seen as that, or you're sunk. The more people there are who see what you are and decide they're for you, the firmer your base is. There's a lot of accident to it. Take my 1970 Election Eve speech. That did more than anything in my political life, but there was a lot of chance to it — the juxtaposition with the President. Unless there is that kind of fortuitous circumstance, then I guess you have to run around to get known, unless someone comes out of the first primary with a big margin. Then the press will give him big coverage — and he may become another George McGovern, or an Ed Muskie and stumble. The press is another problem. It's so easy to become defensive, guarded, suspicious about the press, and also to regard it as conspiratorial in a loose kind of way. And I'm sure I felt all those things in 1972. But that's a mistake. A candidate tends to overlook the fact that most of the members of the press never get a chance to meet him and talk to him and get to know him, so they write what they can or pay attention to those they believe to have access, or they want to be sensational and get attention for themselves. It must be very difficult for reporters to cover this passing scene. They don't have as direct access as we do to the facts on which we have to act."

Muskie returned to talking about the 1972 primaries. "We decided to start in New Hampshire and Florida on successive days," he recalled. "It was tough to do both states well. In Florida I never could catch up, and in New Hampshire it was an effort to get up to the standard the press had set. I was discouraged the night of the Florida primary, and sort of had a feeling that the whole thing had ended. Illinois, the next week, was a great primary. We never got credit for it." Muskie defeated Eugene McCarthy, his only real challenger, in the Illinois primary. "We did consider bypassing Wisconsin. The governors and senators who were supporting me met and opposed that. I think my instincts were right — to avoid another vulnerable situation, with Humphrey and McGovern coming from neighboring states. And I did not do well in multicandidate races. So Illinois was the only good primary, and now, historically, New Hampshire. Really, anyone who can do fifty per cent in New Hampshire — especially in a five-candidate field — is doing pretty goddam well."

Walter Mondale's face gets a pained expression when he is asked about his experience as a potential Democratic candidate in 1976. Re-elected in Minnesota to his Senate seat by a wide margin in 1972, proclaimed a Presidential candidate by Hubert Humphrey that Election Night, Mondale spent a year exploring his chances as the Democratic nominee. On November 21, 1974, he announced that he was withdrawing, because, he said, "I found that I did not have the overwhelming desire to be President which is essential for the kind of campaign that is required." The interesting thing is that he was taken at his word. In the rather cynical political community, the word might well have been that Mondale had pulled out because he wasn't getting anywhere, but it was widely accepted that no such conclusion about his chances could yet be drawn and that Mondale had pulled out for exactly the reason he said he did — that he couldn't stand it.

One day this fall, I asked Mondale to talk about his excursion into Presidential politics. He had been talking easily about other matters, and it was clear that he would have preferred to continue to do so. But he agreed, reluctantly, to cooperate with my inquiry into the Presidential-nominating process.

"The Presidency is the most important office in the world," Mondale said. "The nominating system was unstudied and unanticipated by those who wrote the Constitution. There has been almost no study of it by a President, by Congress. It has just grown. Its growth has been malignant, almost. It's anarchy."

I asked what the process does to a candidate.

"Lots of things," Mondale replied. "One, fatigue. Look at the schedules, travel times, time changes, the absence of weekends for rest. It's not just the physical fatigue; it's the emotional pressure of it all. At every event you have to do exceedingly well — good isn't enough. You might never be seen there again. You have to be up for every meeting, be properly briefed, speak well. So the emotional, psychological pressure, which is hard to define, is worse than the physical fatigue, which is terrible. I was going through the easy, nice time when you can pick your schedule. What are these characters going to do when they get to the primary and caucus time — one primary or caucus on one coast and one on another? One on the Canadian border and one on the Mexican border — all with different rules?"

Mondale went on, "Then, you have the problem of money. You spend days and days and days pleading for money — answering questions, trying to make a good impression on people who have it. Even with the new limits on contributions, you have to do this. You need movers and shakers who can go out and help raise money in thousand-dollar quantities. When you get through with all this, you've got the conflict between what you have to do to be nominated and what you have to do to be a decent President. Some of it's the same. Some of the conflict and emotional pressure is a necessary test for the Presidency. I'm not for the greenhouse approach. You can't be inaccessible and be a candidate, and by being accessible you may learn more than you'll ever learn again. But the way you spend your time is irrelevant to issue development. It's a different life style. Politicians have to be persuasive and able to move people, but when you get to the national scene it's theatre. When you're running for the House or the Senate, you have to grow well on a number of people. When you're running for President, it's like a series of one-night stands in vaudeville — you have to have a good act every night. The good act may carry you farther than the good program."

Mondale continued, "The feeling that bothered me more than anything else was that we were in the control of events we were unable to stop or do anything about. Experts are coming and telling you what you have to do, what positions you have to take — usually it's what they want. Then there are the people who want you to get a speech coach and cut your hair differently. None of that's very important. What's really important is that the goddam news media won't pay you much attention until you've become big. You have to spend years on the road until you get enough percentage points in the polls. The national media won't give you a break until then, and their eyes turn glassy when you talk to them about it. They don't want to hear about it. That's because their business isn't electing Presidents — it's competing with their competitors. The result is that the nation is denied a look at new leadership. If you want to get on the evening news, you have to escalate your rhetoric in order to merit the time. If you're saying something rational and restrained, that's not news. That's one of the reasons politicians look so bad. They're always saying something wild. The news programs don't want to put someone unknown on because their competitor might be putting someone well known on. It's understandable, but why shouldn't there be some national forum where who our next President might be is considered and among those considered are those who are not well known but who have great merit? Now there's no adequate forum for that. So what I had to ask myself was whether I wanted to go through all that was involved not just for two years but maybe for ten years — to get on that lifetime Presidential cycle that some get on. I didn't want to do it. I had to think about whether you should also have some time to be with friends, family, to fish, to have a little balance in your life, or whether the oneness of purpose should consume your life."

One man who has run for Presidential office said to me, "Rich people — you have to go to rich people. These were the worst, most humiliating experiences of my life. There is a certain feeling that they know best, that they're expert. Here I've spent twenty years in government, and some jerk whose father made a lot of money is lecturing me. He doesn't know up from down and he's lecturing me on everything. One time, I was talking with a car dealer. He said, 'You have to smash through with an issue.' I said, 'What issue?' He said, 'I'm got going to get into that.' He makes a lot of money, so he's a political expert. You spend too much time listening to people who have money. Not that they shouldn't be listened to, but they shouldn't have that special access to a politician's ear."

A manager of one 1972 campaign, when I asked him what campaigns were really like, was fairly vehement in his response.

"You start with the basic proposition that, regardless of appearances, campaigns are, by their nature, disorganized, impossible to control," he said. "The better you appear to be doing, the more you attract the parasites, the so-called professionals, for whom you grow to have enormous disdain. There's no such thing as a professional in this business.

"Campaigns generate a king-of-the-mountain atmosphere: a contest to see who can become closest to the candidate — at the expense of someone else, which is the only way to do it. The interests of the candidate diminish at the hands of the staff. This has been true of every campaign I've heard about. The candidate has zero time; his life is no longer his own; he doesn't own his soul. Everyone is telling him what to do. The media managers tell him they need more time. You can't attract the kind of support and ideas you need from intellectuals without giving them time. The fund-raisers demand time. The speechwriters are in constant dispute. The upshot is that long-range planning is impossible. I've left out the constituencies that demand access — labor groups, women's groups, blacks, state leaders. And I haven't mentioned the grass-roots people or the schedulers. You have inherent chaos and conflict among all these warring groups, all of whom see in the candidate their tool to power, and want access, so that when Armageddon is won they will be up there with the heavenly angels."

I asked this man what to watch for in campaigns.

"Look for the obvious gap between the desire for an appearance of harmony and the undertones of conflict," he said. "This is symptomatic of all campaigns. There are always people on the edge of departure because they don't have access to the candidate. That's what matters. Then, there are the professionals, the hustlers. They hire out for pay, but they don't give any pleasure. They don't give a damn about the candidate. They bounce from one campaign to another. They flood the office with memos, and the memos just happen to leak out.

"There is an enormous distance between having a strategy and having the ability to carry it out. Things aren't what they appear. The successes, failures; the harmony, disharmony; getting money, not getting money; having grass-roots followers or not — campaign managers always want to give the impression that they are on top of all of that. The truth is that they are not. The difference in whether they are or not is marginal and accidental."

I asked this man whether he or his candidate had had much time to stop and think.

"The problem amounts to more than that," he replied. "The problem is the system in a country as large as this, with differences in the rules of each state. It's the uncertainty about your allies and the question of whether they have their own axes to grind — whether they are using the candidate. You have to look at the local staff as well as at the national one. You get involved in the selection of campaign posters and pictures. It's a great shell game. It's a silly-ass system."

I asked him if it is possible to run a campaign and think through a program for governing.

He said, "No. No one knows what's going on. No one can monitor a campaign, because it is moving too fast. Almost every campaign tries to set up a system for gathering information — someone responsible for organized labor, a group responsible for blacks, and so on. You do that in the headquarters and in the states. The financial community is a constituency that has to be serviced — they have their views on how to run absolutely everything. If you try to get endorsements from political figures, you do it at the cost of also getting enemies, and then the endorsers want to run your campaign in their own communities, and do it in a way which may be in their own interest instead of the candidate's. It would be almost impossible to describe the day of a campaign manager. To say it's enervating understates the case badly. You feel like a punching bag that Muhammad Ali has been using for two weeks. You're pummelled by staff, by grass-roots, local people. To see to noon the next day is a feat of uncommon accomplishment. When someone asks at 11 P.M. 'What did you do today?' it's amazing if you can remember ten minutes."

Picking up an earlier theme, he continued, "I've overlooked the other constituencies — young people, the elderly. And you can't go on the assumption that labor's labor. There are all sorts of divisions within what is referred to as 'labor.' There's another constituency of the Democratic Party — the 'elder statesmen.' They drive you bananas. It's devastating. They can be ignored only at the staff's peril or the candidate's peril. They're the Washington lawyers who have been around, and there are also people in every state — an ex-Party chairman, ex-governor, ex-university president. Multiply this by every city and county in the United States and you begin to get the picture. They have something to offer, but they are not involved in the campaign. Some take you back to a campaign twenty years ago and insist that that's the way yours should be; some think everything you're doing is wrong."

I asked this man what effect all these elements had had on his candidate in 1972.

"As it grew clear that we wouldn't win, he became very concerned about what it meant to his capacity for continuing in public life," the campaign manager replied. "He would ask, 'Can I continue to be effective?' He would say, 'I've let people down.' It took an enormous toll. He wondered what his old constituents would think. There was lost time with the family to be made up. You either win or lose. That's all there is to it. You win because you're brilliant or clever or had superb media or great staff. He who lost had a lousy campaign, lousy staff, bad media. You start out saying, 'What does it take to get the voters to vote for me in New Hampshire, and what does it take to get them to vote for me in Florida the following week, and what will it take in Wisconsin?' By and large, people in Democratic primaries vote their strongest emotions, their insides: 'Send them a message.' What a way to pick the leader of this country! The whole system stinks. Crazy. Crazy. Crazy."

Power struggles and ego bruises occur in any competitive situation — a business, a university, a church hierarchy — and perhaps it is only fitting that they seem to be most intense where the stakes are the highest: in the race for the Presidency of the United States. But their intensity seems to have grown — as have other problems, such as candidate fatigue — with the changes that have taken place in Presidential campaigns since 1960. In 1960, styles changed, and after that so did the rules — formal and informal. The dilemma is that many of the changes are for the better, but at great cost to the candidate's time and energy. In 1960, John Kennedy won the nomination by having won a few primaries and having had major states "delivered" at the Convention by those who controlled the states' Party machinery: John Bailey and Abraham Ribicoff in Connecticut; David Lawrence and William Green in Pennsylvania; Michael DiSalle in Ohio; Richard Daley in Illinois.

The Party bosses could not deliver to a candidate with no support or stop a candidate with overwhelming support, but they were in a position to have a decisive effect on the outcome of a Convention. It was probably the candidacy of Barry Goldwater for the Republican nomination in 1964 that began to change the rules of the game. Goldwater's grass-roots organizing — a kind of guerrilla action by private individuals against the Party hierarchy — showed new ways to win state caucuses and primaries, and established a model that was followed by Eugene McCarthy in 1968 and by George McGovern in 1972 and is being adopted by a number of the current Democratic candidates. At the same time, after its 1968 Convention the Democratic Party began to establish ground rules for state caucuses and primaries. One result is that the processes are more open and democratic, and invite more participation by citizens. Another is a drastic change in the nature of campaigns.

In recent campaigns for both the nomination and the election, a number of practices have developed. To win in the primaries or the caucuses, candidates must — or think they must — build extensive organizations of people who will attend the caucuses, canvass, and get out the vote. In order to become known or to get coverage, candidates chase from "media market" to "media market" — preferably hitting three in one day, with at least two of the three in different states. If there is no particular reason for a candidate to turn up in an area, a reason must be devised. Finding the reason for a candidate to appear in Pittsburgh a fifteenth time can require some imagination. If there is doubt that the media will see fit to cover what the candidate has to say, or if he has nothing new to say, a "media event" may be concocted: the candidate rushes into a supermarket, holds up a package of hamburger, and decries the rise in the price of meat; the candidate milks a cow, descends into a coal mine. During his 1972 Presidential campaign, George McGovern stopped at a farm in Iowa so that he could be photographed on the porch of an old farmhouse discussing farm problems, and then, for good measure, proceeded, with the camera crews, to the farm's cornfield and pigpen, to be photographed there. What such events do to the dignity of the candidates and also of politics, and how much they contribute to the enlightenment of the electorate, is questionable. In any case, they are part of what consumes a candidate's time, drains his energy, and exposes his nerves.

In late September, I had a talk with Kenneth O'Donnell, who was one of John Kennedy's chief political advisers. O'Donnell is now a businessman in Boston, but, like so many who have been in politics, he still hears its siren song.

"We entered only seven primaries in 1960," O'Donnell pointed out.

"It was a very different ballgame. We had religion as an issue, age as an issue, and an incumbent Vice-President as our opponent. Then we had a beautiful candidate. Geez, we had a candidate. Now you're in a different situation. You have to divide the candidates into different groups. There are those who wait for the Convention. Teddy Kennedy can, Muskie can, Humphrey can — they're known. Then, you have guys like Sargent Shriver, Morris Udall, Birch Bayh — they have to run. Henry Jackson is in that position."

Shifting back to the subject of campaigns, O'Donnell said, "You know what they care about in the Party? Who's going to be sheriff. If I'm sitting with Richard Daley, I'm looking for a candidate who helps the ticket — who elects me attorney general. I care about who's going to be the sheriff, the judge, the D.A. Do you know how much they cared in West Virginia who was going to be President? Zero. Now everybody's talking about SALT and detente — nobody cares about that in Boston. They care about busing and about jobs. About themselves. It's a terrible, horrendous course, you know. People expect you to do things every day. I don't think the fact that you went to three hot-dog plants in the morning makes you a better President. We did it, and it was almost embarrassing. John Kennedy opened his Wisconsin campaign at five o'clock in the morning at an Oscar Mayer plant. Do you think anyone cared? But if you don't do it people think you're lazy and arrogant. If you do it, it means you're willing to work, that's all. Estes Kefauver began it. But people do want to see the candidate and ought to see the candidate."

I asked O'Donnell where he would draw the line.

"I don't know," he replied. "There's a great deal of talk about the question of whether there should be a national primary or regional primaries. That's something we have to think more about. First, you have to get name recognition. The average guy in the street says, 'Who's Birch Bayh?' People say, 'Who's Scoop Jackson?' That's what the problem is. Everybody knows Ted Kennedy's name. They don't know if he's Jack Kennedy or Bob Kennedy or Ted Kennedy. In 1960, between Kennedy and Humphrey, it came down to who could lead the country. We haven't had that since. In 1968, the war was the issue, and Humphrey was trapped. In 1972, McGovern beat Humphrey in the primaries, but he did it in a way that lost him the election. This is a brand-new situation, and nobody knows what it's about. As of now, nobody knows anything."

Among the truisms heard currently is that within the Democratic Party in 1968 and 1972 the Vietnam war was a galvanizing issue, which stirred people into working for Eugene McCarthy and George McGovern, but that no such issue exists now. In those years, it was the cause more than the personalities that defined the Democratic struggle; at present there is no similar compelling cause. It has been the case that those wings of the major parties which are most driven by ideology— for the Republicans, the right; for the Democrats, the left — work hardest in the primaries and caucuses, and thus the results are skewed toward those wings. It was this phenomenon that caused the Republicans to nominate Goldwater, the Democrats to nominate McGovern — each losing disastrously in the general election. Nixon won the Republican nomination in 1968 by spreading himself across the "middle" of the Party, and now several Democrats are trying to figure out how to win the nomination without committing what has come to be known as "the McGovern mistake." The search is for a potion that will arouse nonideological passion.

Fred Dutton is a Washington lawyer who has been involved in the Presidential campaigns of Adlai Stevenson, John Kennedy, Robert Kennedy, and George McGovern. During the Kennedy Administration, he worked in the White House and the State Department. He is an unconventional man, and tends to think about politics in terms of mood and style rather than of mechanics. He is one of the people in Washington who are consulted by politicians and journalists for a sense of what to do or of what is going on. Over lunch one day, I asked Dutton to talk to me not about "who's ahead" but about campaigns.

"The present campaign styles were set by Nixon and Kennedy in 1960," he said. "Both were bright young politicians at the top of their form. The Eisenhower period had burned itself out. Robert Montgomery, as an adviser to Eisenhower, had been toying with TV. Kennedy and Nixon set the new style: standing at microphones, no heavy podium — all sorts of new techniques. They recognized that the idea was to sell themselves, to put across a style. We are still in the dregs of 1960. There is nothing creative. The current candidates are rote figures, automatons, responding in a hack way to 1960. The big changes came when Roosevelt made effective use of the radio, and Kennedy and Nixon used their new techniques in 1960. In fairness, campaign styles haven't changed very often. The early Presidents — Jefferson and the others — offered themselves to the voters in a lofty manner; they spoke from on high, were relaxed, cool. The first big change in style was by Andrew Jackson after he lost in 1824; in 1828 he campaigned like crazy, and personalized contact with the public. In the process, he expanded the electoral base. National political conventions began early in the eighteen-thirties, and then we started to get the bunting, the torchlight parades, keynote addresses. That was the beginning of P.R. in politics; of slogans — guys like William Henry Harrison and Zachary Taylor running on slogans. It was one of the most creative periods in politics, but it came about because the candidates couldn't come to grips with the emerging issues — the diverging economies of the North and the South, slavery. The slogans and the hoopla were to divert attention from substantive questions. In 1896, Mark Hanna, trying to get William McKinley elected, organized county chairmen and outside groups and sent them out on trains to Ohio to see McKinley. Mark Hanna is generally considered the first expert in organizational politics. Roosevelt was the first guy who used the radio effectively; TV wasn't really used with any imagination until 1960. Kennedy and Nixon pulled out all the stops, and we got to the jet-planing and the three stops a day. The problem is that style — the communication of the implicit — has become self-conscious. Everything has become organized, unspontaneous. The implicit and the explicit, the word and the picture should go together. What has happened is that they have diverged, and there is so much that is clearly phony. It is as if Kennedy, instead of relying on his good looks, had worried about getting his picture taken in front of the Statue of Liberty, as Lyndon Johnson did. The Statue of Liberty is a good thing. The Statue of Liberty with a politician in front of it is a phony. By the time Scoop Jackson makes a tour in California, all the humanity and spontaneity are gone. Everything is overorganized. It's the bureaucratization of politics. My guess is that in the next round we're going to get back to substantive people. Someone is going to have to get himself across as a real person. Campaigns should change. The country is going through a withdrawal. It's tired. I tell potential candidates, 'Don't be frenetic. Don't run around the country. Don't do three stops a day. You may have to get around and see power brokers and groups, but take the heat out of it. It's too frenetic.' Then they ask how they would get on television and in the papers. I tell them, 'Get some ideas; get good people around you.' They don't need the daily TV or press story. The real political animal needs to see his name in the paper. They lose all quality control. If they get on Cronkite or Chancellor three times a year with something classy it's better than fifty times a year."

Dutton continued, "People are looking for more spiritual qualities in their leaders. The guy who is going to break through is going to have fresh proposals, and is not going to fit the political stereotypes. All that the candidates are doing now, at a time when people hate politicians, is acting like politicians. These guys who are staying above the battle — the Hubert Humphreys, the Muskies, the Gaylord Nelsons — are being smarter. Mondale was very shrewd. He saw what kind of person he did not want to be, that he would get cut up by the meat grinder, that it was a demeaning process that would make him a lesser man. His was a shrewder judgment than people thought. The best strategy now is to stay out of it and take the chance that nobody will emerge from the primaries and caucuses in a position to win the Convention. Muskie and Humphrey can sit it out, make thoughtful speeches. Like de Gaulle in 1946, going off to the side and waiting to be called. It's one of the oldest tricks in politics."

Early this November, Humphrey, who was being widely touted as the possible Democratic nominee — as was Muskie four years ago — told Jules Witcover, of the Washington *Post*, "It's my judgment that right now the person that has no ambition, no declared ambitions, is more credible," and he added, "He's freer. You don't have to go around weighing every word as you inevitably do when you become a candidate. . . . The minute you get in it, you're just another one of them."

Dutton went on, "I favor the reform rules, but they are making politics more organizational, when what we need is more free form. And if the result is that apathy and cynicism become even greater, we may be worse off than ever. You have more midgets, more faceless people, surrounding campaigns. And the kinds of people you have around in the campaign can determine much more about a Presidency than you think. Nixon ran a Byzantine, secretive campaign and the same kind of Administration."

I asked Dutton if that was not a question of the character of the candidate himself.

He replied, "It's the individual verifying himself in the campaign and then in office. How good is he at putting together a staff? Can he move from state politics to shark-infested national politics?"

I asked Dutton if he felt that campaigns call for the wrong qualities in people.

He replied, "The White House operation is more like a campaign than people think: the number of hardball questions that come in to a President every hour; how much thought goes into a speech. Campaigns are highly imperfect schools for the White House. They are learning exercises. You learn that some issues go and some don't. You don't go out there to preach at people, you go out there to lead. You have to find out where you can lead them. How much stamina do you have? How much can you take the stress of a complicated society? The White House is a hurly-burly job. If you can't stand the strains, you shouldn't be in that league; you should do something else — be a senator, a preacher, a philosopher. A campaign is a frenetic, superficial, compulsive, neurotic process. Can you come across on current technology — not by being handsome but by coming across? Do you understand the mood of the country? The good candidate learns how far he can go, what his stamina is, what the good camera angles are. If you can't reconcile differences within your campaign staff, can't make decisions, you probably can't do those things in the White House. If you can't slow down the pace of a campaign, you can't slow down the pace in the White House. If you can't structure your emotional or decisional process in a campaign, you can't do it in the White House. Ninety-five to ninety-nine per cent of those who run don't think beyond the point of winning; they don't think about accumulating the authority and power to do things once they are in office. Just winning the election is not enough; you also have to come out of it with the power to govern. The candidates run as if they were running for sheriff, yet the next day one of them is going to take over the White House. Eventually, we'll move to new political forms, and then those will become trite, too."

A 1982 GALLUP POLL RE-vealed that Senator Edward Kennedy of Massachusetts was the overwhelming presidential choice not only of Democrats, but of all the people. Gallup found that Kennedy would easily defeat Ronald Reagan in a presidential race. The poll was yet one more indication of the popularity of the Kennedy name, and the attraction of Edward Kennedy as a *hypothetical* candidate. In the following selection, Garry Wills points out that for a long time Kennedy's problem was "how to keep running for president without actually having to *run*."

The Kennedy myth remained greater than the reality until the debacle of 1980, when Kennedy attempted to transform his name into power and lost. The same rank-and-file Democrats who always seemed to admire him from afar voted against him after taking a closer look. They liked Kennedy as a possible candidate, but not as a real one.

It was Edward Kennedy, the *defeated* candidate, who stirred the 1980 Democratic convention into a frenzy. Now out of the race, Kennedy could resume his role as the perennial possible candidate. The 1980 defeat apparently did not destroy his credibility as a potential candidate. He became once more both an adored and feared politician.

Garry Wills analyzes the Kennedy myth in the following selection. Edward Kennedy wears the family's mantle and is sometimes burdened by it. "Just by bearing his name," writes Wills, "Kennedy has come to resemble the aging gunfighter of Western movies, the one every young punk wants to beat as a way of making his reputation." Kennedy is often treated as a surrogate president, a role that he must assume because of his name. As the standard bearer, he is the prisoner of his family's heritage and of popular expectations. Whether he will again seek to become a real president remains to be seen.

3 Garry Wills
EDWARD KENNEDY: THE PRISONER OF POWER

Those whom the splendour of their rank, or the extent of their capacity, have placed upon the summit of human life have not often given any just occasion to envy in those who look up to them from a lower station.
—Samuel Johnson, *Life of Richard Savage*

Harry Truman established for ex-presidents the embarrassing custom of building libraries to themselves (Truman used to act as guide through his own shrine, signing things in the imitated Oval Office, or playing the piano). President Kennedy did not live to preside over his library's construction or arrangement; but one hopes he would have eliminated the more grandiose touches. The worst aspect of the exhibits is an illuminated dateline that runs over all the cases of memorabilia. Below a dividing line are important family dates (from the landing of the first Kennedy on America's shore), correlated, above the line, with events in world history. So, for 1917, we read "John F. Kennedy born in Brookline," conjoined with "Russian Revolution," as if Clio viewed history stereoscopically with a Kennedy always in one slide.

The pairings suggest, in places, more than coincidence — as when, late in 1963, we read below the line "President and Mrs. Kennedy arrive in Texas for political tour" just after reading, above the line, "Diem government in South Vietnam is overthrown."

The events in Edward Kennedy's life march side by side with history's major happenings. The Kennedy family's importance is asserted through this equal billing with World History. But it is hard to shine when one is sharing the stage, always, with Historical Events. Edward Kennedy enters the world, in 1932, partnered with "The New Deal comes to Washington." Some think he is fading from our politics in the same company. And, even aside from such particular chimings, it must be unsettling for one's life to be measured out on such a macroscopic scale — to have wars for playmates, manifestos shuffled with the dance cards, weddings woven into the rise and fall of nations. No man's life should be drawn across the rack of Everything Important supplied by this schedule.

Even if the exhibit were not there, I suppose, people would construct something like it in their minds. Edward Kennedy lives with two great growth charts traced behind him in the air. In every situation, whomever he is meeting, the implicit question hangs there: How does he measure up? Has he got the stuff to be another John F. Kennedy? Somehow Edward acquired, through his late twenties and early thirties, the reputation of being "the family's best politician"; but the 1980 race seems to have destroyed that claim. He lacks the John Kennedy flair, the knowing suggestion of familiarity with ideas, the witty aside that reinforced his poised air of dignity. When Edward poses as an intellectual, he looks uncomfortable. He is not dumb, by any means; but his political feel is for people — preferably other politicians — not for books. His "deep" speeches tend to be delivered woodenly. My wife and I saw that at a 1978 meeting in Philadelphia, where Kennedy addressed a group launching "Project '87" to prepare for the bicentennial of the Constitution's drafting. The audience was made up of fat cats and scholars. For the scholars he met (James MacGregor Burns pointing them out to him), he ran a tape recorder in his head, the importance of the

Constitution today, a perfunctory recital for which he had been programmed.

That night's speech was well researched and well written — a timely argument against calling a new constitutional convention. But the audience was cool, made up of conservative Philadelphia money types (some at our table spoke well of the town's pistol-packing mayor, Frank Rizzo). Those who knew Edward Kennedy only from political rallies full of his supporters were dumbfounded when he spoke so poorly in the 1980 campaign. I was partly prepared for that by his failure to reach out to a skeptical audience in Philadelphia, even with good material prepared for him.

The demands to live up to the president's memory make Edward alternate exaggerated efforts at seriousness with collapses into rowdy relaxation; one minute Peck's Bad Boy, the next an Elder Statesman. When, for instance, he went to a reunion of his Virginia Law School classmates, the same year as that Philadelphia speech, his fellow alumni came to rib him about his school days and his presidential chances. The university president, Dr. Hereford, introduced him by remembering how, as a young faculty member, he rented his home during a sabbatical year to Kennedy and John Tunney. Hereford had some misgivings about turning his house over to students, but these were mollified when he heard that the Kennedy son was bringing a family maid to care for the place. The misgivings revived when he came back to town and heard, from the cabbie who picked him up at the airport, that his address was famous now for the parties thrown, the bands hired, the jolly crowds. As jocular reminiscences were exchanged, Kennedy rose and gave a stiff recital on the privilege of legal training. Just as he is invisibly manacled in the public company of women, so reports of his Charlottesville speeding tickets made him almost a caricature of sober responsibility when he went back to that scene. His name and his past imprison him. It is hard to cross every stage escorting History on your arm.

If Edward is not another poised John Kennedy, he is even less a rumpled and plunging Robert. Robert was a prematurely serious child and he aged into even more childlike earnestness. His haste to be with Cesar Chavez breaking a fast seemed to reflect a desire to make up for lost time, for the vigils in southern churches that Robert had not shared with Dr. King. In the Senate, Robert, the elder, was defiant of custom and lacking in respect for ancient colleagues. Edward, the younger brother, went around picking up Robert's broken crockery. Edward is temperamentally a joiner — Robert was a resigner. I remember speaking just after Edward Kennedy, in 1972, at an antiwar protest held in the Senate caucus room. Kennedy was one of only two senators who showed up, and he spoke earnestly against the war. But the group, which was petitioning for redress of the constitutional grievance of undeclared war, got no encouragement from him in its determination to commit civil disobedience. That is not Edward's way. If Robert had been there, he would have made it clear he shared the group's gut feelings, even if he did not agree with their tactics. Edward Kennedy is a dutiful liberal, not a natural radical. He will be courageous in his choice of goals, but conventional in his pursuit of them. He stands true to old positions — not breaking into new territory, like Robert. His health plan, for instance, is an old measure adopted in most industrial democracies, and he has maneuvered for it in the accepted Senate ways. But in a period of economic retrenchment and noisy "antigovernment" rhetoric, this essentially centrist politician is thought of as the leftwardmost major figure in our politics, the principal target of right-wing political action committees. With a compromise abortion stand close to the majority position, he is considered a villain by antiabortion groups, in part because of his religion. The gun lovers love to haunt his campaigns. He *is* the Left to much of the Right, and his downfall would signal the permanent fall of the Left. It is interesting to see how, as his own position has been eroded, the stature of people scheming against him has diminished. At first it was Lyndon Johnson, who tried to oust the Kennedys and establish his own legitimacy. Then it was Richard Nixon, a president hiring gumshoes to pad around Chappaquiddick. Then Jimmy Carter devoted disproportionate time and effort to the project of "whipping his ass." Now it is John Dolan of the National Conservative Political Action Committee who thinks he holds Kennedy's fate in his hands. Just by bearing his name, Kennedy has come to resemble the aging gunfighter of Western movies, the one every young punk wants to beat as a way of making his reputation.

I asked him, in his Virginia home, if he ever thought of his family legacy as a burden, something that hampers him, by now, more than it helps. "I can't think of my brothers that way. I'm just grateful for all the things they taught me, all the experiences we shared. For the rest, you just have to take that." It was mid-February of 1981, and defenders of the new Reagan administration had claimed *they* were heirs to whatever was good in the Kennedy presidency — leaving the actual Kennedy to take blame for all that was bad. Arthur Laffer, the prophet of Reagan's "supply side" economics, continually invoked the 1963 tax cut as the cause of America's last spurt of prosperity. Kennedy laughed at that: "It is one thing to have a tax cut while maintaining inflation at less than 3.6 percent for three years. It is another matter to impose one with double-digit inflation."

Columnist George Will, who threw a party for the incoming Reagan administration, said that the Republicans now uphold President Kennedy's tough stance against the Russians, the determination to close a defense gap. Edward Kennedy tries to recapture his own name, but is resigned about the prospects of success: "President Kennedy believed the nation must be strong; but he was willing to take imaginative steps like the nuclear test ban." When I press him on the differences between John Kennedy in 1960 and Robert Kennedy in 1968, he says that naturally both men changed with the experience of new things. But Robert underwent especially deep changes in his last years? "He certainly did." One is to presume that John Kennedy would have taken the same course — though it is hard to imagine him at a Cesar Chavez rally.

Edward Kennedy has to keep living three lives at once — or keep giving an account of the lives the other men lived for him. Walking through his empty house, crammed with pictures of the family, one realizes how much of his life has already been lived for him, off in directions he can neither take anymore, nor renounce. At one time, the same-and-different Kennedy smile coming from so many faces clustered on mantel or shelf must have intensified his presence, replicating every aspect of family influence he could bring to bear. Now they seem to drain him — he seeps off into their fading images.

His divorce proceedings have been announced. Only one son is living with him at the moment, and he is at school. Today the senator's press secretary, Robert Shrum, has come out for lunch with us. Otherwise Kennedy lives here alone. But his family is never far from his conversation. He has just come back from a visit with his mother in Florida, where the February rain and cold kept most people from swimming — but not the ninety-year-old Rose. "When she took me to church, there was no one at the altar with the priest, so she said, 'Teddy?' You would have been proud of me, Bob, serving mass." I said I would not know how to serve Mass in the new liturgy, not since Latin went out. "*Ad Deum qui laetificat juventutem meam,*" Kennedy rattles off, in schoolboy tones. Shrum takes up the next response, and I the third. We all agree the *"Suscipiat"* was the toughest response, and prove our point by variously misremembering it.

It was an unnaturally warm day in February: I had seen three chairs lined up before the front door when I parked my car — like deck chairs on a liner, each with its own giant blanket. I went in through the open door and found Shrum, who said, "The senator likes to be outdoors every minute he can." We sat down like a silly version of the three leaders lined up at Yalta, to talk about nuclear disarmament. Kennedy favors a comprehensive test ban (CTB): "President Kennedy took the initiative which led to the first test ban. We need to have some of that imagination."

Is CTB feasible? "In 1974, I explained my proposal to Brezhnev in Moscow, and he said, 'If you had that in your pocket, I could sign it right now' — which surprised me. When I went back in 1978, I asked him why the Russians were opposing our CTB proposal. He said, 'You have changed the terms, from five years to three years. You have added to the number of on-site inspections' — the agreement to have any on-site inspections was a breakthrough that we wasted. 'You have changed from no explosions allowed to none above three kilotons.' "

Why did Kennedy think these changes had been made? "Brzezinski told me we had to get SALT II first, and go for CTB later." In fact the Carter administration, like the Nixon administration before it, resented Kennedy's dealings with Russian leaders as an infringement on their own power to make foreign policy. Kennedy is one of the few men who can be welcomed by foreign leaders as a kind of surrogate president — which infuriates real presidents. He can hurt his own proposals simply by advancing them in his own name. He continues to live inside the pressures that made Robert fear the cause of peace would be hurt with President Johnson if a Kennedy carried its banner. When Edward Kennedy took up the cause of wage and price controls in the 1980 election, he guaranteed that President Carter would never consider that course. Such power to initiate is easily translated into a powerlessness to conclude.

I asked Kennedy if his belief that wage and price controls were needed had been dispelled by the election. "No." Will you continue to call for them while President Reagan actually takes off controls? "I believe in deregulation. We deregulated the airlines and that was even more successful than it appears — part of the savings were eaten up by the increase in fuel costs. But there are forty or so more areas where we can deregulate." Why beat one's head against a wall? If the mood is for deregulation, then deregulate — something, at least, gets done.

Did Kennedy feel the liberal cause was badly damaged by Reagan's triumph, by the loss of so many of Kennedy's liberal colleagues in the Senate? He denies that any overwhelming mandate was won. After all, who can expect an incumbent to win with thirteen percent inflation? "Twelve Democratic senators lost by less than four percent." A few votes here or there and the Senate would still be Democratic. Yet Kennedy is a centrist politician. He says President Reagan should be given a chance to show whether he has a cure for the nation's economic troubles. "I hope he does. We are looking for grounds of agreement. Maybe President Reagan can bring about voluntary price restraint." He does not sound very hopeful. "Well, I guess it can be done; but that would take a tremendous investment of the government's time and energy. I asked Helmut Schmidt how he controls prices in Germany. He said it takes two hundred hours of his personal time during the working year, to keep after labor and business — I wonder how he keeps track of the exact hours?"

Attempts at accommodation with the Reagan people are part of Edward Kennedy's temperament. But a man who could not elicit cooperation from the preceding Democratic administration is unlikely to get much from a White House stocked with right-wing types who think of him as the personification of the Left, or as the heir to certain historical stands — the defense-gap shrillness, the tax cut — they want to *detach* from him and claim as their own. Besides, any chumminess with them would offend his own constituency, labor and blacks and the tattered remains of the New Deal generation. Kennedy shows no desire or design for forging an entirely new coalition. In fact, Gary Hart — one of the few liberal senators to survive the 1980 election — expressly excludes Kennedy as "old fashioned" when he talks of forming a new Democratic program in the Senate. He thinks Kennedy's appeal is based on nostalgia, something that does not stir young politicians trying to build new careers.

If the Right transfers irrational grudges against this or that Kennedy to Edward, the Left nurses an intermittently hopeful disappointment at his failure to live up to its dreams for him. A few liberals are continually running him for president, and he must encourage them (mildly) to protect his eroding position in the Senate. His problem, for a long time, was how to keep running for president without actually having to *run*. In 1980, that difficult juggling act became an impossible one. President Carter gave him no "out" of loyalty or partnership with the Democratic incumbent. And Carter's disastrous personal polls left him no excuse to be drawn from party discipline. All those who had waited for years to see Kennedy run told him, in effect, that it was time to put up or shut up. I saw how these converging pressures worked during the summer of 1979 (that period of "malaise" when President Carter retreated to his mountaintop and consulted every important person in his party except Kennedy). In May, I rode from Washington to Baltimore with Douglas Fraser of the United Auto Workers, Kennedy's principal noncongressional ally in the campaign for governmental health insurance. Kennedy was announcing his health plan, to put it in competition with the president's — and he expected Fraser to be with him in the Senate caucus room when he answered press questions. But Fraser said he could not come unless Kennedy was a declared candidate for president. "If you are not going to take on Carter, I may have to live with him for another four years." Carter was cultivating Fraser with phone calls and White House meetings, which gave labor access and leverage. Fraser would sacrifice that to stand with a *campaigning* Kennedy, but not to help a mere senator promote this bill with a slim chance of passage. At some point, even to advance his Senate projects, Kennedy had to say yes to all those begging him to run.

Fraser was dutiful, rather than begging; he still doubted Kennedy could live down Chappaquiddick. But he joined with Kennedy when he announced. Others were less calm in their advocacy. Multiply the kind of pressure Fraser was exerting a thousandfold, and one sees that Kennedy really had no choice to make in 1980 — he had to run for president. He was not free *not* to. His own lack of enthusiasm for the task showed in the poor preparation he had made. He was only running because everyone assumed Carter had to lose; why prepare for a rough race? Kennedy wants the presidency, if it comes to him by the pressure of events; but he does not have the fire in his belly to rule, like John Kennedy, or the determination of an underdog, like Robert in 1968. Edward rented a private "Air Force One," early in the fall of 1980, and campaigned as an incumbent. The same forces that left him no real choice about running debilitated him when he began the campaign. He was trapped in a race he could not win because he would only undertake a race he thought he could not lose.

It is hard for some to realize that Edward Kennedy is hobbled by his own apparent power. They saw him deliver a stunning speech to the 1980 Democratic convention, and watched the crowd on the floor go crazy with affection for the man and his heritage. Many of those who merely accepted Jimmy Carter as a candidate almost fanatically desired Edward Kennedy. He speaks to them with a voice no one else can equal. That was apparent not only at the party convention of 1980, but at the midterm meeting of Democrats in Memphis two years earlier. Kennedy stole that show with a single speech, in some ways a more powerful one than the televised 1980 address.

President Carter, fearing a miniconvention revolt in 1978, dispatched his entire White House operation to Memphis; then came himself, to sit meekly in two "workshops" while people criticized his record ("Can you imagine Lyndon Johnson sitting there letting others attack his performance?"); and gave a speech too fervent in its rhetoric and too tepid in its delivery. Jerry Rafshoon produced a presidential movie to awe the crowds. Elven White House aides were given the job of countering Kennedy's single appearance at a health-care discussion. To an overflow audience in the largest hall off the convention floor itself, the moderator admitted the reality behind the discussion of various health programs: Governor-elect Bill Clinton of Arkansas said there had been a change in the program, that they were really going to discuss "the relative merits of Georgia peanuts and Massachusetts cranberries."

Joseph Califano led off for the White House, arguing that the economy would not allow any more in health care than the administration was proposing. Kennedy, following, thundered against that timid position. His prepared text, distributed to the press, distilled all his long advocacy on the subject. Charts showed his plan's feasibility. And then, his voice rising, face reddening, Kennedy abandoned his text, stepped forward of the lectern, his voice booming out unaided to the back rows, shouting that every family has disabling illnesses, the Kennedys had, but Kennedys can pay, and senators have illnesses, but senators have ample health insurance, but what of people without these advantages, isn't what's good enough for Congress good enough for *any American citizen?* The audience was up with him, shouting too, euphoric, happily angry. All the exaggerated talk of Kennedy style seemed vindicated. All the memories of his family's suffering, and its sense of caring, all the happier times of social concern at the heart of Democratic politics, made Democrats feel good again — all but dour White House aide Stuart Eisenstadt, who glowered at this demonstration against his boss.

And then the convention went off to vote with Carter on the key measure before it. There had been a moment of rapturous nostalgia, outside the everyday world of political bargaining. They were happy to forget the price tag while Kennedy orated — and were careful to remember it when the vote came. Kennedy was gone from Memphis by the time the real action took place. He had done his job. He had kept alive some memories. The deals were cut without him.

A pattern is emerging. Kennedy is at his best when he is not in the running. That is true not only in Memphis, or at the New York convention; the reporters following him in 1980 noticed a sense of freedom growing in him as his chances faded. He performed best when he was showing his mettle as a survivor, not bidding to take over. Forced by fame, by his name, toward power, he tightens up. Allowed to back off, he relaxes. This is not surrender. He still takes a role, subordinate, one where he can maneuver against the pressures that would *make* him succeed. He seems to be acquiring a sense of power's last paradox — that it is most a prison when one thinks of it as a *passepartout*. When one thinks of it as a prison, one is already partway free.

RONALD REAGAN'S VICTORY seemed assured by election eve, 1980. A Massachusetts bartender told a questioner who was conducting his own straw poll that he was going to vote Republican for the first time in his life. That, by itself, was an almost certain sign of a Reagan victory. More sophisticated pollsters including Patrick Caddell in the Carter camp, knew as well that the die was already cast, that Carter would lose.

Reagan's victory was explained in many ways. Some, especially liberal Democrats, said that it was a vote against Carter. They confidently predicted that the Reagan phenomenon would be short lived, that Democrats would gain in both the House and the Senate in the 1982 elections, and that the party could once again win the White House in 1984.

Reagan's mastery of the media was more widely believed to have been the cause of his success. He had been an actor, after all, and knew how to appeal on television to popular emotions. His image, more than his views on major issues of public policy, was given credit for his victory. During the 1980 presidential campaign Garry Wills wrote that Reagan was the man on the white horse who would save the nation from its past foibles. Wills stressed Reagan's image and style. He was, suggested Wills, "the first serious counter-authority [to government] with an air of authority; the charismatic leader without a vision, just a role."[1] Reagan, concluded Wills, was "both Henry Aldrich and Grandpa Walton, our remembered and our present selves, our fantasy of afternoons with popcorn and the 'real' world of TV politics. Where so little is stable, the emptiness at the center looks eternal. Reagan is the calm eye of history's hurricane; and we hope, by moving with it, never to slip toward the edges into chaos."[2]

While most commentators concentrated upon Reagan's media skills and image to explain his victory, journalist Jeff Greenfield, a TV commentator himself, concluded that Reagan won by following the more traditional rules of politics. He had a superb political organization, and his program offered a clear and apparently popular choice for the electorate.[3]

The Greenfield thesis about Reagan echoed the views of the late political scientist V. O. Key, Jr., who wrote:

> Voters are not fools. To be sure, many individual voters act in odd ways indeed; yet in the large, the electorate behaves about as rationally and responsibly as we should expect, given the clarity of the alternatives presented to it and the character of the information available to it. In American presidential campaigns of recent decades the portrait of the American electorate that develops from the data is not one of an electorate straitjacketed by social determinants or moved by subconscious urges triggered by devilishly skillful propagandists. It is rather one of an electorate moved by concern about

[1] Garry Wills, "Ron and Destiny: Where Will He Lead Us, This Embodiment of Our Everyday Experience?" *Esquire*, August 1980, p. 37.

[2] Ibid.

[3] Jeff Greenfield, *The Real Campaign* (New York: Summit Books, 1982).

central and relevant questions of public policy, of governmental performance, and of executive personality.[4]

Whether voters chose Reagan because of his style, program, or a combination of both, remained conjecture during the first two years of his administration. There was no doubt, however, that Reagan had a program that he intended to carry out. His clarion call to the Conservative Political Action Conference a year after he had been in office reveals his determination: "Fellow citizens, fellow conservatives, our time is now. Our moment has arrived. We stand together shoulder to shoulder in the thickest of the fight."[5] The president had already achieved remarkable success in reducing taxes and government expenditures, but to change the face of government in the way that he wanted far more needed to be done.

Reagan's actions as president, particularly his direct confrontation of the Washington political establishment, which he carefully courted but whose powers he wanted to diminish, surprised political pundits. Reagan apparently meant what he said during his campaign, which made him a political novelty. The following selection, by a journalist who has closely followed Reagan's political career since its inception, depicts his character and style and examines the underlying forces that have shaped him.

4 Lou Cannon
RONALD REAGAN: A POLITICAL PERSPECTIVE

He seemed to many, from beginning to end, a most unlikely leader of the nation. As the United States of America entered the complex, computer age of the 1980s, Ronald Wilson Reagan reached backward and spoke to the future in the accents of the past. His suits were as out of date as his metaphors, most of which derived from the Great Depression or World War II. He quoted freely from the Founding Fathers and from his early hero, Franklin Delano Roosevelt. He viewed Soviet expansionism much as Roosevelt had viewed Nazi aggression. When others protested that he saw the world in stark and simple terms, Reagan would say: "For many years, you and I have been shushed like children and told there are no simple answers to complex problems that are be-

[4] V. O. Key, Jr., *The Responsible Electorate* (Cambridge, Mass.: The Belknap Press of Harvard University Press, 1966), pp. 7–8.

[5] *National Journal*, May 2, 1981, p. 779.

From *Washington Post* Staff Members, *The Pursuit of the Presidency*, ed. by Richard Harwood. © *The Washington Post*, 1980. Reprinted by permission.

yond our comprehension. Well, the truth is there *are* simple answers — just not easy ones."

By the historical standards of the American presidency, Reagan seemed an even more unlikely leader. Though he was vigorous and athletic, he was sixty-nine years old and would be seventy within a month of taking the presidential oath of office. The age showed in the dewlapped wrinkles of his neck. It showed in the Reagan campaign schedules, which were generously endowed with "staff time" that was the euphemistic reference to Reagan's afternoon nap. And Reagan in other ways seemed singularly unprepared for the office which he and others have ritualistically referred to as "the most important in the free world."

He had not held public office in six years. He had no foreign policy experience. He had never worked in Washington. He was a divorced man espousing the values of the family, a wartime stateside noncombatant advocating military preparedness, a fiscal conservative who as governor of California had sponsored the largest tax increases in the state's history.

But despite all this and the majority party and the White House incumbency against him, Reagan was a formidable candidate with an appeal that reached beyond his natural, conservative constituency. He was larger than the sum of his parts. Some said this was because he was a superb television performer whose skills were honed by years of professional experience. Others said he was a lucky politician (as some had said of Jimmy Carter), with the good fortune to face overrated opponents at the time they were most vulnerable. But there was another reason, and it was more important than the others. It was that whatever Reagan lacked in complexity or youth or consistency, he made up for in an unremitting vision of America. The vision was the thing. It was a vision frozen in time, which made it more powerful than transitory visions. Reagan believed in it, which made it even more powerful. A close personal aide, Michael K. Deaver, said this about Reagan's belief: "He's resolved something, his being or what he is, a long time ago. He seems to know what is right."

And whether Reagan did, in fact, know what was right, his vision of America was what made this aging, out-of-date exactor credible to other Americans. Reporters and Reagan aides would smile at one another and head for the press buses when Reagan approached his standard tearjerker ending of the basic speech he used in early 1980. They would laugh outright when Reagan, for the thousandth time, quoted John Winthrop aboard "the tiny Arabella" in 1630 as telling his followers that they should be "as a city on a hill."

"The eyes of all mankind are still upon us," Reagan would conclude. "Our party came into being more than one hundred years ago, born of a great crisis at that time. We led this nation through that crisis. We are being called upon again. Let us keep our rendezvous with destiny, let us build a shining city upon a hill."

This was part of Reagan's vision, and the audience did not laugh at it. Most of the people who heard the speech applauded. A few of them cried. And they came back for the equally simplistic and more materialistic versions of the vision: "At the heart of our message should be five simple familiar words. No big economic theories. No sermons on political philosophy. Just five short words: Family, work, neighborhood, freedom, peace."

Historically, Reagan's vision was rooted in small-town Midwestern America of the early twentieth century — then the real and symbolic heartland of the nation. His values were shaped in a day when most Americans lived not in the great, cluttered urban landscapes of our time but in towns and small cities surrounding a more pastoral land. When he was trying out self-characterizations early in the 1980 campaign, Reagan briefly referred to himself as a "Main Street Republican," a phrase intended to show that he was not a boardroom candidate like John Connally or an Ivy Leaguer like George Bush. The phrase, quietly discarded after the primaries because Reagan's advisers thought it made the candidate seem partisan and out of date, was an appropriate description of Reagan. Like all persons, he is a product of his time and region, his experience and his culture. For Reagan it was small-town Illinois, the quintessential Main Street celebrated in Middle America and satirized by Sinclair Lewis's famous novel of the same name. "Main Street is the climax of civilization," Lewis wrote in the preface to his novel, which appeared in 1920 when Reagan was nine years old. Lewis meant these words sardonically but Reagan would accept them as literal truth. In his autobiography, *Where's The Rest of Me?*, Reagan describes his childhood as "a rare Huck Finn-Tom Sawyer idyll."

"Reagan was shaped by the small towns of the Midwest, and that explains in large part the simple moral and conservative approach he brought to public life," wrote early biographer Bill Boyarsky in *The Rise of Ronald Reagan*. "Where Lewis satirized the Midwest communities, Reagan glorifies them. He enthusiastically accepts the values that Lewis criticized. As a result, he is deeply respectful of business; determinedly conservative; mistrusting of change; unintellectual and slightly suspicious of higher education . . . convinced that, as his father said, 'All men were created equal and man's own ambition determines what happens to him the rest of his life.' "

Reagan's father, John Reagan, known as Jack, was a gregarious, nomadic, hard-drinking Irish-American whose own life seems to have fallen far short of his ambition. He was a Catholic in a Protestant land and in Reagan's childhood a fierce opponent of the Ku Klux Klan, which was at the time a national force in American politics. In his autobiography, Reagan related how his father, then a traveling salesman, was told by a small-town hotel clerk that he would appreciate the accommodations because Jews weren't permitted there. "I'm a Catholic," Reagan quotes his father as saying, "and if it's come to the point where you won't take Jews, you won't take me, either." Jack Reagan then stalked out, spent a cold winter night in his car and became seriously ill.

At the time his second son Ronald was born. Jack was working as a clerk in the Pitney General Store in Tampico. Jack's ambition was to own his own store, a goal briefly realized but quickly crushed by the Depression. Ronald Reagan still seems troubled by what happened to his father. When he announced his presidential candidacy on November 13, 1979, Reagan repeated an oft-told story of Christmas Eve in 1931 when Reagan and his older brother Neil were home from college.

Their father received a special delivery letter he hoped would be a bonus. It was instead a "blue slip" telling him that he had been fired.

Ronald Reagan was born in a five-room flat above the Pitney General Store on February 6, 1911. For the first nine years of his life he lived in a procession of Illinois cities and towns: Chicago, Galesburg, Monmouth, Tampico again, and finally Dixon, the place Reagan still calls his hometown and where he lived until he was twenty-one. His mother, and the anchor of the Reagan family, was Nelle Wilson Reagan. She was a do-gooder, a lifelong member of the Christian Church who practiced what she preached. Reagan and his older brother remember many instances of her finding food or jobs for needy persons. Sometimes the Reagan home became — in a day when the phrase was unknown — a halfway house for released convicts.

Reagan was a prodigy. Born with a remarkable memory, he learned to read at an early age and dazzled his mother, who encouraged him to read newspapers aloud to her friends. Reagan recalls reading an account of the Preparedness Day bombing in San Francisco on July 22, 1916, when he was five years old.

There were other ways in which the Reagan home was avant-garde for Dixon. The Reagan boys called their parents by their first names and they called the boys by their nicknames — "Dutch" for Ronald and "Moon" for Neil. The Reagans were the town Democrats in a place and time devotedly Republican. Both Jack and Nelle participated in amateur theatricals, which stimulated the imagination of their children and which made both of them talk about an acting career.

But there also was the dark side of Jack Reagan's alcoholism. Even the relentlessly cheerful Reagan autobiography, written in 1965 with one eye to his coming political career, cannot disguise Reagan's feelings about his father's drinking. "I was eleven years old the first time I came home to find my father flat on his back on the front porch and no one there to lend a hand but me," Reagan writes. "He was drunk, dead to the world. I bent over him, smelling the sharp odor of whiskey from the speakeasy. I got a fistful of his overcoat. Opening the door, I managed to drag him inside and get him to bed. In a few days, he was the bluff, hearty man I knew and loved and will always remember."

Children are stronger than we expect them to be, and there is no evidence that Jack Reagan's alcoholism cast any permanent blight on the lives of his sons. Ronald Reagan would not drink at all for many years, and he was repelled by the Hollywood cocktail circuit. But by all accounts, including his own, he grew up to be a resolute, cheerful young man, hardworking and unintellectual, interested in football and girls and theatricals. Athletic and well built, Reagan enjoyed the role of local lifeguard, and the varying numbers of persons he saved from drowning became an obligatory part of his political biography. Most of all, he enjoyed talking. He had a nonstop gift of gab that had been encouraged by his mother's showing off of his precocious reading ability. As a freshman at tiny Eureka College, Reagan's fiery speechmaking made him the leader of a student strike (over Depression-cancelled classes that would have prevented some students from graduating) which cost the college president his job. He developed a consuming interest, which has never left him, in the medium of radio, which Franklin Roosevelt was then using to carry the gospel of the New Deal to the countryside. At Eureka, Reagan would listen for hours to sports broadcasts, sometimes interspersed with Roosevelt's "fireside chats." Thirty-five years later, as governor of California, Reagan would use the fireside chats as his model for broadcast and televised reports to the people on the public issues of the day.

The Depression and Hollywood stand with Main Street as the shaping symbols in the life of Ronald Reagan. Reagan still considers the Depression as the single most important influence upon him. The Depression cost his father a partnership in a Dixon shoe store. It sent his mother to work in a dress shop for fourteen dollars a week. Reagan, then working his way through Eureka, sent fifty dollars a week home so that his parents could continue to get credit at the local grocery store. But there were many others in as difficult a predicament, or worse. Often, in his days as governor, when Reagan was asked whether he had been poor as a child, he replied with the bromide that "we were poor but we didn't think of ourselves as poor." Sometimes he used the line when he was talking about limiting welfare, the way out for the modern poor. As a historical reference, however, Reagan's statement is an accurate one. What had happened to the Reagans had happened to America.

In his senior year at Eureka, Reagan won an acting award for his role in *Aria de Campo*, an antiwar play by Edna St. Vincent Millay, and he had thoughts of an acting career. But he had no job and he returned to Dixon, uncertain of his future and thinking of radio as an entry into show business. Reagan applied for work at several Chicago radio stations and was turned down. Then, in the fall of 1932, came a chance to broadcast University of Iowa football games for WHO, the NBC affiliate in Des Moines. Reagan had been a starting guard at Eureka, and he loved football. From his first broadcast, he gave a tense and evocative account of what was going on on the field of play below. When baseball season began, Reagan's proclivity for nonstop talking plunged him into the since-lost art of recreating baseball games from the laconic summaries of the action furnished by Western Union telegraph. At a time when everyone listened to radio, Dutch Reagan became a sportscasting star.

He used radio as his springboard to Hollywood. In 1937 he accompanied the Chicago Cubs to Catalina Island off the Southern California coast for spring training, and a friend arranged a screen test for him at Warner Brothers. Reagan passed easily and Hollywood proved even more suitable for Reagan's talents than had radio. Starting out on low-budget pictures, where his ability to quickly memorize scripts proved an enormous asset, Reagan advanced to become "the Errol Flynn of the B's." He made thirty-one movies in five years, progressing from his $200-a-week starting salary to the princely figure of $1,650 a week in 1941. Popular and invariably cast as a good guy, Reagan had mastered his craft and seemed to be rising to the pinnacle of stardom. Though burdened with "B" pictures, he won critical acclaim for performances in *Brother Rat* (where Eddie Albert made his debut and where Reagan met his first wife, Jane Wyman), in *Knute Rockne* (where Reagan plays the doomed Notre Dame football player George Gipp and Pat O'Brien plays Rockne), in *Dark Victory* (with Humphrey Bogart) and, especially in *King's Row*, where the cast included Claude Rains, Robert Cummings and Charles Coburn.

King's Row, the story of a small Southern town more malevolent than Dixon, was Reagan's best picture. He portrayed Drake McHugh, a playboy whose legs are amputated by sadistic surgeon Coburn as revenge for the seduction of his daughter. "Where's the rest of me?" yells McHugh, coming to without his legs and uttering the future title of Reagan's autobiography. *Commonweal* praised Reagan for a "splendid performance," and other reviews were uniformly good. Reagan liked the film too, and in the tradition of ego-laden Hollywood would often show it to house guests after dinner. After Jane Wyman divorced him, she was quoted as saying, "I just couldn't stand to watch that damn *King's Row* one more time."

Reagan never quite fulfilled the acting promise of this period. His career, like so many others, was interrupted by World War II, most of which Reagan spent in Hollywood making training films with the First Motion Picture Unit of the Army Air Corps. Reagan's career couldn't hit its stride after the war, when newer, younger stars were coming along and Hollywood was fighting its own multifront war with television, labor unrest, foreign films, and domestic investigating committees. At the beginning of the war, Reagan had lost out to Humphrey Bogart for a role in a picture that was retitled *Casablanca*. When the war was over he lost his chance to play in another film classic which also starred Bogart, *The Treasure of the Sierra Madre*. Reagan's choice of films, when he had a choice, had never been exceptional and by now his luck was running bad. Given a role in the movie version of the John Van Druten play, *The Voice of the Turtle*, Reagan objected to playing with a new leading lady and asked for June Allyson instead. The actress he objected to was the richly talented Eleanor Parker, subsequently to be nominated for four Oscars. "It took me only one scene with Eleanor to realize that I'd be lucky if I could stay even," Reagan acknowledges in his autobiography.

Reagan's marriage was on the skids along with his movie career. The low point of the career came in 1951, when Reagan played opposite a chimpanzee in *Bedtime for Bonzo*. His marriage had come to an end three years earlier, during Wyman's filming of *Johnny Belinda*, for which she won an Academy Award. Reagan quipped to a gossip columnist that *Johnny Belinda* should be named as correspondent in the divorce action. If Miss Wyman's testimony in the divorce action is to be believed, a better choice would be the Screen Actor's Guild, which increasingly was taking more and more of her husband's time. The picture she painted, both in court and outside of it, was of a bored wife who no longer shared her husband's interests.

Exit Ronald Reagan actor. Enter Reagan, labor negotiator, public spokesman, and future politician. By the early 1950s, although he was still appearing in occasional films, Reagan had in effect established a new career. As leader of the Screen Actors Guild and six times its president, Reagan had become fully embroiled in the economic and cultural issues which shook Hollywood after the war.

If Main Street represented the climax of American civilization in the 1920s, Hollywood was in this postwar era the undisputed capital of American mass culture. Everything that affected Hollywood was a page one story in Peoria — or in Dixon, where the preferred reading matter was the *Chicago Tribune*. These stories included sensational accusations that the movie industry was honeycombed with Communists, disclosures that a key union was operated by gangsters, the emergence of both television and foreign films as a major competitor and taxation-induced "runaway" of U.S. films to foreign countries. Reagan was in the midst of these battles. During the Red-hunting days which Hollywood now remembers with embarrassment and some shame, Reagan opposed Communists but also disputed the basic thesis of the House Committee on Un-American Activities in these words: "I do not believe the Communists have ever at any time been able to use the motion picture screen as a sounding board for their philosophy or ideology." At the time of the Congressional investigations, his stand fully pleased neither side. But he emerged from that period as an effective and adroit political leader who had kept his union intact.

Reagan's personal life and political views were now changing. He had described himself as a "near hopeless hemophiliac liberal." But in 1952, four years after his divorce from Wyman, Ronald Reagan married Nancy Davis, adopted daughter of a conservative and wealthy Chicago surgeon Loyal Davis. In 1954, he became the host for "General Electric Theater," a new half-hour television series, with a salary of $125,000 a year and generous expenses. The GE contract, which might be said to have launched Reagan's political career, gave him an opportunity to be seen each week on television and to talk to GE employees all over the country.

While some old Hollywood friends ascribe Reagan's increasing conservatism of this time to Nancy or her father, it is probable that General Electric, and Reagan's growing prosperity, had much to do with Reagan's changing political views.

At the outset, Reagan's message in his speeches to GE employees was patriotic, anti-Communist, pro-Hollywood. Reacting to the general nature of his talk, GE Board Chairman Ralph Cordiner suggested to Reagan that "you work out a philosophy for yourself." Increasingly, that philosophy became probusiness, antigovernment conservatism. It was a philosophy more congenial to the Republican party than to the Democrats, at least in California. But Reagan, like many Americans, found it easier to embrace Republican principles than to abandon the political faith of his family. As a Democrat, Reagan had supported Helen Gahagan Douglas in her U.S. Senate race against Richard Nixon in 1950. By 1952, he was a Democrat for Eisenhower. When Nixon ran for president in 1960, Reagan was still a Democrat but this time supporting Nixon. Two years later, when Reagan was speaking for Nixon during his unsuccessful campaign for governor of California, a woman in the audience asked him if he were a registered Republican. Reagan said he wasn't, but indicated his willingness to join the GOP. The woman, a volunteer registrar, marched down the aisle and signed him up as a Republican on the spot.

By this time, Reagan had become a partisan politician almost without recognizing it. He was becoming an embarrassment to General Electric, which did much business with the government Reagan was consistently denouncing. When Reagan used the Tennessee Valley Authority, a major customer of GE, as an example of government waste, the company asked him to delete the reference. Reagan complied, but there were those at General Electric who now wanted to be rid of Reagan altogether. In 1962, GE suggested that Reagan limit his speeches to touting the company's products. By then, "General Electric Theater" also was in trouble, facing competition from "Bonanza," a show which became one of Reagan's favorites. When Reagan balked at the limitations GE wanted to place on him, the company abruptly cancelled "GE Theater." Reagan never knew whether it was his speeches or "Bonanza" which hurt him most.

However, Reagan was now prepared for a political career. He had shaken hands with 250,000 GE employees during his eight years as company spokesman and made speeches from one end of the country to the other. He had a philosophy, name recognition, and a winning smile. He also had money, and owned valuable ranch land in the Malibu hills. Increasingly active in Republican politics, Reagan in 1964 was named California chairman of the Barry Goldwater presidential campaign. The leaders of that floundering effort, short on money and party unity, decided to put Reagan on national television. The result, wrote David S. Broder after that campaign, was "the most successful national political debut since William Jennings Bryan electrified the 1896 Democratic convention with his 'Cross of Gold' speech."

Reagan's emotional speech on the night of October 27, 1964, stirred millions of Americans, but it was familiar to those who had heard him on the GE circuit. Basically, it was the same speech he had given for eight years and would give for another sixteen until it grudgingly gave way to new material in the 1980 campaign. There was the celebration of economic individualism: "We need true tax reform that will at least make a start toward restoring for our children the American dream that wealth is denied to no one." And, there were statistics: "The Defense Department runs 269 supermarkets. They do a gross business of $730 million a year and lose $150 million." And, there was democratic idealism: "This idea that government was beholden to the people, that it had no other source of power except the sovereign people, is still the newest, most unique idea in the long history of man's relation to man." And, finally, inevitably, there was the influence of Franklin Roosevelt, who first discovered an American "rendezvous with destiny" while accepting the Democratic renomination for president in 1936. Americans have been holding clandestine meetings with destiny every since, this one from the peroration of the Reagan speech for Goldwater: "You and I have a rendezvous with destiny. We can preserve for our children this the last best hope of man on earth or we can sentence them to take the first step into a thousand years of darkness. If we fail, at least let our children, and our children's children, say of us we justified our brief moment here. We did all that could be done."

Although Reagan didn't know it then — and though he resisted the idea for nearly a year and a half — this speech stands as his opening address in the campaign for the California governorship in 1966. It raised nearly $1 million for the Republican party and its candidates. And it caused wealthy Republican contributors in California, such as auto dealer Holmes Tuttle, industrialist Henry Salvatori, and the late A. C. (Cy) Rubel, chairman of the board of Union Oil Company, to consider Reagan the best hope to wrest the governorship of the nation's most populous state from the Democrats. When an exploratory committee run by his millionaire GOP backers, "The Friends of Ronald Reagan," raised both money and enthusiasm, Reagan agreed to make the race. The rest, as they say, is history.

Reagan's eight years as governor of California also are history — and there is general agreement among the historians that he was at least an adequate governor and perhaps a good one. State Treasurer Jesse Unruh, a Democratic legislative powerhouse at the time Reagan arrived in Sacramento and the man Reagan defeated to win his second term as governor, offered this balanced viewpoint to the *Los Angeles Times* in 1974: "As a governor, I think he has been better than most Democrats would concede and not nearly as good as most Republicans and conservatives might like to think." Bob Moretti, the Democratic speaker with whom Reagan negotiated his historic welfare bill in 1971, wound up liking and respecting his adversary. In the legislative hyperbole of the time Moretti (and Unruh, and most other Democrats) frequently described Reagan as a heartless, know-nothing foe of the poor, higher education, and racial minorities. But in retrospect, Moretti finds Reagan both a reasonable politician and a man of his word, saying of him: "His bark was worse than his bite."

Any serious evaluation of the Reagan governorship collides squarely with Reagan's own exalted view of his accomplishments. As Reagan told the story on the campaign trail in 1980, it was a golden age during the eight years he served as great helmsman of California's ship of state. "Every time we had a surplus, because I don't think government has a right to take one dollar more than government needs, we gave the surpluses back to the people in the form of tax rebates," Reagan would tell his approving audiences. "We gave back over eight years $5.7 billion to the people of California. We stopped the bureaucracy dead in its tracks, the same way I would like to stop it at the national level."

This account omits as much as it relates. What Reagan does not say is that these surpluses, in part, were a result of his own policies. He does not say that he sponsored what was then the largest tax increase in

California state history and that state spending and taxes more than doubled during his tenure. Corporation, bank, sales, and personal income taxes all rose sharply during the Reagan years. The annual state budget increased from $4.6 billion to $10.2 billion and the operations portion of the budget, over which the governor has more control, increased from $2.2 billion to $3.5 billion. State taxes per $100 of personal income, a better measurement because it adjusts for population and price changes, went from $6.64 to $7.62.

But a case can be made that, despite these figures, Reagan succeeded in his basic goal of controlling the cost of government. "Reagan was not so much an underachiever as he was an overcommitter," says one-time legislative aide Judson Clark of the Sacramento consulting firm, California Research. "He did some important things, but not as much as he said he would do and not as much as he said he did." Among the things Reagan did do was slow the growth of the state work force, which had increased nearly 50 percent during the eight years of his Democratic predecessor, Edmund G. (Pat) Brown. There are different measurements of work force growth, but the generally accepted one shows a 7 percent increase during the Reagan years at a time when state workforces elsewhere were growing far more rapidly. Reagan cut by 40 percent a capital outlay budget which had increased 200 percent during the Brown years. And if the $4 billion which the state gave back in property tax relief is subtracted from Reagan's budgets, they roughly kept pace with inflation during his two administrations.

Had Reagan accomplished this result with the tax structure he inherited, the result would have been that low-income taxpayers would have shouldered most of the financial burden. The supreme irony of his governorship is that the burden was instead thrust in great part on the corporations and middle-class taxpayers which Reagan had been ritually defending in his speeches to conservative audiences. Under Reagan, in that first tax bill the levy on banks was boosted from 9.5 to 13 percent. The tax on corporations increased 61 percent — from a 5.5 to a 9 percent rate. This happened, in part, because of Reagan's ignorance of the way government actually worked. And it happened, also, because even in his ignorance he proved a masterful and intuitive politician.

This combination of ignorance and intuition worked reasonably well for Reagan as he struggled to understand the intricacies of government. At least it did on most issues. Where it failed him was on the emotional issue of abortion. In 1967, sponsors of liberal abortion legislation had chosen California as the testing ground on which to promote the nation's first liberal abortion law. California at the time, like a majority of other states, permitted abortions only to save the life of the mother. The liberalizing U.S. Supreme Court decision opening the abortion floodgates was yet to come, as was the counterrevolution of the pro-life movement. In those days the leading body of opposition was the Roman Catholic Church, which launched a letter-writing campaign that produced more mail than most legislators have ever seen. Reagan, as he puts it, had never thought much about the issue one way or the other. At one critical press conference, after the bill had advanced through key committees, Reagan showed almost total confusion about the measure's provisions, freely contradicting himself and describing as "loopholes" provisions which sponsors said were the major purpose of the bill. On one side, Reagan was lobbied for the bill by physicians including his father-in-law, Chicago surgeon Loyal Davis. On the other, the church brought its big guns to bear, and Francis Cardinal McIntyre called the governor and urged him to veto the legislation. Reagan finally signed the bill after the author had made some amendments which supposedly made abortions more difficult to obtain. The statistics of what happened after enactment tell another story. In 1967, there were 518 legal abortions in California hospitals. In 1978, the last year for which complete figures are available, there were 171,982 abortions. From 1967 through 1978 there were 1,230,359 abortions performed under the bill signed by Reagan, now the ardent champion of a U.S. Constitutional amendment that would impose the restrictions on abortion that were on the books in California when he became governor.

Reagan did better on other issues. He conducted his office with integrity and his governmental appointments, many of them drawn from the business community, were of high quality. So were his judicial appointments, which usually followed the recommendations of the bar. Sometimes this produced a judiciary more independent than Reagan would have liked — as it did when Reagan-appointed Supreme Court Justice Donald Wright tipped the balance in striking down a Reagan-backed capital punishment law.

Occasionally, Reagan approved truly innovative programs, as in authorizing conjugal visits for prisoners with good behavior records. Reagan supported legislation increasing the length of sentences for criminals and more funding for state prisons. Originally, he slashed the funds for state mental hospitals. Then, he restored the funds and gave additional money to community health programs being pioneered in California. State expenditures for mental health doubled during the Reagan administration.

He entered office waging what some called a vendetta against the University of California, scene of a controversial and prophetic "free speech" demonstration. "Obey the rules or get out," thundered Reagan, as he called upon campus authorities to expel "undesirables." Under threat of budget cuts, Reagan tried to force the university to abandon its historic policy of "free tuition" and make students pay more of the costs of higher education. Reagan helped force out University of California administrator Clark Kerr, who had unwisely provoked a vote of confidence, and he did persuade the regents to accept tuition under another name. But the budget-cutting never materialized. Once Reagan had made his point, he was generous to the university. State spending for higher education rose 136 percent during the Reagan years compared to an overall state spending increase of 100 percent and an enrollment growth of 40 percent. Even educators who resented the antiintellectualism of Reagan's approach — he had once accused universities of "subsidizing intellectual curiosity" — praised the governor for the increased funding. There is disagreement to this day, however, on whether the verbal attacks on the university caused intangible damage which cost the university topflight faculty.

It was the performance of the Reagan administration on environmental issues which proved the greatest surprise. "A tree's a tree — how many do you need to look at," Reagan had said during his campaign for governor. Environmentalists viewed Reagan's election as the coming of the dark ages in a state which always has been in the forefront of the conservationist movement. Reagan fought this impression by choosing William Penn Mott, a nationally known park director, as director of state parks. He picked Norman (Ike) Livermore, a lumberman who also was a Sierra Club member, as director of resources. Together, Livermore and Mott compiled a generally enviable record for the Reagan administration — although it was notably pro-industry on smog control issues. A total of 145,000 acres, including forty-one miles of ocean frontage, were added to an already impressive state park system. Two underwater park preserves were set aside off the Pacific coast. A major bond issue for park development was proposed and the endangered middle fork of the Feather River was preserved.

What some think was Reagan's finest hour as governor came on the issue of the Dos Rios Dam, a proposed 730-foot structure on the middle fork of the Eel River, a steelhead-spawning stream that is one of California's few remaining wild rivers. The California water bureaucracy, then considered more powerful than the highway lobby, was enthusiastic about the Dos Rios high dam. When the Army Corps of Engineers joined forces to formally propose Dos Rios under the battlecry of water for populous Southern California, its approval was considered a foregone conclusion. Against an array of big battalions, which included wealthy Reagan contributors, were a few Reagan aides (including Livermore, State Finance Director Caspar W. Weinberger, and Reagan's present chief of staff Edwin Meese) and a few conservationists from Round Valley, which would have been flooded by the impounded waters of Dos Rios. Among these residents were descendants of Indian tribes which had been herded into the valley by army troops late in the nineteenth century. The Indians argued that Round Valley contained gravesites and valley land that was secured by treaty. It was their plea which proved decisive. "We've broken too damn many treaties," Reagan said in turning down the Dos Rios Dam. "We're not going to flood them (the Indians) out."

The major legislative achievement of Reagan's eight years in office was the 1971 Welfare Reform Act. It is one of many bills which looks good on its own and insufficient when matched against the Reagan rhetoric. "When I took office, California was the welfare capital of the nation," Reagan says on the stump. "Sixteen percent of all those receiving welfare in the country were in California. The caseload was increasing 40,000 a month. We turned that 40,000 a month increase into an 8,000 a month decrease. We returned to the taxpayers $2 billion and we increased grants to the truly needy by 43 percent." Most of these figures are exaggerations, or otherwise misleading. The average caseload increase for the two years prior to enactment of the welfare reform measure was 26,000 not 40,000. Reagan's bill did increase the grants for the poorest recipients — which had not been raised a penny during the supposedly liberal regime of Pat Brown — but half of this increase was mandated by federal litigation. The $2 billion which Reagan talks about is a legislative projection which made no allowance for the dropping birth rate or increasing employment in California at this time.

Still, the Welfare Reform Act was good legislation which could be defended as easily in New Deal terms as the ones Reagan used for his conservative audiences. The Urban Institute, a nonprofit Washington research group, called the legislation "a major policy success" in a report issued in 1980. Even taking into account the birth rate, and increasing employment, the institute said that the Reagan program had reduced the welfare rolls by 6 percent under what they otherwise would have been while increasing maximum grants. Frank Levy, the senior research associate who wrote the report, said there were "big symbolic differences in the rhetoric" between what Reagan and various liberals had proposed to improve the welfare system but that the substantive differences were far less than either side was likely to admit. The Reagan program, said Levy, was "reoriented toward fiscal control" but "on balance, more recipients appear to have been helped than hurt." By the time the legislation was passed, there were 1,608,000 persons on the welfare rolls — about one in every eleven Californians. In the next three years the total declined to 1,330,000 — significantly lower but still among the highest in the nation. The Urban Institute study found that the major feature of the control was a simple device requiring each recipient of a welfare check to mail a signed postcard each month certifying income and eligibility. In the face of this rudimentary requirement, welfare fraud seemed to melt away. On the other hand, Reagan's ballyhooed required-work program had little direct effect on the rolls, with only 9,600 persons assigned to jobs during a three-year period.

At ground level, Ronald Reagan is decent, likable, and homespun, used to being the center of attention but reserved to the point of occasional shyness. Unless aroused by some challenge, he is basically a passive person — reacting to Nancy, reacting to staff, reacting to autograph seekers and to questions that are put to him. He seems to like who he is, and the names other men have called him — "Dutch" and "the Gipper" and "the cowboy" — are names of affection and respect. He is considerate of other people. Many who have seen Reagan up close think he is literally considerate to a fault with aides, neither demanding enough of them nor reprimanding them when they do poor work. But he is sensible about some things that other men are not sensible about.

When Nancy Reagan was incensed by an anti-Reagan editorial campaign in the *Sacramento Bee*, Governor Reagan acceded to her request and cancelled the subscription at home. Then he took the paper at the office, confiding that it was a way to have the *Bee* (which he regularly read) and keep Nancy happy at the same time.

Reagan has a genuine sense of humor. When students pressed around his limousine during a college demonstration and yelled, "We are the future," Reagan scrawled a reply on a piece of paper and held it up to the window. "I'll sell my bonds," it said. And when a wire-service reporter of long acquaintance brought him a reissued promotion picture from *Bedtime for Bonzo* showing Reagan and the chimpanzee in bed together, Reagan autographed it with the words, "I'm the one with the watch."

Reagan comes from a milieu where reaction is required. An actor must be prepared, but he awaits the call of others before he can come onto the stage. And the working hours are different, or at least they were in Reagan's day. The phrase "9 to 5 governor" is accurate in a sort of rough-hewn way, but it is not a complete description of Reagan's working habits. As an actor, Reagan might work with great concentration on a film for six weeks or two months and then have a long period of inactivity. He is capable of bursts of very intensive campaigning, as anyone who saw him in New Hampshire in 1980 can attest. But he does not function well working long and hard over an extended period, and he does not want to work that way. "Show me an executive that works long overtime hours and I'll show you a bad executive," Reagan once said. What's more, he really believes this.

Reagan's nature and working habits combine to make him a delegator of authority. Edwin Meese, who served Reagan as chief of staff in Sacramento and then again in the 1980 presidential campaign, once remarked that Reagan was a near-perfect delegator because he gave a grant of authority that was clearly defined. "If you operated within the limits of what he wanted to accomplish, he wouldn't second-guess you," Meese said. "And he was decisive when you brought something to him."

Even those who concede that Reagan delegates well and decides quickly have questions about his basic intelligence. Reagan is, as they say, no rocket scientist. Many find him lacking in imagination. But Reagan consistently has confounded those who have underestimated him. There is a kind of small-town common sense about him that serves him well and shows in moments when it is least expected. And more than most people would suspect, Reagan has an appreciation of his own limitations. "I think any adult man knows his shortcomings and knows his strengths," Reagan has said. "I've never claimed to be the originator of every idea we had in Sacramento, but I do think I have the ability to recognize good ideas. I do think, also, that I set the tone and direction 'in which we wanted to go. We were fortunate enough in surrounding ourselves with people who shared our beliefs and whose talent was turned in the direction of implementing them." These are not the words of a stupid man. But Reagan's intelligence is functional rather than reflective. He is best under pressure — as at the Nashua debate and again on August 9 in the South Bronx where Reagan turned a disastrously advanced event into a triumph by telling a woman who was screaming at him: "I can't do a damn thing for you if I'm not elected."

Reagan's most unnerving quality is his proclivity for giving verbatim memorized responses he has used repeatedly as if he were saying them for the first time. It is like punching the button of a tape recorder and hearing the coded message, complete with sincere gestures and that "aw shucks" smile. Partly, this may be a learned defense mechanism which permits Reagan to talk safely to reporters and supporters on the campaign trail. But he has done this with friends in private conversations, too, and it leaves some of them wondering whether he has an original thought in his head. Others, more charitably, regard the mind-taped messages as a natural consequence of Reagan's combined acting and speaking career and say he gives memorized answers without realizing that he is doing it.

Perhaps Reagan has simply made too many speeches. There is much to recommend the observation of old foe Hale Champion (Pat Brown's last finance director) that Reagan is "the Reader's Digest of politics." At least well into the 1980 campaign, Reader's Digest was certainly Reagan's favorite reading material. "In both cases," wrote Champion in the Washington Post, "their statistics and illustrations have a folklore character. They are, if I may use a nonword, factitious. The figures aren't very good, they often don't prove anything and sometimes they are barely tangential to the issue at hand. But they sound great, and they seem to strengthen the message by making it seem more real, even more concrete." These dubious statistics also enable Reagan, in public or private, to tell his audiences what they want to hear. And this desire to please, more than anything else, has been the source of Reagan's trouble in presidential campaigns. Reagan is almost never embarrassed in direct confrontation, where both the physical and the mental juices are flowing. But before a friendly audience he is likely to say almost anything — once calling for a "bloodbath" if necessary to quell student demonstrations, and, in this year's election campaign blandly referring to the Vietnam war as "a noble cause" before a veterans convention and then four days later questioning the theory of evolution before an audience of fundamentalist ministers.

Reagan's nature and way of doing business make him a natural target for anyone on his staff or in his constituency who wants to foist off a pet proposal on him. Reagan is considerate of others and he wants people to bring ideas to him. While he is pragmatic enough to know that he can't accomplish everything contained in his rhetoric, he nonetheless has real goals and fundamental beliefs.

Watching Reagan struggling to find himself after Noble Cause and Evolution and Taiwan, it occurred to me that he may be more complicated than we have made him out to be. Most of us are. I have been covering Reagan, on and off, since his first campaign for office fourteen years ago, have covered him in office, and have written a book about him. I have seen him on bad days and good, in triumph and defeat. He seems to me a good, if limited, man who has demonstrated that it is possible to govern constructively from a conservative ideological base. And yet there is something about Reagan which remains hidden, never glimpsed in those predictable airplane interviews or in the dreary accounts of how Reagan would use the experience he gained in Sacramento to remake Washington. The something shows occasionally in those "vision of America" endings which drive reporters to the press buses. But it shows even more on those rare occasions when Reagan admits visitors to Rancho del Cielo, the remote fog-shrouded ranch north of Santa Barbara which he has chosen as a haven for himself and his wife Nancy. Watching him tell proudly of how he laid the floors and rebuilt the roof of his understated ranch house and put in the fence around it, watching him saddling horses for the obligatory media ride down the old Western trail, watching him look at Nancy to see if she approved of what he was doing and saying, I thought of the passage in *Death of a Salesman* where the son tells about the porch his father built and says that there is more of Willy Loman in that porch than in all the sales he ever made. I wondered if this were also true of Reagan. He had grown up in Main Street America in the first third of this century believing as his father had told him that the only limits on what he could accomplish were those imposed by his ambition. It is a conceit of our system that anyone can be president and Reagan had taken this idea — this fundamental democratic notion which is close to the wellsprings of our national existence — quite literally. He had become a popular sportscaster, a well-known actor, the leader of his labor union and twice the governor of the nation's most populous state. Now he was the Republican nominee for president. Because of what he had done, Reagan was Everyman. And because this is America, and it is what America expects of its Everymans, Reagan had not been ruined by this, at least not that I could see. He still liked working with his hands, and he liked to ride. He still hammed it up for his friends, as he must have done in Dixon, and he still needed and desired the public and private approval of those closest to him. But he was not riding off into the sunset, at least not this day. The sun was behind him as he rode down into the television cameras. Ronald Reagan was about to put the democratic ideal to one of its sternest tests. And he had every confidence that he could do it.

PRESSURE GROUPS AND LOBBYISTS

Chapter Two

Since the publication of David Truman's classic, *The Governmental Process,* in 1951, many political scientists have become enamored of the "group theory" of politics.[1] Although the origins of group theory date back at least as far as John C. Calhoun, who stated its premises and implications in his posthumously published work, *A Disquisition on Government,* in 1853, real acceptance of the group theory did not come until the twentieth century. There are two essential premises of group theory: (1) individuals function in the political process only through groups; (2) the interaction of political interest groups produces the national interest. Today, group theory is not as widely accepted as it once was. Theodore Lowi, in particular, has led an attack on the group theorists' second assumption.[2] But the idea that politics is essentially a group process, rather than an individual process remains largely unchallenged. The extreme expression of this view treats groups anthropomorphically, that is, as if they are persons. But groups are not mystical entities that can exist apart from the individuals who act as their leaders and members, or from the important intermediaries, such as the Washington lawyers, between pressure groups and government.

Individual character, personality, and style affects the ways in which pressure groups interact with government. The selections in this chapter have been chosen to demonstrate the personal dimension of the group process.

[1] David B. Truman, *The Governmental Process* (New York: Alfred A. Knopf, 1951).

[2] Theodore J. Lowi, *The End of Liberalism,* second edition (New York: W. W. Norton, 1979).

THE REVEREND JERRY FALWELL seemed to burst upon the political scene in 1980 leading the disciplined, charging army of the Moral Majority to the polls to elect candidates who supported the fundamentalist Christian positions on a variety of issues. The evangelical community had been politically apathetic, but Falwell and other evangelists exhorted their flocks to join together to make their religious principles a beacon for political leaders at all levels of government. As the 1980 elections approached, Falwell told the four thousand worshipers who packed his Thomas Road Baptist Church in Lynchburg, Virginia, "The moralists in America have had enough. We are joining hands together for the changing, the rejuvenating of a nation."[1]

For Falwell, rejuvenating the nation required the injection of Christian morality, as he defined it, into public policy. The Moral Majority strongly opposed abortion, and supported voluntary prayers in public schools. Falwell and his movement also attacked the Equal Rights Amendment, homosexuality and gay rights, and pornography, all of which the fundamentalist leaders believe undermine the security, integrity, and central role of the family in society.

As a Southerner, Falwell was well acquainted with the civil rights movement of the 1960s, which had increased the political power of blacks by encouraging them to register and vote. Somewhat belatedly, Falwell took a leaf from the political notebook of Martin Luther King, Jr., and other civil rights leaders when he conducted massive voter registration campaigns among his followers, an estimated 21 million of the faithful.

Outside of his luxurious, church-supported white columned mansion in Lynchburg, Falwell prefers three-piece polyester suits, but within the grounds of his estate he often works in a bathing suit beside his Olympic-sized pool. Adjacent to the pool is a recording studio where he tapes the "Old-Time Gospel Hour," his Sunday service, which is carried by 681 TV and radio stations.

The Moral Majority, like the New Right, represents a rising conservative tide in American politics. Both the presidential and congressional elections of 1980 appeared to reflect the strength of evangelicals and political conservatives. The Moral Majority joined the New Right in claiming credit for the election of Ronald Reagan and for the defeat of a number of liberal Democratic senators, including Frank Church of Idaho, George McGovern of South Dakota, John Culver of Iowa, and Birch Bayh of Indiana.

The following selection examines the world of Jerry Falwell and other evangelical leaders, describing how they have led the Moral Majority into political combat.

[1] *Newsweek,* September 15, 1980, p. 28.

5 THE REVEREND JERRY FALWELL AND THE TIDE OF BORN AGAIN

The Rev. Jerry Falwell fidgeted impatiently as he waited for a colleague to finish thanking the Lord for his bounty. Finally, the Wednesday evening prayer service almost at an end, Falwell strode to the pulpit to address the well-scrubbed congregation of 3,900 that filled the Thomas Road Baptist Church in Lynchburg, Va., a fortnight ago. "Senator [Mike] Gravel of [Alaska] was ousted last night," he told them. "He lost the primary. And that's the beginning." Before the year was out, Falwell intoned, a half dozen more liberal senators would fall: George McGovern of South Dakota and Frank Church of Idaho, John Culver of Iowa and Alan Cranston of California, Birch Bayh of Indiana and Gaylord Nelson of Wisconsin. "The moralists in America have had enough. [We] are joining hands together for the changing, the rejuvenating of a nation."

It was an unconventional litany, to be sure. But such overtly political preaching is an increasingly common — and, to many, worrisome — phenomenon in evangelical churches across the country. Over the last eighteen months a new and potent political force has been taking shape — a "New Christian Right," in the words of theologian Martin E. Marty. Led by religious-TV stars such as Falwell, whose "Old-Time Gospel Hour" reaches an estimated 18 million viewers each week, this movement is attempting to enlist the nation's 30 million to 65 million evangelical Christians in an unabashedly political crusade based on fundamentalist morality. Its ideological bent is distinctly conservative, embracing "pro-family" positions against abortion, the Equal Rights Amendment and gay rights — but also extending to right-wing stands on such secular issues as the strategic arms limitation treaty (which it opposes) and the Kemp-Roth proposal to cut taxes by 30 percent (which it supports). The strategy is more electoral than Biblical. "We want to see more and more politicians in office who believe what we believe," says Charlotte, N.C., TV evangelist Jim Bakker.

To that end, politically oriented groups such as Falwell's Moral Majority and the California-based Christian Voice run massive voter-registration and education drives designed to turn traditionally apolitical elements of the evangelical community into a potent force at the polls. They are committed to partisan combat at every level — from campaigns for town council to the 1980 Presidential race — throwing imposing organizational and financial resources behind candidates who share their born-again priorities. The movement's leaders maintain that their interest is in principle, not partisan personalities, and they insist that they have no intention of hitching their moral wagon to any secular star. But the main beneficiary of their activism, so far at least, has been the Republican Party in general — and GOP Presidential nominee Ronald Reagan in particular. "Christians gave Jimmy Carter his razor-thin margin of victory in 1976," says chief strategist Colonel Donner of Christian Voice. "We plan to reverse that in 1980."

Victories: Politics does not come naturally to the evangelical community, which has long held that the road to salvation lies in the Bible — not the ballot box. But many evangelicals have clearly become convinced that their fiercely held conservative values of God, country and family are threatened by a rising tide of what they call "secular humanism" sweeping through government. "All across the country, Christians are registering to vote like never before," says Gainesville, Fla., minister Gene Keith, who successfully exhorted his flock to take over the local Democratic committee — and who is now a candidate for the state legislature. "We're running for everything from dogcatcher to senator."

And they are winning. In 1978 evangelical activists helped to unseat at least two liberal U.S. senators (Dick Clark of Iowa and Thomas McIntyre of New Hampshire) and elect one governor (Fob James of Alabama). Since then they have helped to block passage of the ERA in fifteen states, disrupt the White House Conference on the Family, impede the most recent Congressional effort at criminal-code reform and force both the Federal Communications Commission and the Internal Revenue Service to back down on challenges to religious organizations. This year their candidates have scored upset victories in primaries for the Senate and House in Alaska, Iowa and Alabama — and though they lost the fight to keep George Bush off the Republican ticket, they did manage to shape large sections of the GOP platform.

The movement's rapid growth and early success worries not only its political opponents, but many mainstream theologians as well. "Its leaders are profoundly immature," says Richard John Neuhaus, a Lutheran pastor and member of the board of the influential Worldview magazine. "They don't really understand the ethical and philosophical traditions of democracy or how to bring about change in a pluralistic society." Even some evangelists themselves are uneasy about the new movement's often strident partisanship and its creative use of scripture to justify the most secular of political positions. "God isn't a right-winger or a left-winger," argues preacher Pat Robertson, president of the Christian Broadcasting Network and host of "The 700 Club," a popular daily religious program. "The evangelists stand in danger of being used and manipulated." In judging political performance on the basis of Biblically derived standards, others contend, the movement is in danger of crossing the constitutionally drawn line between church and state. "They are violating Article Six of the Constitution, which says there must not be any religious test for holding office," says Rabbi Marc Tanenbaum of the American Jewish Committee.

'*Buzzards*': Predictably defensive, evangelical politicians charge that such criticisms are themselves political sour grapes from liberal opponents. "Nobody's ever accused the National Council of Churches of mixing religion and politics," Falwell says. "But when ol' Jerry gets into it, that's violating separation of church and state. The problem isn't violating anything. The problem is that we don't agree with those ·buzzards — and that we outnumber them." Perhaps — although there is a real question whether leaders like Falwell really do represent a huge and potentially monolithic political bloc. According to a new Gallup poll, evangelical Christians are as politically divided as most Americans (see Table). Though as a group they are somewhat more conservative than the nation as a whole, the majority of the registered voters among them nonetheless identify themselves as Democrats, and they favor Jimmy Carter by a wide margin over Ronald Reagan. What's more, a majority (53 percent) support ERA, and only 41 percent favor the extreme position of banning abortion entirely.

Still, there is no mistaking the enormous potential of evangelical politics. The movement's basic raw material is the vast number of fundamentalist Americans who do not normally vote — Christian Voice's Donner estimates it as 25 million — and whose attitudes, as a result, are not reflected in Gallup's findings. So far this year, the movement claims to have registered some 2 million new voters from the ranks of the born-again — and, says Falwell, the total should reach 4 million by Election Day. Even if those figures are inflated, born-again politics could well play a decisive role in this year's Presidential race. "The significance of the fundamentalist vote is not numbers but geography," says Reagan campaign aide Roger Stone. Close elections, he notes, tend to be won or lost in the heartland states of Ohio, Illinois and Michigan — all of which boast growing evangelical communities. "Some of the southern counties in Ohio are as fundamentalist as the Deep South," Stone says. "The return of the fundamentalist vote [to the GOP] will allow Reagan to carry Ohio and, conceivably, the country."

The movement's political gurus are prone to play down their immediate prospects. "Anybody who thinks this group is going to contribute to a political revolution this election is going to be disappointed," says Paul Weyrich, who runs a highly regarded "training school" in Washington for conservative candidates as well as a clearinghouse operation for 30 or so evangelical and secular pro-family groups. But as the strategists see it, the longer-term future is bright. "The basic problem, only now being overcome, is to get people involved," says Howard Phillips, organizer of a right-wing lobbying group called The Conservative Caucus. "Once that is done, this movement will be formidable."

The effort began in earnest less than three years ago, spurred in part by disappointment with the first born-again candidate, Jimmy Carter. "It was a tremendous letdown, if not a betrayal, to have Carter stumping for the ERA, for not stopping federally paid abortions, for advocating homosexual rights," says Donner. The original movers and shakers were mainly political pros, not preachers. The core group consisted of Phillips and Weyrich (who were old comrades-in-arms from the political wars), Robert Billings (a failed GOP Congressional candidate from Indiana who had attended Weyrich's candidate-training school) and Ed McAteer, a veteran marketing man for the Colgate-Palmolive Co. who had come to know hundreds of evangelical preachers around the country. In January of last year they persuaded Falwell to set up a political organization — which Weyrich suggested calling "Moral Majority" and which Billings was assigned to direct. Falwell's backing was crucial; the financial and logistical resources that he commanded were immense.

Allies: There were other allies as well. McAteer had set up a nonpartisan, interdenominational group called the Religious Roundtable. It had just 56 members, but among them were most of the major television preachers as well as an impressive list of New Right politicians. Funded mainly by what McAteer describes as "some gifts from businessmen," it sponsored rallies, seminars and training sessions aimed at increasing the political sophistication of evangelists. Meanwhile, Weyrich had begun holding informal get-togethers for evangelical and pro-family activists every other Thursday in his Washington offices on Library Court, behind the Library of Congress. The Library Court group, as it came to be known, now coordinates strategy for the entire movement.

Another politically potent evangelical group had arisen on the West Coast. Called Christian Voice, it sidestepped IRS strictures on political lobbying by setting up a political-action committee (PAC) called the Christian Voice Moral Government Fund. Unlike the other born-again political organizations, Christian Voice has no compunctions about endorsing specific candidates for office. "We make judgments based on principles," says Gary Jarmin, executive director of the Moral Government Fund. "When you go into a voting booth, you pull a lever for a name, not a principle." Last February it set up another group — called Christians for Reagan.

Agenda: Working together in an informal but very real alliance, these organizations are trying to mobilize a conservative evangelical electorate. The concerns of born-again politics are defined by Falwell's "agenda for the '80s" — a pro-family, pro-life, pro-morality platform that, in a triumph of political packaging, turns out to be considerably more "anti" than "pro." Among other things, Moral Majority — and its evangelical allies — are against abortion, ERA, gay rights, sex education, drugs, pornography, SALT II, the Department of Education and defense cuts. They are for free enterprise, a balanced budget, voluntary prayer in the public schools and a secure Israel.

Using Falwell as its main drawing card, Moral Majority has been holding rallies around the country to spread the word and develop a truly national base. The work is already beginning to pay dividends as a cadre of budding evangelical politicos takes root. Rev. Keith of Gainesville, Fla., is typical — a total neophyte when Moral Majority suggested he attend the weeklong "Campaign Training Conference" run by Weyrich in Washington last November. When he returned to his pulpit at the Southside Baptist Church he persuaded his congregation to run for seats on the local county Democratic committee. Ultimately, they swept 42 of the 53 seats they went after.

Falwell says he is not "candidate oriented." Still, he has managed to lend a hand in several campaigns. At a recent Moral Majority rally in Des Moines, for example, he made a point of praising Senate candidate Rep. Charles Grassley as a "dear friend of ours and a fine Christian." And in Birmingham, Ala., a fortnight ago, Falwell noted pointedly that Moral Majority's local bête noire, Rep. John Buchanan, had "unfortunately" voted to extend the time limit for passage of the ERA. Buchanan lost in last week's GOP primary.

Falwell's political sermonizing doesn't always work out so well. Several months ago he told a Moral Majority rally in Alaska a completely fabricated story about an actual meeting he and other evangelists had with President Carter in the White House last February. According to Falwell's first account, he had boldly asked the President why he had "known practicing homosexuals" on his staff — to which Carter supposedly replied that it was because he considered himself "President of all the American people." When the story got back to the White House, angry Carter aides released a transcript of the meeting — which showed that there never had been any such exchange. "I shouldn't have said it," Falwell conceded recently. "Obviously it was a reckless statement."

Questions: Such gaffes don't really worry him. "There are only two things a preacher just can't afford to be accused of," he says. "One of them is sexual impropriety . . . the other is messing with the church funds." Falwell's reputation as a family man is impeccable. But the Securities and Exchange Commission once raised questions about his ministry's finances (box) — and there are indications that Moral Majority, ostensibly independent, has received favored treatment from Falwell's lucrative religious enterprises. Although contributions have been flowing into Moral Majority lately at the rate of $400,000 a month, the organization has been strapped for cash all year. It has been consistently bailed out by the "Old-Time Gospel Hour," which has allowed Moral Majority to run up debts to it for months — apparently free of any interest charges.

By far the most controversial of the evangelical political groups is the unabashedly partisan Christian Voice. Earlier this year it raised hackles by rating all the members of Congress on how they voted on what it described as "fourteen key moral issues" — ranging from prayer in the schools to the security of Taiwan. On the basis of the ratings, it issued a "hit list" of 36 senators and congressmen, each of whom it accused of having a poor "moral voting record." Though lobbying groups do this sort of thing all the time, Christian Voice's ratings drew heavy fire. For one thing, four ordained clergymen in Congress received among the lowest marks — while Rep. Richard Kelly, one of the Abscam bribery defendants, was given a perfect, 100 percent rating. For another, the

How Far Right?

Despite the conservative message of many evangelical political leaders, a new Gallup poll finds President [Carter] ahead among born-again Christians registered to vote; they are not very far to the right except on abortion and prayer.

If the presidential elections were being held today, which candidate would you vote for?

	Carter	Reagan	Anderson
Evangelicals	52%	31%	6%
All Voters	39%	38%	13%

Which category best describes your own political position?

	Left of center	Middle of the road	Right of center
Evangelicals	20%	31%	37%
All Voters	22%	37%	31%

How They Differ on Issues

	Evangelicals	All Voters
Favor death penalty for persons convicted of murder	51%	52%
Favor government programs to deal with social problems	54%	53%
Favor increased spending for defense	78%	70%
Favor banning all abortions	41%	31%
Favor requiring prayer in public schools	81%	59%

group's equation of Christian morality with political conservatism outraged preachers and pols alike. Even Sen. Jesse Helms, the influential conservative who agrees wholeheartedly with Christian Voice's politics, found the rating system questionable. "I could never take the position that anyone who disagreed with me was less a Christian," he says. "Hubert Humphrey and I didn't agree 90 percent of the time. Does that mean he was more immoral?"

Flood: Unfazed by the criticism, Christian Voice is now gearing up for a massive effort in behalf of Ronald Reagan, including plans to flood the Midwest and the South with 5 million pieces of pro-Reagan literature between now and the election. "The South is reputed to be Jimmy Carter's base," says strategist Donner, "but remember, it's the Bible belt. Our message that Ronald Reagan is *the* Christian candidate of 1980 may sufficiently weaken Carter in the one solid base he still has."

The Reagan campaign takes such analyses seriously, and has been assiduously wooing the evangelicals all year — in the process, hiring Billings away from Moral Majority to become Reagan's liaison with the born-again community. The courtship began in earnest at the GOP convention, to which both Falwell and his Liberty Baptist College choir were invited. Perhaps more important, Falwell and his fellow evangelical politicians got a good crack at shaping the Republican platform.

"Out of the Closet": Reagan further solidified his hold on the evangelical pols by being the only major Presidential candidate to appear at the Religious Roundtable's National Affairs Briefing, a revival meeting cum political rally held in Dallas three weeks ago. More than 15,000 of the faithful turned out for two days of speechmaking and organizing. "It's time for God's people to come out of the closet and the churches — and change America," thundered James Robison, the fire-and-brimstone Ft. Worth evangelist whose weekly TV show is syndicated to 100 stations. Said Reagan: "I know you can't endorse *me*. But . . . I want you to know that I endorse *you*."

Not everyone there shared Reagan's enthusiasm. Preacher Pat Robertson, for one, argues that "active partisan politics" is the wrong path for true evangelicals. "There's a better way," he says: "Fasting and praying . . . appealing, in essence, to a higher power." That feeling is shared by many in the evangelical community who are uneasy over the fact that, as the Rev. Jimmy Allen of Ft. Worth puts it, what is supposed to be "a nonpartisan movement for Jesus . . . always seems to turn into a Republican rally." A sincere concern for traditional values clearly motivates many in the movement, but critics point to an apparent lack of concern for minorities and the poor. "There are more than 300 verses in the Bible on the commitment to the poor, to justice and righteousness, but they are silent on that," complains the Rev. Tom Skinner, a born-again black activist.

What seems to trouble such critics the most is the movement's inexorable reduction of religious and moral values into crude political options. "I would hate for evangelical Christianity to become a spiritual version of the National Rifle Association," says Dr. David Hubbard of the Fuller Theological Seminary, who worries about the possible exploitation of politically naïve evangelicals. And whatever it does to evangelicals themselves, the effect on the rest of society could be devastating. "If in order to be faithful you have to support a certain stand regarding Russia, what's the next step?" asks the Rev. Theodore Edquist of the First Congregational Church of Boise, Idaho. "It strikes at the very heart of the whole notion of religious pluralism and religious and political freedom."

"Mad as Hell": The movement's leaders insist that such worries are wildly overblown. "We're not religious fanatics who have in mind a Khomeini-type religious crusade to take over the government," says Falwell. "We support the separation of church and state . . . we want influence, not control." For the activist liberal theologians who have been in politics for years — fighting for poverty programs, urban aid and an end to the Vietnam War — that argument is hard to dispute. "This is a populist reaction of resentment," says *Worldview*'s Neuhaus. "These are very ordinary Americans and they are mad as hell. It's arrogant and self-defeating for those of us whom they are mad at to pretend they will just go away."

The challenge of the New Christian Right may stir more activism among liberals. But attention will have to be paid to born-again sensibilities. "No group on a crusade is willing to moderate its demands until it feels secure of its place, until it feels recognized as a power to be dealt with," says Neuhaus, adding that many of the liberals who propound the separation of church and state have gone beyond that to the separation of moral judgment from public policy. "They are the ones who have driven us into this current dilemma by trying to purge American life of religion and values — by creating a 'naked public square' where anything goes." What is clear on both the philosophical level — and in the rough-and-tumble arena of politics — is that the Falwells of the nation and their increasingly militant and devoted flock are a phenomenon that can no longer be dismissed or ignored.

A $1 Million Habit

In his dark three-piece polyester suits, the Rev. Jerry Falwell always looks dressed for church. He has to. As chief pastor, executive officer and full-time salesman for his own evangelical empire, Falwell is rarely out of the pulpit. Like a prophet seeking honor in — and for — his own country, Brother Jerry has moved beyond his Lynchburg, Va., congregation to seize vocal leadership of the emerging Christian right, constantly pouring forth a torrent of Biblical rhetoric on behalf of his own conservative vision of a moral America.

To those who know him best, Falwell is a cool, tireless organizer and past master at riding evangelism's new electronic circuit. In a whirl of nineteen-hour days, he darts from board meetings to televised prayer services, jets from political rallies to church conferences, gulps down a dozen cups of coffee daily and rarely misquotes a Bible verse or a financial statistic. His hometown church claims 17,000 members — more than a quarter of Lynchburg's population — but his real constituency is an estimated 21 million faithful who listen to his broadcast sermons every week and support his pyramid of enterprises. Falwell's Sunday service, the "Old-Time Gospel Hour," is carried by 681 TV and radio stations. The yield from this and other fund-raising operations ($1 million each week) supports what is, in effect, Falwell's own Christian denomination — including a children's academy, a Bible institute, a correspondence school, a seminary and Library Baptist College, an as yet unaccredited campus with nearly 3,000 undergraduates (and a former major-league pitcher as baseball coach). To this complex, Falwell last year added Moral Majority, Inc., a political-action organization aimed at unseating politicians who reject his recipe for a righteous republic.

Lapel Pins: Falwell's multifaceted ministry depends on a variety of marketing techniques. Once true believers send in for such premiums as Old Glory lapel pins, their names are added to his massive computerized mailing list. Regular donors (average weekly gift: $12) become Falwell's "faith partners" and are subject to regular computerized pleas for more. In terms of what he calls his "gross ministry," Falwell says he is "neck and neck with Oral Roberts." And by 1981, he predicts, Falwell ministries will lead the evangelical pack.

A driving need to succeed is as much a part of Falwell's pulpit power as his business acumen and folksy fundamentalism. Young Jerry's family was a brawling bunch; his father killed one of Jerry's uncles in a family feud and later died from alcoholism. But Falwell excelled in the classroom and on his high-school football team. He was prevented from delivering the valedictory address only after auditors discovered that he and other athletes had eaten free for a year on bogus lunch tickets. Jerry didn't get religion until a wintry Sunday in 1952 when he went to church in search of girls and found both Jesus and a pretty organist named Macel Pate. In 1956, after dominating the student body at a Bible college in Missouri, Jerry returned to Lynchburg to found his own independent Baptist church, in an abandoned pop-bottling factory, and continued courting Macel — whom he later married. Six months later he aired his first religious show on local television.

At times his knack for fund raising has caused problems for Falwell's empire. Seven years ago the Securities and Exchange Commission sued his Thomas Road Baptist Church for issuing allegedly fraudulent bonds; after an acrimonious trial Falwell agreed to institute more rigorous financial discipline. And some questions still shadow his financial operations. Falwell says, for example, that he spends only 17½ cents to raise every dollar he takes in, but some former financial employees and advisers insist the actual figure is three to four times higher — well above the norm for most charitable causes. Others criticize Falwell's borrowing from Peter to pay Paul — specifically borrowing up to $1 million from the college (with approval of the school's board) to pay his TV expenses.

'Their Way Out': Falwell also makes periodic pitches for money to support specific causes such as the Cambodian refugees in Thailand. There is no way for donors to know how much money such appeals bring in — or where it all goes. Says the Rev. David Brown, who served as controller for the "Gospel Hour" last year: "Jerry would say in his promotional literature that the money raised would be used for a project *and* for other operating costs of the ministry. That last phrase in fine print was their way out." "There's only one problem with a ministry like Jerry's," adds a prominent Lynchburg banker. "He can't stop raising money; if he does, it all falls apart."

There is no evidence that Falwell has ever siphoned off any money for himself. Still, at 47, he lives in comfort. His home (which is owned by a wealthy follower) is a twelve-room Southern mansion complete with portico, swimming pool and verdant lawns — all protected by a high wall and a Bible-quoting guard. Although his salary is only $42,500, Falwell enjoys the perquisites of many big-time entrepreneurs: his ministry affords him an expense account, free life insurance and a private jet that enables him (and often one of his three children) to take in diversions such as World Series games while traveling on "church business." Falwell is hardly embarrassed by these worldly appurtenances. Material wealth, he says, "is God's way of blessing people who put him first."

WHILE JERRY FALWELL IS leading the Moral Majority, Phyllis Schlafly is bolstering the New Right by mobilizing a "silent majority" consisting largely of women who are or intend to become full-time homemakers, coupled with men who support traditional sex roles in the family. This coalition opposes the new feminism and its manifestation in the Equal Rights Amendment (ERA).

Although Schlafly is best known for her successful campaign against the ERA, she was no stranger to politics when the amendment was passed by Congress in 1972 and sent to the states for ratification. Ironically, Schlafly embodied the feminist ideal of a strong, powerful, independent, and career-oriented woman. She was raised during the Depression in St. Louis. When her father became unemployed, her mother supported the family by working as a librarian at the St. Louis Art Museum. Her mother's hard work and frugality enabled Schlafly to attend the elite Catholic school in the city, where she made the highest marks and graduated in 1941 with a full scholarship to a Catholic women's college. She transferred to Washington University in St. Louis, paying for her tuition by working a midnight shift in a St. Louis ordnance plant, testing rifles and explosives. She graduated with a Phi Beta Kappa key in three years, winning a fellowship to Radcliffe where she received an MA in Government after one year.

Although her Harvard professors encouraged Schlafly to stay on for a PhD, she left, going to Washington to work as a researcher for the American Enterprise Association (renamed the American Enterprise Institute in 1962). Unhappy with the life of a single woman in Washington, Schlafly returned to St. Louis where, at the age of twenty-two, she became the campaign manager for a conservative Republican lawyer who was challenging a Democratic incumbent for a seat in the United States House of Representatives.

That Schlafly was hired at such a young age to be a campaign manager was a remarkable feat in itself, for she had to convince a skeptical candidate who was looking for an experienced man for the job. The candidate, who defeated his opponent in a district that had become a Democratic stronghold, later recalled his interview with the young Schlafly. "I was impressed," he said, "by her incredible knowledge of the most nitty-gritty details of St. Louis ward politics. Here was this beautiful young girl sitting in my living room analyzing what I had to do to win, and she had so much plain good political sense, I had to keep looking at her to remind myself I wasn't talking to a fat, old, cigar-chomping ward heeler."[1]

Schlafly's experience and success in the congressional campaign initiated a lifelong involvement in Republican politics. She married Fred Schlafly in 1949, creating "a partnership between two highly intelligent, highly opinionated people who gen-

[1] Carol Felsenthal, *Phyllis Schlafly: The Sweetheart of the Silent Majority* (Chicago: Regnery Gateway, 1982), p. 77.

83

uinely like, respect, and — perhaps most important, considering their strong personalities — agree with each other."[2]

While Phyllis Schlafly's views on the ERA might lead some to think that she believes the proper place for women is in the home, her own life reflects a remarkable union of family and career. She ran, unsuccessfully, for Congress in 1952 when her eldest son was only a year and a half old. She ran again, unsuccessfully, in 1970 when her youngest daughter was five. During the entire time that she was raising six children she was constantly engaged in politics, principally by writing books that articulated conservative issues and views for the Republican party. In 1964 she published privately a book entitled, *A Choice Not an Echo*, which became the theme of Barry Goldwater's presidential campaign. The book attacked the Eastern establishment of the party as an unrepresentative and conspiratorial group that secretly liked the New Deal, and that had helped secure the Republican nomination for liberal candidates who did not reflect a broad cross-section of the party. Between 1964 and 1976 she collaborated with retired Rear Admiral Chester Ward on five books dealing with defense policy. The authors attacked the foreign policy establishment for allegedly plotting to disarm the country. While busily writing and politically active she managed to obtain a law degree from Washington University in Saint Louis in 1978.

Schlafly's books express her conservative views. In 1967 her book on women, *The Power of the Positive Woman*, was published. The ideal woman, argued Schlafly, should always put the family and home first, but once her children are grown she should be able to pursue a career. Compared with the doctrines of the Moral Majority, Schlafly's program offers greater equality between the sexes.

Phyllis Schlafly has always been actively engaged in politics at the same time that she has written voluminously to express her conservative views. She is interested in power as well as ideas. The Equal Rights Amendment gave her a platform from which she could launch her own nationwide organization. Her political skills, which in the past had failed to gain her a seat in Congress or the presidency of the National Federation of Republican Women (NFRW), which she had eagerly sought in 1967, would be tested once again and finally proven when the ERA went down to defeat in 1982.

The following selection describes the Phyllis Schlafly style, which has made her a charismatic leader of the "Silent Majority." The style that is appealing to so many, however, is appalling to her opponents. As the author points out, she is either loved or loathed. Regardless of how one feels about Phyllis Schlafly, there is no doubt that her political leadership was largely responsible for the failure of many states to ratify the Equal Rights Amendment.

[2] Ibid., pp. 83–84.

84

6

Carol Felsenthal

PHYLLIS SCHLAFLY:
THE SWEETHEART OF THE SILENT MAJORITY

Love Her or Loathe Her

On Pearl Harbor Day in 1977, Phyllis Schlafly and I lunched at Chicago's Bismarck Hotel — a hustling, masculine power center frequented by clout-heavy politicians, lawyers, and bankers. I was on assignment from *Chicago* magazine to interview the country's most controversial woman.

Schlafly's porcelain complexion was windburned around the edges and her unadorned hands, tipped by unpolished nails, were stiff from the cold. "I'll never be able to type again," she joked. She had just come from leading a rally against the Panama Canal treaties in the wind tunnel, also known as the Daley (Mayor Richard) Plaza, where twenty-mile-an-hour northerly gusts sent the wind-chill factor plunging to forty below.

In spite of the weather, a busload of Schlafly's "Chicago girls" — members of her Eagle Forum, "the alternative to women's lib" — braved the freeze to hear their leader denounce the treaties and announce, to their profound disappointment, that she would not challenge liberal Republican Senator Charles Percy in the 1978 Republican primary. They joined her for lunch afterward, but most were banished to distant tables in the crowded restaurant, where all they could do was gaze at their guru.

Suddenly, a group of the housewives, eagle pins perched on collars, rose, and, from across the room, offered a heartfelt toast to "Phyllis power." The then fifty-three-year-old, svelte, blue-eyed beauty, with impeccable posture, poise, and upswept streaked hair — who stood out among her disciples like Lauren Bacall at a Tupperware Party — saluted them with a glass of ice water.

Phyllis Schlafly's fans love her with an intensity, a spirit, a loyalty usually reserved for movie stars or members of the Royal Family. She has glamor and guts and intelligence and energy. She is awe inspiring, a phenomenon, a heroine, a star, even, in her inimitable ramrod-straight way, a sort of sex symbol of the right wing. She is an authority — on the ERA, on the Panama Canal treaties, on SALT, on Medicare funding of abortions, on just about every major political issue. Her followers would as soon question her knowledge and commitment as they would question the Pope's.

A month earlier, I was with Schlafly at the Ramada Inn in Houston, where she led what she called a "pro-family alternative to the lesbian and libber-controlled" International Women's Year Conference. Several of her fans watched as she was interviewed in turn by correspondents from ABC, NBC, the BBC, the *New York Times,* and finally, a correspondent from Swedish television. "Can you believe she has six kids?" asked one short, plump woman whose blouse was covered by red buttons bearing the STOP ERA, stop-sign-shaped logo. "Look at this woman God raised up to teach us," gushed another.

As soon as the Swedish crew switched off its lights, the woman rushed up to Phyllis, grabbed her hand, and said, "I want to thank you for what you're doing for us." And they kept coming. "Bless your heart," said the next, and "We love you in Nashville" the next. Soon a long line of "Eagles" formed to get Phyllis Schlafly's autograph, but she had to cut the signing short and duck out. She was a featured speaker that afternoon at a "pro-family" rally in Houston's Astro Arena; a rally that would draw fifteen thousand people — mostly arriving on yellow school buses or CB-connected car caravans — from literally every state in the union, including Alaska.

Phyllis Schlafly's critics, on the other hand, detest her with an intensity usually reserved for history's full-fledged villains. There is no middle ground — love her or loathe her. But, unlike a movie star, Schlafly's enemies can't take her or leave her, can't turn her off — which makes them hate her all the more, especially when she appears not to care what they think. She evokes powerful, emotional reactions, but seems almost oblivious, occasionally even slightly amused, by her foes' fury. She is maddeningly cool.

Later that same day in Houston, the STOP ERA commander and I were eating a very late dinner at the Ramada Inn restaurant. The waitress had just brought two juicy filets, flanked by "Texas toast" dripping garlic and butter. Schlafly — whose last meal had been thirteen hours, four press conferences, and seventeen interviews earlier — gingerly transferred the toast to another plate, handed it to a busboy, cut a small piece of steak, and let it lie there as she continued her elaborate comparison of U.S. and Soviet weapons strength.

As she warmed to the subject and our steaks cooled, an elderly woman wearing pink polyester and sprayed hair approached the table. Interrupted again, I thought, by yet another fan paying homage to her leader — the sixth since we sat down.

Schlafly was still completing her case for the B-1 bomber when the woman barged in, not waiting to be acknowledged. "I promised my friends," she said hurriedly, "that if I ran into you in Houston, I'd tell you what we think of you. You are a traitor to your sex. When you die, the women of this country will rejoice. And you don't have long, Phyllis, believe me." She rushed away, her face as pink as her pantsuit.

There wasn't a crack in Schlafly's composure. Smiling, she summoned the waitress, who, I assumed, would be directed to summon Schlafly's burly press secretary, or the armed sentry outside her suite, or perhaps the Texas Rangers.

"Please bring me some real milk for my coffee, instead of this fake stuff," she instructed the waitress. Then, without missing a beat, she continued her monologue on military budgets of the past five years — the statistics and weaponry jargon flowing smoothly and unstoppably from this self-styled "happy homemaker."

"How do you deal with the fact that so many people hate you?" I blurted.

"You know," she replied calmly, "when women say things like that to me, I just chalk it up to their frustration over the weakness of their arguments. We've beaten ERA in Illinois for six years straight. Last year, only one state ratified. In 1972, before we got organized, twenty-two states ratified. We're winning because we have the truth on our side. They're losing, so they're irrational and mad."

Schlafly had an arsenal of anecdotes to illustrate her point. Debating Betty Friedan in Bloomington, Illinois, in May 1973, seemed to be the encounter she relished most. That one ended when Friedan shrieked, "I'd like to burn you at the stake!"

A short time later, Schlafly debated Senator Birch Bayh (D., Ind.). He came so unstrung by the televised experience that he admitted to wanting "to commit mayhem live and in full color."

Schlafly's critics claim to ignore her. But it's obvious that they can no more ignore Phyllis Schlafly than anti-Vietnam war protesters could ignore Richard Nixon. In fact, feminists seem positively obsessed with her. She is a symbol.

Some ninety thousand ERA supporters gathered in Washington on a scorching day the next July to push for a three-year extension to the time allotted for passage of ERA — without which the amendment would have died on March 22, 1979. President Carter's former women's adviser, Midge Costanza, had only to mention the words "Phyllis Schlafly" to bring the crowd to a frenzy.

National Organization for Women (NOW) President Ellie Smeal, heartened by the huge show of support for ERA, couldn't resist a sure-fire roar raiser: "Mrs. Schlafly, wherever you are, eat your heart out!" Nearby, a group of women burned Schlafly in effigy.

The next October, twenty-four hours after Congress passed the extension, Senator Ted Kennedy brought a crowd of two thousand women's-rights activists to their feet merely by asking, "Phyllis Schlafly, where are you now?" He chided her over and over again, sparking a roar of approval with every dig.

A year later — the extension having not yet produced a single new ratification — ERA supporters held a fund- and morale-raiser. They flew in Midge Costanza to galvanize the troops. The location was carefully chosen — at the home of Schlafly's Alton, Illinois, next-door neighbor Gladys Levis, an ardent ERA supporter. The crowd of women, many of whom liked to dismiss Schlafly as "just a nut, not nearly as important as she thinks she is," couldn't stop gossiping about her, denouncing her. In fact, they spent much more time exchanging rumors about Phyllis than discussing tactics for ratifying ERA.

Chicago Tribune reporter Dorothy Collin recorded snippets of conversation:

"There was a picture of her in the local paper taking a casserole out of the oven. She didn't have any mitts on. You could tell she really baked it."

"She has a staff. I bet she never washes her floor."

One woman captured the attention of the crowd in Levis's "great Gothic stone mansion" by announcing she had just seen Phyllis getting out of her car with an armload of groceries. Several women snorted that they doubted that Phyllis did any of her own cooking.

"That great female impersonator Phyllis Schlafly goes about the country telling women to stay in the kitchen," said Costanza, to thunderous cheers. (In June 1980, after the Illinois house defeated ERA for the ninth year, Costanza drew an even more spirited response by suggesting that Anita Bryant and Phyllis Schlafly would make "a fine set of bookends" for Hitler's *Mein Kampf*.)

Vice-President Walter Mondale was only three minutes into his acceptance speech at the 1980 Democratic National Convention when he too drew massive applause by denouncing Phyllis Schlafly.

ERA backers — nearly every major newspaper and magazine, the White House, politicians of all stripes, the Republican and Democratic national committees,[1] Hollywood stars, talk-show hosts, organizations ranging from the American Bar Association to the AFL-CIO to the League of Women Voters — are baffled, frustrated, and infuriated by Schlafly's success.

---

[1]During the 1980 Republican National Convention, following Schlafly's vigorous lobbying, Republicans dropped ERA from their party platform, ending a forty-year tradition of support for the Amendment. (During most of those years, however, the ERA that Republicans supported contained several exemptions — for example, a clause exempting women from the draft.) A month later, at their convention, the Democrats strengthened their already strong support for ERA by passing a platform plank denying campaign funds and assistance to candidates who oppose ERA.

And their attacks on her — more often than not personal attacks — show it. Gloria Steinem attacked Phyllis Schlafly for being rich. "Are you now or have you ever been a member of the John Birch Society?" was a question invariably asked at Schlafly's press conferences. The reporter asking the question was usually too young to remember Senator Joe McCarthy and too passionately pro-ERA to hide her contempt for Phyllis Schlafly. Schlafly answered "no" on both counts and the reporter's face showed she obviously didn't believe her. The McCarthyesque tactics only added the sympathy vote to an already huge following. And the ERA supporters got angrier and angrier.

"Women's liberationists have come to realize that in order to stop STOP ERA they must also stop Phylis Schlafly," concluded *Alton Telegraph* reporter Mary Scarpinato, echoing a common theme of ERA analyses. Schlafly's family and friends fear that her opponents are beginning to take that conclusion literally. During her "pro-family alternative" to the International Women's Year Conference, her husband stationed a guard at her hotel-room door.

Most of the threats are probably harmless. A woman walked by Schlafly at a Missouri legislative hearing on ERA and hissed, "I'd like to kick you." Activist lawyer Flo Kennedy went on Florida radio and encouraged listeners to stop debating Phyllis and start slapping her. Yippie Aron Kay walked up to her at a Manhattan reception for the Women's National Republican Club and smashed an apple pie in her face, leaving Schlafly, who wears contact lenses, with a painfully scratched eye.

During her Washington "Gala," Schlafly was laughing heartily at her own creation — *the ERA Follies* — parodies she wrote herself, starring STOP ERAers impersonating Bella Abzug and Gloria Steinem. Suddenly the lights came on. Schlafly was frowning, looking furious and a trifle frightened. A grim-faced emcee, Senator Orrin Hatch (R., Ut.), announced that the overstuffed Shoreham ballroom would have to be evacuated immediately. The hotel switchboard operator, he explained, had received an anonymous call warning that two bombs have been placed on the dais "under Phyllis' chair."

And so the "Follies" had an unplanned intermission while a bomb squad swept the room. Schlafly's eldest son, John, a then twenty-eight-year-old law student and talented pianist (the accompanist for the *Follies*), who normally shuns the press, leaned against a wall outside the ballroom talking to me. He seemed a bit shaken by the threat against his mother. "Of course, I'd like Mother to get out of this fight and get out of the headlines. She's already too controversial for her own safety. Too many people hate her for what she has done. I'm scared for her."

A week later, three assistant TV-talk-show producers were planning an end-of-the-decade wrapup. "Who is the most controversial male figure of the decade?" They couldn't agree. So they moved on to the female side. "Who is the most controversial female figure of the decade?" "Phyllis Schlafly," the three answered, almost in unison. A couple of minutes later one asked, "What about Bella [Abzug]?" "In comparison to Phyllis, Bella is about as controversial as Doris Day," answered her colleague. Case closed. . . .

More than anything else — more than her crusade against communism, more than her crusade to get Barry Goldwater elected president, Phyllis Schlafly is famous for her crusade against the Equal Rights Amendment.

Given Schlafly's conservative background, an instant aversion to the amendment was what one would have expected. For as liberated as Schlafly herself was, she was never a fan of the women's liberation movement — with which ERA was closely identified. In her 1970 campaign for Congress, she had blasted the movement as "destructive of family living" and feminists as "selfish and misguided."

She had, after all, grown up in a very traditional family. Her mother worked and brought home the paycheck, but there was never a doubt that her father was the head of the house, the boss. Phyllis passed on that tradition to her children, raising her four boys and two girls with very clearly defined sex roles. She raised all six to be achievers, but she taught her boys that careers should be No. 1 in their lives, and her girls that careers should be No. 2, after family.

One would have thought that a constitutional amendment that was bound to spark unpredictable change and give more power to the federal government would have sparked serious misgivings not only in Schlafly but in most conservatives. However, in 1972, when ERA had passed both houses of Congress and was on its way to the states for ratification, it seemed, to most people, conservatives included, far from radical. ERA was nothing new — not by a long shot. It has been introduced annually in Congress since 1923. Although it might have sounded radical in 1920 when women, against fierce opposition, won the right to vote, a half century later, a constitutional guarantee of equality seemed long overdue. Even most conservative congressmen and state legislators found little wrong with ERA.

Times had changed. It was no longer socially or legally acceptable to discriminate against blacks and other minorities, and women began demanding that it be every bit as socially and legally unacceptable to discriminate against women. So they started agitating to push ERA out of committee onto the floor of Congress. Anyone who believed in simple equality, they argued, had to believe in ERA. It was so downright simple and just. All it said was:

1. Equality of rights under the law shall not be denied or abridged by the United States or by any State on account of sex.

2. The Congress shall have the power to enforce, by appropriate legislation, the provisions of this article.
3. This amendment shall take effect two years after the date of ratification.

Substitute the word "race" for the word "sex" at the end of the first section, women's leaders pointed out, and no politician in his right mind would have dared to stand up publicly and oppose ERA.

So it surprised no one that on October 12, 1971, the U.S. House passed ERA by 354 to 23; or that on March 22, 1972, the Senate approved ERA by 84 to 8. ERA opponents were hard to find. Support came from Democrats and Republicans, the left and the right. Birch Bayh was for it, but so was George Wallace. Ted Kennedy supported it, but so did Strom Thurmond. Bella Abzug promoted ERA as the Great American Panacea, but Spiro Agnew also had nice things to say about it.

Likewise, it surprised no one that, when Congress sent ERA to the states for ratification, it sent the states — conservative and liberal — into a mad scramble to be the first to ratify.

Hawaii could hardly wait. Within hours after word reached Honolulu of the U.S. Senate's approval, the legislature voted to ratify, without a word of opposition or debate. Nebraska, scurrying to be No. 2, passed it the next day, without a single dissenting vote. (Nebraska was in such a hurry, in fact, that it neglected to pass Section II of the three-section Amendment and had to pass it all over again six days later. Alaska passed Section I, but forgot Sections II and III.) The Delaware Senate passed ERA at 3:00 P.M. on March 22, an hour and forty minutes before the U.S. Senate passed it and submitted it to the states for ratification, a fact that brought a court challenge to Delaware's ratification.

Within that first week, New Hampshire, Iowa, Kansas, and Idaho ratified. Kansas, which devoted ten minutes to debate, was typical.

ERA passed by 205 to 7 in Massachusetts, but it also passed by 31 to 0 in West Virginia. Colorado passed it by 61 to 0. In no state was the vote even close.

Within a month, fourteen states ratified. The bandwagon whizzed along and, within three months, twenty states ratified. Within a year, thirty states ratified. Only eight more were needed to make ERA a part of the Constitution. (The Constitution requires that three-fourths of the states ratify [thirty-eight states]. Since 1919, Congress has required that states ratify within seven years. ERA's seven years expired on March 22, 1979.)

In March 1973 — with nearly six years to spare before ERA's time limit expired — women's leaders predicted that within two months the eight states required to bring the total up to thirty-eight would ratify. "ERA will be part of the Constitution long before the year's out," said Martha Griffiths, then congresswoman from Michigan.

The congresswoman, who had shepherded ERA through Congress the year before, failed to take into account one factor — one person — Phyllis Schlafly.

As a religious, traditional woman, Schlafly found ERA distasteful. As a conservative, she found it appalling. A staunch believer that, when it comes to government, "less is better," Schlafly considered the second section of ERA, which gives enforcement power to the U.S. Congress, even worse than the first, which decrees a strict equality of rights under the law. The first section would require states to make vast changes in the laws in such private areas as marriage, divorce, child custody, and adoption. And the second section would effectively give Washington the power to rewrite those laws if they did not meet a national standard. "ERA would virtually reduce the states of this union to meaningless zeros on the nation's map," said Senator Sam J. Ervin — one of the very few critics of the amendment — during Senate debate in 1972.

Schlafly, whose favorite target in speeches had always been "Big Brother" turning a once-diverse, vigorous, and independent country into a standardized, homogenized, helpless blob, agreed. And considering that Section II threatened to transfer some 70 percent of a state legislature's already rapidly dwindling power to the federal government, it was not hard to get a majority of state legislators to agree — especially when Schlafly presented specifics. Under ERA, she warned, the traditional family would become an endangered species.

When ERA was introduced into Congress in 1970, its sponsors omitted the Hayden modification, which had been part of the pending amendment for twenty years and stated: "Nothing in the amendment will be construed to deprive persons of the female sex of any of the rights, benefits, and exemptions now conferred by law on persons of the female sex" (for example, the "right" of a wife to be supported by her husband).

When ERA was on the floor of the Senate, Senator Ervin proposed nine separate amendments to ERA — all of which were defeated. The amendments would have retained preferential laws for wives, mothers, and widows and would have exempted women from the draft and combat duty.

Schlafly was disturbed by the fact that the ERA that was sent to the states compelled absolute equality — no amendments, no exceptions. (She said she would have supported ERA had Congress left in the Hayden modification or the Ervin amendments.)

Once ERA was ratified, the states would be forced to treat men and women equally under all circumstances, meaning that most laws requiring a husband to support his wife would become unconstitutional. Those laws obviously discriminated on the basis of sex because they did not impose the equal obligation on the wife to support her husband. The state of New York, for example, would have to change its law, which read simply, "Husband liable for support of his wife," to require mutual or reciprocal support.

Schlafly saw these changes, which experts on both sides of the issue agreed ERA would demand, as eventually weakening the traditional family. With the divorce rate soaring, young women would be less likely to leave the work force to devote themselves to husband and children. Becoming financially dependent on a male would be too big a gamble for many women to risk, especially because every year of not working would lessen their value in the job market.

The women who had already taken the gamble — the middle-aged, full-time homemakers with no job skills — would be, Schlafly decided, hurt most by ERA. (Not surprisingly, it was from this group that Schlafly drew most of her STOP ERA support.) Those women had gone into marriage in another era when it was assumed that it was the wife's duty to bear and raise children and the husband's duty to provide the support.[2] "ERA does not even include a 'grandmother clause,' " Schlafly was fond of saying.

The fact that ERA allowed no reasonable differences in treatment of the sexes would affect, Schlafly claimed, an enormous number of institutions. Women's colleges that received federal aid (about 99 percent of them) would not be able to continue admitting women only, because by so doing they discriminated "on account of sex." Protective labor laws for blue-collar women — such as those exempting women from compulsory overtime, allowing women extra rest periods and better restrooms, and putting a limit on weights they could be required to lift — would also be unconstitutional.

But to Schlafly these were minor ramifications in comparison with another law that would become unconstitutional if ERA were ratified — the federal law that exempted women from the draft and excluded them from military combat. While there was hot dispute over some of Schlafly's ERA-spawned horrors, there was no dispute over the draft issue. The House Judiciary Committee reported that, under ERA, "not only would women, including mothers, be subject to the draft, but the military, would be compelled to place them in combat units alongside of men." That same year, Professor Thomas Emerson, writing in the *Yale Law Journal*, concurred: "The amendment permits no exceptions for the military. Neither the right to privacy nor any unique physical characteristic justifies different treatment of the sexes. . . ."

While others found the prospect of equality of sexes in the military

---

[2]It is true that many states, without ERA to compel them, have begun to sex-neutralize their family laws. However, Schlafly sees these new laws as fashionable but dangerous trends. Laws can be changed. A constitutional amendment can't be changed — except by another constitutional amendment.

heartening, Schlafly found it horrifying. Aside from the moral implications of men and women sharing foxholes, a coed military to Schlafly meant a weakened defense — according to Pentagon studies women have, on the average, 60 percent of the physical strength of men. The Soviet Army, she said ominously, is less than 1 percent female and its combat troops are exclusively male.

Schlafly saw several other by products of ERA over which there was wide disagreement. The amendment's backers denounced these as "scare tactics," arguments that, they said, were about as sound as the flat-earth theory. Schlafly saw ERA as giving homosexuals the right to a marriage license and so the rights of married couples, such as the right to adopt infants. "ERA bans discrimination on account of sex, and it is precisely on account of sex that a state now denies a marriage license to a man and a man." She was not the first person to make this argument. In testifying before the Senate Judiciary Committee, Harvard Professor Paul Freund said, "If the law must be as undiscriminating concerning sex as it is toward race, it would follow that laws outlawing wedlock between members of the same sex would be as invalid as laws forbidding miscegenation." (Yale Professor Thomas Emerson disagreed: "ERA says you can't discriminate because of gender. It doesn't say you can't discriminate because of sexual preference.")

Schlafly also saw a link between ERA and abortion that has been, perhaps, the most controversial of her anti-ERA arguments. ERA, she said, would give women the constitutional right to an abortion because not to do so is discrimination — denying them their equal right with men not to be pregnant. When on January 22, 1973, the U.S. Supreme Court invalidated state antiabortion laws, finding a right to abortion in the Fourteenth Amendment (ratified in 1868 to give full citizenship rights to blacks), Schlafly pronounced the link strengthened: "No one else had ever seen abortion there for a hundred years, and abortion was clearly *not* intended by those who ratified the Fourteenth Amendment. How much easier it will be to find an absolute, government-financed right to abortion in ERA!"

When Schlafly finished listing what ERA would do, she proceeded to what ERA would *not* do — guarantee equal pay for equal work; a point on which, again, both friends and foes of the amendment agreed. Like most provisions of the Constitution, ERA is directed to government, not individual, behavior. How a private employer treated his employee was not the business of ERA, and, in any case, a federal law — the Equal Employment Opportunity Act of 1972 — already made it illegal for an employer to discriminate against women.

So she quickly labeled ERA the "Men's Liberation Amendment," arguing that it would transfer substantial old rights from women to men without giving women any substantial new rights in return.

For most people, first exposure to Phyllis Schlafly came in the mid-1970s, when she was already in the thick of the ERA battle. So they assume that the statements that opened this selection — that Schlafly was a natural foe of ERA, born and bred to battle the amendment — are accurate. Even her closest associates tend to remember Phyllis Schlafly as opposed to ERA from the very start.

Thus it comes as a surprise to almost everyone that, back in 1971, Phyllis Schlafly, at home in Alton writing about ICBMs and megatonnage and warheads, was apathetic about ERA. In fact, if pressed, she might have supported it. "I figured ERA was something between innocuous and mildly helpful," Schlafly recalled.

That year, Shirley Spellerberg, Schlafly's fellow conservative, was struggling to stop ERA from sailing through Congress and she tried to recruit her friend Phyllis, who declined. "Phyllis and I could have stopped ERA while it was still in Congress," sighed Spellerberg who, in the coming years as head of Florida STOP ERA, would spend hundreds of hours lobbying against the amendment. "I just couldn't get her to move."

Later in 1971, in December, a friend of Schlafly's asked her to come to Connecticut to debate a feminist on ERA. "ERA?" Schlafly replied incredulously. "I'm not interested in ERA. How about a debate on national defense?" Nothing doing. The friend insisted on ERA.

"I don't even know which side I'm on," Schlafly finally said in exasperation. She had other things on her mind, like the SALT I agreements, which would be signed in Moscow that next May and which Schlafly felt marked the beginning of the end of the United States as the premier nuclear power. With the presidential election less than a year away, she also had Richard Nixon on her mind. She could not support him in 1972. His policy on détente, not to mention his national security adviser, Henry Kissinger, had made Nixon completely unacceptable, and she wanted to find a candidate who would be tougher in his dealings with the Russians.

"Look," the friend from Connecticut finally said, "I'll send you some background information on ERA. Just promise to read it. I know which side you'll be on after you do." She was right. Schlafly read the material and did some research of her own. ERA suddenly turned from innocuous to dangerous.

She was determined to stop it. It was too late to block approval in Congress — it had already passed the House, and the tide for passage in the Senate was too strong to turn. So Schlafly focused on the states — three-quarters of which had to ratify ERA before it became the Twenty-seventh Amendment to the Constitution.

The odds were certainly against Phyllis Schlafly. Still, she felt confident that if state legislators "knew what ERA really meant," they would vote not to ratify. At the time, even Phyllis' most fervent fans would have considered her a trifle presumptuous. But in retrospect, she had good reason for confidence. Until then, after all, nobody had mounted a national mass movement against the amendment. The very few individuals criticizing ERA were speaking locally, softly, and irregularly.

Phyllis Schlafly vowed to change all that. "I knew from the start," she said, "that I had found enough seriously wrong with ERA to stop it, or at least stall it, for an awfully long time, if only I could get the message out."

She realized that if she was going to get the message out she had to jump in the battle immediately, marshal the disorganized opposition, and march into the states. To the everlasting despair of ERA's confident backers, she did.

WASHINGTON IS THE MAGnet city for political power seekers. It is the Superbowl of politics, attracting players and spectators from every part of the nation and around the world. Playing the game of Washington politics is a constantly exciting and often rewarding experience.

The Washington political establishment is a closely knit fraternity. Congressmen, bureaucrats, and lobbyists not only know each other but also frequently strive for the same goals. All ambitious members of the political establishment seek to establish their reputations for power. On Capitol Hill, power translates into money for campaign chests and better prospects for reelection, and respect from colleagues. The bureaucrats with a reputation for power have a better chance of withstanding the frequently changing political winds. Lobbyists who can convince their clients that they have power can charge higher fees.

An effective lobbying style maintains the appearance of power. Who the lobbyist is, and what his or her connections may be, are an important part of that appearance. Former members of Congress and their aides often find that lobbying can be an extremely lucrative career, enabling them to stay in Washington and continue to play the game of politics. Former Congressman Dan Kuykendall (R., Tenn.) commented, "A former U.S. Congressman, no matter how capable, is worth more in Washington than any place else — considerably more. Even those members who go to law firms back home end up getting sent back to Washington."[1] The same could be said for former congressional staffers.

The following selection describes the style of a leading Washington lobbyist, Thomas Boggs, Jr., the son of a former congressman and an unsuccessful candidate for Congress himself. Over the years, Boggs has built a reputation for power that enabled him to rise from a $12,000 a year associate to a $500,000 a year partner in what has become one of Washington's largest law firms.

7 Albert R. Hunt
THE WASHINGTON POWER BROKERS

Patton, Boggs, and Blow, one of the capital's fastest-growing law firms, is known as a "full-service lobbying firm."

It represents a multitude of conservative clients ranging from the

[1] *Congressional Quarterly Weekly Report*, December 27, 1980, p. 3643.

97

Business Roundtable to right-wing Guatemalan businessmen. Simultaneously, the firm's most celebrated partner, Thomas H. Boggs, Jr., is
raising campaign funds for some of the most liberal lawmakers in Congress. Over the past fifteen months, the firm has hired two top political
operatives of the 1980 presidential campaign: One worked for Ted Kennedy and the other for Ronald Reagan.

"The Boggs firm," one Washington insider says, "looks more like a
fusion government than a law firm."

Although some senior partners try to play down this wheeling-and-
dealing image, it is these well-advertised political connections that keep
clients coming in droves. "You don't hire Patton, Boggs, and Blow because of their legal expertise," says James Mooney, the executive director of the National Cable Television Association. "You hire them because they have good connections with a broad spectrum" of Congress.
This reputation attracts such contradictory clients as General Motors
Corp., Chrysler Corp., and the Automobile Import Dealers Association.

Although the firm has eighty-two lawyers here, it usually is known
as the "Boggs firm." At age forty-one, Tommy Boggs, son of the late
Democratic Majority Leader Hale Boggs and Democratic Rep. Corrine
(Lindy) Boggs of Louisiana, is one of the capital's most powerful lobbyists.

Mr. Boggs makes about $500,000 a year and recently increased his fee
to $250 an hour from $225. He is widely credited with playing a major
role in congressional approval of the Chrysler bailout bill a few years
ago and always seems to be active in special-interest tax legislation,
including the tax-leasing provision enacted last year.

There are thousands of lobbyists trying to influence policy in Washington ranging from the proverbial, single-issue "little old ladies in tennis shoes" to well-heeled corporate influence brokers. In addition to
law firms, the most successful influence brokers these days include
public-relations practitioners, registered agents for foreign governments, and corporate representatives.

Despite the Reagan administration's pledge to reduce regulation and
the size of government, the political climate never has seemed better
for many of these special-interest pleaders. While some regulatory activities, such as antritrust, may be drying up a bit at some law firms
here, any decline is more than offset for many lobbying operations by
increased activity in other areas, such as taxes and defense. Money,
specifically campaign contributions, is the fuel that generates much of
this lobbying prowess. "I won't even take a client now unless he's willing to set up a political action committee and participate in the [cam-
paign-donations] process," Robert McCandless, a lobbyist, says. Although Mr. Boggs and some others won't go that far publicly, a major
asset clearly is their ability to funnel funds to politicians from clients
and friends.

Tommy Boggs is widely seen as the prototype of the high-powered Washington lobbyist. The affable, moon-faced and slightly paunchy Mr. Boggs is very bright, inordinately savvy, and genuinely engaging. He also is cunning, calculating, and seemingly devoid of any real moral compass, driven mainly by money and success.

In short, Tommy Boggs is a nonmalicious, Washington version of TV's J. R. Ewing.

Mr. Boggs uses more soft-sell sophistication than hard-line pressure, and he shows keen awareness of the political process, especially in the House. "Tommy combines an enormous sense of the way things work with an understanding of where power is and where money is in this town," says Rep. Thomas Downey of New York, a liberal Democrat on the House Ways and Means Committee and a beneficiary of Mr. Boggs's fundraising talents.

Mr. Boggs and his firm have their critics, too. "The Boggs firm, in representing legitimate special interests, contributes to the fragmentation of things," says David Cohen, a former president of Common Cause, the self-styled citizens' lobby. "But unlike the big, prestigious law firms of the past, there's no evidence they play much part in helping government put things back together." And Joan Claybrook, who oversees the Ralph Nader operations here, says: "Some attorneys or lobbyists have a reputation of trying to persuade their clients to do the right thing. Nobody ever says that about Tommy Boggs."

Mr. Boggs isn't comfortable talking about what he hopes to contribute to society or about his political philosophy. But criticism doesn't appear to affect the effervescent lobbyist very much. He says, with a big smile, "I really enjoy playing the game."

He certainly works hard for his clients. He is always prowling the corridors of Congress, talking with members and picking up political intelligence. Some weeks he goes to as many as ten political receptions. "I'll go to two a night if one is for a Ways and Means Committee guy and the other is for defense types," he says. But "it's useless to go to two Ways and Means things," he adds.

That constant motion and energy have honed keen instincts for what motivates politicians. A few years ago, he was helping Marathon Oil Co. fight a move to lower duties on some imported specialty steel that competed against a Marathon subsidiary. He first won over liberal Rep. Charles Rangel, a Harlem Democrat, with the argument that some of the imports would come from apartheid South Africa. Then he won over a conservative, the late Rep. William Ketchum, with the argument that the Marathon subsidiary was based in the congressman's California district. Mr. Boggs still delights in thinking about this left-right coalition.

And he seems omnipresent. When Jimmy Carter was president, a meeting to plot strategy for a "tax reform" bill was held at the White

House. Suddenly, Tom Boggs walked into the session. "I almost fell out of my chair," recalls Robert Brandon, a veteran liberal lobbyist on tax measures. Then, Mr. Boggs, others speculate, was able both to talk about his access to the White House and also to advise business clients what the "enemy" was up to.

Mr. Boggs's reputation is probably exaggerated. He does lose sometimes. Last year, his lobbying on behalf of the cable-TV industry was a decided failure in the Senate. And some congressional aides contend that although he gets much of the credit for the Chrysler bailout measures and some tax breaks, most of the real work was done by others.

Nevertheless, as the belief grows that Tom Boggs can make things happen on Capitol Hill, clients come to the firm specifically for his services. William McGowan, the chairman of MCI Communications Corp., recently insisted that Mr. Boggs personally lobby on the company's behalf before MCI would retain the firm. MCI hired the Boggs firm, one communications expert says, not because of any expertise in that area but because "they wanted the biggest rainmaker they could get."

Money Crucial

It's hard to overestimate the importance of money to all this. Mr. Boggs started off with an advantage — he inherited his father's Majority Leader's campaign fund in 1973 and, with an eye to his own lobbying interests, doled out more than $60,000 over several elections. Now, he gives the maximum legal limit of $25,000 every two years.

More important, however, he funnels much larger amounts of money to strategically situated lawmakers. Six years ago, he advised the American Trial Lawyers Association to start a political action committee as part of its effort to beat federal no-fault insurance legislation. Now, Mr. Boggs and a representative of a Republican lobbyist, William Timmons, advise the lawyers every election on how to dish out some $500,000 from that PAC to congressional candidates.

Mr. Boggs persuaded Chrysler to give to such Democrats as Rep. Tony Coelho, the Californian who now heads the House Democratic Campaign Committee. And he gets his clients to contribute regularly to various Democratic party functions. "Some of these clients are getting had," one Capitol Hill insider charges. "They're giving the money, but Tommy is getting the credit."

Network of Lobbyists

Mr. Boggs also has a network of other Washington lobbyists that he calls on. For example, in trying to raise money for Rep. Fortney Stark, a liberal Californian on the House Ways and Means Committee, Mr. Boggs is seeking $250 each from a list of three dozen lobbyists. "I hit these guys, and I know they'll come back and hit me up," he notes.

He goes to great lengths to keep this network flowing. Shortly after

Tosco Inc., the big oil-shale concern, received a $1.1 billion federal loan guarantee last year, its representatives started getting solicitations to Mr. Boggs's fundraisers and other political activities. A short while later, Patton, Boggs, and Blow started lobbying with Tosco to get its legal business.

When Mr. Boggs deals with a member of Congress legislatively, though, he is the consummate professional. "Tom Boggs never embarrasses me; he never pushes me to vote for something that would be impossible for me to support," Rep. Rangel says. But other politicians acknowledge that Mr. Boggs's fundraising gives him special access, and some say they are inclined to give him the benefit of the doubt on some legislative matters.

Family Ties

Mr. Boggs has come a long way since he joined the law firm sixteen years ago. "When Tommy was first around, everybody thought he was just using his family connections," says his law partner, James O'Hara, who then was a Michigan congressman. After his father died in a 1972 plane crash, it was Tommy, on behalf of the family, who gave Tip O'Neill the green light to run for House Democratic majority leader. His mother succeeded his father in Congress. (This year, a sister, Barbara Sigmund, is running for Congress from New Jersey.)

Tommy Boggs himself ran unsuccessfully for a suburban Maryland House seat in 1970 but says electoral politics is out of his system: "I couldn't afford it." His senior partner, James Patton, thinks that the youthful super-lobbyist aspires to be chairman of a major corporation or secretary of defense someday.

Patton, Boggs, and Blow was started twenty years ago by Mr. Patton, a successful international lawyer with the city's most establishment law firm, Covington and Burling. He hired Tom Boggs, for $10,000 or $12,000 a year," he recalls. The fifty-three-year-old Mr. Patton has directed the firm's enormous growth. A decade ago, the firm had a dozen lawyers; sometime this year, it expects to exceed one hundred attorneys.

Clients number anywhere from four hundred to five hundred, Mr. Patton says, though many are short-term customers. Steady, major clients range from the Mars candy company to Reader's Digest and Northwest Energy Corp. to the state of Louisiana. And yet Patton, Boggs, and Blow (Mr. Boggs became a partner in 1967) isn't considered, among lawyers at least, a top-flight legal firm. Last year, one of its partners left because he wanted to practice substantive tax law instead of always lobbying.

Areas of Expertise

This reputation may be a bit of a bum rap. The firm now has large sections for litigation, international law, administrative practices, and energy. Senior partners say more than 80 percent of their work doesn't involve lobbying.

Still, the political presence of Mr. Boggs and others is ever evident. It is hardly a secret, for instance, that the firm's foreign clients — including retainers of $100,000 a year from the government of Oman and $60,000 from Amigos del Pais, the Guatemalan business group — are based on political connections and not geopolitical expertise. Although the Guatemalan group's chief interest is to spruce up the image here of that country's military dictatorship, Mr. Boggs says he believes that the businessmen are a "moderating influence" and adds that for philosophical reasons his firm wouldn't represent the right-wing government itself.

In keeping with the recent trend in Washington, the firm's lobbying operations have a distinctly bipartisan coloration. The Democratic side is led by Mr. Boggs, former Congressman O'Hara, former Sen. William Hathaway of Maine, and Ronald Brown, a former deputy chairman of the Democratic National Committee and a top adviser to Sen. Edward M. Kennedy's 1980 presidential campaign.

The Republican Side

The Republican services are no slouches, either. They include Ernest Christian, a top tax official in the Nixon administration; Cliff Massa, a former high official at the National Association of Manufacturers; William Colley, a former American Medical Association lobbyist, and Frank Donatelli, who was hired after the 1980 elections, in which he ran the Midwestern-states campaign for Ronald Reagan.

"This political smorgasbord of lawyers," Mr. Patton argues, "gives our clients the whole spectrum of thinking in this town . . . . It can be very exciting and very stimulating."

It also can be very effective politically. For instance, Rep. Barber Conable, the ranking Republican on the House Ways and Means Committee, says he has met Mr. Boggs only "once or twice, and I don't think he has ever been to my office." But asked about Mr. Boggs's partner, Mr. Christian, the New York lawmaker says, "Oh, Ernie is a fine fellow. I talk to him all the time."

Privately, Mr. Boggs also apparently believes that someone with Democratic connections can lobby more effectively for business interests than someone with GOP ties. "Republicans usually vote with you anyway" one corporate lobbyist says. "So Tommy knows he has most of them, and every time he gets a Democrat, particularly a liberal, that's icing on the cake."

Mr. Boggs also sees benefits from the firm's contradictory mix of clients. "With our client list we can build a minicoalition on almost any issue," he declares. A good example, he says, is the controversial tax-leasing provision passed by Congress last year. During consideration of the bill, the firm's leverage on Capitol Hill was increased because the firm represented major retailers, which are potential buyers of tax-leasing plans, and Chrysler, a potential seller.

The firm admits that client interests aren't always the same. But it notes that it represents diverse customers on separate issues; Chrysler on the bailout and tax issues, GM on the Clean Air Act, and import-auto dealers on trade legislation. As for the appearance of conflict of interest in some fields, Timothy May, a senior partner, says: "I've wondered about some of this myself, but we've talked to the clients and they don't see it as a problem."

Neither does Mr. Boggs. He enjoys high-powered lobbying and thinks that in time it may bring respectability as well as money and power. "In recruiting, a few years ago, it was a real disadvantage to say you were a firm that lobbied; we hid it," he says. "But now, it's a recruiting asset. The kids love it. They call lobbying public-policy law."

FREDERICK DUTTON DID NOT make Joseph C. Goulden's list of Washington's superlawyers in the early 1970s, although he had already had extensive political experience at the highest levels of government. But as the decade drew to a close, Dutton had become one of the capital's most influential power brokers.[1]

Dutton was a young California lawyer engaged in a modest practice when he began a political column for the *Los Angeles Times* that eventually brought him to the attention of historian Arthur Schlesinger, Jr., who recruited him for Adlai Stevenson's presidential campaign, launching Dutton's political career. He later served as Governor Edmund Brown's chief of staff, a position he left to join the Kennedy administration. He became secretary of the cabinet, and then assistant secretary of state for congressional relations. Arthur Schlesinger recalled in his chronicle of the Kennedy years that in the latter position, "Dutton joined policy sophistication with political skill in running congressional relations."[2]

Dutton soon became part of the inner corps of Kennedy advisers, a trusted aide not only to the president but to his brother Robert. He worked in the presidential campaigns of Robert Kennedy and George McGovern, all of the time sharpening his political acumen and expanding his Washington contacts. He always carefully cultivated the press.

Today, *Washington Post* executive editor Benjamin Bradlees, *New York Times* Washington Bureau chief Bill Kovach, and NBC-TV anchorman Roger Mudd, attend Dutton's dinner parties, along with the chairman of the Joint Chiefs of Staff and other powerful Washington political figures.[3]

The following selection describes Dutton's Washington style, and how he has become, singlehandedly, a formidable representative of Saudi Arabia.

Steven Emerson
DUTTON OF ARABIA

In Washington's political establishment, Frederick G. Dutton appears to be the embodiment of respectability. His civic and government back-

[1] Joseph C. Goulden discusses what he called the "small and powerful world of the great Washington law firms" in his best-selling book, *The Superlawyers*, (New York: Weybright and Talley, p. 171).

[2] Arthur M. Schlesinger, Jr., *A Thousand Days* (Boston: Houghton Mifflin Co., 1965), p. 445.

[3] Karen Elliott House, "The Power Brokers: A Registered Agent Helps Saudis Fathom and Sway Washington," *The Wall Street Journal*, March 29, 1982, pp. 1, 15.

Reprinted by permission of *The New Republic*, June 16, 1982. © 1982, The New Republic, Inc.

ground is stellar, his reputation among journalists impeccable, his political skill remarkable, and his integrity largely unquestioned by supporters and critics alike. Fred Dutton is also the premier foreign agent for the government of Saudi Arabia. And because of his sterling personal qualifications as well as his influence with his clients, Dutton may even be the preeminent and most powerful foreign agent in the country.

Most of the nine hundred foreign lobbyists registered with the Department of Justice are engaged in activities that could be considered routine. They are paid by their foreign clients to secure special immigrant visas, to help change tariff schedules, to arrange press interviews, and even to disseminate tourist information. Rarely do foreign agents become key political spokesmen for other nations; even less frequently do they become architects of other nations' foreign political strategies. Fred Dutton's work on behalf of Saudi Arabia is a major exception.

Dutton's political career began in the 1950s, when he served in the campaigns of Adlai E. Stevenson and then as executive assistant to Governor Edmund G. (Pat) Brown of California. In 1961, after working for the election of John F. Kennedy, Dutton was appointed to be a special assistant to the president. He later moved to the State Department as assistant secretary for congressional relations. As one friend said, this "proved to be his best preparation for his current role. It gave him hundreds of key contacts." He resigned in 1964 and eventually set up his own law firm. The associates were all liberal Kennedy family devotees. One of them was Herb Schmertz, now vice-president of Mobil Oil Corporation. When Schmertz moved to Mobil, he hired Dutton to provide intelligence and analysis of the "general political climate" in Washington. Dutton also suggested to Schmertz that Mobil sponsor the National Town Meetings, lively Washington discussions on domestic and foreign policy issues which feature journalists and high government officials. Mobil liked the idea, and hired Dutton to run the programs, which, until this year, had been broadcast regularly over National Public Radio. As William Safire discovered last year, because of the Mobil grant, Dutton has also been able "to sprinkle $500 to $1,000 honoraria over hundreds of congressmen and Washington journalists."

In 1968 Dutton was one of Robert Kennedy's principal campaign advisers, and was at his side when he was assassinated. In 1972 he became a key aide in George McGovern's bid for the presidency, and has maintained his contacts in the Democratic party ever since. Dutton was also an early and active opponent of the Vietnam war.

In June 1975 Dutton registered as an agent for Saudi Arabia, first for Petromin, the Saudi state oil agency, and later in the year for the embassy itself. When he first signed up with the embassy of Saudi Arabia in November 1975, Dutton noted on his registration statement that he was "being retained for counseling and legal advice, not public information activities, which registrant understands will be the responsibility of others." Yet, in the seven years that Dutton has served as a Saudi agent, he has helped build an image of moderation and legitimacy for the Saudis, which they desperately sought after the ill will they engendered with the 1973 oil embargo. The Saudis have paid him handsomely: over $1.2 million — $400,000 in 1981 alone for him and his wife — including a virtually unlimited expense account.

Dutton says in his registration forms filed at the Department of Justice that his work consists primarily of legal advice and political counsel, not lobbying or public relations. In an interview, Dutton said, "Ninety-nine percent of my time and work, social or otherwise, is interfacing with the Saudis. I generally have avoided going up to the Hill, don't like it, and made clear I don't want that role. And, for example, I saw one senator and no congressman during the Awacs debate. As for a continuing [public relations] program, no."

Dutton has listed no more than five senators and representatives contacted on behalf of his Saudi clients. He has carefully nurtured the image of a lawyer-client relationship with the Saudis. And it is precisely that professional distance, coupled with his longstanding reputation for integrity, that has enabled him to retain his political credibility.

Some of Dutton's former associates were interviewed by Betty Cuniberti for an article that appeared last October in the *Los Angeles Times.* Frank Mankiewicz, president of National Public Radio, who is described by Cuniberti as "a close friend of Dutton from their high school days in California through the Bobby Kennedy and George McGovern campaigns to the present," said, "I assume someone is going to represent the Saudis. I'm glad it's Fred Dutton, because he's an honorable, decent, thoughtful fellow. Better him than some cut-throat lobbyist. I happen personally not to agree with his stand on Awacs. But would I make a moral judgment on Fred Dutton? Surely not."

Over the years Dutton has cultivated friendships with key senators and various former government officials, and with preeminent members of the national media, including, according to a *Wall Street Journal* article by Karen Elliot House, *Washington Post* editor Benjamin Bradlee, *New York Times* Washington bureau chief Bill Kovach, columnist Joseph Kraft, NBC anchorman Roger Mudd, CBS diplomatic correspondent Robert Pierpoint, and Elliot House herself. In addition to scores of other journalists and U.S. officials, they are guests at his frequent brunches and dinners. Even when Saudi policies are not discussed, the Saudis are well served by these social occasions. One senator says, "When I talk with Fred, I simply never have the feeling that I'm dealing with a foreign agent. I never have the suspicion that Fred Dutton could sell out this country's interest." Even members of Congress not friendly toward Saudi Arabia concede that Dutton has worked miracles for the Saudis. One prominent journalist who has been invited to numerous Dutton dinners says, "If Fred Dutton is their man, how bad can they be?" In 1978 the *New York Times* wrote that "Dutton has long been one of Washington's most useful and reliable sources for political reporters." At the *Washington Post,* Dutton is a well-known fixture, and one staffer says wryly that at the *Post*'s Monday editorial meetings, it's easy to tell who had brunch with Dutton the day before.

The Fred Dutton who works for the Saudis is generally perceived as an extension of the principled Fred Dutton who long ago became outspoken on a wider range of political matters, from freedom of speech to ·the Vietnam war. And, in the 1960s, according to friends, associates, and even Dutton himself, he was a strong supporter of Israel — even "uncritically pro-Israel," in Dutton's own words. Many of the people who know Dutton, including members of Congress and the press, view Dutton's contract with the Saudis as almost incidental. His popularity with journalists is sustained by his fund of imaginative ideas.

But during the Awacs debate, Dutton coined the slogan "Reagan or Begin," which reduced the controversy to an issue of national loyalty. And phrased in such terms, it unleashed undercurrents of anti-Semitism. What caused the change in Dutton's views on Israel to such an extent that he became an agent for Saudi Arabia? According to Dutton, it wasn't simply because a generous offer had been made. "The original contract was not that lucrative to begin with. . . . It has grown with time, as the amount of work, or let's say Saudi trust in me, has grown." He says that then-Senator William Fulbright had recommended him to the Saudis in 1973, and that his decision stemmed from a personal connection with Fulbright. "If almost anybody else had come to me and suggested I do it, no. I don't think I would have done it. It was unusual, but interesting. He was chairman of the Foreign Relations Committee, I admired him, he identified the problem, and so I went over there. But I never even thought about the Arab world, the Middle East, other than from a very uncritical pro-Israeli position. I never thought about representing anybody abroad. All my business had been in California and Washington."

Dutton has long insisted on his initial hesitancy to take the Saudi contract in 1975, and friends and associates say that Dutton has also told them of his unwillingness. This reticence has been critical to the avoidance of a crass hired-gun image. The *New York Times* provided the following account on April 2, 1978:

One day in 1973 Senator William J. Fulbright was discussing the Middle East with Rawleigh Warner, Jr., the chief executive officer of Mobil Corporation, one of Mr. Dutton's clients.

As Mr. Dutton tells the story, the Senator told Mr. Warner that Saudi Arabians "didn't handle themselves well" in Washington and should hire a representative. Mr. Dutton's name cropped up — among others — and Mr. Warner passed Senator Fulbright's advice on to Riyadh.

In 1975 Mr. Dutton was offered a contract by the Saudis, but hesitated. Given the intensely pro-Israeli position of many in the Democratic Party, he feared that working for the Saudis might seem the end of his political career, but he took the job anyway.

The real story is somewhat different. Recently obtained secret oil company documents, confidential correspondence, and information from oil company officials reveal that Dutton solicited the Saudi contract as early as 1973, and began assisting Saudi Arabia, directly and indirectly, through the Arabian American Oil Company (Aramco, the oil consortium consisting of Exxon, Mobil, Texaco, and Standard Oil of California) in December of that year through 1974. The new information shows that Aramco hired Dutton because it was being pressured by the Saudis to prove that it was actively supporting the kingdom's political demands. Furthermore, the documents show that as early as 1973 Dutton conceived of an ambitious public relations program, including newspaper advertisements, films, and an "unannounced" public relations operation with fifteen staff people, aimed at turning American public opinion against Israel and more favorably toward the Saudis.

Finally, the new material provides significant insights into how Dutton got the job, the nature of his public relations activities in the United States, and why he has cultivated such close relationships with the *Washington Post* and the national press.

In the spring of 1973 Saudi King Faisal was becoming increasingly bellicose about American Middle East policy. It was clear to oil company officials that the secret political funding operation which Aramco had conducted since 1967 was not going to be enough. American policy was still aligned with Israel; more had to be done. At the same time a bug had been planted in the ears of oil company and Saudi officials by then-Senator Fulbright, a longtime critic of Israel. He suggested to Rawleigh Warner, chairman of Mobil, that the companies attempt to help upgrade Saudi public relations in the United States.

A search process began in mid-1973 by oil officials for an American adviser for the Saudis — an action taken with concurrence of Saudi officials. The search focused on prominent Washington attorneys. Half a dozen were considered, and by September 1973 Dutton became a finalist.

One former official of Aramco said, "We were interested in this case and in others in getting them an adviser from the U.S. scene who could advise them on whatever subject they wanted — or could direct their efforts of whatever they wanted in the United States. We looked at Dutton, who at that time had no real experience in Middle East but had political experience. He had worked through the Kennedy days and all this sort of thing. We felt he had the kind of a broad expertise on the American scene to offer the Saudis. Up until that point, they looked to Aramco to do it."

According to oil company records, on September 12, 1973, Rawleigh Warner sent a personal appraisal of Dutton to a vice-president of Aramco "as a possible man for the Saudi Arabians." Dutton met Aramco officials in Washington and was told that the Saudis needed an experienced, politically astute, well-connected adviser to help turn American foreign policy toward the Arabs. In one of his meetings, Dutton outlined his plan for a broad public relations operation throughout the United States. Aramco was still evaluating Dutton when he decided to add an extra push. On October 16, 1973 — eight days after the outbreak of the October 1973 war and on the day of a visit to Washington by various Arab envoys bearing the threat of an oil embargo — Dutton wrote a two-page, unsolicited letter to Mike Ameen, then vice-president of Aramco. The letter focused on ways to effect pro-Arab changes in public opinion by use of the media, which Dutton held to be the key to changing American policy. Dutton also warned that Arab threats and warnings about oil cutoffs would only prove counterproductive. Nixon, Dutton added, really wanted a "balanced" policy, but was locked in by public opinion in support of Israel. He wrote:

> I just heard on the morning radio news that a special, high-level delegation of Saudi, Kuwait, and other Arab envoys are coming to Washington today to meet with President Nixon. While that is unquestionably a useful step, I want to urge it is far from enough as a major move even at this juncture — and would seem to misunderstand the overall power system and real decision-making process in this country, especially now.
>
> To the extent the envoys appear to be bearing stern warnings, they only further incite the widespread publicity in the U.S. that the Nixon Administration must not give into threats or oil blackmail. Genuinely effective leverage at least in the U.S. political system must not be a major person but through the public, or key groups, or major news sources. The leverage comes through sympathetic papers, Senators, contributors and such.

Dutton went on to say that Aramco should initiate the public relations campaign he had previously suggested, and should solicit help from sympathetic figures in government and the media:

It must be backed up with the kind of effort we touched on — and quickly. Fulbright and others should be kept briefed; and so should the newsmen here. My own first-hand impression is that the Arabs have far more opportunity in both those sectors than they are beginning to effectively harness. Howard K. Smith on ABC-TV news last evening (nearly twenty million viewers) made a masterful appeal for a more balanced U.S. policy on the Middle East. The Sunday newspapers all contained columns or articles strongly presenting the Arab view. Yet my inquiries of the people writing those (such as Evans and Novak; Smith Hempstone of the *Star-News;* and others) is that they are working out of their own background and digging, not with any real or fresh information. I was at the *Washington Post* again yesterday, and while the paper remains staunchly pro-Israeli in its editorials (as this morning) the working writers there have increasing questions and doubts about the Israeli tilt to U.S. policy. In brief, the opportunity is present for the kind of major effort backing up the diplomacy today suggested above.[1]

In his final paragraph, Dutton reminded Ameen of the need for the special efforts on behalf of Saudi Arabia that cannot be made at the "top" or through regular diplomatic channels. He added, "I do not intend to be implicitly pushing myself to help you in this situation — I am still very much on the sidelines, I realize. But I would think that you might assure there is full understanding of the domestic political, media and particular Congressional aspects and try to bring to bear the necessary steps (the Israelis are massively at work) to assure a balanced policy in this country's own self interest."

In late November Aramco decided to retain Dutton as an adviser. His duties reportedly were to include some of the same services that Aramco had intended for him to provide Saudi Arabia — public relations, political intelligence, and help in planning and arranging visits by Saudi officials to the U.S. It was both Dutton's and Aramco's understanding that it was only a matter of time before Saudi Arabia would agree to a formal employment arrangement with Dutton.

On December 7, 1973, Dutton wrote Aramco another remarkable letter. It strongly suggests that Aramco hired Dutton and pushed for his employment by the Saudis because of its need to prove its loyalty to the Saudis. In four pages, Dutton detailed a massive public relations program that Aramco could take on its own, "responsive to what I assume is a fundamental need to demonstrate to the Saudis that Aramco is taking real steps here to carry forward your and their common interests." Dutton impressed upon Ameen Aramco's self-interest in such a program: "The huge stake that Aramco has there would seem to make that especially important over the next three to six months, with the impending negotiations, oil embargo and underlying struggle looming so

---

[1] © 1978 by The New York Times Company. Reprinted by permission.

large. Not making a genuine effort over the months immediately ahead would seem, in fact, to be readily subject to interpretation by them as that the company is ducking in the really critical clinch." He urged throughout that only programs of a certain type be initiated: those that would result in "press clippings," or that could be "directly verifiable to the Saudis" in other ways. "Sophisticated Saudis like Yamani must be well aware of how much more influential TV has become than newspapers with the White House, Congress, and general public; and showing tapes of films can even make a more indelible impression than thumbing through batches of newspaper stories." Dutton's suggestions included five-minute documentary TV commercials, fifteen-minute radio programs, advertisements in the New York Times, and lectures, seminars, and speeches by pro-Saudi Americans at major universities.

Saudi oil minister Sheik Yamani was scheduled to visit the United States in early December of that year, and Dutton provided some assistance to him during the visit. In his talks with Kissinger, Yamani reaffirmed Saudi Arabia's refusal to lift the oil embargo unless the United States acceded to Saudi Arabia's demands that Israel be forced to withdraw immediately from all the occupied territories. At the conclusion of the visit, Dutton delivered a book to Yamani at the Madison Hotel. The book, Dutton wrote in an accompanying note, was "intended as a very small token of appreciation for all you have done on this trip, from those here who believe in an even-handed U.S. policy toward the Middle East. I hope there will be many renewing follow-ups on behalf of that from many sources."

In the course of his work, Dutton also prepared, apparently on his own initiative, a proposed three-page advertisement, to be signed by King Faisal or Sheik Yamani, for publication in the United States. The advertisement, entitled From Saudi Arabia to America, defended the Arab view on the Middle East, attacked Israel, and justified the embargo. In the advertisement, Dutton attributed the sole source of Middle East instability to Israel — including its encouragement of Jewish immigration — as the reason for the oil embargo: "The stepped-up recent building of permanent settlements on occupied territories and the international campaign launched for still greater immigration into the area inescapably forewarned for yet further expansionism onto Arab soil and larger injustices if resolute corrective action was not sought."

In a letter dated December 15, 1973, just after Yamani left the U.S., Dutton wrote Aramco chairman Frank Jungers to tell him, "Yamani's trip here was superb, with much good coming of it. But vastly more is needed — and quickly." Dutton then outlined a whirlwind press tour by Prince Saud and Sheik Yamani during their prospective visits to the U.S.

Dutton also suggested an increased role for himself in helping to schedule future visits to the United States by Prince Saud and Sheik Yamani.

> Leaving the development of the scheduling for a Saudi visit to the Saudi Embassy in Washington or the State Department will not accomplish what has to be done. None of the Arab embassies here has a feel for these matters; and the State Department is neither sensitive or imaginative enough about the domestic front, as I learned while Assistant Secretary of State under Kennedy and Johnson.

In his concluding paragraph, Dutton expressed his pleasure in meeting Jungers and added:

> And I want to thank you, too, for the opportunity to meet Yamani, who I sensed is about as fascinating an individual as John F. Kennedy, whom I came to think while his Secretary of the Cabinet was about the most interesting political figure (even with his faults) I would ever come to know.

According to correspondence to Dutton from high-ranking Aramco officials, Dutton was to be working under the Saudi official, Kamal Adham, if a contract with the Saudis could be agreed upon. Adham was described by Aramco officials as "special adviser to the King," but, in fact, he was the head of the Saudi secret police. As King Faisal's brother-in-law, Adham also positioned himself to be a middleman for billions of dollars of Western contracts with Saudi Arabia, and he is considered to have been the principal CIA liaison in Saudi Arabia. Adham's nephew, Prince Turki, who has since succeeded Adham as head of Saudi intelligence, was to work with Dutton.

Dutton also conceived of a public relations "operation" for Saudi Arabia to be set up in Washington under the aegis of a high Saudi official, and heavily dependent upon staff personnel from Mobil, SoCal, Texaco, and Exxon. According to an outline, the operation was to "have a low profile" with no announcement made of its creation. "Simply go to work," wrote Dutton. "Set up goals, assignments, small staff. Do through others. Use 'free' outlets to the maximum extent possible." The "staff nucleus" was to consist of a "TV and radio news specialist," "newspaper experts for contact," writers, research assistants, and liaison people with the Senate and House of Representatives. In addition, over ten staff personnel "detailed from the Aramco companies" were to be placed in charge of numerous public relations programs. Senators, representatives, and "major news people" were to be invited to Saudi Arabia. Lucius Battle of the Middle East Institute was to be commissioned to give press interviews throughout the United States. Dutton also suggested setting up college seminars, producing film documentaries, preparing newspaper advertisements, and scheduling Aramco and

Saudi officials to speak in the United States and abroad. Targeted groups included the "business community," "blacks," "environmental groups," "peace groups," "individual VIPs," "governors, mayors, and others."

Dutton insisted on being exclusively in charge of the operation and working directly with Kamal Adham and top Aramco officials. Quoting a fee of $1,000 a day for top Washington lawyers, Dutton asked for a $600,000, three-year contract and added, "I will likely be giving thirty days a month for a long time to come, and long evenings." Dutton also added, "I would be burning many bridges to do this — have family obligations." The contract would be subject to cancellation "if Fulbright informally indicates [that I am] not performing or for other grounds." (Incidentally, appraising the adequacy of Dutton's work for the Saudis would have been an interesting role for the chairman of the Senate Foreign Relations Committee to play.) In the final line of the three-page outline, Dutton wrote, *"Start Immediately* — should have started six months ago, or twenty-five years ago" (the year in which Israel was created).

By February 1974, Aramco led Dutton to believe that the Saudis would finally agree to a formal contract. Dutton had met with Adham and Turki several times, in the United States and in Saudi Arabia. He drew up a "Statement of Understanding" with eight clauses enumerating his duties as a "consultant," rates of compensation, method of payment, and expense reimbursement. The contract was to begin on February 15. Dutton stipulated in clause two that he "shall be guided by and report to Sheikh Adham and shall not be assigned to work regularly under a ministry or bureaucracy, nor under other Americans." The contract was to run for three years "because of the almost certainly protracted nature of the problem to be dealt with concerning Saudi Arabian-U.S. ties and because other sources of income and work for me will be affected by my taking this responsibility."

But no contract was signed. At the end of Dutton's visit to the kingdom in early February, where he met with top Saudi officials, Dutton wrote to Jungers expressing his appreciation for making the trip possible. He hoped that "a working relationship with Kamal Adham goes together as it provides striking opportunities for getting at the real problems of these times both here and more broadly."

In a memo sent to Aramco, Dutton detailed a "small vignette" that indicated to him that there was "some dark thinking going on in Washington." On Friday, February 22, 1974, Dutton was scheduled to have a "quick, informal" dinner with Fred Graham and David Halberstam. The oil embargo was still in effect at the time. The three of them dropped by a hotel to see Eric Severeid and Theodore White, whom Dutton had known for a long time. After Dutton mentioned to White that he had recently visited Saudi Arabia, White, in Dutton's words, "immediately assailed me and began a long diatribe of how no little country of 2 million people (he even had his figures wrong) should be able to cause so much trouble to all the industrial nations of the world." White, according to Dutton, continued in his "warped, distorted, incredible diatribe by what is supposed to be a highly intelligent man and certainly an influential one . . . including more with U.S. political leaders (especially Nixon) than the reading public. No argument or moderating could change his attitude. The scene was frankly grotesque. But it is mentioned here because I have run into varying degrees of it with respected political writers at several Washington dinners and several of the younger editorial writers at the *Washington Post*."

By late May 1974, the Saudis had still not signed an agreement with Dutton, despite repeated Aramco requests to Saudi officials. On May 27, Aramco's vice-president, Mike Ameen, promised Dutton that he would finally confront Adham to "get this matter settled once and for all." Why were the Saudis holding up a formal agreement? According to an Aramco official in Saudi Arabia at that time, the delay was due to the "procrastination and deliberations associated with all Saudi endeavors."

While awaiting a formal agreement, Dutton provided services for the Saudis in 1974 for which two high-ranking Aramco officials thought Dutton should be paid. They urged that he submit a bill to the Saudis in May. Even though this arrangement was apparently agreed to by Adham, Ameen advised against it lest the Saudis "misinterpret" the bill. "I feel it best," Ameen wrote Dutton, "that we continue to attempt to have him [Adham] enter into an agreement signed, sealed and delivered."

It was not until December 1975, nearly two years after he began providing public relations ideas to Saudi Arabia, that Dutton registered as an agent for its embassy. Dutton has worked hard to convey the image of a lobbyist who is above the level of crass influence peddling or manipulative public relations, and that image has been the key to his credibility with the national media.

When confronted about his earlier unreported work for Saudi Arabia and Aramco, Dutton said that he was not involved in public relations for the Saudis, and "was not made aware of Aramco's dealings with the Saudis" regarding his employment with Saudi Arabia: "I went to work for Aramco in early 1974, as Aramco was trying to assess where it stood in the midst of the oil boycott. I was not paid by the Saudis, but by Aramco, to analyze problems and the changing situation on energy." But as the new information shows, it is difficult to distinguish between Dutton's work for Aramco and his work for the Saudis.

In the end, the issue is not that Dutton solicited a lucrative contract with the Saudis, but that the petrodollar has come to play such an extraordinary role in American society. It can buy more than goods — it can buy influence, prestige, and the services of men like Fred Dutton. And its real target is the foreign policy of the United States.

THE MEDIA
AND POLITICAL
CONSULTANTS

Chapter
Three

The First Amendment's guarantee of freedom of the press both reflects and protects the political power of an institution that has always played an important role in the nation's politics. The publishers and pamphleteers of eighteenth-century America considered freedom of the press a natural liberty, and acted accordingly. Their criticisms of British and colonial authorities helped to plant the revolutionary seed in the minds of the colonists. Colonial governors were aware of the dangers of a free press, and sought unsuccessfully to control it by requiring government licenses for printing. Moreover, the authorities did not hesitate to bring charges of seditious libel against journalists who criticized the government.

The freedom of the press that was won in the eighteenth century created an environment in which political journalists could and did flourish. Reporters could build successful careers by covering politics at state or national levels, although Washington inevitably became the mecca for the political press.

By the time of the New Deal, the Washington press had become a firmly entrenched establishment force in the nation's capital. Jonathan Daniels, an experienced Washington hand who had served as President Franklin D. Roosevelt's press secretary, commented, "It would be difficult to find a body of men who more clearly represent Washington than the gentlemen of the press who report it. There are notions, carefully cultivated, that they are in Washington but not of it, and that they stand in scrutiny but also in separation. Actually, of course, they are probably more representative of the good and the bad on the Capital scene than any other body of bureaucrats. As they stay in Washington, which most of them hope to do, they are at least as remote from the country as the administrators are."[1]

[1] Jonathan Daniels, *Frontier on the Potomac* (New York: The Macmillan Co., 1946), p. 159.

The media is a powerful political force at all levels of the government. A century before the advent of radio and television, Tocqueville pointed out that the diversity and power of the press is a major characteristic of democracy, and particularly of a government such as that of the United States, which contains so many political subdivisions. "The extraordinary subdivision of administrative power," remarked Tocqueville, "has much more to do with the enormous number of American newspapers than the great political freedom of the country and the absolute liberty of the press."[2] Newspapers, concluded Tocqueville, can persuade large numbers of citizens to unite for a common cause. Moreover, "The more equal the conditions of men become and the less strong men individually are, the more easily they give way to the current of the multitude and the more difficult it is for them to adhere by themselves to an opinion which the multitude discard. . . . The power of the newspaper press must therefore increase as the social conditions of men become more equal."[3]

The press has always attempted to create, in Tocqueville's terms, associations of citizens to back causes and candidates. The press attempts to be the kingmaker for many of the ten thousand or more elected offices throughout the nation.

The growth of the electronic media, radio and television, added a new dimension to the traditional political role played by the press. While newspaper publishers and correspondents are free to express their political views, supporting whatever candidates they choose, the electronic media are in an entirely different position. The airwaves used by the electronic media to communicate information are technically "owned" by the public. The government licenses broadcasting stations for a three-year period, after which it reviews the licensee's conduct in relation to statutory and administrative standards to determine whether or not the license is to be renewed.[4] One of the regulatory standards governing broadcasting requires impartiality in the expression of political views. When a station editorializes it must give "equal time" for the presentation of opposing opinions. Broadcasters, unlike publishers, do not often endorse political candidates.

While broadcasting is supposed to be politically neutral, it is inevitably drawn into partisan politics. All news and public affairs programs

[2] Alexis de Tocqueville, *Democracy in America*, Vol. 2 (New York: Vintage Books, 1954), p. 121. Tocqueville's volumes were first published in 1835.

[3] Ibid., p. 122.

[4] In fact, almost all license renewals are automatic, making the licensees virtually permanent owners of their stations.

have a slant, which indirectly shapes citizen attitudes on important issues. Statements about public policy are often made simply by the choice of subjects to be covered. The White House, which is so frequently the focus of media attention, complains constantly that it is not being treated fairly. Republicans attack the "Eastern liberal establishment" press, while Democrats always echo President Harry S Truman's lament: "I was sure that the American people would agree with me if they had all the facts. I knew, however, that the Republican-controlled press and radio would be against me, and my only remaining hope of communicating with the people was to get the message to the people in a personal way."[5]

However much politicians may criticize the media, they increasingly depend upon it to project their personalities and communicate their views to the electorate. Political consulting, which began in California in the 1930s, has become a major industry.[6] By 1952, 45 percent of the households owned television sets, and not surprisingly, that year marked the advent of political television in a big way in presidential campaigns.[7] General Eisenhower, portrayed as the simple and sincere man from Abilene, easily won over the sometimes acerbic but always witty Adlai Stevenson of Illinois. The Stevenson campaign spent only $77,000 on television, compared to a Republican expenditure of $1.5 million on its media campaign. The use of media consultants and the expenditure of large sums of money for public relations has been considered *de rigueur* for almost all political campaigns, presidential, congressional, and at the state level, as television has become the principal political medium. Media consultants are the new political gurus.

The vignettes in this chapter reveal how the press can be a kingmaker, the character and the style of a powerful political consultant, and the way in which one presidential administration attempted to manage the news.

[5] Harry S Truman, *Memoirs,* Vol. 2 (Garden City, N.Y.: Doubleday and Co., 1956), p. 175.

[6] See Larry J. Sabato, *The Rise of Political Consultants* (New York: Basic Books, 1981), pp. 10–13, and *passim*.

[7] Ibid., p. 113.

NEWSPAPERS ARE PEOPLE, and as such, they reflect, above all, the voices of their publishers, powerful editors, and insofar as politics is concerned, the views of their political correspondents and columnists. While newspapers reflect many disparate viewpoints on a wide range of topics, they also speak with a collective voice that defines their character, style, and orientation to overriding matters of social, economic, and political concern. Newspaper publishers are power brokers, often influencing, behind the scenes, the selection and presentation of political candidates. One of the most powerful newspapers in the country is the *Los Angeles Times*, and as the following selection describes, one of the most fateful decisions made by its publisher — the Chandler family — and their star political correspondent — Kyle Palmer — was to launch and sustain the political career of Richard M. Nixon.

9 David Halberstam
THE POWERS THAT BE

The *Los Angeles Times* . . . was [not] a joke to . . . [most] people who lived in Los Angeles in the thirties and had to deal with the paper socially or politically each day, a situation made worse by the fact that the main alternative to the Chandler paper was Hearst. For all of Norman Chandler's personal attractiveness he published a paper devoid of fairness and justice. He did not know better and he did not intend to know better. His paper slew his enemies — Democrats, labor unions. Norman Chandler was publishing in the tradition of his father and grandfather, and publishing for his peers, the big boys in the California Club, the conservative anti-labor barons of Southern California. The friends of the Chandlers were written about as they wished; their enemies were deprived of space, or attacked. What was not printed was as important as what was printed. The *Times* sanitized and laundered the operations of a rich anti-labor establishment and its politicians; it repeatedly used red scares to crush any kind of social-welfare legislation. It gave its enemies no space and no voice. If a newspaper at its best reflects and hears all factions of the community, letting them play their will out as openly as possible, examining the legitimacy of each case on its merits, trying to limit the emotions and passions, then the *Times* was a manifestly unfair newspaper; it appealed to ignorance and prejudice and it fanned passions.

It was intensely, virulently partisan. The *Times* was not an organ of the Republican Party of Southern California, it *was* the Republican Party. It chose the candidates for the party; if anything the Republican Party was an organ of the *Times*. Fairness had nothing to do with it. In 1934, Turner Catledge, then a young political reporter for *The New York Times*, went out to the West Coast to do a story on Upton Sinclair and his radical political movement. Sinclair was then running for governor in a passionate and heated campaign against Frank Merriam, the Republican candidate. Catledge picked up the Los Angles *Times* after he arrived, looking for news of Sinclair. There was none. He thereupon looked for a schedule for Sinclair so he could at least find out where the candidate was speaking and perhaps drive out to hear him. He found none. All he could find about Sinclair was a story saying that Sinclair was attacking the Bible and was un-Christian. That night Catledge went out for dinner with the *Times*'s chief political correspondent, Kyle Palmer, and, still wanting to cover some Sinclair rallies, asked Palmer where Sinclair was speaking. Kyle, who was very charming, replied, "Turner, forget it. We don't go in for that kind of crap that you have back in New York of being obliged to print both sides. We're going to beat this son of a bitch Sinclair any way we can. We're going to kill him." Which they did.

. . . In 1958, a year in which California politics was particularly turbulent, Don Irwin of the New York *Herald Tribune* went out to do a major piece. He dropped by to see Kyle Palmer, and found him very pleasant, very gracious, and quite informative about the Republicans. What about the Democrats? Irwin asked. "Oh, we don't bother with them," Kyle answered.

That was his job, that was his mandate. He knew whom he worked for and what they wanted. He exercised awesome power over four decades, he was the voice of the *Los Angeles Times*; Harry Chandler had begun it, he had created Kyle Palmer, and in time Kyle Palmer and the Los Angeles *Times* created Richard Nixon. Palmer was that powerful, a Dick Daley of Southern California. He was wonderfully ingratiating, and cynical. He made careers and he broke them, sometimes the same career. He chose the candidates for the Republicans, dictated policies, floor-managed legislation in the California legislature, told governors which bills to sign. He was a journalist and a political writer, but in a real sense he was a kingmaker. . . .

Kyle Palmer, political correspondent and kingmaker, had picked Nixon out very early and nurtured him. Nixon, he told his friends, was the best young politician he had ever seen, the best tactician. It was born into him, Palmer said, his very reflex was for tactics, he had an intuitive sense of the chessboard. He was the quickest to learn. Palmer had decided from the start that Nixon had the quality and the scope to go national. Kyle Palmer had not been a member of an informal group in Los Angeles — Whittier that had advertised for young enterprising congressional candidates, but his friends were part of it (indeed, Jack Garland, Norman Chandler's favorite brother-in-law, was a member), and Palmer had been looking for someone like Nixon. The presence of Jerry Voorhis, steadfast New Dealer, in the House seat was a constant irritant, particularly to a political czar who controlled almost everything else. Worse, many of the Chandlers and their friends lived in Pasadena, which was included in the Voorhis district. There are two versions of what had happened. The first was that the original committee was something of a front for Palmer and that he had picked Nixon from the start. The other was that the committee picked Nixon and that Palmer very quickly fastened on him, sensing that Nixon was doing well, and shortly thereafter took him to Norman Chandler for the official laying on of hands. The latter story is more likely the right one. It is unlikely that Palmer would pick up Nixon and invest seriously in him until he thought he had a reasonable chance of winning; Palmer did not like losers. But he quickly took Nixon under his wing in that campaign, urged him to hit hard on the anti-Communist line. The New Deal era was passing, he said, so Nixon should tag Voorhis to it, to the CIO-PAC, attack the bumblers in Washington, put him on the defensive. At the same time, in the pages of the *Los Angeles Times,* often in Palmer's own column, *The Watchman,* there began the evolution of the White Knight Nixon. Young, Clean-cut. War veteran. Quaker background but not afraid to fight. Family man. Straight shooter. Not afraid to duck the issue of Americanism. ("Nixon has ability and courage. He will stand up and fight for what he believes to be right and he swings from the floor.") . . .

The campaign was carefully orchestrated, and there was no doubt, among those in Washington who knew how the *Los Angeles Times'* political coverage worked, about who was the sponsor of it. . . . Voorhis could get no real coverage of his campaign; nothing that he said explaining his record could make this or almost any other paper in his district. He could not even get his daily schedule printed. If he wanted the *Times* to print the announcement of a rally he had to buy an advertisement, and even then they sometimes edited it. Midway through the most difficult campaign of his career, fighting for his political life, he could feel himself becoming a nonperson.

Richard Nixon had no complaints about the press coverage of that campaign. There was a traveling claque which went around with him and which often seemed not just to applaud Nixon but to drown out Voorhis. It bordered on bully-boy tactics. This was the beginning of Nixon. He was the local boy ready to make good, upwardly mobile, ambitious for all the good things that his sponsors seemed to have, unquestioning of them, their values; status and power were their own rewards and bore their own legitimacy. He was bright, eager, a winner. He had run against Voorhis and beaten him, they were in his debt as much as he was in theirs; Voorhis had been a special thorn and Nixon had removed that thorn; now Kyle Palmer adopted Nixon. He guided him on issues, emphasizing that Communism was a no-lose issue, it put Democrats on the defensive, no one wanted to defend Communism, thus it always worked. He made sure that Nixon saw Norman and Buff Chandler, and their friends, and he tutored him on the various members of the inner circle — . . . what they were like, their interests, their vulnerabilities. He told Nixon that when he came back from Washington and went to dinner with his sponsors, he should always give them a nugget, a bit of gossip, a feeling of being on the inside, something they would not get elsewhere. He made sure that when Norman and Buff were in Washington, Nixon would find ample time to see them, to escort them around, to give a dinner in their honor. Washington and Nixon became linked together. At the same time that Palmer was explaining to Nixon how to deal with his new sponsors, he was selling his new protégé to the elite, particularly to Buff and Norman. This young man was not just a congressman. He was going to be a senator. Not just that, but there was nothing stopping him from being a *President*. He was the best young politician Kyle had ever seen, Norman and Buff should take him very seriously, be proud they had a special relationship with him.

Thus began the connection. It was a very special relationship. The *Times* sanitized Nixon, printed whatever would make him look good, and ignored anything that might be damaging. Kyle Palmer was the sole journalist who had access to Nixon at all times, who could walk in and see him without an appointment, without even checking with Rose Mary Woods. It was an almost fatherly relationship; in fact, in 1950, preparing a Senate seat for Nixon, Palmer had written: "Nixon is young enough to be old, and wise enough to be prudent and his perceptive qualities are exceptional. In fact the flattering references which our fathers formerly made to an exceptionally promising junior — that he had an 'old head on young shoulders' — applies with all its homely implications to this young man who grew up here, became a lawyer, went to war, and returned to win a spectacular victory in his first bid for public office." The connection of the *Times* was through Kyle; Norman and Buff stood back just a bit. They were not that directly involved, they were not that personally close to Nixon, but he was useful to them, and potentially even more so; his future, if Kyle was right, seemed limitless.

Yet he was of a different class, he was not *of* them, and they did not want to be any closer to him than necessary. Buff had always found something lacking in him, and years later, when it all had gone sour and he had disgraced himself, she would remember that she always thought he was a little tacky. Indeed, the first time she had met him, on election night in 1946, when all the good winners dutifully came by the *Times* building (as they now go by the television studios) for the anointing by Palmer, she had not liked him. Nixon with his parents and brothers had gone upstairs to the Chandlers' private suite in the building, where there was a buffet. Someone asked the Nixons what they wanted to drink and the Nixon women said milk, so the Nixon men also said milk, and then as Buff was going out the door for milk, Nixon had taken her aside and asked for a bourbon — "Can you get me a straight bourbon? I don't want my mother to see me drinking it." It was a quick flash, but she did not like it, a grown man concealing a drink from his mother. But she did not let it stand in the way of the *Times*'s sponsorship of Richard Nixon. The Nixons, after all, were politicians, people to be used, not liked. They would use him, he would use them. They did not need to be friends. . . .

Nixon's relationship with the *Los Angeles Times* continued to be very profitable and the Hiss case had not hurt him with his sponsors back home. He got wonderful coverage, his every attack on the Reds printed, applauded, his deeds written large and heroically. The easiest of political deeds in the late forties, a HUAC speech, was transformed into a gutsy, courageous stand. Not only were his assaults upon his enemies amplified, but their rebuttals silenced. Typically, the slush-fund incident of 1952, the biggest story in the nation at the time, did not make the *Los Angeles Times* for three days, and when it finally did it was written, on Kyle Palmer's instructions, as a *rebuttal*, NIXON ANSWERS CRITICS. The paper gave Nixon enormous leverage and clout at home, but it was not by any means the healthiest of relationships; it spared Nixon from the normal give-and-take of politics and journalism, it bred in this most fragile of egos a sense that he could attack others without being attacked in return; it allowed him to rise to higher and higher levels of politics without ever testing his ability to take the normal strain and criticism of politics. It made him think that no one would dare attack him — for few in California did — and it made him believe that his lesser moments, if known to journalists, would not be printed, and that finally, if journalists did write normal, balanced, tough-minded analytical stories, they were virtually personal attacks. Few other major politicians came out of a metropolitan area so pampered.

It all created in Nixon a sense that he could get away with things, that the press was crooked and could be bought off. That there were, in fact, special rules. It meant that other politicians in his own area and in his own party lived in fear of him. (In California, Earl Warren, Goodwin Knight, and Bill Knowland, all three Republicans, despised Nixon and deeply distrusted him and believed he was less honest than other politicians, but they were very cautious about it, he was the Chandlers' boy, if they crossed him in any incident a Nixonized version might appear in the *Times* to their detriment.) In 1954, when Goody Knight was governor, Nixon made a deal with Knight that gave Knight the right to name the chairman and the vice-chairman of the California delegation, and Nixon the right to name the treasurer. Knight thereupon went sailing on a honeymoon and Nixon immediately broke the agreement and moved to name the top men. It was a real power struggle; control of the California delegation in 1960 was potentially at stake. Knight, alerted by a ship-to-shore radio of Nixon's move, returned, rallied his troops, and held his turf. It was, by most newspaper standards, a wonderful story, the two top figures in California politics, both potential presidential candidates, struggling over the state's delegation, one of them clearly having broken his word, but no word of it ever appeared in the state's most powerful paper. It was not, by the standards of the *Los Angeles Times*, a wonderful story — it showed Nixon breaking his word to a fellow Republican.

But that was the way the *Los Angeles Times* did it. In late 1949 Kyle Palmer called Richard Nixon in Washington and asked, "Dick, have you thought of running for the Senate?" Nixon answered that he had not thought of it at all, which was not exactly true. In truth, he had for several years thought of little else. "Well," said Kyle, "I wish you'd give some thought to it because we'll all support you if you do." Later Palmer phoned his friend and money raiser Asa Call. "My friend," he said, "the telephone is an astonishing instrument. It is absolutely amazing what you can do with just one call." Thus was it done. A Senate seat from one of the two most powerful states in the Union arranged for a two-term congressman. The oligarchy was all lined up, a few more phone calls were made, the money was arranged. (It was all very simple. After the election there was a deficit of $5,000. Call hated this, he hated untidiness, so he went home and mentioned it to his wife, and Mrs. Call said she would like to make up the difference for Mr. Nixon and so she wrote a check for $5,000, it would be her pleasure.) There would be plenty of money, the oil companies were not displeased, tidelands after all was the central issue of the time. There would be access to the media, Norman and Kyle would fix that. So the seat was cleared. There was a misguided Republican named Raymond Darby who wanted to run for the Senate himself, but Kyle made it plain that this was not his year; Darby, somewhat innocent, was more insistent than most, so Kyle struck up a deal: What about running for lieutenant governor? *Raymond Darby would make a terrific lieutenant governor.* Lieutenant governors often became governors. We can promise you, Kyle said, the support of the *Los Angeles Times.*The support of the *Times.* Ray Darby knew what that meant and he stepped aside and technically, yes, the *Times* did support him, but Kyle was interested in Goody Knight for lieutenant governor that year, Goody was still quite conservative in those days, and Kyle wanted a check on Earl Warren (later he would use Pat Brown as a check on Goody as Knight became too close to labor). So he pulled the rug out from under Darby, and while the *Times*'s official support went to Darby, its real support — full coverage — and the money of its friends went to Knight; Darby predictably perished in the primary.

So it was set up for Nixon to run against Helen Gahagan Douglas. Here again the *Times* was instrumental. The issues of the campaign were totally redefined. Instead of tidelands and the rights to offshore oil, the central issue of the campaign and the principal one upon which Mrs. Douglas was running, it became Communism. It was all red-baiting. Pink lady. If anything, the editorial voice of the *Times* was even harsher than that of Nixon. Mrs. Douglas's voice was never heard. She was never covered; she was only attacked, that was all that was permitted. Any conservative Democrat who backed Nixon made page one. If a Marine fighting in Korea sent back a five-dollar campaign contribution to Nixon — to keep America the way it had been when he left — it was fully reported. Any women's volunteer group was given great news space ("This is the group that did such a fine job in the primary and they want to repeat it and keep Helen Gahagan Douglas out of the Senate next November 7"). There was no way, other than buying ads, that Mrs. Douglas could even get her schedules into print. It was a wonderful free ride for Nixon; he could speak to civic clubs and by raising his eyebrows even imply that there was something sexual going on between Mrs. Douglas and Harry Truman (there was not, of course), and it was never reported. There was no attempt by any newspaper to assign a reporter to a candidate and have the reporter record the charges of that candidate; thus the candidates were unusually free to say what they wanted without any real accountability.

That Helen Gahagan Douglas was in trouble even in a clean campaign was beyond doubt. The Cold War was at its height, Stalinism seemed a dark and immediately threatening specter. The country, disillusioned, was turning inward from the liberalism of the thirties and forties. Mrs. Douglas seemed the embodiment of a period that people were now turning away from, liberalism on domestic issues, trust of the Soviet Union. When the Korean War began in June, her position was made even more vulnerable; when, in October, the Chinese Communists entered the war, her candidacy became hopeless. Up to then she had been doing quite respectably in the polls. With the entrance of the Chinese, her position collapsed, the nation became even more nervous and conservative. . . .

POLITICAL CONSULTING IS A growth industry that is becoming more and more profitable as the costs and skills required to campaign in the modern technological age increase. Consultant fees, commissions, and expenses account for approximately 20 percent of campaign costs.[1] Consultants charge fees ranging from $10,000 to $100,000 to handle electoral campaigns. In addition, they bill candidates for their expenses and collect commissions that may range up to 33 percent on the costs of media advertising.

In many cases, the names of consultants have become as prominent as the candidates they advise. California consultant Stuart Spencer gained widespread publicity after successfully managing Ronald Reagan's gubernatorial campaign in 1966. He was a leading Reagan consultant in 1980. David Garth was credited with making Ed Koch mayor of New York, and winning reelection for incumbent New Jersey governor Brendan Byrne in 1977 against long odds. Gerald Rafshoon, who handled Jimmy Carter's publicity in 1976, gained national prominence after the election of the former Georgia governor. Consultants who become stars are often masters of the electronic media, using their creative talents to mold the television images of their candidates favorably and place opponents in an unfavorable light.

Some political pollsters have also reached stardom. Patrick Caddell's wizardry reputedly helped to elect Jimmy Carter in 1976. Caddell's polls kept the campaign staff aware of shifts in opinion, and pinpointed ways in which the candidate could improve his image. Caddell's view of politics, like that of many consultants, is that "too many good people have been defeated because they tried to substitute substance for style."[2]

While the Stuart Spencers, David Garths, and Patrick Caddells of the political consultant corps gain the most notoriety, the direct-mail consultants have taught candidates how to use the mundane facilities of the post office to raise money — the lifeblood of the political process. Some consultants see direct mail as an essential communications channel to build political constituencies.

Richard Viguerie, the subject of the following selection, is the undisputed master of the direct-mail consultants. Viguerie is the force behind the National Conservative Political Action Committee (NCPAC), which spends millions of dollars to support conservative candidates. NCPAC claimed credit for the defeat of a number of liberal Democratic senators in 1980, including George McGovern of South Dakota, whose direct-mail techniques in the 1972 presidential campaign so impressed Viguerie that he later copied them. McGovern's direct-mail consultants had amassed a 600,000 member list of potential contributors by the time the South Dakotan de-

[1] Larry J. Sabato, *The Rise of Political Consultants* (New York: Basic Books, 1981), p. 52.
[2] Ibid., p. 144.

128

clared his presidential candidacy in 1971. The list yielded over $12 million for the McGovern campaign.[3]

Viguerie has used the most advanced computer technology to target conservatives for fundraising and votes. His skills have helped conservatives to outdistance their liberal opponents by a wide margin in the race for money. Viguerie also uses direct mail to convey his passion for the conservative cause. His character and style are portrayed in the following selection.

10 Sidney Blumenthal
RICHARD VIGUERIE:
THE POSTMASTER GENERAL OF THE RIGHT

Just as Hollywood producers once found starlets sipping sodas at Schwab's Drugstore, the New Right now discovers candidates at meetings in motel function rooms called to protest issues like the Panama Canal Treaty or Salt II. The rise to power of U.S. Senator Gordon Humphrey (R., N.H.) is a case in point. Humphrey, a thirty-eight-year-old commercial airline pilot, got his start when he was invited to a gathering against the canal treaty. Nine people showed up, and Humphrey volunteered to serve as chairman of a "Keep Our Canal" rally. This time, five hundred people attended. From that group, Humphrey built up the Conservative Caucus in New Hampshire to fifteen hundred members, providing a network of support for his candidacy. When Humphrey won the GOP nomination, the New Right summoned its considerable resources. Huge sums of money were raised, enough to buy into the Boston television market, which blankets southern New Hampshire, and to hire expensive political consultants. The result: Humphrey unseated the popular sixteen-year Democratic incumbent, Thomas McIntyre.

Was Humphrey's victory a lucky accident? Not quite. His name originally surfaced on the mailing list of political entrepreneur and generalissimo of the New Right, Richard A. Viguerie. "Things don't happen by accident," he says. "They're planned. They're organized. We don't have a notebook with the whole thing carefully mapped out, although that's not a bad idea. But we have plans."

[3] Ibid., p. 231.

Forty-six-year-old Viguerie has become a very powerful man in a short span of time. He's the publisher of a flotilla of publications ranging from the mass circulation *Conservative Digest* to the insider's newsletter *New Right Report*. Several political action committees are run by his associates, providing modern consulting methods to specially selected candidates. Several U.S. senators owe their seats to Viguerie in some way. Senator Jesse Helms (R., N.C.) was dubbed the Six-Million-Dollar man last year when he ran for reelection, a reference to the amount Viguerie raised for him as a result of direct-mail solicitations. (Viguerie, incidentally, keeps a hefty chunk of the loot; in some cases more than 75 percent of what he raises goes to him and his subsidiaries.)

Viguerie's IBM tape decks and high-speed printers work twenty-four hours a day, with time off only on Christmas, Thanksgiving, and Easter. In the vault of his computer room, to which entry is permitted only by a security guard, is his treasure of 11 million names on tape. This is the core of the New Right.

Viguerie is ready for the presidential election year, another milestone, he hopes, in the progress of the New Right. At first, Viguerie's candidate was Congressman Philip Crane of Illinois. In the eleven months after his announcement in August 1978, Crane raised $2,490,276 in funds through direct mail. But he paid out $1,191,847 to five companies of which Viguerie is an owner, officer, or director. Crane disagreed with Viguerie about the direct-mail strategy. He wanted to resolicit those on the "house list." Viguerie wanted to keep "prospecting" for new supporters. Eventually, Crane and Viguerie had a falling out.

Meanwhile, Viguerie approached another presidential contender, John Connally. "He was interested and we got married," says Viguerie. "Connally and I agree on 75 percent of the issues. And he has the best chance of beating Ted Kennedy." This factor is paramount to Viguerie. He is terror stricken by the thought of a Kennedy presidency. He believes Kennedy will attempt to put the New Right out of business by promulgating campaign contribution reforms and by political use of the Justice Department. If Kennedy is the candidate for the Democrats, Viguerie sees the election as a life-and-death struggle.

"It's a sign of our strength that there is no candidate in the Republican party who is going to run a left of center campaign for president," says Viguerie. "I think the new vitality of the conservative movement definitely is responsible for that. This will be the first time in our lifetime that no one who is a serious candidate will appeal to that liberal perspective. Slowly but surely we're moving the political balance much more to the center. Not to the right. But things are definitely moving our way. We've got some momentum."

One of his confederates, Massachusetts conservative Howard Phillips, believes that Viguerie's mailing lists are at the base of the New

Right's sudden influence. It was Phillips's Conservative Caucus that "discovered" Gordon Humphrey in New Hampshire, courtesy of Viguerie's computerized lists. "They're indispensable," he says. "Without assembling that body of names we couldn't have achieved anything. As Jesse Unruh said, money is the mother's milk of politics. Unless you have money you don't have anything. Without the magic of direct mail, conservatives would be relegated to part-time activity. There would have been no fight over the Panama Canal Treaty unless there was a New Right. We helped defeat instant voter registration. If the New Right wasn't involved, the two parties would take the same position and there would be no debate."

Viguerie is the High Tech Lenin of the New Right. He didn't come to the right through disillusionment or defeat. He isn't brooding or starkly resentful. He's relaxed in his corner office, surrounded by paintings of famous golf courses. His head is a gleaming sculpted dome with a few strands of hair brushed across it. He's at ease with himself, not threatened by conversations with journalists. On the contrary, he welcomes these exchanges. He's animated, yet completely self-possessed. He's eager to state his position. He wants challenges. Interviews are exercises, preparatory drills, jogs in anticipation of the long-distance run. He bubbles with optimism.

"If I had been in a lot of the foxholes a lot of the conservatives have been in for thirty years and been shot and shelled and just torn apart and suffered all the defeats and have a what-the-hell attitude . . ." Viguerie shrugs and plows on. "That's just not the attitude of the new conservatives. We believe we will win and prevail. There isn't a Communist leader in the world worth his salt who doesn't feel that Communism isn't the wave of the future. They just believe that they are the stuff of history. There's not a leader I know of in the Free World who believes freedom is the wave of the future. That's what we have going for the conservatives now: the conservatives believe that they will govern America. They see themselves as winners in life. They are totally convinced that they have the ability to govern and that they *will* govern in the foreseeable future. There's an electricity, an excitement that wasn't here six years ago."

Viguerie is a fundamentalist in his political beliefs. What sets him off from mossbacks of previous generations is his sophistication. He knows that without a contemporary approach his ideas would remain ethereal, unconnected to real politics. He wants to win. He's reaching for power. He knows how to work the levers and his intentions are clear. All of this makes him an original American political type, unlike the old rightists who were nurtured on failure and developed what the late historian Richard Hofstadter termed "the paranoid style in American politics."

Richard Viguerie is a modernist. He may not accept the precepts of the New Deal, but he abides the canons of advertising as if they were eternal verities. He's pragmatic in his use of technique. He wants to use what works. Viguerie has been willing to learn from sources other than fellow rightists. He is an apt pupil of George McGovern, the New Left, and the AFL-CIO, all Satan incarnate to old rightists. But Viguerie is confident that he can truck with the devil without being marked. He emerges stronger in his convictions and surer in how to realize them.

"We've taken close to 100 percent of the left's tactics," he confesses unashamedly. "What we're doing is what they did. We have been thirty years late in realizing how the left did it. We're into making a list of all the things they do and doing the same things." The methods he's adopted are simply common organizing techniques, at least common to the labor movement, the peace movement, and the civil rights movement.

On Viguerie's desk, when I paid him a visit, was a thick book containing copies of the direct-mail solicitations from the 1972 McGovern for president campaign, which Viguerie holds in high professional esteem. "I'm studying it," he says. "I'm trying to build a movement. I don't know if you've heard that word much. Among us conservatives that's a word that's used constantly. The movement." Hearing him speak in the shorthand of the left is eerie. The word *movement* resonates oddly when Viguerie uses it. But the right, after all, has momentum. It is in movement. It is a choice, not an echo.

Viguerie's achievement is considerable. He has forged a distinctive New Right, moving it beyond its narrow complaints, melding it into a movement. Previously, the right embraced a politics of nostalgia for a past that never existed; the right expected and needed defeat because defeat certified its opinions. Its politics were concerned with loss of status in a rapidly changing world. Viguerie has helped the right transcend status politics to become a brand of interest-group politics, a far more efficacious approach. The New Right often seems to be a collection of motley single-issue groups, very particularized, dependent on the old anxieties. But within the new structures the right is able to have much more of an effect. Viguerie has wedded the substance of status politics to the form of interest-group politics. It's a real advance for the right, a signal change in its methodology. Viguerie has pushed the right into the modern era, educating conservatives in the craft of marketing and advertising, essential instruments of American politics. The New Right is much more dangerous because of his pedagogy.

"Years and years ago, I decided that I wanted to do something in a major way to help the conservative movement," he says. "There were different routes I could have gone." He ticks off the names of influential conservative writers. "Bill Buckley, Bill Rusher, Russell Kirk. I could have gone that route. I probably wouldn't have amounted to a hill of beans. That wasn't my nature. I didn't have the educational background for that. What we didn't have, what we had zero people doing, was having someone take the ideas, the writings, the books and market them to the masses. A new cause came along, a new candidate, we didn't really have someone who understood how to market them on a national scale. So I set out for myself to become the best marketer I could be. I wanted to communicate with the masses, to market ideas. And I did that. It may not have occurred to other conservatives. It's not an easy thing to do. It requires certain skills. I had to train myself, to teach myself. I've been doing it a long time, but I've got a long way to go yet. I went to college to learn one profession and then I had to learn a different one. Not a lot of people are willing to do that, put in those kind of hours. I majored in political science at the University of Houston. I went to law school for about a year and a half. I always, always, always wanted to be a politician. I didn't understand *how* I was going to do it. I just knew I *was* going to do it."

An optimistic rightist like Viguerie had to have been born and raised on the cusp of the sunbelt. Richard Viguerie is a sunny new-wave reactionary. He is idea and act, free of cobwebs. He was born in Golden Acres, Texas, a town outside Houston. His father was a middle-level petrochemical executive, his mother a practical nurse. "My parents were the silent majority out there," he recalls. "Their instincts were conservative. We don't disagree on hardly anything philosophical. But there wasn't a situation where I can remember discussing politics in the evening at dinner. It's something I picked up on my own. My philosophy wasn't counter to my parents, but they weren't very political."

When he was very young, perhaps seven, he became enthralled with American Indians. He was very shy and small for his age, even as a teenager. Although he had never actually seen an authentic Indian he was obsessed with their plight. Movies, which mainly portrayed Indians as ignoble savages, perked his interest. He immersed himself in books on the subject. At some point he linked victims of Communism with Indians. The Communists were the white men. The American way of life — entrepreneurial capitalism — was imperiled. It could be wiped out like the Indians. America was the underdog. Communists were closing in. For a boy in Texas, the end of the frontier was vivid.

In college Viguerie had two heroes — "the two Macs" he calls them — General Douglas MacArthur and Senator Joseph McCarthy. When the Army-McCarthy hearings were broadcast Viguerie was riveted to the radio. These hearings, more than anything else, led to McCarthy's demise. During them, McCarthy's penchant for character assassination and coarse tactics was revealed unadorned on nationwide television. As McCarthy went down, Viguerie, listening attentively in his dormitory room, rooted for him. "Here was a man fighting Communism," he says. "So I became a fighter."

His start in politics wasn't auspicious, a typically undistinguished beginning running the Houston headquarters of Senator John Tower. The following year he moved up the ladder to become the first executive secretary of the Young Americans for Freedom, William F. Buckley's finishing school for future conservative leaders. As part of his job Viguerie was supposed to raise money for the organization. He did not like asking rich people for contributions directly. He decided to write them letters, and his first direct mailings worked. Soon he made the plunge into business. With a $300 investment he rented a one-room office on Capitol Hill in 1965; today he grosses over $15 million a year, a conservative estimate. He was like an oil wildcatter, an independent driller in politics. He sank his lines and hoped for a gusher. It was just a trickle to begin with. Direct mail, while part of an overall political consulting media package, wasn't regarded by most operatives as lucrative enough to base a firm on. It was fine as a supplement to television, but in itself it was patently inadequate. Viguerie kept at it.

Then came three big breaks. The first of these was the 1972 McGovern campaign for the presidency, which demonstrated conclusively the power of direct mail. McGovern's campaign was a sterling example of a faultless direct-mail operation. "George McGovern," explains Viguerie, "ran over the Henry Jacksons and the Hubert Humphreys of the world because he understood the new technology. He was a creature of direct mail. McGovern was thinking direct mail from the beginning." The reason McGovern was thinking direct mail was because he had to. He didn't have the backing of the regular Democrats, the AFL-CIO, the urban machines, or the ethnic groups. In early polls his standing with Democrats wavered between 2 and 3 percent. He had no wealthy supporters. His candidacy seemed particularly farfetched then. He desperately needed a means to nourish his campaign in its lean phase, at least until it could take off. McGovern contacted Morris Dees, the most successful political direct-mail operator in the country. Dees, a liberal Southerner, built the biggest direct-mail company outside New York and Chicago, sold it, and, when McGovern contacted him, was devoting his time to public interest law and civil rights. (Dees had begun his career as a student at the University of Alabama selling birthday cakes to students' parents.) Dees calculated that the right pitch would enable the McGovern campaign to carry itself through its nascent stages. He wrote a letter asking recipients to contribute ten dollars a month to the McGovern for President Club. A coupon book for making payments was enclosed; those who signed up were sent an "insider's" newsletter and monthly reminders to pay their "dues." By early 1972 monthly income from the scheme totaled about $100,000. "The club idea proves that Alexis de Tocqueville was right when he observed almost 150 years ago that America was a nation of joiners," Dees declared. Viguerie took notice of Dee's scheme. In his own work, Viguerie began to write fundraising appeals with participatory gimmicks, asking recipients to send in an enclosed poll or an odd dollar contribution for a specific purpose. He was catching on.

His next leap forward was provided by Arthur Bremer. When George Wallace's putative assassin incapacitated the Alabama governor in 1972, Wallace's 1976 presidential campaign was cast into doubt. Wallace had little personal control over the political efforts on his behalf. The collection of money, which would determine if there would even be another run, was farmed out to Richard Viguerie, whom Morris Dees suggested as ideologically compatible. In eighteen months Viguerie raised $2 million and spent as much in the effort. Eventually he garnered $6.9 million for Wallace. Viguerie was Wallace's life-support system, sustaining him for one final campaign.

Wallace's campaign was the real making of Viguerie and the New Right, for it provided a list of 600,000 names, sifted from a larger list of contributors, that was as good as gold. While Viguerie did a lot for Wallace, Wallace was a godsend for Viguerie. His campaign gave Viguerie free-and-clear proprietary rights to the hardcore of the New Right. Unintentionally and indirectly, however, it also contributed to the rise of Jimmy Carter, whose 1976 primary victories over Wallace in Southern states made him the leading candidate, acceptable to blacks and liberals.

The third and perhaps most important boon for Viguerie was Watergate. Besides the removal of Richard Nixon from the Oval Office, the most tangible result of Watergate was a campaign reform act passed by Congress that limited contributions to $1000. Supposedly, this would inhibit arm twisting of corporate executives by presidential hopefuls, democratize the political process by making parties less dependent on major contributors, and involve more citizens who would feel that their small gifts carried weight. It didn't exactly work out that way. The principal beneficiary of this reform, enacted mainly at the behest of liberal Democrats, was Richard Viguerie.

It was a bonanza for him. With his Wallace list he could sell his services to appropriately reactionary candidates to help them reach the small contributors they now urgently needed. Through a series of campaigns Viguerie piggybacked his list, gathering more and more names, prospecting for the best ones to add to his computer tapes. The list expanded geometrically. The Wallace campaign itself depended upon these small givers. Watergate made his jackpot seem almost inevitable.

Suddenly, Viguerie was in the big time. But he continued to see everything through an ideological lens. He considered his fortuitous elevation to a position of influence to be more than a simple political victory: it was a triumph of modern marketing. "The left has missed a lot of things," he advises. "They think of direct mail as fundraising. They miss the whole boat if they think that. *It is a form of advertising*. It is not an evil conspiratorial thing. It is just a fact of life, which I haven't found anybody to deny, that the major media of this country has a left of center perspective. The conservatives can't get their message around this blockade, except through direct mail. It's a way for conservatives to bypass the monopoly the left has on the media. It's a way of mobilizing our people; it's a way of communicating with our people; it identifies our people; and it marshals our people. It's self-liquidating and it pays for itself. It's a form of advertising, part of the marketing strategy. *It's advertising*."

Viguerie began his thrust for leadership of the New Right in 1974, when Gerald Ford nominated Nelson Rockefeller to serve as his vice-president. This appointment was the final affront to the New Right. Viguerie moved into action to attempt to block the selection. He telephoned more than a dozen conservative movers and shakers and invited them to his office to formulate tactics. The meeting was a disappointment. "The conservative leaders of America in that room didn't know how to go from point A to point Z," recalls Viguerie. "I saw very dramatically that nobody knew how to organize."

It was then that Viguerie started to develop his theory of leadership, a conception of a counterrevolutionary vanguard that would take command of the right by giving it direction. "There is a lot of planning and communication within the conservative movement that didn't exist half a dozen years ago," says Viguerie. "It's basically happening because of a dozen or so key leaders who are moving in a very bold, dramatic, decisive way. Of all the problems the conservative movement has had over the years it has been lack of leadership that's hurt the most. We've had people who were well known, who were very articulate, who could write very well, could speak, had charisma. Naturally everyone would think that's a leader. But there's a difference between a spokesman and a leader. We've had our spokesmen and now we have our leaders."

Viguerie's desire to form a vanguard is derived from his sense of history. He believes that history is the story of great men, that personalities are the driving force of events. The masses to him are inconsequential compared to their leaders. "This country is here today," he explains, "because of a few dozen people. Maybe twelve. It wasn't the million that demanded the freedom from England. Take away a Washington, a Franklin, where would you be? The same with the conservative movement today. Take away that dozen and you've got problems."

This somewhat imperious attitude, however, generates extraordinary passion in Viguerie. The day I spent with him he was up at four in the morning to write a fundraising appeal. He reserves his most fervent evangelism for his copywriting. His true pulpit is in an envelope. "I feel," he says, "that when I have spent five or six hours writing a letter, I am the audience. I am the person I am writing to. When I am finished I am physically wrung out. I am exhausted because I put myself in there emotionally. I am in my copy. I feel for the people, for the cause. It's very emotional. A lot of my clients don't like the copy because they say it sounds too cornball, too conversational, it's not dignified. But people respond to emotionalism. The successful and effective speakers are emotional."

His feelings aren't wasted. There's more to these solicitations than just a visceral release for Viguerie. Direct mail is part of a grand strategy. It fits in with his theory of the counterrevolutionary vanguard; he believes that a vanguard without a movement is simply a sect. Viguerie doesn't just tender advice to candidates and single-issue groups for a fee. He is building a movement that will support a certain kind of candidate. He is working from the bottom up to create a constituency to back his politics. In the language of the left, he's base building.

Direct mail is not Viguerie's only organizational tool, however. He has created a political conglomerate with satellites spinning around the direct-mail operation. Viguerie keeps extending his frontier with a sense of surety; he believes in political manifest destiny. Political action committees (PACs) expedite his missions. They spend millions: in 1972 congressional races, established conservative groups dropped a mere $250,000; but in 1976, with Viguerie geared up, conservative groups raised close to $5.6 million. Viguerie's PACs differ from the corporate PACs in that they're much more ideological. They're also more organizationally minded. Corporate PACs just give their money to candidates they feel best represent their interests. Viguerie wants more than that from his PACs. He wants commitment; he wants more movement activists. So his PACs are designed to train politicians. One of his PACs, the National Conservative Political Action Committee (NCPAC), which helped elect fifty-five New Rightists to office in 1978, prefers to give candidates material services rather than outright grants of money. NCPAC will provide politicians with an ensemble of modern techniques — polling, media advice, and campaign management training. When U.S. Senator Frank Church of Idaho felt threatened by NCPAC support of an opponent in the 1980 race for his Senate seat, he reacted by raising the issue of a Soviet brigade in Cuba in connection with passage of the SALT II treaty. Church was running scared, and thus was influenced by Viguerie's cohorts on this very important matter.

Another of the Viguerie sponsored PACs, the Committee for the Survival of a Free Congress (CSFC) selects the candidates it wants to elect and then runs them through a training seminar. In 1978, CSFC helped elect twenty-six congressmen and five U.S. senators. The key to the success of this PAC is a precinct organization plan, which is presented as a revelation. It calls for an organization of precinct workers to be assigned voter turnout goals and to be supervised by area chairmen. The average twelve-year-old in Chicago could devise a more complicated scheme. But to the New Right this approach is novel.

The group that best reflects the comprehensive Viguerie viewpoint — combining the vanguard with the base, the single-issue campaigns with political races — is the Conservative Caucus. Headed by Howard Phillips, it is located in a rabbit's warren of offices occupied by other New Right groups above Papa Gino's on Tremont Street in Boston. (The offices are rent-free since the owner of Papa Gino's is a New Rightist and on the executive board of the Conservative Caucus: Ideology to go.) Phillips is burly and forceful. Viguerie attests to his political acumen. "Howie's one of the six key people," he confides. In 1978, Phillips ran as a Democrat for the Senate nomination, which struck most Bay State Democrats as ludicrous. Phillips, after all, is a former official of the Nixon administration. But his move indicated the drift of New Right strategy. What happened to his particular candidacy is relatively unimportant. What was meant by it is far more significant.

Phillips's ideas reflect his experience. He doesn't engage in idle theorizing. Obviously, he has a strong impact on Viguerie and the rest of the New Right. He carries weight. "In 1968 I was a conservative Republican," he says. "In 1979 I'm a conservative period." He received his education at the hands of Richard Nixon. When Phillips was a student government leader at Harvard in 1960, he was a fervent Nixon backer. Nixon was his hero. Now he sadly admits, "I'm without heroes." To New Rightists, Nixon is the great betrayer. Democratic presidents simply carried out the tasks they set out for themselves; they were liberals. But Nixon promised something new, fulfillment of the conservative dream, an evolutionary antireformism, unraveling the liberal program. They feel he had power in his grasp, but never used it. He shattered their expectations, which were probably somewhat naive to begin with. Nixon was far too centrist for the far right. "He damaged everything I hold dear," says Phillips. "He was the most liberal president in American history, except for Gerald Ford. He's a fundamentally weak man who groveled for Establishment recognition. He just wanted to look good in the history books, have the *New York Times* say nice things about him. At the same time, he hated them. He didn't have the courage of his intestines. I owe him a great deal because I got an education in his administration. My real education is that even presidents are flawed."

In 1974, Phillips formed a group called CREEP II, Conservatives for the Removal of the President. He was afraid that Nixon would make concessions to the Russians as he tried to fend off the Watergate inquiry. After Nixon's abdication, Phillips blueprinted plans for the Conservative Caucus. "I went to Viguerie," he says. "And we sent out material in the mail. Had it not been for Viguerie we couldn't have made much progress. Direct mail has done more than give us money. It gives us a way to get to our people."

Once outside the Nixon administration Phillips explored political options. Perhaps he learned the most from the left. "People in the conservative movement today aren't conventionally ambitious. It's the same way on the left," he says. "A lot of conservatives have read Saul Alinsky. I read all the liberal publications including the *Progressive*, the *Nation*, *Working Papers*. If something works, we're for doing it. In terms of the Caucus, the strategy comes out of trial and error. We need a grassroots organization and we're developing a system for doing it broadly."

Phillips's Conservative Caucus can take credit for Gordon Humphrey's victory in New Hampshire. Less directly, the New Right has influenced other elections, mainly by creating a favorable conservative climate. "The greatly expanded base of conservative strength permitted Democratic primary upsets," the *New Right Report*, Viguerie's newsletter, gloated. "And the best news is this: This is not a temporary trend. This coalition will be bigger and stronger in 1980."

The New Right strategy calls for support of conservatives, whether they're Republican or Democrat. Before the 1976 election, William Rusher, publisher of the conservative *National Review*, argued, in a book entitled *The Making of the New Majority Party*, for a conservative party to replace the Republicans. For a while, New Rightists embraced the Rusher thesis. Now they've jettisoned it. They're for building coalitions across party lines that maintain ideological consistency. Much of this tack derives from Phillips's experience. "My experience in the Nixon administration persuaded me that parties are less important than I had thought. It doesn't matter which party succeeds. Principles matter."

Viguerie's empire will be at the eye of the coming political storm. Yet he is being criticized by old-style conservative Republicans for his business practices. From three of his PACs, for example, his companies clear 83 percent of the total take. Certainly, he makes piles of money. But it seems out of character for these conservatives to attack a political rival for his entrepreneurial zeal. Isn't that what they're fighting for? Viguerie is an exemplar of economic individualism. He embodies the Ayn Rand ideal, suggested in the title of one of her books, *The Virtue of Selfishness*.

There's more than a touch of Horatio Alger to Richard Viguerie. He's driven to self-improvement, up at four in the morning. But Viguerie isn't a conventional go-getter. He believes that free will is tied to postmortem punishment. "I believe in reincarnation," he asserts. He doesn't know who or what he was in the past, but he's doing his best not to wind up another species next time: if you don't do the right thing you might become a cockroach. Viguerie is hammering himself into line out of fear of metamorphosis. Strangely, he sees this as a liberating concept. "After I began to understand reincarnation," he says, "the idea that we are all responsible for ourselves, that things don't happen to us accidentally, it was exciting. You reap what you sow. Sometimes you're going to reap it in this life, sometimes in the next life. Life is a learning experience. There's a law out there. You violate the law, you're going to be punished. You stick your hand in an electric socket, it's going to hurt. Life is not luck, it's not chance. It's a question of choice. Anything that I do that's not Christ-like I'm going to have to pay for it. This time or the next time. Doggone it, I want to get it right this time."

His mysticism suffuses his politics with confidence. Viguerie's religion gives him a sense of divine direction. More, his religiosity is a justification for his practicality. He feels free to pursue his career, certain that it meets with heavenly approval. He is in control of his life and his machines.

He doesn't fear his computers. "Technology is neutral," he says. "It's just a tool." For him, science is the servant of ideology. Although Viguerie maintains a sure hand on his IBM machines he still reveals doubt about the effect of the new technology on politics generally: "It's seldom that you will find older, established candidates that will be interested in using direct mail. Things you don't understand you don't feel comfortable with. When I'm sixty years old, I may not be any different than they are. It's fear of the unknown. You feel comfortable with what you've done for twenty or thirty years successfully. Why do it a different way? Why change? But there are people doing it a different way and they're running over the older politicians. It's possible to get elected today with the computers and the direct mail and the telephones and not really know how to govern. You can use these techniques to win the nomination and the election, but not know how to govern. That's right, you become a permanent campaigner. Take old Lyndon Johnson. He had all kinds of problems, but he knew how to govern. He knew how to make the bureaucracy work. He knew how to run things and administer things. He wasn't out of place in the Oval Office. The old politicians might understand how to govern better than a lot of the new ones. The new ones are relying on technology that is basically being applied by others. The old ones don't know how to campaign and the new ones don't know how to govern. There might be something to that."

Does this mean that he worries about the depth of commitment of some of the New Right candidates who owe so much to him? He expresses no such feelings. He's upbeat, 1980 promises to be a good year, and after that things look even better. "We're definitely going against the anti-ideological grain," he says. "And we're succeeding." He believes the left is beginning to retreat before his advancing legions. He thinks he can set the order of battle. "If the AFL-CIO wasn't worried about my direct mail, they wouldn't stay up nights worrying about me," he says. "It's a defensive posture by basically older people who don't know how to stop it. You can't stop it. Ask the French how defense works. It doesn't."

"Offense picks the terrain," I suggest.

"Exactly," Viguerie replies. "That's good," he muses. "I'll have to use that."

BEFORE RICHARD NIXON boarded over the indoor White House swimming pool to make a press-briefing room, presidential aides going to their offices in the West Wing walked through a press lounge. There, one White House aide told the author, the "piranha" eagerly waited to devour White House staffers. In the paranoiac atmosphere that so frequently pervades politics, the press is always the enemy unless it is controlled. Every president in the modern era, from Franklin D. Roosevelt to Ronald Reagan, has attempted to manage the news. William Safire defines managed news as "information generated and distributed by the government in such a way as to give government interest priority over candor."[1]

The media are, to use the phrase of Douglass Cater, the fourth branch of the government.[2] The press, which now includes the electronic as well as the print media, has appointed itself guardian of the public interest. Although many members of the press have a cozy relationship with public officials, upon whom they depend for valuable information, the theory of the press that is taught in journalism schools requires reporters to distance themselves personally from the subjects of their stories. The adversary relationship between investigative reporters and the government enables a reporter to ferret out the facts no matter how unpleasant they may be.

While the Washington press includes reporters like Bob Woodward and Carl Bernstein, whose investigations of the Nixon White House's coverup of the break-in at the Democratic National Headquarters in the Watergate office complex led to impeachment proceedings against the president and his resignation, they are exceptions and not the rule. Understandably, the seductive Washington environment, in which power and status mean everything, has co-opted many reporters. The press has become part of the Washington establishment because it has learned to play the game of power politics itself. The Gridiron Club, an old and exclusive organization of newspaper people, symbolizes the press elite. Annually it invites members of the political establishment to join it in a fun-filled session of humor and satire. The spirit of camaraderie that prevails at such a gathering can best be appreciated by those on the inside. President and Mrs. Reagan were the highlights of the club's meeting in 1982, as the First Lady skillfully performed a skit that satirized the prevailing press view of her activities.

The Gridiron Club may roast politicians, but its members recognize that the press and the politicians are in the same broader club of the politically powerful. Washington reporters recognize that to be at the top of the newspaper profession they must have access to the top of the political world.

[1] William Safire, *Safire's Political Dictionary* (New York: Random House, Inc., 1978), p. 397.

[2] Douglass Cater, *The Fourth Branch of the Government* (Boston: Houghton Mifflin Co., 1959).

The linkage between success and power often softens the adversary stance of the press.

Washington's political centers of power recognize that the press is an important fourth branch of the government. Presidents, members of Congress, and even Supreme Court justices know that managing the news will buttress their power and may even be a key to survival. Presidents, especially during their first few years in office, feel besieged by a press that they consider hostile and unfair. Even before he became president, John F. Kennedy went out of his way to warn an aide about the press, "Always remember that their interests and ours ultimately conflict."[3]

Kennedy cultivated political reporters, and his good press relations not only helped him to win the presidential election in 1960 but also buttressed his presidency. Richard Nixon blamed his 1960 defeat on an unfair press, an attitude that was intensified after he lost his race for the California governorship in 1962. Nixon understandably put managing the news at the top of his agenda when he became president. In the following selection, one of Nixon's closest aides describes how the Nixon White House went about controlling the press.

11 John Ehrlichman
MANAGING THE PRESS

There has been some arrant nonsense written about Richard Nixon and the press, and some of it has been written by people who should know better.[1] Former newspaper people like Ray Price and Herb Klein argue that Nixon was the victim of a sort of transient, uncontrollable dementia where the press was concerned. That, as they saw it, accounts for his disregard of all their good advice. It is more likely that *most* of Nixon's conduct of his press relations was calculated and deliberate.

Before and during his presidency, Nixon manifested no illusions about his press problems, although his well-rationalized reasons for journalists' dislike of him were unconvincing. All of his press world was divided into two parts, and the larger was made up of his enemies. "They hate me," Nixon would say, "because I have beaten them so often." He had nailed Alger Hiss, whom Nixon saw to be the darling

[1] Nixon, interestingly, has not written much about the press in his memoirs.

of the press Establishment. The Checker speech had frustrated their effort to sink him. He'd come back from his 1962 California defeat in spite of the media's universal political obituaries. In simplest terms, he believed that they were liberal and he was conservative and most of the people out in the country believed with him, not them. The press couldn't stand that, and so they were his sworn enemies.

During the years I worked for him, Nixon was usually capable of a passionless and penetrating analysis of his press opportunities. He was a talented media manipulator. I often watched him successfully plan how he or his spokesmen would dominate the evening news, capture the headlines and right-side columns of the front page of the *Washington Post* or the lead story in *Time* or *Newsweek*. Richard Nixon could think like an editor.

Nixon knew how to bait a hook to catch a columnist. Many of the most prominent columnists, including Hugh Sidey, Stewart and Joe Alsop, James Kilpatrick, and Evans and Novak, have given Richard Nixon their allotted space, sometimes unwittingly, when he went after it.

As president, Nixon could also demand prime-time television for major policy statements and get it. He could speak to the people over the heads of the press and the commentators, commanding huge audiences which sometimes could find nothing but Richard Nixon to watch on their television sets.

Nixon was convinced that the vast majority of reporters and commentators would be unfair to him if left to their own devices. They had to be prevented from airing their biases, therefore, by whatever means were available. Television pictures of an event, a crowd or a person would preclude distorted comment; people could see a picture and could know what the truth was for themselves; so Nixon thought a lot about "visuals" and "photo opportunities." And he counted on the fact that most reporters would use handouts before they would dig for their own stories, because most Washington reporters were basically lazy or burned out. The prudent politician gives them well-written press releases full of facts, briefings, research and background information.[2]

Nixon believed in freezing out any reporter who revealed his or her bias against him. As president, he headed the most bountiful source of news in the nation. A reporter who was barred, so that he couldn't get news from the White House, was in trouble. Before long his assignment editor would move him out of there in favor of someone who could produce stories. Or at least, so the president believed.

Nixon came into the White House determined to exercise the fullest possible influence over what the press said about him and his admin-

[2]Later, Nixon and Charles Colson were to attempt more coercive tactics to counter media bias — including bringing direct influence to bear upon television-network executives.

istration. He and Bob Haldeman shared the view that no previous president had properly organized and staffed the White House to manage the news. They set about constructing an apparatus that would appear to serve the White House press corps while, at the same time, sending volumes of information over their heads to small newspapers and television stations out in the hinterlands. For the first time the White House would systematically propagandize the general public.

It was Nixon's premise that the small group of old-timers who constituted the regulars in the White House press room were so jaded by their years of covering presidents that they constricted the outward flow of news. If Nixon were to play with his dog — this is hypothetical, of course — there would be little or no coverage because Kennedy and Johnson had played with their dogs; dog-play was old stuff to the White House press corps. Therefore, the White House staff must include people who had the skills to have the president and his dog mentioned on evening television news. And there must be people who could write president-and-dog news releases and send them to the American Kennel Club newsletter for dissemination. A house photographer must take pictures of man and dog to be given exclusively to *People* magazine, the wire services, *Life,* or the pet publications. A Navy film crew should be on hand to photograph dog-play footage which could be released to the television news organizations. And someone should write canned editorials about the President and Man's Best Friend for weekly newspapers and trade publications, to be disseminated by the hundreds.[3]

It took Bob Haldeman several months to get the propaganda mill fully staffed and in operation. Its first major project would be to counter a huge antiwar demonstration planned for mid-November 1969.

Bob Haldeman and Charles Colson were Nixon's principal propaganda planners. They assembled a sizable staff and budget. Haldeman recruited Jeb Stuart Magruder, an ambitious young California businessman, to be his executor of the White House public relations plans. Herb Klein, too much of an old Nixon retainer to be wholly excluded, was designated "Director of Communications," but he was largely a figurehead. Jeb Magruder took his orders directly from Haldeman and Colson, and caused the Communications Office to produce the reams of news copy, the pictures and the editorials that poured out every day.

A couple of staff committees were formed to provide general advice to Haldeman, Colson, and Magruder. The president's writers — Jim Keogh, Bill Safire, Pat Buchanan, and the others — the scheduler,

---

[3] There actually was a photo opportunity featuring Nixon and King Timahoe, his red setter, on the beach at San Clemente. Manolo, the President's valet, released the dog a hundred yeards up the beach, and King Timahoe ran straight for Nixon, who opened his arms wide. But Timahoe was chasing a sea gull and ran right past the president and on down the beach half a mile, leaving Nixon unrequited (and unphotographed — except by me).

Dwight Chapin, the press secretary, and occasionally some of us dealing with substantive matters were convened to "run it up the flagpole," "vet it" and "bounce it off the wall."

Most of these meetings were a waste of time, and I seldom attended. Richard Nixon would ultimately decide what would and wouldn't be done on these subjects, and it mattered little what any PR committees recommended. In the last analysis, Nixon would listen to Colson and Haldeman — and less often one of us others — and then do what he wanted to do.

I would estimate that Richard Nixon spent half his working time on the nonsubstantive aspects of the presidency, and probably 40 percent of that half dealing with the problems of communication. (I recognize that a good argument can be made that communication *is* the substance of the presidency. But from where I sat, George Shultz, Henry Kissinger, and I were dealing in substance — policy and its implementation — while Bob Haldeman's element of the staff was concerned with process and appearances.) I have watched Nixon spend a morning designing Walter Cronkite's lead story for that evening, then send Ron Ziegler, Henry Kissinger, or me out to a press briefing to deliver it in such a way that Cronkite couldn't ignore it.

Sometimes the subject matter alone would be enough to capture the top slot on the news. Other times we devised phrases or slogans to catch a news editor's attention. One day I was sent out to charge that the president was faced with an irresponsible "credit card Congress." Another time it was enough to call some appropriations bills "seven Trojan horses lumbering down Pennsylvania Avenue toward the White House."

In any administration the press secretary's office grinds out reams of handouts for its journalistic clientele. Mimeographed statements, announcements, proclamations, statistical collections, abstracts and analyses, photographs, and schedules pour into the laps of the White House press. On most days the press secretary holds a "briefing" in the press room. The reporters may ask any questions they wish, but there are a couple of limitations. First, the television people may not photograph or sound-record most of these briefings. Second, there is no requirement that the press secretary must answer the questions.

An adroit press secretary can usually pump out into the nation's news columns the content that his president wants placed there. If the flow of the briefing didn't reach every subject Ron Ziegler wanted to peddle on a given day, he could call the wire-service reporters to his office and tell them what he wanted them to know. Ninety-nine percent of the time the wire services would dutifully carry the handout.

In February 1970 I was treated to a Nixon homily that emanated from his decision to veto a veterans' education bill. "Not on television," he instructed. He didn't want to be seen disapproving money for the vets.

"You can do too much television, you know. You have to weigh giving news to the writing press or to television. It's not *what* presidents do but how they do it that matters. That's what gives an administration its personality — how the president works."

It wasn't until the end of this talk that Nixon used the word "image," but it was obviously what he had in mind as he ticked off a list of ingredients:

"— hard work, his guts, a restoration of dignity, the family, church, square," he said, looking at me as if expecting an argument. I looked back without expression. Nixon continued:

"He [the president; himself; Richard Nixon] came in with the press against him. They said he couldn't handle TV. Now there's been a complete shift in 'the man's' image."

"You know, it's been harder because I won't let Ziegler be a pimp for me like Jack Valenti was for Johnson. Instead we've built a mythology about the president."

"Teddy Roosevelt is a good example. Taft was a much more effective president than T.R. But Roosevelt is recorded by history as the 'greater' president. It's fine to be the good managers. But we've got to get the story out!"

"At press conferences I never have friendly questions planted. I never 'can' or memorize answers," Nixon added, gratuitously.

A month later, as we were discussing school desegregation, Nixon began to tell Bryce Harlow and me how his presidential message on the subject should be news-planned. "It should have the broadest possible circulation," he began. "I want Fentress [of *Time*] backgrounded. You should brief [James] Kilpatrick and [Irving] Kristol. Call in black officials and preachers, including Reverend King. Brief our staff and Bill Rogers — he was attorney general once, of course — and the Democrats in Congress, especially Stennis and Russell. Ed Brooke, too.

"I want them to understand what was possible. The object is to unite the country behind a program of desegregation that's *achievable*. Tell them how the statement was written: many people worked on it. My old law partner Len Garment was one. They sent me many alternative drafts. Twelve drafts. Say that I'm still making changes in it. You can cite them that phrase about 'stripping away hypocrisy, ignorance, and prejudice' and tell them how carefully chosen it was.

"As in preparing the November 3 speech, the president has curious work habits," he dictated to us. "He reads, works, talks to the staff on the phone until midnight. The schedule the past three or four days has been brutal. [It hadn't been.] The president has slept only four hours a night. He goes to bed at eleven or twelve, then awakens at two and works from two to three. That's when he does his clearest thinking. Then he sleeps until seven-thirty."

Most of Nixon's speeches and statements were designed to reach beyond the press, directly to the people. A State of the Union address to a joint session of the Congress was a fully televised presidential speech with a potential for high drama. Nixon prepared for this annual address with scrupulous care. It would ride the main line straight to the people.

On January 12, 1971, I had a series of Sunday phone calls from the president as he worked on the State of the Union he would give later that month. He had just received a proposed draft from Ray Price, the writer he'd assigned to help with that speech, and Nixon was not happy. His first call was to tell me that the proposed draft was terrible and that if *he* was to have to do this speech work, unassisted by competent writers, then we couldn't expect him to do any of the other chores around the office. "Tell everyone there's to be no further contact with the president for the next two days. Tell Henry [Kissinger] and Bob [Haldeman]. Henry wants to resign again. Tell him I just can't see him. I'm going to have to do this speech."

Two hours later he called again to explain that *his* speech would not be a "laundry list" of administration proposals. He would have it short; the draft had to be boiled down. Each thousand words would be cut to one hundred. He would speak only of concepts; the details could be given later.

"I've read every inaugural speech ever given," Nixon said. "And I've read many of the State of the Union speeches. None of them that were over three thousand words were any good.

"This speech should be about ideals, goals, and directions. You don't write one of these for the press; you explain it to them later. You just give the Congress a great concept and quit and get out.

"John," he went on, "you are probably unaware that I cut forty percent out of the State of the Union they [the writers] sent me last year. You have to take out all the details. It's much harder to write a conceptual speech; a clerk can write up a laundry list."

Nixon was always ambivalent about doing pure "PR" events. He wanted the results — he wanted good press and public support — but he was reticent about doing most of the things his publicists and the other staff advisers urged him to do. Some of his mind knew that the president had to personify the presidency, but the rest of him wished that that were not so. He kicked, bucked, and dragged his feet when we suggested he get up from his desk and venture forth among the people. But paradoxically, he would sometimes do public things on impulse that demonstrated a latent love of the limelight and a good sense of the right thing to do.

When Wilkes-Barre, Pennsylvania, was devastated by a flood, Nixon called his man-on-the-scene, Frank Carlucci, to come to Camp David one Saturday for a firsthand report on Federal relief efforts. As Frank described the progress he'd made in emergency housing, cleanup and subsistence relief, Nixon began to think about going to Wilkes-Barre. He asked how long it would take to fly there from Camp David. It was the Jewish sabbath, he noted, so Pennsylvania Governor Milton Schapp would not be there to hog the limelight. Today would be the best day to go, to show the people that the president cared about them.

In five minutes I'd whistled up a helicopter and our Secret Service detail and we were off — just Nixon, Carlucci, and I. And Nixon's personal photographer, Ollie Atkins, of course.

We landed in a schoolyard in Wilkes-Barre, drove to the flood-destroyed area in a borrowed police car and walked the streets among amazed citizens. At least once an hour the president devised some highly photogenic event that made me yearn for a network-television camera crew. He sat in the living room of someone's trailer and sympathized with old ladies about their tragedy. He talked with the workmen who were shoveling out mud and debris. At a town meeting he volunteered to buy the hot dogs for a community picnic for the flood workers. (We sent up hundreds of pounds of picnic food from the White House kitchen the next weekend.)

As we were leaving town, the president suddenly ordered our driver to stop the car in a suburban street. He had seen a bride and groom just coming out the doors of a church; he jumped out of our car and hurried across the street to them as their families and the minister were gathering on the church steps. Nixon visited with the wedding party for about fifteen minutes, posing with the bride and groom for the wedding photographer and Atkins. Then, putting fifteen dollars (of my money) into the Reverend's hand for the poor box, he bade the dazed crowd farewell and ran back to the car.

Flying back to a field near Camp David, Nixon dictated rapid-fire instructions to me. He was overflowing with ideas to help Wilkes-Barre. And he liked the little jet we were flying in. He would henceforth move around the country in a JetStar rather than *Air Force One*. He didn't need all the staff and press that usually went about with him. He would do more events on the spur of the moment. It was good to be out among real people.

But back at Camp David, the White House correspondents were raising hell. Their job was to cover the president, and they had been left at home. They lodged such a strong protest that Ron Ziegler promised they would never be left behind again. Then Ziegler came to Nixon to plead with him not to travel without at least a "death-watch" press pool, which could cover possible accidents or illness. Nixon reserved the right to escape the press, but from then on he would cite the inescapable need for a press pool as a good Catch-22 reason not to do some of the other worthwhile events that were proposed.

Sitting in the office, sheltered, Nixon told himself that he preferred not to go out to do such things. Once out among the people, he performed well and seemed to enjoy the interaction.

Perhaps it's fair to generalize in this way: Richard Nixon genuinely enjoyed the spontaneous. But he abhorred what he called "hokey" public-relations events, and would turn down about 90 percent of the PR proposals that came to him. With sixty or seventy reporters in train, almost anything a president does is devoid of spontaneity. Thus, the dilemma: When the press was around him, Richard Nixon was stiff and stagy. So reporters filed stories about the wooden, insensitive man who looked at his watch as he shook hands with well wishers. In Wilkes-Barre he was sensitive, genuine, and inspired as he moved about among the flood victims, unreported.

Occasionally a journalist got a glimpse of the unreported Nixon, but the resulting reportage usually alleged that Nixon had "changed," not that he was multifaceted. So Nixon's propagandists were dealing with a paradox. They were not unlike florists who were trying to sell a flower that would bloom only in absolute darkness. . . .

At the end of 1969, the *Wall Street Journal* ran a long article about the president's worsening press relations. Ron Ziegler came into the president's office with the newspaper one winter morning as the president was telling me what he wanted me to say about rumors that we would seek a value-added tax.

Nixon (who invariably professed indifference to the views of his critics) immediately read the *Journal* article. He looked up, partway through reading, and said to Ziegler, "You're doing just what you should. The press is hostile, and we'll continue to go over their heads to the public." At that moment Henry Kissinger walked in to join us. The president showed him the *Journal* article. Kissinger read the article, nodding. "Ron is the best press secretary in history, the members of the press corps tell me," Kissinger said.

We were then offered a Nixonian parable: "Henry, one time on a trip I had a long talk at a bar with an old-time White House reporter," Nixon began. "He was a little drunk, and he told me that everyone in the press hates the president. You know why? Because he goes right over their heads to the people, that's why. Seventy-five percent of them hate my guts because they don't like to be beaten. There was Alger Hiss, and Khrushchev in Moscow, and Caracas.

"Understand," Nixon went on, "the press's dislike of me is not personal. No, it's not personal. Their hate is based on the fact that they don't roll me very often. The only time they are nice to you is when they think you are finished."

The conversation moved to other subjects, but Nixon wanted to talk more about the press. Nixon was now talking to himself, not to the three of us in his office. "You know, in the Hiss battle I was alone. Ninety-five percent of the columns and news stories were against me. They all said Whittaker Chambers was lying."

Kissinger chimed in: "Hiss was the epitome of the Eastern Establishment, Mr. President. You and Chambers were outsiders. The wrongness of Hiss really rankled the press."

Nixon nodded. "Intellectuals can't stand a fight and they can't stand to lose."

In organizing the White House staff in late 1968, Nixon had decided there would be no press secretary in the pattern of Bill Moyers, George Christian, or Jim Haggerty. Nixon wanted Ron Ziegler to run the press office, but it would be a far less important place than in the past. Ziegler would conduct the ministerial aspects of the office — the routine postings and announcements and press logistics — but he would have no discretionary functions. The president would hold his own press conferences from time to time to deal with policy matters. And in between, Ziegler would say what Nixon told him to say at regular press briefings.

Nixon had been president for six months when he instructed Kissinger, Burns, Moynihan, and the rest of us to get busy and dominate the news. Herb Klein and Ron Ziegler were assigned to provide us with lists of the friendlies and unfriendlies among the media, which they dutifully did. In mid-July, I received a twenty-six-page catalogue of columnists, print-media reporters and radio/television reporters, listed by categories. "Those We Can Count On" was a short list. "Those We Can Never Count On" ran two and a half pages. Each reporter was described in a capsule biography:

4. **Richard Valeriani** — NBC — Unfriendly — *Valeriani*, if given a chance, will go with negative slant. Must be forced to the positive. . . .
6. **Bob Pierpoint** — CBS — Neutral — Pierpoint is admitted liberal Democrat but does report fairly, generally, except on matters relating to civil rights and liberal domestic matters. Tends to allow personal emotions to enter into reports. . . .
10. **Cliff Evans** — RKO General — Friendly — *Evans* very much leans to administration. Often used to guide briefing questions. Unfortunately small audience. . . .

Herb Klein's personal report included:

ABC's Frank Reynolds is unpredictable. He is objective and on a few occasions when he has not been, I have worked on him through Jim Haggerty. . . .

ABC — Bill Gill — a sensationalist who is more negative than positive, and is not over-intelligent. He is just unpredictable and sometimes even friendly.
The most vindictive is Sander Vanocur. You know him. . . .

Klein wrote: "I don't have the opportunity to see television as much as I would like but I think we are getting a great deal of coverage, and our objective has been to decrease the negative. All the network executives are aware of the fact that we are watching and they hear from me both ways."

Richard Nixon was watching too. Among others, he was watching Henry Kissinger, and he outspokenly disapproved of Henry's self-aggrandizing leaks and posturing, but he almost never spoke to Henry about his unhappiness. Instead, he told Bob Haldeman to chastise Henry for his tête-à-têtes with Joseph Kraft, Henry Brandon, and James Reston.

In my case Nixon was less reticent. Early in 1969 he told me flatly that I was never to see "Scotty" Reston of the *New York Times* for any reason (and I did not). When I had given interviews to Hugh Sidey of *Time* or John Osborne of the *New Republic,* Nixon would patiently explain to me that these men were not our friends; I should favor our friends and freeze out our enemies among the press.

But John Osborne was the bell-cow of the White House press corps, and I had a good experience with him. He had covered Washington for years, for several news publications, including *Time,* and he was a skilled practitioner of his art. He was always superbly prepared for an interview, but it was hard to see it. He asked questions like an old-time trial lawyer, obliquely, apologetically, behind enough of a smoke screen that the unwary would miss seeing the snare he'd laid by the path. John smoked constantly, mumbled and lost his notes, snuffled and snorted and seemed to ramble all over the place, but in ten or fifteen minutes he'd gotten me to tell him enough to permit him to write the most lucid, full-of-thought and genuinely perceptive column I'd see all week. In spite of Nixon's admonitions I continued to see Osborne, mostly because I liked to watch him work. Secondarily, I knew the other reporters talked to him a lot, and if I could convince John Osborne some domestic effort of ours was worthwhile, I was a long way toward finding approval in other reporters' news stories and columns.

In 1972 and 1973 I totally lost the right to see the reporters to whom I wanted to give interviews. Bob Haldeman told me that the president wanted all press contacts cleared with Ron Ziegler in advance, without exception.

From then on, routine requests for appointments with journalists were phoned to Ziegler when they came in. Often it took a day or two to get Ziegler's reply. I figured that in fact, Richard Nixon himself was passing advance judgment on my contacts. And I'm sure that he knew that I knew. The Ziegler fig leaf avoided an otherwise unpleasant confrontation with the president, which was all right with me. When I really wanted to see a reporter I just forgot to ask Ron.

Richard Nixon at times seemed to believe there was no national issue that was not susceptible to public-relations treatment. And he knew there were certain problems that were especially related to public attitudes.

After a 1970 year-end meeting with Dr. Arthur Burns, the president mulled over Burns's pessimistic report on consumer confidence. Christmas sales were down, while savings were the highest in history. General Motors was on strike. Shoppers were buying only inexpensive goods. There was a lack of confidence that there would be an economic recovery, Burns had said.

"What's the trouble?" Nixon asked me. "I doubt they're worried about inflation. Is it unemployment? There are ten days left until Christmas. I want to know how sales are going, regularly.

"We may need a media campaign about the economy," he continued. "All this recession talk can infect people, can't it? Can't there be a psychological recession? The question is, how can we un-create it?

"From 1961 to 1963 what did the three television networks say about recession?" Nixon asked, thinking back to the Kennedy years. "There was plenty of unemployment then. It was 6.7 percent in 1961. What was NBC saying then? You take responsibility for this," Nixon said to me. "How many stories did NBC run on the economy in 1961?"

A quick check disclosed that there had been no material difference in the television networks' concern for the economy ten years before. And Paul McCracken, George Shultz, and our other economists felt the depressed consumer confidence they saw was based on much more than mere television talk.

But Nixon persisted in his feeling that a White House public-relations effort could affect the economy one way or the other.

When Arthur Burns and others persuaded the president to adopt an "incomes policy" and impose wage and price controls, it was from its inception to its fadeout as much public relations as it was substantive. And throughout, Richard Nixon was the architect of the PR aspects of wage and price controls. His theme was that government was at last doing something about prices, inflation, the cost of living, and buying power. The president stood for lower prices and fairness in the application of controls. Controls were only temporary. As soon as the "fire of inflation" abated, the controls would be removed and all Americans would realize the fruits of their sacrifice. If controls were largely an exercise in public relations, and if controls failed, the Nixonian syllogism would conclude that better PR would have made them succeed. . . .

Tom Brokaw said he and others had an impression that I was hostile to the press who covered the White House. It may be that I appeared that way. But in fact, I only wanted the press people covering the domestic side to be more diligent, more accurate, and better informed. Perhaps I held them to a higher standard than that to which they held themselves.

The *Christian Science Monitor* ran a particularly incorrect editorial one day on some aspect of the budget for social programs. So I called Joseph Harsch, then the person in charge of the editorial page of the *Monitor*, and asked him to come talk about it the next time he was in Washington. As a Christian Scientist, I had more than ordinary interest in the performance of the *Monitor*. I was frequently available to Courtney Sheldon and Budge Sperling of its Washington bureau. (I once invited its prized columnist Richard Strout [also known as TRB] to come in for a talk in 1969. I was disappointed to find him to be extraordinarily unpleasant and hostile; upon sitting down he announced that he was not a Christian Scientist — obviously he didn't approve of my religion — and he didn't think much of Richard Nixon, either. I said that at least some of that could be seen in his *Monitor* columns. I was interested in helping Strout understand what we were trying to do. I began to offer him whatever help I could, but it appeared he was interested only in antagonizing me. In his memoirs Strout contends that I tried to co-opt him during that brief session, but the fact is that his offensive personality so put me off that I decided to end the meeting quickly and to avoid Mr. Strout thereafter.)

When the *Monitor*'s editorialist, Joe Harsch, dropped by, I had a file of facts and figures ready for him. The budget people had collected welfare statistics and other information on the subject of the *Monitor*'s recent editorial, and I invited Joe to take the data with him. I told him how greatly concerned I was that the *Monitor* — of all papers — be accurate in matters of this kind, and I wanted to help in any way I could.

Joe had his problems up there at the *Monitor* in Boston, and he began to share them with me. It is hard to be accurate when you are shorthanded to begin with and then some of your people are out (excuse the expression) sick.

"Maybe it would be better to just not print a doubtful editorial if you can't check the facts," I suggested.

"Listen," Joe said, "if we are right *half* the time, I've got to be satisfied." Joe didn't seem happy with the situation at the *Monitor*, but he was resigned to it.

I was to hear substantially that same surprising defense from Hugh

Sidey in 1970. He was the Washington bureau chief for *Time* magazine when *Time* ran a long story on our health policy that was studded with errors. I met Hugh for lunch at the Hay-Adams Hotel to talk to him about our version of the facts. I had come armed with *Time*'s story pasted on sheets of paper with much of our data in the margins, annotating the story to show *Time*'s mistakes.

Sidey listened, but neither the facts nor I moved him. He began telling me about his impossible deadlines, the trouble his Washington people had with *Time*'s New York researchers and editors, and his difficulty getting access to Nixon people who would talk to his reporters about the facts. On balance, *Time* had run a pretty good story, Sidey said.

"But," I protested, "it's full of mistakes."

"Every story contains mistakes," he said. "A reporter on deadline just does the best he can. You have to expect mistakes."

It took a while, but eventually I did come to expect mistakes in reporting; but I never got to the point where I could join Sidey and Harsch in their passive tolerance of the errors.

I seldom criticized the press in a general way; I preferred to talk to individuals when I spotted mistakes. But one day in June 1972 in Los Angeles, Robert Abernathy asked me on NBC Television why the president was not holding more press conferences, and I made some general comments which really aroused the press. Abernathy noted that there had not been a televised presidential press conference for many months, and he asked why.

I began my answer with approved doctrine: the president used many avenues of communication to reach the American people. Of all of those, the televised East Room extravaganza was one of the poorest.

The Associated Press reported the details of the rest of my response this way:

Nixon Aide Says Reporters
Ask Dumb Questions

Los Angeles (AP) President Nixon's domestic affairs adviser says one reason the President has few news conferences is that newsmen ask dumb questions.

"He doesn't get very good questions at a press conference, frankly," said John D. Ehrlichman. "He goes in there for a half hour and gets a lot of flabby and fairly dumb questions and it doesn't really elucidate very much.

"I've seen him many times come off one of those things and go back in and say, 'Isn't it extraordinary how poor the quality of the questions are?' "

Asked during an interview taped Tuesday for showing on KNBC television Saturday why Nixon has had only one news conference this year, he said, "He's been very busy, and he communicates with the American people in a lot of different ways."

In a typical news conference, Ehrlichman said, "You have 300 people jumping up and yelling, 'Mr. President,' and all that kind of thing and it just isn't a very useful way of communicating with the American people. . . .

"I think some of them may be preoccupied with their own interests or their bureaus may have fed them things that they're asked to ask, but the long and short of it is that you don't get very much out of it.

"It seems to be a great deal more . . . could be developed as interesting news and valuable for the people out of a one-on-one with Dan Rather (CBS White House Correspondent), where he could follow up and press and so on."

Asked at one point whether he was accusing the Washington press corps of being flabby and dumb, Ehrlichman replied, "No — I said the questions are flabby and dumb."[3]

Then, the next day, at another press conference, I took six or seven questions about what I'd said. Los Angeles reporters seemed very much upset that I had criticized their Washington colleagues. That led me to deliver a short remonstrance that resulted in this UPI story:

Nixon Aide Says Newsmen Like 'Insecure Ladies'

John D. Ehrlichman, one of President Nixon's top aides, Wednesday compared newsmen to "insecure young ladies" in love.

Ehrlichman, the White House domestic affairs adviser, was asked at a Los Angeles news conference about his remark the day before that President Nixon does not hold many news conferences because the reporters ask "a lot of flabby and fairly dumb questions."

Responded Ehrlichman: "When people at the White House get together with the press, newsmen are sort of like insecure young ladies and they keep asking us if we love them. Then, when we tell them the truth, there is a hurt feeling that sets in.

"It would be better if you didn't ask us if you didn't want to know."

By the time I returned to Washington, the White House press corps was lying in ambush for me. When the Secretary of Health, Education, and Welfare, Elliot Richardson, joined me to announce an education bill the president had signed, I tried to defang the subject by saying, at the end of our press conference: "While I am here, I want to congratulate everyone on the apparent muscle tone and wit of the questions today."

The reporters laughed, but one of them called out, "We wish we could say the same for the answers."

Editorial writers all around the country picked up the "flabby and

[3] © 1972 Associated Press; reprinted by permission.

dumb" phrase to either blast Nixon for not having more press conferences or criticize the Washington press corps for their lack of diligence.

Finally, at his next in-the-office press conference, Nixon was asked:

> QUESTION: Mr. President, is Mr. Ehrlichman correct when he says that you sometimes get irritated with us for our dumb and flabby questions, so-called?
>
> THE PRESIDENT: You are not dumb and flabby. No, I noted that comment and expected a question on it. I am afraid if I begin to characterize the questions you will begin to characterize my answers, but you probably will anyway. In any event, as far as questions are concerned, I think what Mr. Ehrlichman was referring to was the tendency in the big East Room conferences for questions to come in from all over the place and no follow-up, as there can be in a conference like this.
>
> Sometimes the questions may appear somewhat less relevant. I have found, for example, although we do not rule out the big conference where everybody gets to come, I have found that these smaller sessions do provide an opportunity for members of the regular White House press, who study these issues day by day and who know what is relevant and what is not relevant and who can follow up, I think that the possibility of dumb and flabby questions is much less and I don't, frankly, complain about it.
>
> The other point that I should make is this: in looking over the transcripts of various press conferences, I have not seen many softballs, and I don't want any because it is only the hardball that you can hit or strike out on.[4]

But on July 7, out at San Clemente, Nixon and I had an early-morning meeting to prepare for a session with his economists. He was disturbed by a report from the news summary editor, Mort Allin, that the media were being "soft" on George McGovern.

"They are biased, of course," the president said. "But I want Agnew kept out of the subject of media bias now. He is to make no public statements that the media is against us. Get others to do it." Agnew was too harsh and vindictive, Nixon said.

"Kicking the press is an art," Nixon continued. "Your flabby-and-dumb crack was good. You let them have it without rancor. That's what you have to do."

[4] © 1972 United Press International; reprinted by permission.

THE
PRESIDENCY

Chapter

Four

The administrations of Lyndon B. Johnson and Richard M. Nixon changed the perspective of many Americans about the presidency. In spite of the bitter partisanship that always precedes presidential elections, the office of the presidency had before Lyndon B. Johnson always been treated with great reverence, which often led to reverence for the man who occupied the White House. This is not to suggest by any means that presidents had always been extolled for their virtues and placed on a kingly throne, for anyone familiar with American history knows that there have always been bitter personal attacks on presidents by a wide assortment of critics. And these presidential critics were not above calling their prey "mentally unbalanced." Nevertheless, most presidential biographies concentrated on the heroic and not the neurotic qualities of their subjects. An eloquent illustration of this was Carl Sandburg's biographical volumes on Abraham Lincoln. All the resources of the poet were directed toward enshrining President Lincoln in the Temple of the Gods. Contrasting Carl Sandburg's biography of Abraham Lincoln with more recent works on presidents by such authors as James David Barber or Doris Kearns, not to mention Bob Woodward and Carl Bernstein, reveals the major differences between past and present approaches to assessing presidents.[1]

Although the administration of Lyndon B. Johnson seemed entirely rational to his supporters, other persons, particularly critics of the Vietnam War, believed the president to have relentlessly, single-mindedly, and more importantly *irrationally* embarked on a highly destructive policy. David Halberstam began an extensive study of the history of the war in order to determine how the United States became involved. His best-selling book, *The Best and the Brightest*, published in 1972, emphasized the role of personalities, not so much of the president himself as of his top level advisers, in making the critical decisions com-

[1] See James David Barber, *The Presidential Character* (Englewood Cliffs, N.J.: Prentice-Hall, 1972); Doris Kearns, *Lyndon Johnson and the American Dream* (New York: Harper & Row, 1976); Bob Woodward and Carl Bernstein, *The Final Days* (New York: Simon & Schuster, 1976).

159

mitting the country to the war.[2] In the same year, political scientist James David Barber published his ground-breaking book, *The Presidential Character,* in which he made personality profiles of a variety of presidents in order to determine the effect of presidential character on performance. With the publication of Barber's book, psychopolitics came of age.

James Barber attempted a complex classification of different character types, and came to the conclusion that the best presidents were what he termed "active-positive." The active-positive president is achievement-oriented and productive, and has well-defined goals. He is rational, "using his brain to move his feet." Above all, he is flexible; he can change his goals and methods as he perceives reasons for altering his course of action. He has a sense of humor about the world and, more importantly, about himself. John F. Kennedy was, according to Barber, an ideal active-positive president.

Perhaps even more significant than the active-positive presidents are the "active-negative" presidents. These are the presidents that may do irreparable damage, according to Barber. They have a compulsive need to work because of personal problems and a misguided "Puritan ethic." They are ambitious and power-hungry but lack goals beyond that of rising to power. They tend to be politically amoral, as was Richard Nixon, but may take on false and misleading goals, such as making the world safe for democracy, as did Woodrow Wilson. The great energy of the active-negative type is frequently directed in irrational ways, and once set in a course of action the active-negative president tends to become very rigid, especially in the face of opposition and criticisms from the outside. Because of personal insecurity, the active-negative president surrounds himself with yes-men in order to fortify him in confrontation with the hostile world outside. Barber's portraits of various active-negative presidents, including Richard Nixon, when taken in conjunction with the portrait of President Nixon in Bob Woodward's and Carl Bernstein's *Final Days,* is truly frightening. Because of the enormous power that presidents possess, it is especially important to examine their characters and styles, which set the tone of presidential administrations.

The selections in this chapter illustrate various dimensions of presidential personality, and what is frequently overlooked, the way in which the personalities and styles of the President's staff can influence the political process.

[2] David Halberstam, *The Best and the Brightest* (New York: Random House, 1972).

JIMMY CARTER'S 1976 CAMPAIGN promised "nothing but the best." Running as an outsider against the Washington establishment, Carter caught the imagination of a large number of voters who had become disillusioned with government. Voters outside of Washington, not familiar with the ways of the power establishment of the city, believed Carter's rhetorical exhortations that his election *would* make a difference. And, many voters who were knowledgeable about the Washington power establishment and its ability to stymie change voted for Carter, because they wanted to believe in him. All who put their trust in Jimmy Carter were confident that he meant what he said, that he would bring the highest standards to government, never lie to the people, and passionately strive to right the wrongs of the past.

James Fallows, who was chief White House speech writer for President Carter during his first two years in office, and who became the Washington editor of the *Atlantic Monthly*, was a sophisticated observer of the Washington scene who worked for Carter's election. Fallows put his trust in the Georgian, confident that a Carter White House would bring a refreshing approach to government. In the following selection Fallows contrasts the promise and reality of the Carter administration, emphasizing how the character and style of the president affected his performance.

12

James Fallows
THE PASSIONLESS PRESIDENCY

In the spring of 1978, as the primary election season drew near, Jimmy Carter began a long march across the country, ready to help off-year Democratic candidates who might later reciprocate by helping him. This was a tiring trip, which caught the President at a tired time. Within the previous month, he had traveled halfway around the world and across the country many times. More of the same lay immediately ahead. On the first leg of this trip, in Chicago, Carter made an interminable appearance at a Cook County Democratic banquet, speaking briefly to party members in six separate ballrooms, then launching into an hour-long address in the main hall.

Of the many things being demanded of him, Carter was tired most of all of giving speeches. He told Jody Powell, who passed the word to me as the presidential speechwriter, to change the plans for his appearance next day before the Illinois state legislature in Springfield. We should release the text of the speech that we had prepared — a sobersided discussion of the "iron triangle" of bureaucratic interests, congressional committees, and outside lobbying groups that kept things in the government from ever being reformed — but, Carter said, he did not intend to deliver it. Instead, he would stand before the legislators, endorse the sentiments expressed in the advance text, and then take questions from the floor.

In the Springfield capitol building the next morning, I sat among the reporters and watched the revised plan unfold. Carter announced his intentions and read introductory comments from his note cards — and then, unexpectedly, he began talking in a deeper register, a more heartfelt style; a graceful natural cadence replaced his familiar singsong. Carter was speaking once more as he had spoken during the campaign, not about a specific policy or the rationale behind his acts, but about himself, his values, the emotions he felt day by day. He had once referred to his job as "one big multiple choice exam," and he told the rapt crowd about the tests he would soon face. He told them of his difficulties — "It is not easy to negotiate with the Russians on a SALT agreement. . . . A Panama Canal treaty was not a popular thing." The Mideast arms sales were "almost impossible to resolve to the satisfaction of the American people. It took a lot of courage to make those decisions."

Carter told them of his faith in the American people, whose goodness he had seen in the small towns. Our people, he said, are "basically decent, basically honest, basically have great common sense." And he was determined to reflect those virtues. He had been a businessman, a farmer, in touch with the cells and organs of American life. As the American people would respond to hard questions, so would he. As they were hardworking and honest and brave, so too must he be.

Carter then began taking questions, but I stopped listening; so much that had puzzled me was becoming clear. Sixteen months into his Administration, there was a mystery to be explained about Jimmy Carter: the contrast between the promise and popularity of his first months in office and the disappointment so widely felt later on. Part of this had to do with the inevitable end of the presidential honeymoon, with the unenviable circumstances Carter inherited, with the fickleness of the press. But much more of it grew directly from the quality Carter displayed that morning in Illinois. He was speaking with gusto because he was speaking about the subject that most inspired him: not what he proposed to *do,* but who he *was.* Where Lyndon Johnson boasted of schools built and children fed, where Edward Kennedy holds out the promise of the energies he might mobilize and the ideas he might enact, Jimmy Carter tells us that he is a good man. His positions are correct, his values sound. Like Marshal Pétain after the fall of France, he has offered his person to the nation. This is not an inconsiderable gift; his performance in office shows us why it's not enough.

After two and a half years in Carter's service, I fully believe him to be a good man. With his moral virtues and his intellectual skills, he is perhaps as admirable a human being as has ever held the job. He is probably smarter, in the College Board sense, than any other President in this century. He grasps issues quickly. He made me feel confident that, except in economics, he would resolve technical questions lucidly, without distortions imposed by cant or imperfect comprehension.

He is a stable, personally confident man, whose quirks are few. He told the several Rhodes scholars on his staff that he had not won one of the scholarships, that this had been a great disappointment to him, but that he'd made out all right, heh, heh, hadn't he? He tends to exaggerate his background ("I am a nuclear physicist"; "I directed the Head Start program in Georgia") and to tamper with truth on small matters. As character flaws go, these are small change. Apart from occasional profanity, I saw him form no argument and strike no pose that would make him look a hypocrite if publicly revealed. . . .

Carter is usually patient, less vindictive than the political norm, blessed with a sense of perspective about the chanciness of life and the transience of its glories and pursuits. I left his service feeling that when moral choices faced him, he would resolve them fairly; that when questions of life and death, of nuclear war and human destruction were laid upon his desk, he would act on them calmly, with self-knowledge, free of interior demons that might tempt him to act rashly or to prove at terrible cost that he was a man. One factor in our choice of Presidents is their soundness in the ultimate moments of decision, when the finger is poised over the button and the future of the race is at stake. Of all contenders on the horizon, none would be saner or surer than Carter in those moments. In his ability to do justice case by case, he would be the ideal non-lawyer for the Supreme Court; if I had to choose one politician to sit at the Pearly Gates and pass judgment on my soul, Jimmy Carter would be the one.

But if he has the gift of virtue, there are other gifts he lacks.

One is sophistication. It soon became clear, in ways I shall explain, that Carter and those closest to him took office in profound ignorance of their jobs. They were ignorant of the possibilities and the most likely pitfalls. They fell prey to predictable dangers and squandered precious time.

The second is the ability to explain his goals, and thereby to offer an object for loyalty larger than himself.

The third, and most important, is the passion to convert himself from a good man into an effective one, to learn how to do the job. Carter often seemed more concerned with taking the correct position than with learning how to turn that position into results. He seethed with frustration when his plans were rejected, but felt no compulsion to do better next time. He did not devour history for its lessons, surround himself with people who could do what he could not, or learn from others that fire was painful before he plunged his hand into the flame. . . .

I worked for [Carter] enthusiastically and was proud to join his Administration, for I felt that he, alone among the candidates, might look past the tired formulas of left and right and offer something new. These early hopes impose a special burden of explanation on people like me; before we find fault, we must explain why we thought things would be different. Carter had no experience in Washington or in foreign affairs; to blame him for that now seems somehow unfair. He had grown unpopular as governor of Georgia; why should it be different in the White House? On paper, as a provincial businessman and one-term governor, Carter promised to perform just about the way he has.

But there were two factors that made many of us ignore these paper limitations. One was Carter's remarkable charm in face-to-face encounters. All politicians must be charming to some degree, but Carter's performance on first intimate meeting was something special. His intelligence and magnetism soon banished all thoughts of the limits of his background. When working at the White House, I often felt persuaded by Carter's argument — and, even more, of his personal merit — while talking with him, although I knew, on calm reflection, that his argument was wrong. This was not simply the malleability of a young employee; I met very few people who, having sat and talked with Carter by themselves or in groups of two or three, did not come away feeling they had dealt with a formidable man.

He was fully aware of this power and used it whenever he could. Early in the campaign, when trying to convince people that his candidacy was not a joke, he placed high hopes on his meetings with newspaper editorial boards. After Gerald Rafshoon's arrival in the White House, Carter invited editors and publishers to dinner, usually to good effect. He always felt in foreign affairs that if he could only get his adversaries into the room with him, he could win them over. This he demonstrated most spectacularly with Sadat and Begin at Camp David and in his dramatic and courageous resuscitation of the Egyptian–Israeli peace negotiations this year. Lyndon Johnson had the same faith in his famous "treatment," but it was based on his intimate knowledge of the other party, which told him how to flatter, threaten, and cajole. Carter's faith was in himself, and in the impression he would create.

The other factor was a subtler thing, though clearly visible in retrospect. I always thought Carter awkward at the deliberate manipulation of symbols, but he was a genius at using a phrase, a gesture, a code word that his listeners assumed to be of greater significance than it was. He led call-and-response like a preacher in a black church; he talked with environmentalists about the sins of the Corps of Engineers; he told the American Legion about his family's three centuries of military service; and he told everyone in back-room meetings that, while he could not promise a single appointment to a single person, "I think you'll be pleasantly surprised by the choices I make," and "I think you'll agree with what I do 95 percent of the time." Espying these chunks in the water, each onlooker viewed them as tips of icebergs, indicating vast, hidden extensions below.

I realize now how people were led on by these hints; I was led on myself by the hope that Carter might make sense of the swirl of liberal and conservative sentiment then muddying the political orthodoxy. Never did I feel it more strongly than after my first meeting with Carter, in August 1976, when he was receiving petitioners in Plains. Shortly after I joined the campaign staff, I accompanied a friend and former employer, Ralph Nadar, when he went to call on Carter. From 9 P.M. until long past midnight on a steamy summer night, I sat in the back of Carter's study while Nader delivered a lecture on the way the government works. What Boswell must have felt when Burke and Johnson had their fine moments I thought I was feeling then, as Nader distilled into three hours the lessons of a dozen years. They were not programmatic, or even "liberal," points, but practical warnings about the way administrations went wrong. Carter must do everything possible to eliminate third-party payment systems, Nader said; they always bust the budget. He must find ways around the unions' guild mentality if he wanted to put poor teenagers to work and to rebuild the cities. He must control, from his first moment on the job, the way he spent his time, so that when the crises came, as they inevitably would, his other efforts would go on. He must avoid the ancient seductions of foreign affairs, and must constantly search for ways to make the people in government feel that he was looking over their shoulders day after day, encouraging, inspecting, reproving, an ever-present focus for loyalty and healthy fear.

Nader did most of the talking that evening, but when Carter spoke it was to show that he *understood*. . . .

The first jarring note was struck after two months in office, when large pay increases were allotted to the White House staff. Many people got a raise just by joining; Carter could have hired nearly everyone for half the starting pay; except for a few lawyers, such as Robert Lipshutz and

Jack Watson, those entering public service were making no financial sacrifices. I was twenty-seven years old when I starting working at the White House. The year before, I had made about $20,000 as a magazine writer. On Inauguration Day, my pay rose by 87.5 percent, to $37,000. Two months later, with the general pay increase, it went up another $5000, to $42,500. After two more unpublicized, automatic, "cost of living" raises, I was earning $47,000 when I resigned at the end of November 1978.

Of all complaints about Carter, overpayment is the most ironic, for he was the most notorious tightwad in town. But it was a sadly typical complaint, for it showed that Carter's inner values mattered less than his naiveté about organizations and the effect of symbolic acts. By going along with the pay increases, Carter gave the clearest possible sign that it would be business as usual in his Administration. His later talk about inflation would be forever undermined by this demonstration that restraint did not start at home. . . .

There came other signs that Carter was not alert to bureaucratic perils. If there is any constant in the literature of presidential performance, it is that the President must husband his time. If he is distracted from the big choices by the torrent of petty details, the big choices will not get made — or will be resolved by their own internal logic, not by the wishes of those who have been elected to lead. Carter came into office determined to set a rational plan for his time, but soon showed in practice that he was still the detail-man used to running his own warehouse, the perfectionist accustomed to thinking that to do a job right you must do it yourself. He would leave for a weekend at Camp David laden with thick briefing books, would pour over budget tables to check the arithmetic, and during his first six months in office, would personally review all requests to use the White House tennis court. (Although he flatly denied to Bill Moyers in his November 1978 interview that he had ever stooped to such labors, the in-house tennis enthusiasts, of whom I was perhaps the most shameless, dispatched brief notes through his secretary asking to use the court on Tuesday afternoon, while he was at a congressional briefing, or a Saturday morning, while he was away. I always provided spaces where he could check Yes or No; Carter would make his decision and send the note back, initialed J.)

After six months had passed, Carter learned that this was ridiculous, as he learned about other details he would have to pass by if he was to use his time well. But his preference was still to try to do it all — to complain that he was receiving too many memos and that they were too long, but to act nonetheless on everything that reached his desk. He believed in the clean-desk philosophy. During his first month, he said, "Unless there's a holocaust, I'll take care of everything the same day it comes in." When he moved toward the more usual presidential course — letting his aides worry about the details, and acting on their advice — he neglected the usual corollary, which is that the aide should live or die on the quality of his judgment. His counsel, Robert Lipshutz, examined the comptroller's report on Bert Lance in August 1977 and told Carter it presented a clean bill of health. At that, Carter flew down from Camp David to say, "Bert, I'm proud of you." In the lower reaches of the staff, the dismay at Lipshutz's interpretation was exceeded only by the incredulity that he suffered no visible sanction or remonstrance for his poor advice. Indeed, the criticism Lipshutz received in the press made Powell and Jordan all the more dogged in their defense of him. Lipshutz was one of *them*, one of the southern boys, being persecuted by a hostile northern press.

If often seemed to me that "history," for Carter and those closest to him, consisted of Vietnam and Watergate; if they could avoid the errors, as commonly understood, of those two episodes, they would score well. No military intervention, no dirty tricks, no tape recorders on the premises, and no "isolation" of the President. When it came to setting up the White House, this meant avoiding a recreation of the "Berlin Wall," the Haldeman–Ehrlichman bulkhead that had blocked out Nixon's other assistants. Carter stressed that his nine main aides had equal access to him, and that another two dozen people (of whom I was one) had free access in memos, if not in the flesh.

This arrangement reflected not only Carter's reading of recent history but also his personal style. His affections were constant toward his retinue of loyal helpers; he did not scramble to hire someone with a talent that Powell, Eizenstat, Jordan, or Rafshoon did not happen to possess. None of them would have made a good chief of staff, so that function simply did not enter into the organization chart. Carter would do it himself, as he would everything else, whether it be the Administration's long-range planning or improving the grammar in the proclamations we wrote for him.* . . .

A far graver managerial error was that of "Cabinet government," another outgrowth of Carter's truncated historical view. Like no other President since Eisenhower, Carter seemed to think that organizations would run in practice as they did on paper: people would perform their assigned functions and seek no others; orders, once given, would be carried out; when people were asked to direct specific bureaus or departments, their loyalties would still lie with the larger interests of the Administration. Recent history was taken by Carter to prove his point:

*President Carter announced in his press conference on July 25, 1979, the appointment of Hamilton Jordan as Chief of the White House Staff. In effect, Jordan was to become an assistant president. Carter's announcement reflected his recognition of the very failures that Fallows discusses in this article.

one of Nixon's worst sins was his abuse of Cabinet departments — he stacked them with political flunkies and destroyed the secretaries' control over their own shops. With Watergate over and Nixon deposed, "Cabinet government" became a good-government rallying cry. Carter took up the cry, eagerly accepting a naive book by Stephen Hess which proposed that the secret of efficient management was to give Cabinet secretaries free rein.

The book — and the policy — were wrong because they omitted the necessary caveat: if a president wants to allow Cabinet secretaries full day-to-day control, he must make special, almost daily efforts to find out how that control is being used. Otherwise, when a president declares "hands off the departments," a depressingly predictable sequence will begin. The White House staff will defer to the departments — until the first big calamity happens. A secretary might play to the department's constituents rather than the President's — as Patricia Harris of Housing and Urban Development was suspected of doing with her truculent demands for more money for housing programs. A big scandal might arise — at the General Services Administration, for example, or at Labor or Health, Education and Welfare, where they seem to crop up regularly. A secretary might appear to be building his own empire — as Joseph Califano was suspected of doing at HEW, with his LBJ-like determination that everyone in his department work only for him. Deception, inefficiency, a dozen other ills infecting the various government departments, whatever the origin, will make a president angry. He will feel frustrated, as John Kennedy has been portrayed as feeling when he discovered, during the Cuban missile crisis, that his orders to remove our missiles from Turkey had been ignored. He will feel especially frustrated if, like Carter, he has put extra stress on governmental performance and results. If he cares about his policies and his political future, he will feel compelled to act. He will send in his own people, good loyal people, to "get the job done right." That is what Richard Nixon did, even after making claims more fulsome than Carter's about his Cabinet "with the extra dimension," and it is what Jimmy Carter began doing in 1978. At Camp David he held a session with Cabinet officers and told them to stop freewheeling and start following the White House lead. Hamilton Jordan began holding weekly meetings with Cabinet representatives, and took to dressing down those who had most offended against the company line. Tim Kraft, an old campaign hand, started controlling appointments to the second- and third-level jobs in the departments — appointments which, the first time around, had been left entirely in the secretaries' hands. The pendulum swung the White House way, as it had so often before.

More than mere time was wasted; all the relationships were poisoned by the clumsy experiment of the first several months. Department officials began to think of the White House as the enemy, not as a source of patronage. In turn, those in the White House blamed their problems on evil people in the departments, not on foreseeable, preventable bureaucratic trends. Cabinet secretaries were judged more and more on their personal styles. The hot dogs, the show-offs — Califano, Harris, Blumenthal — came to be detested for those qualities. When preparing for a bill-signing ceremony involving HEW, I asked whether Califano would attend. "He never does anything for us," Rafshoon said. "Why should we do something for him?" The warmth was reserved for such men as Cyrus Vance and Harold Brown, whose departments were so inherently strong that they could afford to be modest, self-effacing gentlemen, tugging deferentially at their forelocks and seeming embarrassed when the spotlight fell on them.*

There was one other indication that Carter had missed a familiar lesson about the management of his time. No matter what his original intentions, foreign problems were sure to preoccupy him deeply. Like every other President who has served since the United States became a world power, he would inevitably be drawn into the whirlpool of foreign affairs. Already on his desk when he arrived were the SALT negotiations, the Middle East tensions, accommodation with China, eruptions in Africa, and the chronic economic pressures imposed by the oil-producing nations and our ever-richer allies. Additional crises would make these more, not less, demanding as his term wore on.

There were also the familiar allurements of foreign affairs: the trips on fabulous Air Force One, the flourishes, twenty-one-gun salutes, and cheering multitudes along the motorcade routes. More important was the freedom to negotiate with foreign leaders without constant interference or nit-picking from congressmen and senators, the heady dips into worldly secrets in rooms lined with lead to protect against eavesdroppers — all the excitement and trappings that go with dealing in momentous global matters that can mean life or death for all mankind.

But Carter was not only preoccupied by the serious international problems that lay before him; he — and those around him — became virtually transfixed by them. The president seemed to foresee neither the temptations nor the demands of foreign policy, nor the ways to prevent them from stealing his concentration away from other pressing business of his office. As he grew more deeply involved in his international human rights campaign, the Panama Canal negotiations, the delicacy of détente with Russia, and especially, his quest for peace in the

* After the Camp David Summit in the summer of 1979, President Carter fired HEW Secretary Joseph Califano and Secretary of the Treasury Michael Blumenthal. Their independent stances and unwillingness to cooperate closely with the White House had angered the president and the White House staff, particularly Hamilton Jordan.

Middle East, his efforts on the domestic front suffered from his inattention. Returning from a triumphal journey to Nigeria or Germany, his eyes would noticeably glaze as he forced himself to discuss such a matter as reorganization of the Commerce Department. The exhilaration that followed the Camp David agreement seemed to dull even further his appetite for home affairs. Next on his plate after Camp David was the most pressing domestic issue of all — inflation — but he appeared bored and impatient throughout high-level deliberations over what to do about it, unhappy with the half steps his advisers served up, and plainly eager to return to shaping international history.

During the first year came other indications that Carter did not really know *what* he wanted to do in such crucial areas as taxes, welfare, energy, and the reorganization of the government. In each of these areas, Carter's passionate campaign commitments turned out to be commitments to generalities, not to specific programs or policies. After taking office, he commissioned panels of experts to tell him what to do, usually giving them instructions no more detailed than his repeated exhortation to "Be bold!" . . .

Carter, who was able to learn from experience in a once-burned, twice-shy way, showed no inclination to prevent the burns by seeking associates who had been there before. Nowhere was he surer to need help than in his dealings with the Congress. His experience there was minimal, his campaign tone had been hostile, his skin crawled at the thought of the time-consuming consultations and persuasion that might be required to bring a legislator around. He did not know how congressmen talked, worked, and thought, how to pressure them without being a bully or flatter them without seeming a fool. He needed help from someone who knew all those things, who had spent time absorbing that culture. But for his congressional liaison, he chose a Georgian named Frank Moore, a man whose general aptitude was difficult for anyone outside the first circle to detect, and who had barely laid eyes upon the Capitol before Inauguration Day.

Although Carter himself wakes up each morning popping with ideas, very few others in the Administration have been induced by him or by themselves to feel any passion to *do*. Most of the "Georgians," those who have been with Carter long enough to feel a personal commitment to his success, owe their first loyalty to the welfare and advancement of Jimmy Carter. In that they are little different from JFK's Irish Mafia, or LBJ's Texas Rangers, or any other group that has ever served a President. What makes them different is that they seem to have nothing in second place, no axes they are particularly eager to grind in their years in government. If there has been little abuse of power, it may be because they have so little sense of what power is and how it might be exercised. . . .

. . . In two years in the government, I had not one serious or impassioned discussion with a member of the senior staff about what all those countless government programs meant, which of them, if any, really worked, how the government might be changed. I think it must have been different in other days.

I do not particularly admire people who can say, as Jack Valenti did in his silly book *A Very Human President,* that "working on the White House staff is the ultimate seduction," but I came to think that emotion of that sort might be a necessary ingredient for getting the job done. There was so little of that glimmer and drive in this White House that I began to realize that the absence of passion was as serious a weakness as the lack of sophistication.

I started to wonder about the difference between a good man and an inspiring one; about why Jimmy Carter, who would surely outshine most other leaders in the judgment of the Lord, had such trouble generating excitement, not only in the nation but even among the members of his own staff. One explanation is that Carter has not given us an *idea* to follow. The central idea of the Carter Administration is Jimmy Carter himself, his own mixture of traits, since the only thing that finally gives coherence to the items of his creed is that he happens to believe them all. Hubert Humphrey might have carried out Lyndon Johnson's domestic policies; Gerald Ford, the foreign policies of Richard Nixon. But no one could carry out the Carter program, because Carter has resisted providing the overall guidelines that might explain what his program is.

I came to think that Carter believes fifty things, but no one thing. He holds explicit, thorough positions on every issue under the sun, but he has no large view of the relations between them, no line indicating which goals (reducing unemployment? human rights?) will take precedence over which (inflation control? a SALT treaty?) when the goals conflict. Spelling out these choices makes the difference between a position and a philosophy, but it is an act foreign to Carter's mind. He is a smart man, but not an intellectual, in the sense of liking the play of ideas, of pushing concepts to their limits to examine their implications. Values that others would find contradictory complement one another in his mind. During the campaign, he used to say that our nation was the first to provide "complete compatability" between liberty and equality. This pained me more than anything else he said. I sent him notes and told him in person that these two terms were like city and country, heaven and hell; the tensions between them shape much of American society. But Carter continued to make the same statement, and I realized it was not because he was vulgarizing his ideas for the crowd, but because he genuinely believed what he said.

Carter thinks in lists, not arguments; as long as the items are there, their order does not matter, nor does the hierarchy among them. Whenever he gave us an outline for a speech, it would consist of six or seven subjects ("inflation," "need to fight waste") rather than a theme or tone. . . .

For certain aspects of his job — the analyst and manager parts — Carter's methods serve him well. He makes decisions about solar power installations and the B-1 on the basis of output, payload, facts, not abstract considerations. But for the part of his job that involves leadership, Carter's style of thought cripples him. He thinks he "leads" by choosing the correct policy; but he fails to project a vision larger than the problem he is tackling at the moment.

In domestic policy, this caused frustration, since it thwarted all attempts to explain a domestic philosophy. In foreign policy, it opened the door to genuine tragedy, for it left Carter unable to defend the course he had taken. Carter did not choose the circumstances in which he operates: our dependence on foreign oil, our economic vulnerability to our allies, the resistance to military intervention left over from Vietnam. Under these difficult circumstances, he has tried to set a steady, prudent policy, keeping his eye on our real national interest, not acting out of bluff or bravado, steadfastly pursuing the things that we need and ignoring those that we don't or that we can't control. The policy should win him respect; but because Carter cannot explain what he is doing, he is an easy mark for a Moynihan or a Reagan or a Connally who can speak with passion about the decline of American power. . . .

The clearest example of this difficulty was Carter's speech at the U.S. Naval Academy in June 1978. The speech was intended to set the record straight on U.S. policy toward the Soviet Union, which was then very muddied because of the varied comments coming from Brzezinski and Vance. It was widely, and correctly, assumed that there were two different outlooks within the government, Vance's emphasis on a SALT treaty and Brzezinski's habitual pugnaciousness in the face of the Soviet Union. Vance had sent a memo to Carter arguing the need for a presidential speech to explain our policy; Carter agreed and asked Brzezinski, Vance, Andrew Young, Stansfield Turner, and several other advisers to submit memos suggesting the tone and content of the speech.

Carter then assembled the speech essentially by stapling Vance's memo to Brzezinski's, without examining the tensions between them. When he finished rewording the memos, the speech was done. It had an obvious break in the middle, like the splice in a film; as one news-man who had read the advance text said, after hearing Carter come to the end of the conciliatory material and move into the Brzezinski sec-tion, "And now — War!" The Washington *Post*'s story the next morn-ing was titled "Two Different Speeches," an accurate and obvious in-terpretation, but one that galled Carter and those around him. Hadn't he laid it all out for them, all the elements of his thought, all his views? What more could they want?

Carter's problems as an explainer were compounded by his tendency to talk down to his audience. He didn't do this when speaking extem-poraneously — at those times he used words from the engineering books and Brzezinski's fanciest theories — but he couldn't avoid it in his prepared speeches. While working on the first fireside chat, I re-ceived a lecture from the president. I should not use words such as "cynical," because average people wouldn't understand them. Carter said that whenever he worked on a speech he thought of a man at a cer-tain gas station in Georgia (not his brother). If that man couldn't under-stand it, it should be changed. Instead of "cynical," I should use the word "callous." "Working people understand callouses. They see their hands get hard."

The sentiment was admirable but too broad. When simplifying words, Carter too often simplified ideas as well. I always thought the public could tell the difference between a clear, simple image — such as Franklin Roosevelt's garden hose to symbolize Lend-Lease — and a deceptively simple thought. When they heard Carter's constant talk of harmony, respect among nations, happy times at home, the men at the gas stations knew they were hearing less than the full truth.

Nor did he distinguish among the audiences he had to address. For some — but only a few — of his televised appeals, it was important that a speech be understood by every hearer. In most other cases, that was a false goal. In a television interview in 1960, Walter Lippmann said that an effective President "must be articulate. He must be able to talk in language which is not the lowest common denominator, but the best. What you must lead in the country are the best of the country and they will carry it on down. There's no use of the president trying to talk down to a fellow who can just about read and write. Let somebody else do that. He must talk to the people who teach the man to read and write." I came to believe very deeply in a hierarchy of information and attitudes. Once an idea took hold in the serious magazines and the edi-torial pages, it would make its way down through the news columns, the reports in *Time* and *Newsweek*, and eventually to the television com-mentators, who shape most people's view of public affairs. In many cases, the real audience for a speech should be not the 5000 people who are present for the occasion but the editors, academics, politicians, and columnists who will read the text and adjust their view of the president accordingly. Such speeches are the best, sometimes the only, way a president can show that he understands the complications in his policies, the problems ahead, the hard questions that have been raised about his course. Except for one or two speeches on foreign policy — where he was more willing in general to buy the conventional wisdom than he was in domestic affairs — Carter never consented to such speeches.

All these oratorical problems were made worse by his refusal to learn how to speak. By his natural gifts, Carter is a good off-the-cuff speaker and a poor formal orator, and he never bestirred himself to improve in either way. It seemed to me the height of arrogance that Carter refused oral practice before his campaign debates against Gerald Ford.

   To the day I left the White House, he never really practiced a speech — not in the sense of subjecting his performance to the scrutiny of others and letting them say plainly how he must change. Before a big speech, Carter would read through the text once or twice — once into a little cassette tape recorder he could play back to himself, once with the TV lights on, after which Jerry Rafshoon would say, "That was good," or "Go a little slower." One of Carter's excuses for not practicing more was that his voice wore out, and three or four rehearsals would have left him unable to deliver the speech. The first lesson in any speech class is that hoarseness indicates a strained speaking style; barring illness, it is a sign all by itself that the style should be changed. The correction is easy, but not until you admit you might be doing it wrong. John Kennedy's hour of practice to get *Ich bin ein Berliner* down straight was embarrassing to him, revealing too clearly the limits of his linguistic gift. But Kennedy spent that hour, and while the practice is forgotten, the phrase lives on. When we prepared a German couplet (*"Alle Menschen werden Brüder wo dein sanffter Flügel weilt,"* from Schiller's "Ode to Joy") for Carter's speech in Bonn, he had the interpreter, Harry Obst, read it into a cassette, which Carter could listen to by himself, in his cabin at the front of the plane, and practice without Obst there to tell him he was doing it wrong. As a result, the couplet, perhaps the most famous in all of German letters, left the crowd looking around in puzzlement about what the American President was trying to say.

Throughout most of my last year at the White House, I kept asking myself, Why should a man as well-meaning and intelligent as Carter blithely forgo the lessons of experience and insist on rediscovering fire, the lever, the wheel? Why not temper the fresh view he brought with the practical knowledge of those who had passed this way before? Why, in a man whose language was peppered with "bold" and "competent" and "superb," was there so little passion to learn how to do the job?

The first clue to the solution of these questions was Carter's cast of mind: his view of problems as technical, not historical, his lack of curiosity about how the story turned out before. He wanted to analyze the "correct" answer, not to understand the intangible, irrational forces that had skewed all previous answers. When he spoke of cleaning up the bureaucracy, he spoke like a Peace Corps volunteer explaining hygiene in Malaysia, imagining that such scientific insights had never occurred to the listeners before. When he said that, this time, tax reform was going to happen, it was not because he had carefully studied the tales of past failures and learned how to surmount them, but because he had ignored them so totally as to think that his approach had never been tried. In two years, the only historical allusions I heard Carter use with any frequency were Harry Truman's rise from the depths of the polls and the effect of Roosevelt's New Deal on the southern farm. The rest of Roosevelt's record, especially his style of educating the public and getting the most out of his employees, was uncharted territory to the leaders of the Administration. Once, at dinner, Jody Powell was drawn into bitter argument with one of my historically minded friends. As Powell fulminated against the sins and arrogance of reporters, my friend warned him that people would think of him as another Spiro Agnew if he went on that way. "We weren't here then," Powell replied — and Powell, who was a graduate student in history and who prides himself on his Civil War scholarship, is the most sensitive to history of all those around the President.

Carter occasionally read history — he loved David McCullough's book on the Panama Canal — but history had not become a part of him. Shortly before I left, I was startled to see, in Carter's private study, shelves crammed with books on American history. Later I read that he had decided history was important, and that he needed a better background for his job. This realization came at the same time as did many others — about Cabinet government, the need for staff coordination, the value of Washington's old hands. Half of one term had been wasted before Carter absorbed what I had once thought he knew on the first day.

There was a second clue, more obvious during the first year, when Carter's southernness was still novel. Beneath the jokes about peanuts and grits lurked the notion of the southerner as moron; Carter was determined to prove that he and his associates had not stepped straight out of Dogpatch. During the campaign, he had enjoyed receiving the busloads of eastern experts, wrinkled and cranky after the three-hour ride from Atlanta to Plains — knowing that they'd tell their friends at

Brookings and Harvard about the brilliance of the simple country boy, knowing also that they'd call him a dumb southern redneck when he made his first mistake.

The Georgians saw this prejudice behind every slight — in the use of the phrase "the Georgians," in Brother Billy's rise as the stereotypical idiot from the South, and most of all, in the savagery visited upon Bert Lance. Between the two levels of the Administration, there was very little discussion of Lance. Those on the lower tier — non-southerners, mainly, careerists who would be in Washington when Carter was long gone — gossiped among themselves about how many days Lance had left. Those on the upper tier — Georgians, Lance's friends — grumbled among themselves about how unfair it all was. Bert was being destroyed, they knew, because he was an outsider who had not changed his southern ways. Jody Powell immediately, and intelligently, apologized for his attempt to discredit Lance's accuser, Charles Percy, but he privately felt that he, like Lance, had been a victim of the insiders' game. His story about Percy accepting rides on a corporate aircraft was wrong, but just a little wrong, Powell felt; he had only missed a few of the details. But because Percy was an insider while Powell and Lance were not as yet, the press ate the southerners alive. Frank Moore's problems, too, were written off to anti-southern snobbery. Although it was hard to deny the evidence of Moore's repeated missteps, this was an officially unmentionable topic at the White House, like Hamilton Jordan's early comments about Vance and Brzezinski, and Carter's promise to cut the defense budget. Powell and Jordan defended him with angry, knee-jerk loyalty, for Moore, unlike his critics, and unlike the sneering members of the junior staff, was one of them. His survival was part of the South's survival; together, all who had come from Georgia would prove they could do it their way.

Like this southern defensiveness, Carter's notion of populism and privilege gave him a reason to resist learning things in the usual way. His "populism" was no straightforward sentiment. He was more comfortable with businessmen and bankers than with the community organizers who protested against them; when he vacationed on St. Simons Island at the home of Smith Bagley, the Reynolds tobacco heir, he felt completely at ease. His "populism" was reflected in his pride, even arrogance, about having seen all sides of life close-up in his small town, and in his disdain for the elite, "socially prominent" (a favorite phrase) professionals whose privilege shielded them from such knowledge. At one meeting on welfare reform, he dressed down a team of experts from HEW who were lecturing him about the unemployability of the underclass. These were the people he had lived with, Carter said; they may not have been educated, some may have been lazy and drunk, but most of them understood the meaning of dignity, self-sufficiency, and work. No one could miss Carter's real message: unlike anyone else in the room, he was talking about people he had seen.

No group better exemplified what Carter despised than the Washington mandarins — the Cliffords, Califanos, Valentis, and Kissingers — who had come to do good and stayed to do well. Before joining Carter's Cabinet, Califano was making half a million dollars yearly as a lawyer; Valenti, nearly that much at the Motion Picture Association. They had their names in the society columns and their children in private schools; they protected each other with networks of mutual support. Joseph Alsop might be discredited in journalism, but not in Washington, because he was a charming guest at Katharine Graham's. The Iranian ambassador lost his job and his country, but he would never lack for friends in Washington because of the years of caviar and champagne. These were the people Carter was talking about when he told the Democratic convention that "too many have had to suffer at the hands of a political and economic elite who have shaped decisions and never had to account for mistakes or suffer from injustice." They happened also to be the people who knew how Washington worked.

Carter was right in railing against their insularity; I attributed much of his success in the primaries to the voters' suspicion that there was a conspiracy of self-protection at work in the capital. But the insiders were right to scoff at him, for they understood how much he did not know. His problem as he took office was like China's on the eve of modernization: how to get the technical know-how without accepting the cultural detritus, how to get the steel mills without the discos, the computers without Larry Flynt. Carter needed the insiders' wisdom about the power game if he was to succeed in office — but he needed to remember why he, instead of one of them, had been elected. Maintaining this balance required a keen awareness of how much he needed to acquire, and an even keener sense of what he needed to avoid. The tragedy of Jimmy Carter was that he knew neither.

At the start of the Administration, as in the general election campaign, Carter and his captains felt omniscient; they had done what no one else had known how to do. Why should they take pains to listen to those who had designed the New Deal, the Fair Deal, the Great Society? The town was theirs for the taking; it would have required nothing more than allowing the old warriors a chance to help. But Powell and Jordan and Carter let these people know that they could go to hell. Where had they been, with all their sage advice, when the campaign was out of money and no one knew who Jimmy Carter was? What were they doing when Carter was drawing crowds of ten and twenty in tiny

Iowa towns? Spite is an expensive luxury in government, but Carter thought he could afford it, not realizing then how badly his operating account would soon be overdrawn.

Carter paid the price for this arrogance with the blunders of the first year; then, burned enough, he began reaching out. Clark Clifford became Lance's champion; Anne Wexler and Robert Strauss joined the White House staff. There were informal brainstorming sessions with those who had been through all the cycles before. But Carter's people made the second mistake, forgetting what made them different at the start.

Ten days after I left the White House, I went to a Redskins game in Robert F. Kennedy Stadium. Across the field, in the box of Redskins owner Edward Bennett Williams, sat a casual sampling of Washington's permanent ruling groups — the *Post*'s editor, Benjamin Bradlee, Joe Califano, Senator Muskie, Art Buchwald, other friends. Next to Williams sat someone new to the scene: Hamilton Jordan, wearing a suit. If he had been there two years earlier, it would have been a cheering sign that the outsiders knew how to get what they needed. Coming when it did, it made me think that the earlier hostility had been mere defensive reverse snobbery. Now that Carter's people were sure they'd be accepted, they were glad to join the club.

That same week, President Carter granted a second television interview to Bill Moyers. In the first, in May 1976, everything that was new and original in Carter's intelligence had come across like a fresh breeze. This time, Carter sounded like all the grizzled veterans he had defeated in 1976. Moyers asked him about inflation, and whether the fight against it wouldn't throw people out of work — the poor, the black, those most recently employed. The Carter of the first interview would have said, of course, that was true, that the agony of the job lay in choosing between such evils. This time, after two years in office, Carter answered "no" — fighting inflation would not cost people their jobs, the question was simply wrong. It was the sort of answer other politicians might have given, because, having now seen what they saw before, Carter had grown like them in basic ways. Never again would he preach sweeping tax reform, scorn incrementalism, pretend that the government could be changed. Like Hamilton Jordan, he was ill prepared to maintain what was best in him while learning what he needed to know.

These clues told me part of the answer, but there was one part missing, the most fundamental of them all. Carter's willful ignorance, his blissful tabula rasa, could — to me — be explained only by a combination of arrogance, complacency, and — dread thought — insecurity at the core of his mind and soul.

For a while, I thought the arrogance was the unfortunate by-product of life in a small town. If his secure position and effortless supremacy in Plains had made Carter calmer than Nixon or Kennedy, it seemed also to have given him too high an estimation of his own gifts. It would have helped him to have spent a little while in a law firm in Boston, or with a movie company in Los Angeles, or as a broker in New York, to acquire that edge of neurosis and compulsion to get the best ideas out of the people on his staff. That Jimmy Carter would have been a less pleasant person; a different background might have denied him the very traits that are now his greatest strength. But it might also have made new ideas seem crucial to him; it would not have left him satisfied, as the real Jimmy Carter too often is, with what burbles up in the usual bureaucratic fashion and with the people who happen to come to hand. In Plains, he had run the business himself, relied entirely upon himself. He did not need to search constantly for people to push and test him, because his unpushed abilities were good enough.

This characteristic could be called complacency — the last word one associates with the Jimmy Carter of the speed-reading lessons, the carefully timed jogs around the South Lawn, the typed-up list of the classical music he will be listening to during the day. But while Carter accepts challenges to his ideas and is pleased to improve his mind, he stubbornly, complacently resists attempts to challenge his natural style.

At some stage in our lives, we learn to depend on others for the challenges that will make us do our best — or we manage to resist those challenges while privately correcting our defects. I shrink before the prospect of pop psychology from a journalist, but it seemed to me that things were so ordered in Jimmy Carter's universe that he never faced such challenges.

Carter has virtually no one in the White House with the right combination of age, experience, and personal standing to challenge him seriously. Robert Lipshutz is gentle and unassertive; Robert Strauss knows the sources of his power and the limits of his role; Walter Mondale assents to Carter's preference for harmony above all other virtues; Zbigniew Brzezinski marvels to the President about his fresh and powerful insights into complicated foreign issues. That is why I thought it a tragedy that Bert Lance had to leave; in my one brush with footnote-history, playing tennis with Lance, Carter, and Jordan the day that Lance resigned, I could see that Lance behaved with Carter in a way that no one else could. They were friends, who jabbed and teased with as much equality as is possible when one of the friends is President. Carter's only peers now are his wife, Rosalynn, who has given no sign of thinking that anything her husband might do could be wrong, and Charles Kirbo, who stops by for a visit every few weeks.

Those who are close enough to Carter to speak to him frankly —
Powell, Jordan, Rafshoon, perhaps Moore — either believe so totally in
the rightness of his style, or are so convinced that it will never change,
that they never bother to suggest that he spend his time differently,
deal with people differently, think of his job in a different way. Even
that handful speaks to him in tones more sincerely deferential than
those the underlings use. No one outside this handful ever has an opportunity to shoot the breeze with Carter, to talk with no specific purpose and no firm limit on time.

If he persists in walling himself off from challenge and disorder,
Jimmy Carter will ensure that great potential is all he'll ever have.
Teaching himself by trial and error, refusing to look ahead, Carter
stumbles toward achievements that might match his abilities, and asks
us to respect him because his intentions have been good. I grant him
that respect, but know the root of my disappointment. I thought we
were getting a finished work, not a handsome block of marble that the
chisel never touched.

THE WORLD OF THE WHITE House staffer is unique. In the rarefied atmosphere of the west wing of the White House the president's press secretary, national security adviser, top personal assistants and troubleshooters, and other staffers who are particularly close to the president work near the oval office. Occupying physical space that is near the president is of enormous symbolic significance, being generally taken to reflect a close relationship with the president himself. Not all of the White House staff works in the west wing; many occupy offices in the old and new executive office buildings which are respectively adjacent to and directly across Pennsylvania Avenue from the White House. The formal office of the vice-president is in the old executive office building with a view directly overlooking the west wing. President Carter moved Vice-President Walter Mondale into an office in the west wing to symbolize a close presidential–vice-presidential relationship (the former vice-president's office is occasionally used for ceremonial functions and stands ready to receive vice-presidents in the future).

The White House staff is a relatively new institution; President Roosevelt created it in 1939 as part of his reorganization plan establishing the executive office of the president. The White House staff, however, did not come into its own as an independent force until much later. While it always included powerful and influential persons, its original purpose was best expressed by Harry Truman: "The Presidency is so tremendous that it is necessary for a President to delegate authority. To be able to do so safely, however, he must have around him people who can be trusted not to arrogate authority to themselves."[1] Truman continued, "Eventually I succeeded in surrounding myself with assistants and associates who would not overstep the bounds of that delegated authority, and they were people I could trust. This is policy on the highest level: it is the operation of the government by the Chief Executive under the laws. That is what it amounts to, and when that ceases to be, chaos exists."[2]

President John F. Kennedy put together a dynamic and forceful staff that was later inherited by Lyndon B. Johnson and described as "the best and the brightest" by journalist David Halberstam.[3] Halberstam argued persuasively that major White House decisions escalating the Vietnam War during the Johnson administration could be traced directly to powerful White House staffers such as Walt Rostow, McGeorge Bundy, and Robert McNamara (who later changed from hawk to dove and resigned his position as secretary of defense to become president of the World Bank).

It was during the Nixon years that

[1] Harry S Truman, *Memoirs: Volume 1, Year of Decisions* (Garden City, New York: Doubleday and Co., 1955), p. 228.

[2] Ibid.

[3] David Halberstam, *The Best and the Brightest* (New York: Random House, 1972).

the White House staff, controlled by H. R. (Bob) Haldeman and John Ehrlichman, arrogantly wielded power around Washington in the name of the president. The Nixon White House staff was dubbed the "Palace Guard," because of its reputation for preventing direct access to the president by cabinet officers and other top officials. Like Truman, Nixon recognized the need to delegate power, but unlike Truman, he did not recognize the critical importance of retaining absolute control over his own staff. Many of the acute embarrassments to the White House that occurred during the Nixon administration, including possibly the Watergate break-in itself, might have been avoided had the president been less optimistic about the system of broad delegation of powers that he established in the White House.

Regardless of who is president, the tendency of those on the White House staff is to aggrandize their personal power. White House staffers continually seek to be in the good graces of the president, which not only may involve backroom intrigue among different individuals and groups of staffers, but also tends to mute honest criticism of the president if he embarks on what an ambitious staffer feels to be the wrong course of action. In the following selection George Reedy, a longtime associate of Lyndon B. Johnson, both on Capitol Hill and in the White House, provides a succinct personal account of the way in which the institution of the presidency affects staffers. Reedy was Lyndon Johnson's press secretary in 1964–1965, after which he returned to private life, only to be summoned back to the White House in 1968 as a special adviser to the president on domestic matters. When Johnson was in the Senate, Reedy served with him at various times, both as a staffer on the committees Johnson chaired and as a member of the senator's personal staff. Reedy's thesis is that the atmosphere of the White House tends to breed "blind ambition," to borrow John Dean's phrase (see Selection 11, p. 165), on the part of staffers, even though their personalities might not have revealed this trait before they entered the White House.

13 George E. Reedy
THE WHITE HOUSE STAFF — A PERSONAL ACCOUNT

The most frequently asked question of any former presidential assistant is whether he misses the White House. My answer is a heartfelt no!

It is an institution which can be regarded with a far higher degree of approbation from the outside — where reverence softens the harsh

From George E. Reedy, *The Twilight of the Presidency*, pp. xii–xvii. Copyright © 1970 by George Reedy. All rights reserved. Reprinted by permission of Harry N. Abrams, Inc.

lines of reality — than from the inside. Like any impressionistic painting, it improves with distance. . . . The factor that I have missed in
most of the works on the presidency I have read is the impact of the institution on individuals. The literature on the subject seems to assume
that the White House somehow molds the man and his assistants into
finer forms and that the major problem of government is to assure channels through which these forms will have full expression. It is virtually
taken for granted that the proper objective of a study of our chief executive is to identify those inhibiting factors which frustrate his efforts to
resolve national problems and to devise mechanisms which will remove
those frustrations. This is a type of study which should be continued on
a priority basis. The frustrations are many and could be catastrophic.

But the analysis is inadequate. It ignores the fundamental reality of
society, which is that institutions are manned by individual human
beings and that government — regardless of the managerial flow charts
produced by the behavioral scientists — is still a question of decisions
that are made by people. The basic question is not whether we have
devised structures with inadequate authority for the decision-making
process. The question is whether the structures have created an environment in which men cannot function in any kind of a decent and
humane relationship to the people whom they are supposed to lead. I
am afraid — and on this point I am a pessimist — that we have devised
that kind of a system.

To explain this, I must start with a highly personal reaction. The
trouble with the White House — for anyone who is a part of it — is that
when he picks up a telephone and tells people to do something, they
usually do it. They may sabotage the project, after they have hung up
the phone. They may stall, hoping that "the old son of a bitch" will
forget about it. They may respond with an avalanche of statistics and
briefing papers in which the original purpose will be lost and life will
continue as before. But the heel click at the other end of the wire will be
audible and the response — however invalid — will be prompt. There
will be no delay in assurance, however protracted may be performance.

This is an unhealthy environment for men and women whose essential business is to deal with people in large numbers. It is soothing to
the ego, but it fosters illusions about humanity. It comforts the weary
assistant who may have gone round the clock in his search for a solution
to an insoluble problem, but it paves the way for massive disillusionment. And for the very young, the process is demoralizing. It creates a
picture of the world which is ill adapted to that which they will face
once the days of glory come to an end. There should be a flat rule that no
one be permitted to enter the gates of the White House until he is at
least forty and has suffered major disappointments in life.

My own heart is back in the Senate, where I spent so many years of my adult life either as a newspaperman or a staff assistant. This is not because the people at the other end of Pennsylvania Avenue are any better in terms of character, wisdom, or goals. It is simply that their egos must face daily clashes with similarly strong egos who stand on a par and who do not feel any sense of subordination. In the Senate, no course stands the remotest chance of adoption unless a minimum of fifty-one egotistical men are persuaded of its wisdom, and in some cases the minimum is sixty-seven. These are preconditions under which even the most neurotic of personalities must make some obeisance to reality.

The inner life of the White House is essentially the life of the barnyard, as set forth so graphically in the study of the pecking order among chickens which every freshman sociology student must read. It is a question of who has the right to peck whom and who must submit to being pecked. There are only two important differences. The first is that the pecking order is determined by the individual strength and forcefulness of each chicken, whereas in the White House it depends upon the relationship to the barnyard keeper. The second is that no one outside the barnyard glorifies the chickens and expects them to order the affairs of mankind. They are destined for the frying pan and that is that.

The White House does not provide an atmosphere in which idealism and devotion can flourish. Below the president is a mass of intrigue, posturing, strutting, cringing, and pious "commitment" to irrelevant windbaggery. It is designed as the perfect setting for the conspiracy of mediocrity — that all too frequently successful collection of the untalented, the unpassionate, and the insincere seeking to convince the public that it is brilliant, compassionate, and dedicated.

There are, of course, men who seethe inwardly over this affront to human dignity — most of whom either go smash or leave quietly, their muscles set rigidly to contain an indescribable agony. There are, of course, the warm and relaxed permanent White House staff members, secure in their mastery of the essential housekeeping machinery of the mansion and watching with wry amusement and some sympathy the frenetic efforts to shine forth boldly of those who have only four years out of all eternity to grab the brass ring. But the men of outrage are few and for some reason avoid each other after they slip out the side door. There are experiences which should not be shared. A reunion would lead only to a collective shriek.

It is not that the people who compose the menage are any worse than any other collection of human beings. It is rather that the White House is an ideal cloak for intrigue, pomposity, and ambition. No nation of free men should ever permit itself to be governed from a hallowed shrine where the meanest lust for power can be sanctified and the dullest wit greeted with reverential awe. Government should be vulgar, sweaty, plebeian, operating in an environment where a fool can be called a fool and the motivations of ideological pimpery duly observed and noted. In a democracy, meanness, dullness, and corruption are entitled to representation because they are part of the human spirit; they are not entitled to protection from the harsh and rude challenges that such qualities must face in the real world.

It is not enough to say that the White House need not be like this if it is occupied by another set of personalities. It is not enough to point out that I may subconsciously be exaggerating the conditions which I describe in overreacting to the reverence that has characterized most studies of the presidency. The fact remains that the institution provides camouflage for all that is petty and nasty in human beings, and enables a clown or a knave to pose as Galahad and be treated with deference.

Is my reaction purely personal disappointment or shaped by service in a specific White House in a specific administration? Obviously, no man can be truly objective about an experience so central to his life and so vital to all his goals and his aspirations. All I can say is that I am fully aware of the treacherous nature of one's sensory mechanisms in surveying the immediately surrounding universe. I have taken this factor into account and tried to allow for it in every possible way — which is why this book has been so long delayed. I believe that what I am saying is more than the conclusion of one man in a unique set of circumstances.

The thirty years I have spent in Washington have been punctuated with a number of telltale incidents. I have observed, for example, that former White House assistants are reticent about their experiences. When pressed for a description they invariably resort to words like "richly rewarding" and "fulfilling" — the clichés that men always use when they wish to conceal, rather than to convey, thought. And their congratulations to newly appointed assistants begin always with perfunctory "best wishes" and then shift to heartfelt friendly tips on how to survive. Only once have I felt a genuine flash of fire. It came from one of the top "assistants with a passion for anonymity" of the Roosevelt days. I described to him White House life as I saw it and his response — which was passionate — was: "Don't worry! That's the way it has always been and that's the way it will always be!"

I have a feeling that Camelot was not a very happy place. Even the gentle language of Malory does not fully cloak hints of intrigue, corruption, and distrust — reaching as high as Guinevere. And the "Table Round" seems better adapted to boozing in a vain effort to drown disappointment than to knightly discourse on chivalrous deeds and weighty matters of state.

In fact, Malory makes virtually no effort to describe Camelot as a seat of government. King Arthur was presumably beloved by his subjects because he was wise and valiant. But how did he handle roadbuilding, public charity, or the administration of justice? Such questions had to wait several hundred years for the advent of Mark Twain, whose entirely fictitious (and wholly irreverent) account was probably much closer to the reality than that produced by the original sources.

It is this aspect that gives cause for concern. The psychological ease of those who reside in Camelot does not matter except to the individuals themselves. But the type of government that Camelot produces affects every individual and, ultimately, can determine the character of the society in which we all must live.

It is my highly pessimistic view that Camelot will no longer suffice — however effective it may have been in the past. As a rallying point for men who would beat off dragons and ogres, it was superb. As a device to lead us through the stresses of modern life, it is wholly inadequate. And one of the few historical principles in which I still retain faith is that an inadequate government will either fall or resort to repression.

There is no reason to believe that the United States is exempt from the forces of history. We have no special writ from the Almighty which will substitute for normal human wisdom. There is no evidence that such wisdom is being applied effectively to the overwhelming problems that beset us nor is there any light on the horizon. And while it may seem premature at this point, we may well be witnessing the first lengthening of the shadows that will become the twilight of the presidency.

ALTHOUGH THE NIXON WHITE House was anything but ordinary, the feelings of John Dean when he first approached the southwest gate of the White House to put in his first day on the job were in many respects typical of new White House staffers. From the very beginning Dean's chief desires were to enter the inner circle of the president, and to acquire both the symbols and the realities of power. Dean entered the White House with a sense of awe; he left it with bitterness less than three years later, after being fired by President Nixon. Dean could not imagine on that first day at the White House the quagmire in which he would eventually find himself. Everyone in politics has ambition, and many have "blind ambition." It was the latter that led Dean to become part of the Watergate coverup conspiracy, a blind ambition that was characteristic of the Nixon White House during the Watergate era.

14

John Dean

MY FIRST DAY AT THE WHITE HOUSE

I arrived early for my first day on the new job, July 27, 1970, and drove to the southwest gate of the White House grounds. A guard found my name on his clipboard and instructed me to park in one of the visitors' spaces, since my permanent spot had not yet been assigned. Bud Krogh pulled in a few spaces away. He waved a greeting at me and hurried off, mumbling like the Mad Hatter that he was late. He would see me later, he called. It was not yet eight in the morning. *Late*, I thought. I had been worried about getting there too early. No one had told me when the work day started.

I'd barely got acquainted with my new office in the Executive Office Building when Bud called in, "Hey, John, have you had a chance to take a real look around yet?"

"No, I haven't."

He seemed pleased. "Let me take you on a tour and show you some of the places no one sees." There was a look of mischief on his face.

Bud Krogh — Egil Krogh, Jr. — was a long-time friend of John Ehrlichman and his family in Seattle. After spending much of his childhood in the Ehrlichman home, he had joined Ehrlichman's law firm and then followed Ehrlichman to the White House as his assistant. Such intimate sponsorship from Ehrlichman gave Bud a head start in the White House, and he made the most of it. Despite his youth, he was already known in the Administration for his quick grasp of complex issues and his forceful presence. Even when he was largely ignorant of the subject matter, he was sharp enough to dominate meetings and win the participants' respect. Already he was the White House man in charge of relations with the District of Columbia government, with responsibilities ranging from reviewing its budget to overseeing its response to the massive antiwar demonstrations of the early Nixon years. He was also in charge of the White House effort to combat heroin and other dangerous drugs, a subject of great concern to the President. Later he would be selected to run the highly secret Plumbers' Unit that was to stop up leaks, and still later he would go to jail for his activities there.

Bud Krogh was someone I considered a friend. We took off toward the basement of the Executive Office Building like the Hardy Boys. Hidden in the depths we found the telephone switchboard headquarters, and behind it a massive equipment room filled with transformers, generators and electrical circuitry. Bud introduced me to the chief operator, who seemed pleased by our visit. "This equipment we have, Mr. Dean, could handle a whole city the size of Hagerstown, Maryland," she said proudly. I wondered why she picked Hagerstown, of all places, but her domain was certainly impressive, as were the skills of the women who worked as operators. They could locate anyone, just as they had found me for Larry Higby when Haldeman wanted me to fly to San Clemente. (Only once did I abuse this skill, when I asked one of the operators to track down a woman I had met who would not give me her unlisted telephone number.) Bud and I lingered briefly and then pressed on to the basement of the White House's West Wing and the Situation Room.

The Situation Room, I had heard, was where Henry Kissinger took his dates to impress them. It operated twenty-four hours a day to keep the President aware of what was happening throughout the world, Bud explained. I pictured this nerve center as a gleaming room packed with uniformed admirals and generals seated at long computer consoles, surrounded by lesser-ranking aides and walls of incomprehensible charts and maps. Wrong. The room was dreary and overcrowded, jammed with cluttered desks and staffed by a few young military men wearing out-of-date civilian clothes and a secretary checking the antique-looking teletypes. Even the windowless wood-paneled conference room, designed to prevent eavesdropping, was boring. This vital communications post was far less imposing than the switchboard rooms, and I decided that Kissinger must have something more than the Situation Room to impress the ladies.

Outside the "Sit Room" we peeked into a large storage area beside the mess, where workmen were building an executive dining room for senior staff and Cabinet officers, which would resemble a private men's grill at a posh country club. We walked on, peering into the White House barbershop, the limousine drivers' waiting room, the photographer's office, the vault safe for sensitive Presidential papers, and a Secret Service command post.

We went upstairs to the first floor of the West Wing, where the President's Oval Office is located. Bud was amazed that I had never seen it. As we approached, he pointed out a small monitoring device that kept constant track of the President's whereabouts. It indicated that the President was in his hideaway office at the Executive Office Building next door. An Executive Protective Service officer was posted near the monitor. A thick velvet rope guarded the door to the Oval Office, which was standing open. Bud, never shy, asked the officer to remove the rope so that we could take a closer look. He obeyed reluctantly, with the request that we step *just* inside.

"This is The Man's office," said Bud. "What do you think?"

"Not bad, not bad at all. In fact, it's damn impressive." I could feel the importance of the office as I took it all in. My attention was caught by the conspicuous rug and the huge desk. The oval rug was deep blue, with a ring of gold stars and a huge gold eagle in the middle, a replica of the President's seal of office. It struck me as surprisingly flashy for Richard Nixon, who had such strong feelings about appearing dignified and Presidential. He would not, despite the advice of his television experts, wear a blue shirt. Blue shirts weren't Presidential, he said, and he didn't care if his white shirts made his dark features appear harsher on television; white shirts were Presidential. His blue-and-gold rug, like the short-lived Bavarian-guard uniforms he commissioned for the White House, was in odd contrast to all that.

His desk was enormous and had allegedly been used by Woodrow Wilson. Two Presidents, maybe four, could have worked at it without disturbing each other. There was a story about the desk around the White House. The President liked to sit with his feet on it, and his heels had scarred the top. Once, when he was out of the country, someone noticed the damaged mahogany surface and sent the desk out to be refinished. When he returned, Nixon noticed that his heel marks had been removed. "Dammit, I didn't order that," he snapped. "I want to leave *my* mark on this place just like other Presidents."

We moved on to the East Wing, with Bud pointing out places of interest along the way — the doctor's office, the chief butler's office, the Map Room, the Lincoln Library, the kitchen, the secret tunnel. We stopped briefly at the door of the secret tunnel, which ran from the basement of the White House to the Treasury Department a block away. Bud said the Secret Service had contingency plans for bringing troops through the tunnel if a hostile demonstration ever got out of hand. But the only trooper to use the tunnel was Chief Justice Warren Burger. On the day his Supreme Court nomination was announced, the tunnel enabled him to enter the White House unnoticed by the press.

Down we went to the East Wing basement, until halted by a large steel door posted "Restricted Area." Bud ignored the sign, and I followed him through a room of furnaces, low-hanging pipes and huge valves to a second steel door with a small window. He rang the doorbell, and a face appeared that recognized him. The door opened and Bud stated his purpose: "I want to show Mr. Dean, the new counsel to the President, the area we use as a command post during demonstrations."

We walked through a corridor maze until we came to a small suite of rooms. "This," Bud announced, "is the President's bomb shelter." I looked around. Ventilated air. Stored supplies. Beds. An appropriately Presidential desk flanked by flags. And a conference room with three built-in television sets, plus radio equipment and telephones everywhere. It *looked* like a President's bomb shelter.

Bud said Ehrlichman found this an ideal command post for monitoring demonstrations, which puzzled me. It was remote, to say the least, and totally out of touch with what would be occurring on the streets. I conjured an image of "Field Marshal Ehrlichman," whose interest in demonstrations Haldeman once likened to that of a firehouse Dalmatian at a blaze. I knew I wouldn't use the shelter for monitoring demonstrations, although Haldeman had told me that that would be one of my responsibilities. The only time I ever returned there was for a secret screening of *Tricia's Wedding,* a pornographic movie portraying Tricia Nixon's wedding to Edward Cox, in drag. Haldeman wanted the movie killed, so a very small group of White House officials watched the cavorting transvestites in order to weigh the case for suppression. Official action proved unnecessary; the film died a natural death.

As Bud and I went past the offices of the White House staff members, I noticed furniture and files being moved. The White House, far more than any other government office, was in a state of perpetual internal flux. Offices were constantly exchanged and altered. One day I visited the President's Congressional-liaison man, Bryce N. Harlow, in his first-floor West Wing office (which later belonged to Clark MacGregor and then to William E. Timmons) and found a team of workmen busy constructing a new wall where a door had once been. Bryce explained he had been forced to give up his private bathroom because the stairwell from the basement to the second floor was being made smaller so that Henry Kissinger's office could be expanded. "In a way, I'm glad to know the place I used to shit will be Henry's office," he said with a wry smile. "That tells me who's who around here." Harlow was perhaps the only man in the White House who did not care about losing space; he was planning to leave anyway.

Everyone jockeyed for a position close to the President's ear, and even an unseasoned observer could sense minute changes in status. Success and failure could be seen in the size, décor and location of offices. Anyone who moved to a smaller office was on the way down. If a carpenter, cabinetmaker or wallpaper hanger was busy in someone's office, this was a sure sign he was on the rise. Every day, workmen crawled over the White House complex like ants. Movers busied themselves with the continuous shuffling of furniture from one office to another as people moved in, up, down or out. We learned to read office changes as an index of the internal bureaucratic power struggles. The expense was irrelevant to Haldeman. "For Christ's sake," he once retorted when we discussed whether we should reveal such expenses, "this place is a national monument, and I can't help it if the last three Presidents let it go to hell." Actually, the costs had less to do with the fitness of the White House than with the need of its occupants to see tangible evidence of their prestige.

Our tour ended and it was time to go back to my "temporary" EOB office and work. By all White House standards my office was shabby. The walls needed painting and the furniture looked like military discards. I was across and down the hall from Special Counsel Charles W. Colson, whose growing staff had lovely views of the White House and its tree-filled south lawn from their freshly decorated offices. From my window I could gaze on an interior asphalt courtyard filled with delivery trucks and parked cars plus the rear ends of air conditioners in other office windows.

I spoke with Larry Higby about this situation, which I felt did not befit a man with my title. "Larry, I don't want to sound like a complainer, but I'm embarrassed to invite anyone to my office for a meeting, it's such a dump. Also it's sometimes hard to concentrate, listening to the urinals flush all day, since you've got me right beside the men's room."

"It's only temporary," he said. He agreed to have the walls painted and some decent furnishings delivered, but added a teaser: "Bob hasn't decided where he wants to put you yet." Then he dangled "possibilities" before me — nice big offices of people Haldeman might move out in order to move me in. I did not have to be told what was happening. I was being tested and my performance would determine what I would get. I was at the bottom of the ladder, and instinctively I began to climb.

For a thousand days I would serve as counsel to the President. I soon learned that to make my way upward, into a position of confidence and influence, I had to travel downward through factional power plays, corruption and finally outright crimes. Although I would be rewarded for diligence, true advancement would come from doing those things which built a common bond of trust — or guilt — between me and my superiors. In the Nixon White House, these upward and downward paths diverged, yet joined, like prongs of a tuning fork pitched to a note of expediency. Slowly, steadily, I would climb toward the moral abyss of the President's inner circle until I finally fell into it, thinking I had made it to the top just as I began to realize I had actually touched bottom.

POLITICS GENERATES, PARTICularly at the highest levels, an attitude among the participants that often borders on paranoia. In politics, as in war, the enemy must be found and destroyed. Politics, like poker, requires a steady hand, and the ability to feign to win. The most skillful players can, over the long term, win fairly consistently. As in Western movies, however, villainous players seek to guarantee winning by cheating, which may involve a card up the sleeve or spying through intermediaries upon one's opponents.

Political players at the top, in the White House, the bureaucracy, and Congress, are often unwilling to play the game strictly by the rules. Winning is too important to them because the stakes, both for themselves, and sometimes in their view, for the country, are so high. John F. Kennedy and Lyndon B. Johnson were not above using the Internal Revenue Service and the FBI to pressure and spy upon their opponents. FBI Director J. Edgar Hoover built his empire by, among other things, maintaining dossiers detailing the private lives of a wide range of congressmen and other political leaders.

Politics is a combat sport, an extraordinarily rough game that is played for keeps. In professional football and hockey, the players at times view the rules as a veneer for the spectators; for themselves rules can be violated if necessary to win. National Hockey League players have occasionally even attacked umpires for enforcing the rules.

President Richard M. Nixon and his staff saw politics as a particularly hazardous sport, one requiring that all stops be pulled to win. The attempt to spy on the Democratic National Headquarters at Watergate, directed from inside the White House, if not by the president himself, was an example of the kind of political overkill that results from the paranoia of politics. Moreover, as George Reedy pointed out (Selection 13), presidential aides are often more concerned with maneuvering for power in the White House than they are with the external world.

When Henry Kissinger joined the Nixon White House as the president's national security adviser, he was no stranger to politics. He had worked in many capacities for Governor Nelson Rockefeller of New York, and had been a foreign policy adviser to the State Department and the White House on many occasions. Kissinger learned a great deal more about politics from his experience in the Nixon White House, which he has entertainingly and provocatively described in his memoirs. He is a particularly acute observer of the impact and interplay of personalities upon politics. In the following selection he describes the way in which the president and his closest aides responded to the growing Watergate revelations, and his own early reactions to the crisis. It is a revealing portrait of the president's personality, and of the continual power game played by White House aides as they sought to solidify and expand their influence. The Nixon White House played "hardball politics," but not always by the rules.

15
Henry Kissinger
A RUDE AWAKENING

The moment when all hopes for a period of healing dissolved can be precisely charted. It was on a weekend in the middle of April 1973.

On the evening of Friday, the thirteenth of April, the Federal City Club of Washington — its membership predominately Democratic — in a gesture of goodwill, bestowed its public service award on me, a senior representative of the Nixon administration, and on Senator John Sherman Cooper, a senior Republican senator. The Federal City Club of Washington was founded in the early 1960s as a protest against the admissions policies of the dominant, prestigious, and staid Metropolitan Club. Leading figures of the Kennedy administration and sympathetic journalists had resigned from the latter and founded a new club a few blocks away in the Sheraton-Carlton Hotel. Unfortunately, its finances did not equal the idealism of its founders; it consisted essentially of one large dining room, a bar, and a small terrace wedged between high and undistinguished office buildings.

The Nixon administration did not have much use for either club. Its key members mistrusted the Federal City as too liberal and the Metropolitan as too Establishment. Nothing could better signify their isolation from the permanent community of the nation's capital and political life — an isolation that contributed to their undoing.

That evening a distinguished group had assembled; nearly everybody of importance in Washington was there to honor two leading Republicans — except for other senior members of the Nixon administration only recently reelected with the second largest margin in American history. Senator Cooper and I brought to the occasion an appeal for national unity. My theme was the hope that, with Vietnam behind us, the nation's foreign policy could combine the exuberant idealism of the Kennedy administration (which I had served briefly and inconspicuously) with the unsentimental emphasis on national interest of the Nixon administration. . . .

My remarks were received warmly. There was in the room a glow of goodwill, conciliation, and budding optimism.

My awakening the next day, Saturday, April 14, was rude. I was still buoyed by the evening's mood of reconciliation and the geniality of the audience when Leonard Garment called at my office at the White House. What he told me shattered everything.

Len Garment was one of that small group of liberal Republicans whom Nixon had added to his entourage partly for protective coloration, partly because they genuinely appealed to his gentler and more sensitive side. Like their conservative counterparts — the speechwriter Patrick Buchanan, for example — some of the "liberals" imagined that they alone represented the "true" Nixon, although Garment was too perceptive for such a sentimental misjudgment. The fact was that there was no true Nixon; several warring personalities struggled for preeminence in the same individual. One was idealistic, thoughtful, generous; another was vindictive, petty, emotional. There was a reflective, philosophical, stoical Nixon; and there was an impetuous, impulsive, and erratic one. Sometimes one set of traits prevailed; sometimes another; occasionally they were in uneasy balance. One could never be certain which Nixon was dominant from meeting to meeting. Nor was it wise to act upon an impulsive instruction without making sure that the reflective Nixon had had a crack at it. Indeed, it was the failure of some more literal-minded White House advisers to understand the requirements of his complex personality that gave such momentum to Watergate. Strangely enough, the thoughtful analytical side of Nixon was most in evidence during crises, while periods of calm seemed to unleash the darker passions of his nature.

Garment had met Nixon when they were partners in a New York law firm. Len was a man of many talents. He was at ease in the world of the arts as in that of the law — he was himself an enthusiastic clarinet player — and credit for the Nixon administration's enormously expanded federal support for the humanities is due to him as to no other single person. If this decency reduced his effectiveness in the more brutal sparring of high-level government, it also gave depth to his role as a conscience for the president and as confidant to his friends. His title, Special Consultant to the President, was grand enough, but without a specific area of responsibility; he had no regular access to the president or a day-to-day schedule.

As a general rule, influence in the White House must not be judged by job descriptions. Many unwary neophytes are enticed into service by promises of constant contact with the president. But influence on presidential decisions depends more on the substantive mandate than on theoretical access to the Oval Office. Whatever the president's intentions, he is usually overscheduled. Inevitably, he faces problems requiring more decisions than he can comfortably handle. Conversation not related to his agenda, no matter how stimulating or instructive, soon becomes a burden. If the adviser agrees with the bureaucracy, he is a waste of time. If he disagrees and even if he should convince the president, he raises the problem of how to marshal bureaucratic support so as to implement the suggested course. I can think of no exception to the rule that advisers without a clear-cut area of responsibility eventually are pushed to the periphery by day-to-day operators. The other White House aides resent interference in their spheres. The schedulers become increasingly hesitant in finding time on the president's calendar.

Garment had reduced these inherent disabilities to the maximum degree possible through unselfish conduct and the high regard others had for him. Still, his emergence into prominence was usually a good signal that Nixon was in some distress and required a steadying hand. It was also noticeable that in recent days he had spent an increasing amount of time with Nixon, though it was not clear what matters were discussed. To explain why was the purpose of Garment's visit to my office on April 14.

In his deceptively casual manner he slumped into the blue-covered couch against the wall that faced the ceiling-to-floor windows overlooking the White House front lawn and Pennsylvania Avenue. I sat in an easy chair at right angles to the sofa, next to my desk. Never one to beat around the bush, Garment opened the conversation by raising a question unlikely to receive an objective answer: "Have you lost your mind?"

Without waiting for a reply, Garment somewhat wearily unfolded an astonishing and shattering tale: Within a matter of days my evocation of national reconciliation would look like a plea for mercy and be submerged in a crisis that would make the turmoil over Vietnam seem trivial. Nixon's lifelong enemies were about to be handed the weapon that they had been seeking. In the tornado of suspicion about to overwhelm us, my appeal to idealism tempered by a stern perception of national purpose would sound vacuous if not cynical. The outcome of the recent election might well be reversed; there was likely to be a battle to the death.

"Watergate" was about to blow up; its ramifications went far beyond the break-in at Democratic National Committee headquarters in the Watergate apartment complex. There had been other break-ins sanctioned from the White House for several different purposes, some as yet unclear. Also, a plan had existed to kidnap presumptive leaders of potential demonstrations against the Republican National Convention and to fly them to Central America. Prostitutes were to be used to compromise and to blackmail delegates to the Democratic National Convention. Garment said the "sordid mess" had many dimensions, only part of which he knew himself. It could not have developed without the cooperation of the highest levels of the administration. Garment thought that Special Counsel to the President Charles W. Colson had probably been the "evil genius" behind it. Yet the scale of the wrongdoing really made it impossible to imagine that Assistants to the President H. R. (Bob) Haldeman and John Ehrlichman, whom the press had nicknamed "the Germans," had been unaware. There was a puzzle here, for Halde-

man's and Ehrlichman's dislike of Colson was proverbial. And if Haldeman and Ehrlichman were involved, it was nearly inconceivable that
the president had been completely ignorant.

Whoever was the culprit, in Garment's view, only radical surgery
and the fullest admission of error could avert catastrophe. But if the
president was involved even indirectly, full disclosure would not be the
course selected; hence the administration might bleed to death amidst
a cascade of revelations gleefully exploited by the host of opponents
Nixon had managed to acquire over the years. Garment was convinced
that the administration would have to be ripped apart and reconstituted
in procedures as well as personnel. Nixon would have to put himself at
the head of this movement of reform, brutally eradicate the rot, and
rally the American people for a fresh start.

I was stunned. From the White House, somebody had implemented
presidential musings that could only be regarded as juvenile; had
adopted the tawdriest practices of the hated antiwar radicals; and had
set at risk both our social cohesion and our ability to fulfill our international responsibilities. For four years I had sustained myself through
the anguishing turmoil of Vietnam with the vision of a united America
turning at last to tasks of construction. And now through acts that made
no sense, discord would descend once again on a society already weakened by ten years of upheaval. I felt like a swimmer who had survived
dangerous currents only to be plucked from apparent safety by unex-
pected and even more violent riptides toward uncharted seas.

As I considered what this portended for foreign policy, my heart sank.
A nation's capacity to act is based on an intangible amalgam of strength,
reputation, and commitment to principle. To be harnessed, and applied
with care and discrimination, these qualities require authority, backed
by public confidence. But if Garment was right, political and moral authority inexorably would start draining from the presidency. The dream
of a new era of creativity would in all probability evaporate. Even pre-
serving what we had achieved — the Indochina settlement, for example — would become precarious. There was real peril. Without the
impression of American authority, aggressors would be tempted. Delicate balances in regions where American commitments were crucial to
peace would be less stable. Our ability to mediate conflicts, or to inspire
friends, would erode. We were threatened with stagnation in our foreign policy, and a rearguard struggle to avert a wholesale unraveling.

Exactly what had triggered this avalanche? When the Watergate
break-in occurred in June 1972 I had been en route to China. I had paid
little heed to the sparse news reports I read. I could not imagine that a
president as politically experienced as Nixon would permit the White
House to be involved in so pointless an exercise. I thought that at worst
some egregious minion had conducted a childish private enterprise.

In the months that followed, Watergate — then specifically associated in the public mind, as in mine, with the June 17 break-in — was
never discussed at the White House meetings I attended. The White
House assistants are both partners in a joint endeavor and competitors
for the president's attention and favor. The latter consideration often
predominates — at least it tended to in the Nixon White House. Each
assistant tenaciously defends his turf, which is best accomplished by
maintaining some exclusive jurisdiction.

Thus in the Nixon White House there was an almost total separation
between the domestic and the foreign policy sides. The relation of the
various Nixon aides to one another was like that of prisoners in adjoin-
ing cells. They might hear something about the scale of the activity;
proximity did not invite participation or intimate knowledge. To all
practical purposes I was excluded from domestic issues and Ehrlichman, who handled domestic policy, from foreign policy discussions.
Haldeman, who attended both, invariably confined himself to political
and public relations concerns. There were large daily staff meetings,
which both foreign and domestic advisers attended, but they were
preoccupied with public relations; sensitive matters were never discussed there.

I was aware, of course, of the pervasive sense of beleaguerment that
resulted from a combination of the president's personality and the violent, occasionally extralegal assaults of the antiwar critics. And I had
come to know a dark side of Nixon. Nevertheless, in the summer of
1972 I did not believe it possible that the White House was involved in
the Watergate affair; I accepted Press Secretary Ronald L. Ziegler's public position that it was a "third-rate burglary attempt" involving no
White House personnel. The morning staff meetings seemed to bear
this out. The few references to Watergate were always by junior staff
members who complained of the media's unfairness. The avuncular approval this elicited from Haldeman, who presided, reinforced the sense
that nothing serious had occurred.

Once, in the summer of 1972, I asked Haldeman what Watergate was
all about. "I wish I knew," he replied; and changed the subject. On
another occasion I mentioned Watergate to John Ehrlichman. In late
January 1973 I had run into Joseph Califano, a former Johnson aide and
old friend from the other side of politics, and gossiped on the street for
a few minutes with him. To my smug remark that I did not see how the
Democrats could recover from their electoral debacle, Califano said Watergate would bring a Democratic revival. It was wrong to think of judges
as unaffected by the public mood. Enough media attention had been
focused on Watergate to make it extremely likely that the forthcoming
trial of the Watergate burglars could cause the judge to crack down and
force further revelations. I passed this view on to Ehrlichman. Ehrlich-

man, smarting under the media's tendency to contrast me favorably with "the Germans," tended to give me short shrift whenever I ventured within the three-mile limit of domestic jurisdiction. He snorted, "Wishful thinking! If that is what they are counting on, they will be out of office for thirty years."

There was, hindsight makes plain, something that should have alerted me early in 1973. It was the behavior of Nixon himself. I found it difficult to get Nixon to focus on foreign policy, to a degree that should have disquieted me. In the past, even in calm periods, he had immersed himself in foreign policy to enliven the job of managing the government, which ultimately bored him. Now it was difficult to get him to address memoranda. They came back without the plethora of marginal comments that indicated they had been carefully read. On at least one occasion Nixon checked every box of an options paper, defeating its purpose.

I ascribed this lassitude to his characteristic depression after success. Through my acquaintance with him, absence of tension provoked not elation but lethargy. Nixon's most capricious actions had occurred in times of quiet, not in reaction to crises. Calm periods seemed to drive him to disequilibrium as if he could find his own balance only in tension.

Throughout this period I remember only one conversation with Nixon that related directly to Watergate. In early April 1973, as Senator Sam Ervin's Senate Select Committee on Presidential Campaign Activities (the Watergate Committee) began its investigations, we were in San Clemente. One afternoon the president called me to his office and asked whether Haldeman should testify. I replied, naively as it proved, that this would be an admission of guilt and that only those with direct knowledge of the break-in should appear. Nixon gave no sign that based on his knowledge I had just put forward a proposition that contradicted itself. Impassively, he told me to repeat my views to Haldeman, a suggestion whose extreme ambiguity did not strike me for several weeks. When I did, Haldeman listened equally impassively and urged me to repeat my views to Ehrlichman. Ehrlichman, in turn, shrugged off the observation with the air of a man whose patience was barely equal — but might not always be — to my invincible ignorance of political matters.

Now that Watergate was about to explode, I pondered Nixon's options. I had my doubts about Garment's proposed solution. The vision of Nixon's putting himself at the head of a reform movement to clean up his own administration stretched credulity. Nor was it all that certain to work. A massive purge in the fifth year of a presidency raises profound doubts about the incumbent's judgment for not having spotted the malfeasance earlier. Moreover, I thought that Garment's diagnosis precluded his remedy. Anyone familiar with Nixon's way of conducting affairs would know that he needed a strong chief of staff to carry out *any* plan, that in the absence of delicate pressure from those he trusted he would procrastinate; his usual coolness under fire always needed reinforcement by trusted aides. In other words, only Haldeman could get Nixon to fire Haldeman, an unlikely proposition. If Haldeman was involved even indirectly, there was no one else to shepherd such a program past our chief's psychological defenses. On Garment's diagnosis the administration seemed headed for prolonged turmoil without a foreseeable outcome.

If this was true, my duty as I perceived it was to rally those unaffected by the catastrophe for the ordeal ahead. I asked Garment's permission to inform a few in the White House whose probity and integrity would help us preserve public confidence — George Shultz and Arthur Burns in particular. Garment agreed; I immediately set up a meeting for Sunday evening, the first time they were both available.

In the meantime, on Saturday evening, April 14, I attended the annual dinner tendered by the White House correspondents. The guest of honor is putatively the president, together with the cabinet. I say "putatively" because a point is usually reached in an administration — it came rather early in Nixon's — where the president feels that his daily harassment by the media exhausts his tolerance for their company. Listening to the uneven sarcasm that is the staple of these evenings is not a duty foreseen by the Constitution. Presidential attendance begins to slip. Nixon used his absence to pretend an imperviousness to the journalists assigned to cover him — only reinforcing the reciprocal hostility and sensitivity of the president and the press.

On this occasion, however, Nixon decided to show up. The evening went well enough; at least I remember no untoward incident, though the atmosphere was redolent with resentment. Afterward, several newspapers gave parties in various suites. While attending one of them, I was called to a phone. It was the president and he was highly agitated. It was not unusual for Nixon to call at all hours, nor for him to pose an odd-sounding question and hang up. But this evening the question sounded weird even for a late night call. "Do you agree," he asked "that we should draw the wagons around the White House?"

We know today from the mountains of Watergate revelations that the day had been one of frenzied meetings between Nixon, Haldeman, Ehrlichman, and former attorney general and campaign manager John Mitchell. But I was not aware of them. I would like to be able to report that I said something helpful or constructive to the obviously distraught president. But few advisers possess the fortitude to tell their president that they do not know what he is talking about, or that his query indicates a propensity toward melodrama. Nor did I feel up to it that evening. I mumbled something noncommittal that Nixon, not unreasonably, construed as assent. "All right," he said, "we will draw the wagons around the White House." He gave that enigmatic metaphor no further content before hanging up suddenly. Had it not been for my conversation with Garment a few hours earlier, I would not have known what agitated the president so much.

Stung, I mentioned Garment's worries to John Ehrlichman when he called me about something or other on Sunday, April 15. "Garment," replied Ehrlichman, equably enough, "is a nuclear overreactor. Pay no attention to him. Our major problem is to get John Mitchell to own up to his responsibility." Mitchell indeed! Did he have the major responsibility for the Watergate break-in — or was he chosen as the fall guy? I asked myself the question without any idea of the answer. What was clear was that if Mitchell was involved, the scandal would be uncontainable. John Mitchell, that epitome of loyalty, would never have acted without at least believing that he was carrying out presidential wishes. Indeed, whatever hypothesis one considered — Garment's, which saw Colson as the chief villain with Haldeman and Ehrlichman in supporting roles; or Ehrlichman's, which now apparently placed the blame on Mitchell — Watergate was bound to rock the nation. It simply was not credible, least of all to those of us who knew how the White House operated, that Nixon's paladins had acted totally on their own on a matter with such grave implications for the president.

Thus, unless it could be shown unambiguously that the president was not involved, we would soon face a monumental crisis of institutions. Clearly, the president was severely wounded. Whatever the unimaginable outcome, Nixon would have to alter his system of management. He would no longer be able to dominate the government through White House assistants, harassing or bypassing the regular bureaucracy. The trusted political aides who, as part of the postelection shake-up, had been placed into every key department as a means of keeping an eye on the cabinet member who was titular head, would lose their clout if not their positions. Challenges to White House predominance were increasingly probable. It was imperative to adopt rapidly a mode of government less dependent on solitary decisions at the top. However necessary existing procedures may have appeared to brave the Vietnam period, the moral, psychological, and political basis for them had now disappeared.

My meeting with George Shultz and Arthur Burns was the evening of that same Sunday, April 15, in Shultz's White House office. Shultz at that time combined the positions of secretary of the treasury and assistant to the president in charge of economic policy. Burns was chairman of the Federal Reserve Board but wielded a wider influence than that title would indicate. The later debacle of the Nixon administration has obscured the extent to which it included men and women of extraordinary character and intelligence.

Shultz had entered the cabinet as secretary of labor, had been moved to the Office of Management and Budget when it was given policymaking functions, and had succeeded John Connally as secretary of the treasury in the summer of 1972. I met no one in public life for whom I developed greater respect and affection. Highly analytical, calm, and unselfish, Shultz made up in integrity and judgment for his lack of the flamboyance by which some of his more insecure colleagues attempted to make their mark. He never sought personal advancement. By not threatening anyone's prerogatives, and, above all, by his outstanding performance, he became the dominant member of every committee he joined. He usually wound up being asked to sum up a meeting — a role that gave him influence without his aiming for it. If I could choose one American to whom I would entrust the nation's fate in a crisis, it would be George Shultz.

It was easy to underestimate Arthur Burns. As he puffed on his pipe while considering a proposition, he seemed to be a fuzzy-minded, slightly abstracted academic, and indeed he had been a professor at Columbia University for three decades. His deliberate manner of speaking might be occasionally taken by the unwary as a reflection of the pace of his mind. But Burns had an unusual ability to get swiftly to the heart of any problem. He was both brilliant and incredibly persistent; and he proved to be one of the canniest bureaucratic infighters in Washington. He had not been filling his pipe reflectively throughout the Eisenhower and Nixon administrations without studying and learning what made government tick. He worked patiently at lining up support for his position; he lost few battles while I observed him in action. Yet this did not diminish the admiration for his integrity, dedication, and subtle intelligence held by those of us whom he usually outmaneuvered.

When I confided Garment's news to my two colleagues they were at first unbelieving. But we all shared a sense of impotence. We did not know the dimensions of the looming scandal. We agreed to keep each other informed of whatever we learned; we would tell each other of conversations with the president relevant to our concerns so that we would, if possible, offer unified advice. We would try jointly to develop policies and initiatives to maintain the confidence of the American people in their government even in the midst of a political crisis. The administration had, after all, nearly four years to run; presumptuous as it may seem, we thought a duty had fallen on us to preserve as much moral substance for the national government as could be salvaged.

F EW PRESIDENTIAL ADMINISTRA-
tions have been free of scandal.
While presidents themselves are
not often implicated, one or more
presidential aides invariably get
themselves into trouble because of
conduct that the press and other outside critics perceive to be an abuse of
their position and power. Even the
most minor indiscretions are grist for
the political mill, as investigative reporters seek to cash in on their
scoops, and political opponents strive
for ascendancy.

Presidents largely determine the
ethical tone of their administrations.
Although most presidents have ad-
hered to the highest ethical standards
and have expected their aides to do
likewise, at least one major scandal
has accompanied most modern presi-
dencies. Presidential style and personality determine to a considerable
extent the way in which the White
House confronts and deals with the
reality of scandal. Whether or not
presidents stand by their accused
aides often depends upon White
House politics, an important part of
which is the president's need for loyal
and trusted advisers. A president faces
the most difficult dilemma when the
subject of a scandal is a long-time associate who has remained loyal to him
throughout his political career.

The following selection depicts the
different styles of modern presidents
from Franklin D. Roosevelt to Ronald
Reagan in dealing with their staffs and
cabinet members. The character of the
president, and his relationship with his
aides and top administration officials
can go a long way in determining
whether or not scandal will arise in the
first place, and if it does what the outcome will be.

16 David Wise
WHY THE PRESIDENT'S MEN STUMBLE

Almost unnoticed by official Washington, the Republican National
Committee recently hired Richard V. Allen as its foreign policy and
national security adviser. Allen, the former assistant to the president
for national security affairs, remains a consultant to the presidential
advisory board on foreign intelligence. He is also a "distinguished fellow" of the Heritage Foundation, a conservative research institution
with close ties to the Reagan administration.

For all of these august titles, Allen, at forty-six, is now a man on the
periphery of power. He was forced out last January in the first scandal
of the Reagan White House, a $1,000 "misunderstanding" that arose

The New York Times, July 18, 1982, page 14. © 1982 by The New York Times Company. Reprinted by permission.

when three visiting Japanese tried to hand the cash to Nancy Reagan after an interview Allen helped to arrange.

While the reasons that presidential advisers get into trouble vary widely, they may involve lack of judgment (often the case), outright larceny (rare), and past activities that come to light after an official reaches the White House (fairly frequent).

Ironically, in Richard Allen's departure was sown the seeds of the stunning resignation of Alexander M. Haig, Jr. as secretary of state six months later. Haig got rid of a rival when Allen left, but as part of the shuffle, the power of the president's national security adviser was restored to its traditional level. Allen had reported to presidential counselor Edwin Meese III. Allen's successor, William P. Clark, Jr., a former Haig aide, reports directly to President Reagan. And, by most accounts, Clark's growing power was a key factor in Haig's decision to quit.

Other members of President Reagan's inner circle have recently been the focus of embarrassing allegations:

A Federal special prosecutor found "insufficient credible evidence" to indict Secretary of Labor Raymond J. Donovan or to link him to organized-crime figures. A key witness in the inquiry was found murdered in a car trunk in lower Manhattan, leaving an untidy loose end to the affair that is still under investigation by the Justice Department and the Federal Bureau of Investigation. President Reagan has declared that he would "stick with" Mr. Donovan, but for how long is a matter of much conjecture.

Attorney General William French Smith, perhaps with one eye on a Supreme Court seat, decided to give back a $50,000 "severance payment" from a California company and to limit his tax deductions on two controversial drilling deals to the cash he actually invested.

Joseph W. Canzeri, who was supposed to be a presidential troubleshooter, himself got into trouble when it was disclosed that he had bought a town house with $400,000 borrowed from Laurance S. Rockefeller and Donald M. Koll, a California developer, neither of whom seemed to require any immediate interest payments. Canzeri, who was a deputy assistant to the president, also submitted expense claims for the same trips to both the Federal government and the Republican National Committee. (The Justice Department later absolved Canzeri on both counts, and he reimbursed the government for his trips.) When the storm broke, Canzeri, an old political hand who had worked for Nelson A. Rockefeller for seventeen years, knew what to do and resigned instantly.

Few modern presidents have been immune from staff troubles. Scandals, conflict-of-interest, and ethics cases involving White House aides have occurred with remarkable frequency since World War II. Of the eight postwar presidents, only John F. Kennedy and Gerald R. Ford, neither of whom served full terms, escaped major scandal among their closest advisers.

Why does it happen? Why do men at the pinnacle of power, presumably chosen because of their sure-footed political skills, regularly commit errors of judgment that embarrass the presidents they serve? Errors that at a minimum cause damaging publicity, or at worst lead to resignation, dismissal, or even prison.

On a quiet Saturday afternoon, James A. Baker III, chief of staff to President Reagan, and possibly the second most powerful man in America, sits in his large corner office in the White House, talking very softly and with surprising directness about the Richard Allen episode, and the dilemma such cases pose for a president.

As scandals go, the affair was somewhat unusual. Allen had, after all, been cleared of any misconduct by both the Justice Department and an internal White House investigation. Why, then, was he forced to walk the plank? Because the president or Mrs. Reagan had been embarrassed? Because he performed poorly on the National Security Council? Because he scrapped too much with Al Haig?

"I'd have to say it was probably a combination of those factors," Baker replies. But most important was "the political damage to the president. And the likelihood that the damage would continue well into the future."

"The president," continues Baker, "feels very strongly that you have to bend over backward to be fair. A career, a man's life, and reputation hangs in the balance. He also believes that you don't toss somebody over when he's being investigated. A president is really put to a choice of tossing somebody over the side and being inherently unfair, or taking the political damage that will result from not doing anything."

"It became clear to me that it wasn't going to subside," Baker says. "And the good of the president, and the good of the presidency, has to prevail whether someone's done something wrong or not."

In examining why the president's men fall from grace, one could, of course, begin with ethical or moral lapses by presidents themselves. Warren G. Harding experienced the joy of sex in the White House coat closet. Dwight D. Eisenhower accepted many thousands of dollars worth of equipment, livestock, and trees as gifts for his farm in Gettysburg, Pa. John F. Kennedy apparently shared the favors of a woman with a Mafia figure who was trying to assassinate Fidel Castro for the Central Intelligence Agency. Richard Nixon was an unindicted co-conspirator who accepted a presidential pardon from his successor, Gerald Ford, for all Federal crimes that he had "committed or may have committed" during Watergate. And President and Mrs. Reagan have been criticized for the more than $30,000 in gifts they have accepted since coming to the White House.

These cases — along with Spiro T. Agnew's alleged acceptance of more than $100,000 in bribes from Maryland contractors while governor and vice-president, which forced him to resign as vice-president — are fascinating, but they do not necessarily shed a great deal of light on the problem.

However, from extensive conversations with present White House aides, former presidential advisers — including some who were central figures in scandals — leading presidential scholars and present and former Washington correspondents, a fairly cohesive set of possible answers does emerge. Five factors recurred most often in the discussions: the tendency of power to cloud judgment, the effect of professional and personal backgrounds, the confusion created by a double standard of morality in government and in the private sector, the level of scrutiny focused on the White House, and the example set by the president himself.

"You sit next to the Sun King," says Jack Valenti, a former aide to President Lyndon B. Johnson, "and you bask in his rays, and you have those three magic words, 'the president wants.' And all of a sudden you have power unimagined by you before you sat in that job. And if you don't watch out, you begin to believe that it is your splendid intellect, your charm, and your insights into the human condition that give you all this power. You can go to the highest reaches of this government and abroad and cause an otherwise strong man to blink. That really has an effect on you."

"And even people who would like to discipline themselves are sometimes caught off guard," Valenti adds. "The arrogance sinks deeper into their veins than they think possible. What it does after a while is breed a kind of insularity that keeps you from being subject to the same fits of insecurity that most human beings have. Because you very seldom are ever turned down. You are lionized in Washington. There are stories in *Newsweek* and *Time* about how important you are. I'm telling you, this is like mainlining heroin. And while you are exercising it, it is so blinding and dazzling that you forget, literally forget, that it is borrowed and transitory power."

Joseph A. Califano, Jr., another former Johnson aide, remembers the day that work was completed on LBJ's first legislative program in 1965. The president told his cabinet that he could not personally coordinate every single issue. "And I'm just sitting there against the wall in the cabinet room, and Johnson says that Joe Califano's going to do this and when he speaks, that's my voice you hear. You know, that's fairly heady for a thirty-four-year-old kid from Brooklyn."

Johnson's former press secretary, George E. Reedy, has compared the executive mansion to a monarch's court. "After a while," he says, "it's very easy to get the impression that the whole world should revolve around you." Reedy, now a professor of journalism at Marquette University in Milwaukee, adds: "It's only derivative power, but that doesn't matter. Anyone that you call in the entire executive branch of the government is just going to be as respectful and subservient; it's incredible."

Joseph Laitin, who survived in the White House and in other senior government public affairs posts during six administrations, agrees that "a chemical change seems to come over you in that place, from the president on down to the messenger boy. A driver told me once that during the Eisenhower administration, one of the secretaries at the White House had to stay late, so she sent an Army sergeant in a White House car out to her house in the suburbs to turn on the lights so her cat wouldn't be lonely."

The privileges that go with a job in the White House add to the sense of power. Dom Bonafede, chief political correspondent for the *National Journal*, stresses the euphoric effect of the perquisites. "They have a car and chauffeur, if they're high enough up; the use of a swimming pool, and a tennis court, the presidential box at the Kennedy Center. They have their own mess, where they're served by Filipino stewards. They can requisition priceless paintings from government art galleries. They can even order furniture made for their office — they have their own cabinetmakers. After a while they think they're invulnerable, untouchable."

Typically, White House aides are young, and often have no administrative experience to prepare them for the vast responsibility they are suddenly called on to exercise. More often than not, they come straight from the campaign trail to the executive mansion. And the skills that may elect a president are not necessarily the same ones needed to run the government.

"The thing about the White House," emphasizes Robert J. Donovan, author of books about Presidents Truman, Eisenhower, and Kennedy, "is that every four or eight years you bring in a raft of amateurs to run the country. Can you imagine if IBM did that?"

In the Nixon White House, for example, John D. Ehrlichman had been a Seattle zoning lawyer, H. R. Haldeman had been an advertising man, and Ronald Ziegler, also a former ad man, had once been a tour guide on the Jungle Cruise boat at Disneyland.

Professor Thomas E. Cronin of Colorado College, a perceptive student of the American presidency, suggests that the kinds of people who go into public life and make it to the White House may also have a bearing on the problem. "You have to be a risk taker. You have to have a lot of ambition. Usually, you have to be someone with fundraising experience. And it's very difficult to separate fundraising from bribery. There's a very thin line." Cronin, a Democratic candidate for Congress in Colorado this year, also points out that "people involved in campaigns deal with the brutal realities, the sleazier aspects of our system. Often, people in politics have low pay and high expenses. And the temptations are high at the White House."

There is, too, the double standard of morality. "If we were to get a true norm of behavior of people similarly situated in the private sector," says Nelson W. Polsby, professor of political science at the University of California at Berkeley, "we would not view the political behavior of White House assistants as so deviant from that of people in other segments of society."

Robert Donovan agrees. "Look at the whole history of the human race," he says. "There has always been corruption. Corruption in business dwarfs corruption in government. Every year, white-collar crime runs into hundreds of millions of dollars. Take local zoning — my God. If you except something like Watergate, the White House may be quite clean."

Another veteran Washington journalist, James Deakin, who reported on numerous scandals as the longtime White House correspondent of the *St. Louis Post-Dispatch,* says: "You run into particular trouble with the businessmen. They've been running corporations, so it's inevitable that an awful lot of them come here and try to run the government like a business."

If a double standard of morality is applied in the case of public officials, who may be pilloried for behavior that would not seem out of place on Main Street or in the corporate suite, that is perhaps as it should be. Voters expect public officials to shed their private standards of morality when they enter the White House.

The intense level of press scrutiny under which presidential advisers operate may be another hazard. If a mid-level official in the Agriculture Department is wined and dined by a lobbyist in one of Washington's plush K Street restaurants, hardly anyone will notice, or care. But if Ed Meese goes for a moonlight sail on a lobbyist's yacht, it may well be noticed, and reported.

Although there has been more emphasis on "investigative reporting" since Watergate, the fact is that investigative reporting has been around much longer than the use of that term. It was, after all, a re-porter, Paul Y. Anderson of the *St. Louis Post-Dispatch,* who helped to force the reopening, after five years, of the Teapot Dome case, which sent a former cabinet member, Interior Secretary Albert B. Fall, to jail, and won Anderson a Pulitzer Prize.

Despite the Watergate scandal, we may not be living in a particularly corrupt political era. The nineteenth century — with its robber barons, the Crédit Mobilier financial thievery, the Whisky Ring liquor tax frauds, and the other scandals of the Grant administration — was not a time of overwhelming ethical purity. But in the climate of post-Watergate mo-rality, there may be an increased sensitivity to scandal on the part of the press and the public. There are more people peering in the fish-bowl. And, to some extent, the game has new rules. The Ethics in Gov-ernment Act of 1978, for example, requires senior government officials to make annual financial disclosure statements. Another provision of the same law provides for the appointment of a special prosecutor, or at least a preliminary investigation at the drop of an allegation.

Above all else, the president sets the tone. A Lyndon Johnson who, whatever his own flaws, rides herd tightly on his staff, may have less trouble than a Harry Truman, whose fierce loyalty and benign attitude toward his aides may be unappreciated by the electorate.

"The White House staff is what the president wants it to be," de-clares John Ehrlichman, counselor to President Nixon. "The Nixon White House was destroyed because Richard Nixon involved himself in Wa-tergate."

Ehrlichman says he has no knowledge of whether Nixon knew about the break-in at the Democratic National Committee headquarters be-forehand. But another former senior Nixon aide, who prefers to remain anonymous, says he has little doubt about it: "No way would anybody ever think of doing anything at all, even feeding King Timahoe, with-out checking with the president."

Alexander P. Butterfield, the presidential aide who revealed the ex-istence of the Watergate tapes, testified that Nixon concerned himself with whether or not salad should be served at state dinners and "whether or not the Secret Service would salute during 'The Star-Spangled Ban-ner,' and sing." "The president was 100 percent in charge," Butterfield concluded.

One obvious reason why White House staff scandals are, by and large, a postwar phenomenon is that prior to the administration of Franklin D. Roosevelt the White House staff, in the sense that it operates today, simply did not exist.

George Washington had exactly one staff assistant, his nephew,

Lawrence Lewis, whose salary he paid out of his own pocket. After Washington, other presidents had only one or two secretaries, usually relatives, also paid from personal funds. Not until Andrew Jackson moved into the White House was a government clerk assigned to assist the president.

By the beginning of the twentieth century, the White House payroll had begun to expand, but the staffs were still mostly clerks, file managers, and secretaries. With the coming of Franklin Roosevelt's New Deal, the picture changed measurably. "The president needs help," a study committee headed by Louis Brownlow, a public administration expert, wrote in 1937. And these White House aides, the report said in a phrase that was to become famous, should have "a passion for anonymity."

Two years later, FDR established the Executive Office of the President (EOP), an umbrella agency that today includes such key presidential units as the National Security Council and the Office of Management and Budget. Within the Executive Office is the smaller White House Office, also established in 1939. This is the group of men and women, mostly housed on the three floors of the West Wing, that is usually referred to as "the White House staff." Under Ronald Reagan, the EOP has 1,520 employees and an annual budget of $91,624,000. Of this total, the White House staff numbers 314 and costs $19,652,000 a year.

No major staff scandals surfaced under FDR, who kept everyone on a very tight leash. One of Roosevelt's brain trusters, the Washington attorney James H. Rowe, Jr., recalls: "Once, FDR saw my name in the paper, in a story saying I'd been at a cocktail party. 'If I see your name in the paper much more,' he told me, 'you'll need a new job.' "

Rowe, who was twenty-eight when he went to work in the White House in 1938, thinks youth had something to do with the New Deal's relative purity. "They were mostly young, idealistic people and they didn't know how to steal. People weren't interested in money. I don't even remember being offered anything."

"Another reason,' Rowe says, "was Harold Ickes's goons. They were all over the place," toiling for Ickes in his dual capacity as Interior Security and Public Works Administrator. "Once, a top lawyer for Ickes found that his mail had been opened by Ickes's security men. It was a dividend check from AT&T. The lawyer was outraged, but Ickes said, 'Well, we wanted to know why you were getting mail from big corporations'!"

"There were three Democratic national committeemen who came here and opened up law practices," Rowe recalls. "Roosevelt announced publicly one day that they'd all resigned from the national committee. They hadn't! But then two of them did. FDR watched that sort of thing, but there wasn't much of it."

FDR's staff had at least one blot on its record, however. It centered on Louis McHenry Howe, the gnomelike former newspaperman who served as Roosevelt's secretary. Frank Freidel, author of a multivolume biography of Roosevelt, recalled "the Civilian Conservation Corps' 'mess kit' scandal early in the New Deal. Howe had arranged with some old friend of Roosevelt's — not a very savory character — to sell 200,000 mess kits to the CCC boys at a very high price. But there wasn't a nickel in it for Howe."

Gifts to White House aides — sometimes linked to official favors by the recipients, sometimes not — have frequently figured in the troubles that have caused scandal in the president's house. Perhaps the quintessential gift taker was President Truman's jovial, poker-playing friend and aide, Major General Harry H. Vaughan, who indelibly stamped the word "crony" on the history of the Truman administration.

"Vaughan and Truman met as young lieutenants during World War I," says Robert Donovan. "Vaughan was not in any sense a corrupt man. But the White House was not the place for him. He was used to doing favors for people when Truman was vice-president, and he carried that mentality over into the White House."

"Vaughan got in trouble," says Donovan, "because a friend visiting the White House overheard him talking on the telephone about Mrs. Truman's problems with food spoilage out in Independence. Next thing you know, seven freezers were being shipped. Vaughan got one, for the White House Mess, and so did Mrs. Truman." Vaughan kept a freezer for himself and the rest went to other Truman administration officials.

Professor Richard E. Neustadt of Harvard University, who worked for a time in the Truman White House as a budget aide and later as a special assistant, may be the only eminent scholar of the presidency to have actually eaten a meal prepared from Harry Vaughan's freezer: "Early in the Truman administration, they organized a little lunchroom for the staff down in the basement of the West Wing. Vaughan talked some messenger at the White House into serving as chef. They had a crummy old stove and used to serve terrible meals. Vaughan went around scrounging free, cast-off equipment for the galley. Somebody gave him a freezer. After that — great scandal."

To the Republicans, at least, the freezers became the symbol of the Truman administration, along with the $8,540 royal pastel mink coat that a Washington lawyer, Colonel Joseph Rosenbaum, bestowed upon a White House stenographer, Lauretta Young, whose husband, an influence peddler, specialized in obtaining loans for businessmen from the Reconstruction Finance Corporation.

Gifts were also the undoing of Harry Truman's appointments secretary, Matthew J. Connelly, who served six months in a Federal prison after accepting a $3,600 oil royalty, a topcoat, and two suits from the lawyer representing a St. Louis shoe manufacturer, for whom Connelly intervened in a tax case. In all, nine Truman administration officials served prison sentences.

"The Truman scandals were serious," says Robert Donovan, "but not even Truman's worst enemies ever connected him with any of the scandals. After all these years, one is confident Truman was an honest politician. He never had any money."

Dwight Eisenhower promised to clean up "the mess in Washington." But during his first presidential campaign, the "Nixon Fund" story broke, revealing that a group of California businessmen had contributed $18,235 to pay Nixon's political expenses as a senator. Nixon went on national television and delivered his celebrated "Checkers" speech, declaring: "Pat doesn't have a mink coat. But she does have a respectable Republican cloth coat."

None of the string of scandals that ensued in the Eisenhower administration reached directly into the White House until Sherman Adams, the president's chief of staff, got into trouble. Adams, a former governor of New Hampshire, was generally portrayed as a man of granitelike integrity, the last person who would be mixed up with a wheeler-dealer textile manufacturer like Bernard Goldfine. So the shock was even greater when it was revealed that he had accepted a $700 vicuña coat from Goldfine and intervened on his behalf with two Federal regulatory agencies who were after Goldfine for, among other sins, mislabeling his wool (Goldfine's vicuña contained nylon). Although Adams had accepted more than $6,000 in gifts and hospitality from Goldfine, it was the coat that remained fixed in the public's mind.

In testimony before the House subcommittee investigating the case, Adams conceded that he could have acted "a little more prudently." The next day, Eisenhower defended his staff chief and declared, "I need him." Harry Vaughan graciously offered Adams the use of his freezer in which to store the vicuña coat over the warm summer months. Adams hung on until fall, but when the Republicans lost the Senate and gubernatorial elections and two of three House seats in Maine that September, Adams had to go.

John F. Kennedy's White House was, more or less, scandal-free, although Frank D. Reeves, a special assistant to the president, was forced to resign when it was disclosed that he had been billed by the District of Columbia for $741.90, in delinquent taxes.

According to Meyer Feldman, a Washington attorney who handled highly sensitive economic matters as an assistant to President Kennedy, a very big contributor to the Kennedy campaign complained incessantly about the extended antitrust investigation of his company by the Justice Department under Robert Kennedy. Feldman finally arranged a face-to-face meeting with the president. At the conclusion of the campaign contributor's argument, Feldman says, President Kennedy looked at the man and said, 'Mr. ———, there's one thing wrong with this administration. We don't have an attorney general we can fix.' "

Despite Lyndon Johnson's reputation as a wheeler-dealer, and his involvement with Robert G. (Bobby) Baker — who went to prison for crimes committed while a Senate aide to LBJ — the Johnson White House was considered generally free of scandal except for the Walter Jenkins case. Last October, however, an article in the *Atlantic* charged that Johnson, as a congressman and vice-president, accepted "envelopes stuffed with cash," which he used to help the campaigns of other politicians, and as president handled business affairs that were supposed to be in a blind trust. When the author of the article, Robert Caro, was criticized for not documenting his charges, he said he would do so in the first volume of a book about Johnson to be published in a year's time.

Jack Valenti thinks he knows why the Johnson administration fared as well as it did: "Johnson bullied, humiliated, harassed his assistants, saying, 'You never ran for sheriff and all these people are courting you. By God, they want you — Valenti, Moyers, Califano — because they think you've got my ear. You think it's because they like you? They don't give a ——— about you, but they damn sure give a ——— about what you can do through me, so by God, you'd better be careful.'

"Nobody in the Johnson White House could ever make an appointment for anyone at Treasury, Defense, or the Justice Department. He used to say, 'Remember Matt Connelly, remember Matt Connelly. One day you'll make an appointment over in Defense and the ——— will turn out to be a fraud and you'll be up before some Senate committee answering questions, and you won't be able to answer them right and they'll put you in jail. By God, I'm not going to have it, and I'm going to fire your ——— or anybody else's that ever violates that rule.' As a result, we were frightened to death of something like that."

LBJ's dire warnings apparently worked. The one exception was Walter Jenkins, who was arrested on a morals charge at a YMCA one block from the White House in the midst of the 1964 presidential campaign. Valenti was in New York with Johnson at the Walforf Astoria when press secretary George Reedy called with the doleful news. "The president was very stony-faced," recalls Valenti. "He said, 'George, get Walter's resignation immediately.' Now, you have to understand, this man was like a brother to Johnson; he'd been with him for twenty-five years. But he did not hesitate. Because he was going to protect the presidency."

The trouble that Jenkins, married and the father of six children, got into was, of course, of a different nature from the conflict-of-interest or corruption cases that felled other White House aides.

There is an epilogue to that story that is not generally known. Johnson, Valenti says, "never saw Walter while he was president, after that. But the minute he got out of the White House he resumed his long friendship with Jenkins."

Under Richard Nixon, who found it necessary to proclaim that he was not a crook, the White House became involved in a continuing scandal that ultimately consumed and destroyed his presidency. There were enemies lists, wiretaps, break-ins and buggings, as well as obstruction of justice, perjury, political spying, forgery, and other high and low crimes and misdemeanors. These were the men, Senator Lowell P. Weicker, Jr. said at the start of the Senate Watergate hearings, "who almost stole America." An astonishing ten top White House aides marched off to jail before it was over: H. R. Haldeman, John D. Ehrlichman, Charles W. Colson, John W. Dean III, E. Howard Hunt, Jr., G. Gordon Liddy, Dwight L. Chapin, Egil Krogh, Jr., Jeb Stuart Magruder, and Herbert L. Porter. And Richard Nixon became the first American president forced to resign his office in utter disgrace.

Gerald Ford's staff was not around long enough to get into much trouble, and its members were presumably a bit cautious, in the wake of Watergate. But trouble was not long in coming to Jimmy Carter's White House. The tangled and dubious banking practices of his close friend and budget director, Bert Lance, were making headlines by the summer of 1977. Most of Lance's questionable activities had taken place before he joined the administration, but by defending Lance instead of dismissing him outright, Carter compounded his difficulties. Lance did not resign until that September.

The embarrassments continued. Three months after Lance left, guests at a dinner party attended by Egyptian Ambassador Ashraf Ghorbal and his wife reported that presidential assistant Hamilton Jordan had peered down Mrs. Ghorbal's cleavage and remarked that he had always wanted to "see the pyramids." Jordan denied the allegation, but soon afterward the columnist Rudy Maxa wrote in the *Washington Post Magazine* that Jordan had spit Amaretto and cream down the front of a young woman's blouse at a Washington singles bar, a report that led the House Minority Leader, Representative Robert H. Michel, Republican of Illinois, to comment that the Carter administration had "gone from great expectations to great expectorations." The Carter White House put out thirty-three pages of documents in an effort to refute the story.

Then Dr. Peter G. Bourne, Carter's principal adviser on drugs and narcotics, had to quit because he wrote a false name on a drug prescription for his assistant, Ellen J. Metsky. And special prosecutors found insufficient evidence to act on separate allegations that Jordan and Tim Kraft, another White House aide, had used cocaine, which both denied. The cases took place against an obbligato of murky charges about the financial operations of the Carter family peanut warehouse and, of course, "Billygate," which involved $220,000 in "loans" to the president's brother, Billy, from the government of Libya.

Which brings us back up to President Reagan and Richard Allen. In an interview with this writer, Allen charged that "the real reasons" he was forced out were "to eliminate my views" on foreign policy. He said that he and Alexander Haig had "important and enduring policy differences, reflecting on the one hand one fellow's determination to uphold the mandate on which the president of the United States was elected, versus having that mandate supplanted."

Allen admits to "human error" in handling the $1,000 that the Japanese visitors attempted to give to Mrs. Reagan. Allen says he "intercepted" the money and told a secretary to turn it over to "appropriate officials" but that she forgot. "I suppose, with 20/20 hindsight, you could have given it back." But he didn't, and he was out. And, like a character in a Kafka novel, he was never really sure what the charges against him were.

In fairness to Allen, almost no one in the White House, even now, fully understands the complex, overlapping laws and regulations governing acceptance, or handling, of gifts. In general, small gifts are all right and large ones are not, but how big is small? Things were easier in the old days when there were no size limits. Calvin Coolidge accepted a hippopotamus from Liberia.

"If you want to get along, go along," House Speaker Sam Rayburn was fond of saying. It is perhaps in the nature of politics for the players to go along, to engage in a wide variety of favors, back scratching, and mutual aid and admiration. In politics, a "contract" refers not to a written agreement but to an understanding to use one's influence to help a political friend; both sides know that the favor may have to be returned sometime. It is easy enough for political operators to carry that attitude into the White House where it could cause them major difficulties.

No doubt, there are other reasons why presidential appointees continue to get into trouble. Perhaps one is the national appetite for scandal. Both press and public seem to relish the fall from grace of a high official. This is particularly true in the nation's capital: Washington loves a victim.

Americans, observes Professor Cronin, are proud of their country but "hate government and politicians; always have. I think Americans yearn for flaws in politicians. So when scandals break, they say, 'There, that's just what I expected.' There's a great distrust of politicians. It's one of the reasons we designed a system of checks and balances. If men were angels, we would need no government."

THE
CONGRESS

Chapter
Five

Congress is a fascinating amalgam of individual characters, personalities, and styles, which help to shape the institution. Personality is particularly important as it affects congressional leadership, both of party leaders and of committee chairmen. Different personality types in positions of power within Congress develop contrasting styles that influence the way Congress operates. For example, the Senate under the majority leadership of Lyndon B. Johnson operated very differently than it did under Mike Mansfield. Johnson's active-negative character was evident in the Senate as in the White House. His personality compelled him to seek control over the Senate, which he managed through knowledge of the strengths, weaknesses, and needs of his colleagues, skill in manipulation of institutional procedures, and an extraordinary ability to persuade others. Each senator became a challenge to Johnson, who sought personal loyalty above all else. The aggressive and dominating style of Lyndon Johnson as majority leader of the Senate was similar to, but much more flamboyant than that of his mentor, House Speaker Sam Rayburn, and it stemmed from different personal needs.

In sharp contrast to Johnson's style as majority leader was the style of Mike Mansfield, who was elected majority leader in January 1961, and served until his retirement at the end of the Ninety-fourth Congress in 1976. Mansfield's style was, to say the least, more muted than Johnson's. He treated each senator with great respect and as an equal. No attempt at a personal cult of leadership was evident during Mansfield's tenure. Johnson was highly effective as a personal leader, whereas Mansfield's effectiveness was as a team player. The contrasting personalities of Johnson and Mansfield go a long way toward explaining differences in Senate operation during their periods of leadership. Under Mansfield, senators were far freer to pursue their own legislative interests without fear of retaliation if they happened to disagree with the majority leader. Mansfield's style became the model for his successor, Robert Byrd. Howard Baker too leads by consensus, not by command,

217

in a Senate that would no longer tolerate LBJ's system of unilateral control.

Personality is as important in the House as in the Senate in determining who runs for positions of party leadership, and what their styles of leadership will be. Sam Rayburn, Speaker of the House for seventeen years, enforced discipline in the House. Like Lyndon Johnson in the Senate, Sam Rayburn knew every member of the House, their constituencies, and their needs and aspirations. He was able to use this information to consolidate his power as Speaker. Again like Johnson, Rayburn operated on a highly personal basis in the House. The House was his constituency, as the Senate was Johnson's, and he did not hesitate to involve Republicans as well as Democrats in his decisions as Speaker. The election of John McCormack as Speaker of the House in 1962 brought about profound changes, primarily because of the contrasting personalities of Rayburn and McCormack. Robert L. Peabody says:

> Peaceful succession brings on more incremental change, but the impact of such *different personalities* as Rayburn and McCormack on the Office of the Speaker was considerable. McCormack's style was both more institutional and partisan than Rayburn's. He called more meetings to discuss legislative strategy and involved the Majority Leader and Whip to a much greater extent than Rayburn did. . . .
> The telephone was one of McCormack's most effective weapons — "I'd call the Devil if I thought it would do any good." In contrast, Rayburn operated on a more independent and personal basis. He preferred the intimacy and informality of after-the-session gatherings of the "Board of Education." The Whip organization was used less frequently and Rayburn almost never called a party caucus beyond the opening meeting.[1]

Both Rayburn and McCormack, although differing in their personalities and styles, provided effective leadership to the House. Carl Albert, of Oklahoma, became Speaker in 1971, and his personality and style were criticized as weak and ineffective. Peabody points out that "One reason he easily advanced to the Speakership was summed up in a widely affirmed statement — 'Nobody's mad at Carl.' "[2] Being a "nice guy" is usually a reflection of inability to make hard decisions that inevitably antagonize others.

After an extensive analysis of congressional leadership, Peabody concludes:

[1] Robert L. Peabody, *Leadership in Congress* (Boston: Little, Brown, 1976), p. 309. Italics added.

[2] Ibid., p. 155.

218

Of the twenty variables highlighted in this analysis, the most pervasive and continuing influence upon leadership's selection for party office has been exerted by the personality and skill of the candidate and, especially, of the incumbent. Every leader in Congress, as in other organizations, brings to office a unique set of characteristics: age, ambition, education, health, personal skills, prior political and professional experience — in sum, a personality. Not only does this personality affect the opportunities he may have to obtain a leadership position, they also, in part, influence the extent to which he can maintain office and perhaps even alter the scope and potential of a given party position. A leader's personality, his strengths and liabilities, also is the single most important variable that affects his ability to withstand or succumb to a challenge.[3]

Personality is also a factor in the selection of committees and in the functioning of committee chairmen. The Senate Government Operations Committee (renamed the Governmental Affairs Committee in 1977), under the chairmanship of Senator Joseph McCarthy from 1953 until 1955 operated very differently than it has at any other time. The personality and the style of Senator McCarthy were responsible for this difference. The Senate Foreign Relations Committee under the chairmanship of Senator J. William Fulbright from 1959 until his defeat in 1974 was quite different than it became in 1975 under the chairmanship of Senator John Sparkman of Alabama.

South Carolina Republican Strom Thurmond runs the Senate Judiciary Committee in an entirely different way than did his predecessor, Massachusetts Senator Edward Kennedy.

Weak chairmen, strong chairmen, chairmen who seek the limelight, and those who use chairmanships for "grand-standing," all have contrasting personalities and styles. The committee system is an important institution of Congress, and the way it functions largely depends on the personalities of committee members. Committees are used to advance the goals of their chairmen and key members, who are attempting to gain power and status within and without Congress. Thus the legislative work of committees is often undertaken as much to serve personal ambition as to respond to constituents' needs; legislators may use the committee hearing and investigation process for personal aggrandizement, as well as for legislation.

[3] Ibid., p. 498.

TENNESSEE REPUBLICAN HOWard Baker's Senate career began in 1966, when the Democrats had firmly controlled the body for thirty of the preceeding thirty-four years. The Democrats, particularly those from the South whose seniority awarded them committee chairmanships, had profoundly shaped the character of the institution. The minority did not really exist in an important sense. Not only were the Republicans denied access to committee chairmanships, they were not allocated staff, which is an important adjunct of power in the Senate, on an equal basis with the majority members.

While Republican senators were excluded from committee chairmanships and other perquisites of power, they could still be a decisive legislative force in a body where party discipline was difficult if not impossible to maintain. Howard Baker's father-in-law, the wily and flamboyant Senator Everett McKinley Dirksen of Illinois, exercised extraordinary power as Senate minority leader from 1959 until his death in 1969. Dirksen often held his Republican colleagues together, joining with Southern Democrats to make a voting majority on important legislative issues.

Howard Baker lost no time in announcing his candidacy for minority leader after Dirksen's death, even though he had served for less than three years. One of his Senate colleagues said of Baker at the time, "He has a great deal of charisma. He's an eloquent speaker — there isn't a member here who wouldn't welcome Baker coming into his state to speak for him at a fundraising dinner or political rally. He handles himself well on the floor."[1] Baker lost his first race for the minority leadership by a 19–24 vote. Oregon Senator Robert Packwood, one of Baker's supporters, commented after the vote, "We had most of those who were philosophically tuned to Howard, and we had many of the younger members who wanted newer, more dynamic leadership. But there were just enough older members who couldn't bring themselves to vote for a guy who had only been here for two and one-half years."[2] Baker lost to Pennsylvania Senator Hugh Scott, a Capitol Hill and party veteran, who had been elected to the Senate in 1958.

Baker finally won a close contest for the minority leadership position in 1977. Never did he dream that some day he would become majority leader, but the conservative tide in 1980 that swept Reagan into the White House also voted for a Republican Senate. Baker was again chosen to be the Republican leader, but this time on the majority tide. The following selection describes Baker's personality and political style, which have made him the head Republican on Capitol Hill.

[1] Robert L. Peabody, Leadership in Congress (Boston: Little, Brown and Co., 1976), p. 430.

[2] Ibid., p. 434.

17 Martin Tolchin
HOWARD BAKER: POWER IN THE SENATE

Midnight had passed, and the Capitol was all but deserted, the echoes of occasional footsteps reverberating on tile floors. Outside room S230, the office of the Senate majority leader, a dozen reporters clustered, awaiting word from within where a dozen congressional leaders were in a deadlock on a major budget item with an administration group that included James A. Baker III, the White House chief of staff; and Treasury Secretary Donald T. Regan.

The reporters milled about impatiently, missing deadlines, until finally the door opened just a crack to reveal the majority leader himself, Tennessee's Howard H. Baker, Jr. He pointed his Leica at the reporters, focused, snapped off a few shots and, with a slight shrug, returned to the battle, carefully closing the door behind him.

Weeks later, in that same office, which looks out over the Mall and the Washington Monument, Senator Baker recalled the incident. "I knew what I wanted to do," he said, in his soft, measured way. "When the door opened, I wanted to take a picture of whatever was out there. I got a great picture."

The camera is never far from Howard Baker's side. No matter how deeply involved he becomes in affairs of state, he is never so involved that he does not pause to capture the moment on film. Part of him is always detached.

"There are two tracks in my personality," he said. "One of them tries hard to do the job here. The other runs along more or less parallel, sort of watching what's going on."

Was it an overstatement to say that the camera reflected his own view of himself as an outsider? "No, it's not," he replied. Did he, for example, feel an outsider at the White House? "I am, and always have been," he said — and then, gesturing at his Senate surroundings, added, "and sort of an outsider here."

Mr. Outside and Mr. Inside, observer and participant, casual and calculating, Howard Baker is a hard man to pigeonhole. Those who know him have different ideas as to his personality, his politics, his goals. His public image as a political moderate, for example, is at odds with his substantially conservative voting record. Yet there is basic agreement among both his friends and foes in the Senate that Mr. Baker last year compiled one of the most extraordinary records in the history of that body — keeping the frail Republican majority intact on vote after

vote with occasional forays into opposition ranks; consistently out-
flanking, outthinking, and outfighting the Democratic leadership.

"He's a genius at finding the compromise point and pushing it
through," said Senator Jim Sasser, Mr. Baker's Democratic colleague
from Tennessee. And on a snappy February morning, at the other end
of Pennsylvania Avenue, a newcomer to Washington added his praise.
As sun streamed into the Oval Office, and a fire crackled in the fire-
place, President Reagan told a visitor: "I'm frank to say that I don't
think we could have had the successes that we've had up there without
his leadership." . . .

Howard Henry Baker, Jr. was born to politics on Nov. 15, 1925, in
Huntsville in the eastern, Republican part of Tennessee. His paternal
grandfather was a judge; his maternal grandmother, a county sheriff,
and his father served in Congress from 1951 until his death in 1964.
Then his stepmother took over the House seat.

Young Howard and his two sisters grew up as gentry among the
hillbillies. "The first thing that happened to me that had a jolting effect," the Senator recalled, "was when my mother died. I was eight.
Next thing after that was when my father remarried. I was eleven. I
resented her. It took a while for all that to settle down."

After high school at the McCallie military academy in Chattanooga,
he enlisted in the Navy's V-12 program and studied engineering, receiving his Navy commission just in time for the Japanese surrender.
Mr. Baker went on to the University of Tennessee Law School, where
he was elected student-body president. He ran on a platform that called
for mending fences between fraternity members and the independents
on campus — an early example of Mr. Baker's lifelong devotion to coalition politics.

Shortly after graduation, he wed Everett Dirksen's daughter, Joy. Says
Professor John Bakke of Memphis State University, a student of the senator's career: "His marriage could not have been better politically arranged if it had been made in the courts of Europe." (The Bakers have
two children, Darek, 29, a computer specialist, and Cissy, 26, who is
continuing the family tradition by running for Congress in Tennessee's
Fourth District.)

Howard Baker set out to carve a court career, specializing in murder
trials. A long-time idol was Ray Jenkins of Knoxville, who later served
as special counsel during the Army-McCarthy hearings. "The most successful bit of courtroom theater I've ever seen," Mr. Baker once said,
"was Ray Jenkins representing the victim's family. He just sat there in
the hot courthouse, with the sweat from his face dripping down on a
grindstone, and stroked the murder weapon back and forth, sharpening
the blade on the wet stone." In time, Mr. Baker himself won fame in
Tennessee courtrooms as "Old Two-to-Ten" in honor of the low prison

terms his clients received. He also prospered as attorney for coal operators, insurance companies, and banks and on a major investment in lumber.

In 1964, when his father died, Howard Baker might have easily taken the vacant House seat, but he left that to his stepmother and chose to try for the Senate. He was buried in the Lyndon Johnson landslide. Two years later, he ran for another seat and won, the first Tennessee Republican ever to be popularly elected to the Senate. During that interval, he had made at least one dramatic change in his stance. With Barry Goldwater at the top of the ticket, Mr. Baker had said he would have voted against the Civil Rights Act had he been in the Senate. By 1966, he had reversed himself and was able to capture a sizable number of minority voters in Boss Ed Crump's Memphis, a conservative Democratic stronghold, along with many a moderate Democrat. Asked to explain the change, Mr. Baker said: "It took from 1964 to 1966 to convince me that I had been wrong."

It did him no harm to have the endorsement of the liberal Nashville newspaper, *The Tennessean.* "I really thought he represented a moderate, stable approach to government," said John Seigenthaler, the editor and publisher, who also was impressed with Mr. Baker's character. "There are things that Howard Baker will not do. There are things he will not say. You can count on him to be rational. He cleaves to the middle of the road as if the Holy Grail was there."

In Washington, the Senator went his own way, socially and politically, eschewing the party circuit, growing roses in the greenhouse of his luxurious rented home just off embassy row. Mr. Baker still spends at least one weekend a month in his ancestral and emotional home in Huntsville, which boasts acres of rolling lawns and the county's first tennis court.

In the Senate, Mr. Baker often differed with his father-in-law on legislative issues — the principle of one man, one vote, for example, which Mr. Baker supported.

When Senator Dirksen died shortly after Labor Day, 1969, Mr. Baker's aides passed the word that he would campaign for the job. "It wasn't appreciated," said one legislative veteran. "He had been in the Senate only two and a half years." Hugh Scott of Pennsylvania, the candidate of the Northeast liberals, was elected to the post, and Senator Robert Griffin of Michigan was appointed whip.

Senator Baker handily won reelection in 1972 and 1978. Much of his national exposure came because of his habit of helping presidents, regardless of party. His first major test was as the ranking Republican and vice-chairman of the Senate Watergate committee. At the hearings, he sought to separate Mr. Nixon from the actions of his underlings, pounding away at an artful question, "What did the President know and when did he know it?" According to John Seigenthaler, Mr. Baker thought Mr. Nixon would be absolved. "The meanness of the Nixon administration," he said, "is something Howard Baker did not believe."

During the brief presidency of Gerald R. Ford, Mr. Baker was a loyal supporter in the Senate and supported Mr. Ford in his 1976 primary campaign against Ronald Reagan. There was speculation that he might have been Mr. Ford's vice-presidential running mate but for a family problem. Upon the death of her father, in 1969, Joy Baker developed a drinking problem, and subsequently became one of the first political wives to tell the public of her battle against alcoholism.

Mr. Baker also cooperated with the Carter White House. According to Stuart Eizenstat, chief domestic adviser, Mr. Carter highly valued Senator Baker's help on domestic issues, such as energy legislation, as well as on the Panama Canal treaties.

In 1977, with the retirement of Hugh Scott from the minority leader's post, Howard Baker ran hard for the job and won it, narrowly defeating Senator Griffin. As his floor duties increased, many Tennesseans thought they noted a growing lack of interest on the part of the senator in local politics. That has not always been the case. One controversial instance: his cosponsoring of legislation for the government to purchase a tract of land owned by a Tennessee company which Mr. Baker had once served as lawyer and director. Even last year, during the budget-cutting crunch in the Senate, such major Tennessee projects as the Clinch River breeder reactor and the Tennessee-Tombigbee Waterway had miraculous survival powers. Yet Mr. Baker has given nearly all state patronage to Governor Lamar Alexander, a longtime Baker protégé, and Mr. Baker himself says of the governor, "He is the head of the Republican Party in Tennessee."

In fact, there was a feeling that Howard Baker was becoming bored with his Senate job itself, that he was ready to retire when his term ended in 1984. Then came the Reagan victory. Suddenly, it was a new ball game in the Senate, with a Republican majority and the majority leader's post waiting to be filled. Any thoughts of retirement vanished as Mr. Baker thought of the new challenges and opportunities up for grabs.

He was an automatic and vigorous contender, but there were potential problems. The freshman class of senators was, as a group, considerably to the right of Mr. Baker. Many of them, for example, had not forgiven him for supporting the Panama Canal treaties. He knew that his only potential challenger was Senator Paul Laxalt of Nevada, a conservative who also happened to be the president's closest friend in the Senate. But was he in the race? The day after the election, Mr. Baker called Senator Laxalt at 7 A.M. Nevada time with a request. He asked Mr. Laxalt to nominate him as majority leader.

"If Laxalt says 'no,' I know I have a problem," Senator Baker told an aide. "If he says 'yes,' I know I'm home free." Mr. Laxalt readily agreed to speak for Mr. Baker. "There's very little enthusiasm for that job from former governors," Mr. Laxalt said in an interview afterward. "We've been there. That's heavy responsibility. That's being on the point."

The Republican members of the United States Senate had spent the better part of a quarter-century perfecting their skills as guerrilla fighters in innumerable parliamentary ambushes; they had freely indulged their individual egos and ideologies — "the luxury of being dissidents," as Senator Mark O. Hatfield, Republican of Oregon, put it. The dawn of the Reagan era changed that. Said Mr. Hatfield: "We had to make this thing work."

The presence of Ronald Reagan in the White House was a central factor; the Republican senators wanted him to succeed, and they knew that it was he who set the congressional agenda. But the explosive personal and ideological mix in the Senate had to be harnessed, and, for that task, Howard Baker was the key. "If you're looking for somebody who could put us all in a pot and make us come to a boil," said Senator Dole, "he's the one. He's the chef."

As the Republican minority leader of the Senate in the 1960s, Everett Dirksen, Mr. Baker's father-in-law, had been famous for his oracular, highhanded approach to the job — threatening, for example, to withhold coveted committee assignments or hold back floor action on particular legislation as a means of forcing recalcitrant senators to vote the party line. It was a familiar technique in an era when senators spent a lifetime in the chamber, amassing political IOUs and nursing grudges. Today, fifty-four senators are in their first term. They have little sense of institutional devotion and no disposition to be bullied.

Howard Baker's approach to the job reflected the changing makeup of the Senate — he enlarged attendance at leadership meetings, for example, inviting freshmen and those with a special interest in the particular piece of legislation under discussion. His approach also reflected a very different personality: Mr. Baker is a patient builder of coalitions, generous with his time and slow to anger. He is also one of the great listeners of all time and a man of considerable personal charm and humor. Last year, for example, when Senator Slade Gorton, Republican of Washington, wondered why the majority leader was sitting out a debate, Mr. Baker offered one of his down-home epigrams: "Ain't got no dog in this fight."

Not that calm always prevailed. "There were times when we'd be shouting," Senator Hatfield recalled, "and Senator Baker would say, 'Let me turn up my hearing aid.' He'd let everyone talk and talk, and then he'd say, 'I want you and you and you to get together and talk this thing over and give me a brief memo on the options.' This created a delay, and by the time we came back, we'd gotten it out of our system. More times than not, we'd come to some consensus."

Howard Baker's first legislative campaign as majority leader was the effort to win Senate approval for the raising of the debt limit to $1 trillion. Democrats in years past had generally voted for such measures — and then been forced to listen to Republican candidates portray them as wasteful big spenders on the basis of that vote. This time, the Democrats announced, they would vote to extend the debt limit only if a majority of the Republicans voted for the measure. Mr. Baker's problem: Thirteen of the sixteen Republican freshmen, having campaigned on a hold-down-the-debt platform, flatly refused to reverse themselves, even at the president's request.

The majority leader turned for help to conservative veterans, including Strom Thurmond, John Tower of Texas, and Pete Domenici of New Mexico. He put them together with the recalcitrant freshmen. "You guys are all rookies on this team," Senator Tower told them, "and the quarterback has called a play." In the end, Mr. Baker had his votes.

His greatest come-from-behind victory last year — and a case study of the skills the majority leader's job requires — was in persuading the Senate not to block a proposed sale of five Awacs radar planes to Saudi Arabia. "We had twelve votes when we started on this thing," Senator Baker recalled. The House had been against the sale by the lopsided vote of 301–111. A resolution of disapproval had been sponsored by fifty senators — just one vote short of the number required to shelve the sale.

Mr. Baker's first move was to convince the White House to make a new approach to the Saudis, seeking their acceptance of some scaling down of the package, but the Saudis balked. Then he reached out to Democrats, including Sam Nunn of Georgia, an expert on military affairs, and David Boren of Oklahoma, head of the informal conservative caucus of Senate Democrats. He also appealed for help from John Warner, Republican of Virginia, a former secretary of the navy.

The answer came, Mr. Baker said, from Senators Warner and Nunn — the idea for a letter from the president to the Senate, containing assurances that the Saudis had consented to a "detailed plan" as to just how the Awacs would be used. "Jim Baker and I took that and started building on it," Senator Baker said.

One early turning point was in the Foreign Relations Committee, where the vote of Senator Larry Pressler, Republican of South Dakota, spelled the difference between victory and defeat. The majority leader put in a call to Maxwell Rabb, ambassador to Italy and a personal friend of Mr. Pressler's. From Mr. Rabb, Mr. Baker learned that Senator Pressler felt he needed a telephone call from the president requesting his vote. Mr. Baker called the president who, a scant twelve minutes later, telephoned Senator Pressler. The South Dakotan thereupon informed the committee that he had just heard from the White House and that he was going to vote for the sale.

The battle was tough and gritty, with the outcome in doubt as late as two hours before the 5 P.M. roll-call. Senator Baker's patience was strained again and again. He found it particularly galling, for example, that Senator Robert C. Byrd of West Virginia, the former majority leader, had failed to support the Awacs sale. Support of the president on a controversial foreign-policy initiative was one of the obligations of Senate leadership, Mr. Baker felt, citing his own support of President Carter's Panama Canal treaties.

For all of the emotion over the issue, Mr. Baker managed as usual to maintain his detachment. During the vote, he looked up at the galleries and saw Georgie Packwood, wife of the Republican Senator who had led the fight against Awacs. He dispatched an aide to bring her a rose.

Mr. Baker's most singular achievement last year was in keeping his Republican majority virtually intact during scores of votes on the Reagan budget; each item in the $37 billion in budget cuts sought by the White House brought forth violent protests from groups that had become accustomed to increases in Federal largess over the years. The White House strategy was to place all the cuts in one package, subject to one up-or-down Senate vote, preventing lobbyists from picking off the trims one by one.

"My evaluation," said Senator Baker, "was that it was unchartered, and I was unsure we could do it. But when the president asked me if I thought it was the best shot that we had, I told him I thought it was." Mr. Baker also thought, he recalls, that a success on the package of cuts would make for increased cohesion among his troops. "With the majority of the Senate," he said, "every time they stick together, it makes it just a little easier to stick together the next time."

Stick together the Republicans did, fending off scores of Democratic efforts to embarrass them by offering amendments to the package seeking to restore funds for popular individual programs, such as Medicare and child nutrition programs. The Senate voted for the package, 88 to 10.

Motioning a visitor toward a wing chair, President Reagan took the seat alongside and talked of Howard Baker and his achievement in the Senate. Mr. Baker frequently provided "very realistic summations of what the problems are on the Hill," said Mr. Reagan, who also spoke of Mr. Baker's "good sound advice." But the president's voice took on added enthusiasm when he spoke of his personal relationship with Mr. Baker.

"A very typical thing about him," Mr. Reagan said, "was in '76, when obviously there was some feeling because I was a candidate in the primaries — he supported the incumbent President, which I think was proper — but when I found myself campaigning in his vicinity, he had Nancy and myself as houseguests, he and Joy, at their home."

Senator Baker has, by and large, been a staunch supporter of his president, and not only in pushing his legislation. Early [in March 1982], for example, Senator Bob Packwood, the Oregon Republican who is chairman of both the Commerce Committee and the Senate Republican Campaign Committee, said that the president's "concept of America" as male, white, Protestant, middle class and above forty years of age was hurting the party's long-term chances to capitalize on the 1980 victory. Senator Baker met with Mr. Packwood the following morning and persuaded him to apologize for expressing his views in public, though he did not apologize for the views themselves.

The first major national test of the Reagan administration will come with the fall elections. Mr. Baker expressed some modest optimism. "I think we're going to keep our majority in the Senate," he said. Republican chances are helped by the fact that only twelve Republican seats are up for election while there will be contests for 20 Democratic seats.

The real key, Mr. Baker said, was the economy: "I think we've got more time than most people think. If the market decides we're on the right track and the Fed decides we're on the right track, the country will decide we're on the right track." He said he was looking for an economic upturn by early fall.

As to his own future, the senator was typically forthright. "I make no bones about it," he said. "I want to be president."

In 1984, in the event that Mr. Reagan does not seek a second term, Mr. Baker will almost certainly be among the leading candidates for the Republican presidential nomination, along with Vice-President Bush. Other possibilities include Senator Laxalt, Representative Jack F. Kemp of Buffalo, and Illinois Governor Jim Thompson. Ronald Reagan will have either triumphed or failed, and a contender will have to be able to identify with or back away from Mr. Reagan and his administration. How will Mr. Baker be positioned for such a run?

His voting record suggests that he will be ready in either eventuality. On the one hand, he supported all of Mr. Reagan's proposed cuts in social programs last year, including cuts in food stamps, child nutrition, and child immunology. He also voted to reduce inspections by the Occupational Safety and Health Administration, for the neutron bomb, and against delaying the MX missile. That added up to a 17 rating, out of 100, from Americans for Democratic Action and an 81 rating from the Americans for Constitutional Action. On the other hand, for all his conservative votes, Mr. Baker is perceived by large groups of the public to be quite liberal, in part because of his civil-rights position.

Given his record as majority leader to date, Mr. Baker may well be able to don the Reagan mantle in 1984 as a loyal lieutenant and a logical heir. Yet if there is, at that point, a need to distance himself from the Reagan administration, Mr. Baker will have the ammunition.

As early as last fall, he led the fight against the president's "September offensive," a request for new, deeper cuts in social programs. He has taken selected positions against some administration initiatives — the plan to dismantle the Department of Education, for example. And he has criticized the president's proposed budget, not simply at private meetings, but at numerous news conferences.

Mr. Baker's chances for the Republican nomination, however, are not likely to be helped by his 1980 campaign, which convinced few politicians that he would make a compelling candidate. He was an early dropout. One problem was poor organization — the failure, for example, to schedule the candidate at events where he would pick up a large audience. Part of the problem was the difficulty of running for president, at least a full-time job, while still being subject to the demands of a senator's life. That would be true in spades for a majority leader. In fact, Mr. Baker said, he would quit the Senate if he were to try for the presidency again.

A more serious problem with his campaign two years ago, according to some of his aides, was their candidate's casualness. Mr. Baker told his usual down-home stories. ("There was the time," he might begin, and then he would repeat the question somebody asked Will Rogers: "Is it true Congress is all made up of thieves and rascals?" And then the senator would recount Will Rogers's reply: "Of course it's true, but it's a good cross-section of its constituency.") He was his customary amiable self. But he lacked, the aides said, the fire that could ignite an audience — or a possible financial contributor.

Early [in 1982], talking with a reporter about his future, Howard Baker seemed his usual objective and detached self, moving smoothly and contentedly along two tracks.

"I don't have any great compulsions or overweening ambitions," he said. "I'm happy to do what I'm doing. I'll be happy to run for president, or not. That may sound complacent or self-satisfied, but it's a remarkably comfortable state of affairs."

Well, perhaps.

LYNDON B. JOHNSON, A MEMBER of the Senate freshman class of 1948, was majority leader from 1955 until 1960, when he was elected vice-president. His experience in Washington predated his Senate career; he had been a congressional staff member in 1931 and at the age of 28 had defeated seven other candidates in a special election to fill the seat of the 10th Texas congressional district left vacant by the death of the incumbent representative.

Johnson was a consummate politician from the very beginning of his stay in Washington. He embraced the New Deal, and became a favorite of President Franklin D. Roosevelt; he even supported the president's ill-fated court-packing plan, which was opposed by many of Roosevelt's Washington supporters.[1]

While still a congressman, Johnson ran and was defeated in a special election for a Senate post vacated by the death of incumbent Senator Morris Sheppard in 1941. Johnson continued to serve in the House (with a brief leave in 1942 to serve as a naval re-serve officer) until, with John Connally as his campaign manager, he defeated arch-conservative Governor Coke Stevenson in the Democratic primary in 1948 by 87 votes out of almost a million cast. Since there was essentially no Republican opposition in Texas at that time, the election in the Democratic primary was tantamount to victory in the general election held in November.

When Johnson became majority leader the "Johnson era" began in the Senate. The "Johnson system" of power reflected his personality and style: he unhesitatingly rewarded his friends, from whom he demanded loyalty, and punished his enemies. His formal powers as majority leader were minimal. His chairmanship of the Democratic Steering Committee, for example, did not automatically guarantee him personal control over Democratic committee assignments. But Johnson exerted such control. He developed an informal network of power, and a dazzling style that came to be known as "the treatment."

18 Roland Evans and Robert Novak
THE JOHNSON SYSTEM

To build his Network, Johnson stretched the meager power resources of the Majority Leader to the outer limit. The mightiest of these was his in-

[1] In 1937 Roosevelt recommended legislation to Congress under which he would be given authority to appoint one new Supreme Court justice for each justice over seventy years old. At the time there were six septuagenarian justices, so that Roosevelt could easily have "packed" the court with his own appointments.

From *Lyndon B. Johnson: The Exercise of Power* by Roland Evans and Robert Novak. Copyright © 1966 by Rowland Evans and Robert Novak. Reprinted by arrangement with The New American Library, Inc., New York, N.Y.

fluence over committee assignments. Still, it was not comparable to the absolute power enjoyed by Nelson Aldrich a half century before. As chairman of the Democratic Steering Committee, Johnson steadily widened the breach in rigid seniority rules, working delicately with a surgical scalpel, not a stick of dynamite.

In January, 1955, his ally and adviser, Clinton Anderson, pressed his claim for an overdue assignment on either Foreign Relations or Finance. Each committee had one vacancy. But former Vice President Alben Barkley, who had just returned to the Senate as a "freshman" from Kentucky in the 1954 elections, asked for the Finance Committee — a request that could scarcely be denied. A further complication was the still unresolved problem of Wayne Morse, the Oregon maverick who had bolted the Republican party in the 1952 campaign and, after two years in the political wilderness as an "Independent," now joined the Democratic caucus in 1955. Morse's decision was vital to Johnson. It provided him with the narrow one-vote margin he needed to cross the bridge, incalculably important in terms of power, from Minority Leader to Majority Leader. Thus, it was incumbent upon Johnson to give Morse a good committee assignment, and Morse wanted Foreign Relations.

Johnson duly explained these facts of life to Anderson, who agreed not to insist (as he well could have) on either Finance or Foreign Relations. But Johnson remembered his old friend's personal loyalty and, on a 1956 speaking engagement in New Mexico, he publicly — and unexpectedly — promised that Clint Anderson would become the next chairman of the Joint Atomic Energy Committee. That post, because of New Mexico's Los Alamos atomic installation, would solidly enhance Anderson's prestige. To make good his promise, Johnson was required to jump Anderson over none other than Richard Russell, who outranked Anderson on the joint committee.

The Foreign Relations maneuvers temporarily drew the sharp-tongued Morse to Johnson, in sharp contrast to a year earlier. In January, 1954, Morse had told an ADA Roosevelt Day Dinner in Texas: "Johnson has the most reactionary record in the Senate. Look at his voting record. If he should ever have a liberal idea, he would have a brain hemorrhage. . . ."[1] But a little more than a year later, ensconced on the Foreign Relations Committee, Morse gently confided to the Senate: "During the past year, I have been the beneficiary of one kindness after another from Lyndon Johnson. I consider him not only a great statesman but a good man."

---

[1] Johnson retaliated in kind: "Texas doesn't need any outsiders to come in and tell them [sic] how to vote. I don't think Texas will pay any more attention to him than the Senate does." In those early days of his leadership, Johnson was far more ready to engage fellow senators in a war of words than he would be later.

And as chairman of the Joint Atomic Energy Committee, Anderson was even more pleased than he would have been on Foreign Relations. The only grumbling over Johnson's ingenious shuffling came from Russell, who had not agreed in advance to step aside for Anderson. But the grumbling was private and soft, not public and bitter. Lyndon Johnson could count on Dick Russell not to make a public fuss about such matters.

Two years later, Anderson was the center of far more devious committee maneuvers by Johnson. After the presidential election of 1956, Estes Kefauver of Tennessee and John F. Kennedy of Massachusetts, who had competed on the National Convention floor at Chicago for the vice-presidential nomination the previous summer, were competing again — this time for a single vacancy on Foreign Relations. Johnson, who had backed Kennedy against Kefauver at Chicago, was not trying to bring Kennedy closer to his orbit. He was determined to have the vacancy go to Kennedy over Johnson's old foe, Kefauver. But how to get around Kefauver's four-year seniority bulge over Kennedy? In December, 1956, long before Congress convened, Johnson telephoned Anderson with a most curious question: "How are you getting along with your campaign for the Foreign Relations Committee?"

Anderson was puzzled. Could Johnson have forgotten that his "campaign" had ended two years earlier? But Johnson persisted.

"This may be your chance," he said.

Before Anderson could reply that he had his hands full as chairman of Atomic Energy, Johnson rushed on.

"You have seniority now over Jack Kennedy," Johnson explained. "But if you don't claim it, Estes Kefauver may get there first."

Johnson's ploy suddenly came through to Anderson. Both Anderson and Kefauver were members of the Class of '48 and therefore had equal seniority. If they both applied for the one vacancy on the Foreign Relations Committee, Johnson could throw up his hands in the Steering Committee, declare a standoff — and give the vacancy to Kennedy. Anderson went along with this neat strategy, and Kennedy was given the seat, just as Johnson wanted.

Johnson's use of power to influence committee assignments cut both ways. "Good" liberals, such as Humphrey, could be prematurely boosted into the Foreign Relations Committee, and a "bad" liberal, such as Kefauver, could be made to cool his heels for years. A "bad" liberal such as Paul Douglas could be barred from the Finance Committee for eight long years, while five fellow members of the Class of '48 (Kerr, Long, Frear, Anderson and Johnson himself) and one from the Class of '50 (Smathers) were finding places there.[2] Senators who dared to func-

[2] This extraordinary treatment of Douglas also reflected Johnson's desire to keep the Finance Committee free of Northern liberals opposing special tax advantages for the oil

tion too far outside the Johnson Network waited long to get inside the prestige committees.

In these clandestine committee maneuvers, Johnson seldom exposed his hand. But in the routine committee shifts, he enjoyed wringing out the last drop of credit. One evening in early January, 1955, shortly after the committee assignments for the 85th Congress had been settled and announced, Johnson invited a couple of friends into his Majority Leader's office in the corner of the Capitol for a political bull session over Scotch and sodas. Nothing relaxed him more than these feet-up, hair-down chats. They invariably lasted well into the night and they invariably ended in long, often hilarious LBJ monologues, full of ribald yarns and racy mimicry.

Suddenly, he interrupted himself. "My God," he said, "I forgot to call Senator Stennis and congratulate him." Stennis had been valuable to Johnson a month earlier in the McCarthy censure fight, and now had just landed a coveted seat on the Appropriations Committee — thanks to Lyndon Johnson. Johnson reached over, cradled the phone between his shoulder and chin, and dialed.

Mrs. Stennis answered the phone, and the conversation commenced. "Ma'm, this is Lyndon Johnson, is your husband there? . . . He isn't? . . . Well, I must tell you, Ma'm, how proud I am of your husband and how proud the Senate is, and you tell him that when he gets home. The Senate paid him a great honor today. The Senate elected your husband to the Appropriations Committee. That's one of the most powerful committees in the Senate and a great honor for your husband. I'm so proud of John. He's a great American. And I know you're proud of him, too. He's one of my finest Senators. . . ." Accompanying this monologue were nods and winks in the direction of Johnson's fascinated audience.

Johnson went on to tell Mrs. Stennis how the Steering Committee had selected her husband unanimously for the Appropriations spot and how the full Senate had unanimously concurred, but implicitly he was belaboring the obvious — that it wasn't the Steering Committee or the full Senate that really was responsible. It was LBJ.

Johnson quietly commandeered other bits and pieces of Senate patronage that previous Majority Leaders ignored. To cement his budding alliance with Senator Margaret Chase Smith, for instance, he arranged for a special staff member of the Senate Armed Services Committee to be appointed by her and to be responsible to her alone, even though she was a Republican on the Democratic-controlled committee, and only fourth-ranking Republican at that.

---

and gas industry. But if Douglas had been a "good" liberal in the Humphrey mold, Johnson could have shaved a point, since the Finance Committee was already so stacked in favor of the oil and gas industry.

Although in the past, office space for Senators, a source of sometimes intense competition, had been distributed by strict seniority as a routine housekeeping chore of the Senate's Sergeant-at-Arms, Johnson quickly perceived its value as a weapon of influence and fitted it into his growing system of rewards and punishments. When Paul Douglas lost that top-floor Capitol office to Johnson in 1955, the Senate took notice. It was a dramatic sign of the consequences of a lack of rapport with the Majority Leader. Johnson skillfully exploited the gleaming New Senate Office Building in 1958, with its spanking new suites, as an inducement for help on the floor. Senator Mike Monroney of Oklahoma, sometimes troublesome for Johnson, was brought into line on one bill with the award of a handsome corner suite that Johnson knew Monroney coveted.

Johnson also kept his ears open to discover which Senator — or Senator's wife — was really anxious to go on which Senatorial junket abroad. At a cocktail party early in 1957, Johnson was chatting with the wife of Frank Church, the young, newly elected liberal Democrat from Idaho. Mrs. Church innocently revealed that she had always wanted to see South America. Knowing that Frank Church might become a valuable addition to the Johnson Network, the Majority Leader saw to it that he was named to the very next delegation of Senators to visit South America.

Even before that, however, Frank Church had reason to be grateful to Lyndon Johnson. Bitterly opposed by the Idaho Power Company and other private-power interests because of his public-power stand, Church was hard-pressed for funds in his 1956 campaign for the Senate. He sent an S.O.S. to the Senate Democratic Campaign Committee in Washington. Senator Smathers, chairman of the Campaign Committee, was dubious about pouring money into what seemed a hopeless cause in a small Mountain State. But Johnson and Bobby Baker argued Church's cause, and their wishes prevailed.

De facto control of the Campaign Committee's funds was one of Johnson's least obvious but most effective tools in building his Network. He controlled the distribution of committee funds through both its chairman — first Earle Clements and later George Smathers — and through its secretary, Bobby Baker. More often than not, the requests for campaign funds were routinely made to Baker, and the money was physically distributed by him. Johnson further tightened his control when Clements was named the committee's executive director after his Senate defeat in 1956. Johnson got the most out of the committee's limited funds (at that time a mere four hundred thousand dollars) by shrewdly distributing them where they would do the most work. In the small Mountain States like Idaho, a ten-thousand-dollar contribution could change the course of an election. But in New York or Pennsylvania, ten thousand dollars was the merest drop in the bucket. Johnson and Baker tried to reduce contributions to Democrats in the industrial Northeast to the minimum. Since Senators seldom bite the hand that finances them, these Westerners were naturally drawn into the Johnson Network, while the Eastern liberals tended to remain outside.

But this ingenious stretching of the Majority Leader's limited stock of patronage could not by itself explain the brilliant success of the Johnson Network. The extra, indeed the dominant, ingredient was Johnson's overwhelming personality, reflected in what came to be known as "The Treatment."

The Treatment could last ten minutes or four hours. It came, enveloping its target, at the LBJ Ranch swimming pool, in one of LBJ's offices, in the Senate cloakroom, on the floor of the Senate itself — wherever Johnson might find a fellow Senator within his reach. Its tone could be supplication, accusation, cajolery, exuberance, scorn, tears, complaint, the hint of threat. It was all of these together. It ran the gamut of human emotions. Its velocity was breathtaking, and it was all in one direction. Interjections from the target were rare. Johnson anticipated them before they could be spoken. He moved in close, his face a scant millimeter from his target, his eyes widening and narrowing, his eyebrows rising and falling. From his pockets poured clippings, memos, statistics. Mimicry, humor, and the genius of analogy made The Treatment an almost hypnotic experience and rendered the target stunned and helpless.

In 1957, when Johnson was courting the non-Senate Eastern liberal establishment, he summoned historian and liberal theoretician Arthur Schlesinger, Jr., down from his classroom at Harvard. Wary at the prospect of his first prolonged meeting with Johnson (whom he suspected of disdaining the liberal cause), Schlesinger had in his mind a long list of questions to ask Johnson. Never known for shyness, Schlesinger was nevertheless on his guard when he entered Johnson's Capitol office and sat in front of the great man's desk.

The Treatment began immediately: a brilliant, capsule characterization of every Democratic Senator: his strengths and failings, where he fit into the political spectrum; how far he could be pushed, how far pulled; his hates, his loves. And who (he asked Schlesinger) must oversee all these prima donnas, put them to work, knit them together, know when to tickle this one's vanity, inquire of that one's health, remember this one's five o'clock nip of Scotch, that one's nagging wife? Who must find the hidden legislative path between the South and the North, the public power men and the private power men, the farmers' men and the unions' men, the bomber-boys, and the peace-lovers, the eggheads and the fatheads? Nobody but Lyndon Johnson.

Imagine a football team (Johnson hurried on) and I'm the coach, and

I'm also the quarterback. I have to call the signals, and I have to center the ball, run the ball, pass the ball. I'm the blocker (he rose out of his chair and threw an imaginary block). I'm the tackler (he crouched and tackled). I'm the passer (he heaved a mighty pass). I have to catch the pass (he reached and caught the pass).

Schlesinger was sitting on the edge of his chair, both fascinated and amused. Here was a view of the Senate he had never seen before.

Johnson next ticked off all the bills he had passed that year, how he'd gotten Dick Russell on this one, Bob Kerr on that one, Hubert Humphrey on another. He reached into his desk drawer and out came the voting record of New Jersey's Clifford Case, a liberal Republican. You liberals, he told Schlesinger, are always talking about my record. You wouldn't question Cliff Case's record, would you? And he ran down the list and compared it to his voting record. Whatever Johnson had on those two lists, he came out with a record more liberal than Case's.

Johnson had anticipated and answered all of Schlesinger's questions. The leader rolled on, reiterating a theme common to The Treatment of that time. He'd had his heart attack, he said, and he knew he'd never be President. He wasn't made for the presidency. If only the Good Lord would just give him enough time to do a few more things in the Senate. Then he'd go back to Texas. That's where he belonged.

Breathless now, ninety minutes later, Schlesinger said good-by and groped his way out of Johnson's office. Eight years later, he was to record his impressions. Johnson had been "a good deal more attractive, more subtle, and more formidable than I expected." And, he might have added, vastly more entertaining.

The Treatment was designed for a single target or, at most, an audience of three or four. In large groups, what was witty sounded crude, what was expansive became arrogant. It was inevitable, then, that when Johnson allowed The Treatment to dominate his "press conferences" a sour note entered his relations with the press. Reporters en masse didn't like being on the receiving end of The Treatment. Johnson's failure to understand that annoyed the press, which in turn made Johnson increasingly wary and suspicious. Unable to tame the press as he tamed so many Senators, he foolishly took offense at routine questions, and was quick to find a double meaning in the most innocent point raised by a reporter. Although Senate reporters and Washington's top columnists were captivated in their *private* sessions with Johnson in his office or at the LBJ Ranch, his press conferences were fiascoes. They simply could not be harnessed to The Treatment. . . .

EDWARD F. KENNEDY AND ROBert C. Byrd have fundamentally different personalities, which have shaped their respective Senate careers. Each, like most of his colleagues, has sought power and status on Capitol Hill. But the route to power each has selected reflects a different background, character, and style. Kennedy is a star and has embraced an individualistic style; through the astute use of the committees he chairs he has sought to put the Kennedy imprint upon legislation, investigations, and committee reports. Kennedy's style represents the "new Senate," in which individual senators are more independent of their colleagues. They seek power not so much through the traditional emphasis upon collegial cooperation, but by gaining personal recognition among colleagues for hard work on

committees, specialized knowledge, and legislative accomplishments. There remains an important collegial aspect to these efforts, but in the modern Senate an increasing number of members tend to focus on the separate worlds of their committees more than upon the collective demands of the institution.

Robert Byrd, in contrast to Kennedy, adopted a collegial style of operation; he sought positions of leadership in the Senate body rather than emphasizing his individual power through committees. Because of his service to fellow senators, Byrd was elected majority whip and majority leader. His personality is more muted than that of Kennedy, his style less flamboyant and aggressive. As the following selection makes clear, each has made an important contribution to the Senate.

19 Laurence Leamer
ROBERT BYRD AND EDWARD KENNEDY: TWO STORIES OF THE SENATE

The Capitol is the greatest public building in America. Visitors can sit in the House and Senate galleries, climb the broad staircases, roam the marble halls, and ride the elevators. They can go almost anywhere they choose. Yet hidden within the Capitol are offices and nooks and gathering places that are private. On the House side of the Capitol, down a back staircase from the House floor, stands an unmarked door. Behind the door is a dark room shrouded in drapes, with an old desk and a few chairs casually arranged. Here Speaker Sam Rayburn's "Board of Education" used to meet each afternoon over bourbon and water to talk politics. Fifteen years after Rayburn's death the star of Texas is still there, painted in ornate style on the far wall.

From *Playing for Keeps in Washington* by Laurence Leamer. Copyright © 1977 by Laurence Leamer. Permission granted by The Dial Press.

On the Senate side of the Capitol there are fifty-four private rooms used by senators. Some are no more than rude accumulations of government-issue desks, chairs, and paintings. Others are exquisitely decorated with antiques, political memorabilia, ornate telephones. The largest office is a three-room suite that can be reached by going down a narrow staircase just off the main corridor. These are the offices out of which Bobby Baker, the assistant to Senate majority leader Lyndon Johnson, operated. Baker had worked there until he was convicted of abusing his position and sent to prison.

These are the rooms that Edward "Ted" Kennedy of Massachusetts claimed as his own in 1969 when he was elected Democratic whip, the number-two position in the Democratic leadership. Then the offices had all the sweaty urgency of a political boiler room. The suite was full of Kennedy people. The phones rang constantly. Journalists hurried in and out. Now and again Kennedy came bursting in for a few minutes before rushing off somewhere else. There was always something happening. There had never been anything quite like it in the Senate.

In 1971 Robert C. Byrd of West Virginia defeated Kennedy and took over the suite. From all appearances, Byrd did not think the suite a grand prize but more a gift kept for occasional use. The doors might stay locked for days. Byrd decorated the rooms with just enough pictures and artifacts so that the suite became indisputably his. On the wall he put mounted whips that Senator Joseph Montoya of New Mexico had given him and a copy of a *Parade* magazine story about himself ("Senate Whip Bob Byrd: From Poverty to Power").

On the wall of the outer office hung pictures of the fourteen men who had served as Democratic whip. From Jay Hamilton Lewis to Hubert Humphrey, from Morris Sheppard to Russell Long, from Lister Hill to Lyndon Johnson, the first twelve faces looked forth with the fleshy, canny confidence of the professional politician. But Kennedy and Byrd were different. Kennedy's picture had the perfect looks of a Hollywood publicity glossy. Byrd, for his part, looked half-embarrassed, as if in the act of allowing himself to be photographed he was giving away something that he did not want to give away.

As much as Kennedy and Byrd were different in appearance from the twelve men who preceded them, so were they different from each other. They were two of the most powerful men in Washington. They did not like each other. They did not like each other's politics. In their distinct ways they symbolized what power had become in the modern Senate.

Senator Robert Byrd walked down the main corridor of the Capitol, down a narrow staircase, and unlocked the door to the whip's office. Many senators travel with a flotilla of aides, but Byrd almost always walks alone. He is a little man with a chalk-white face and black-and-white streaked hair swept back in a high pompadour. He looks like a wary sparrow, with a face that could be found up most any hollow in Appalachia, the face of a man who had missed some basic nutrient. It belonged to the man who was on the verge of becoming the Senate majority leader — the most powerful and prestigious position in Congress.

Byrd is a man of religious intensity, both public and private, the personification of the self-made man, a man of deep, unfathomable ambition, beyond perhaps anyone else's in the Senate. He sought power, wooed power, lived with and for power. . . .

The Senate that Byrd was sworn into in January 1959 was still dominated by Southerners like Lyndon Johnson of Texas and Richard Russell of Georgia. A conservative might believe that a certain lassitude and the petty corruption of privilege were merely the exhaust fumes given off by the Senate as it made its stately way through history. Senator Thomas Dodd of Connecticut, for instance, had an elderly retainer known as the "judge" who slept blissfully at a desk outside the senator's office.

The Senate had not yet spread out into the nearly completed New Senate Office Building. Donald R. Matthews, an academician, was finishing work on a book on the Senate, *US Senators and Their World.* He broke Senate offices down into two general types: the bureaucratic and the individualistic. In the bureaucratic offices, "the senator has delegated considerable nonroutine responsibilities to his staff, established a fairly clear-cut division of labor and chain of command." The individualistic offices were "vest pocket operations in which the senator has delegated only routine tasks and in which the staff has little influence and less authority."

Byrd was arriving in the Senate as it was going through a profound evolution. The old Senate, the Senate of "individualistic" offices, had just been portrayed in *Citadel: The Story of the United States Senate,* a book by William S. White. White wrote of the US Senate as "an institution that lives in an unending yesterday where the past is never gone, the present never quite decisive, and the future rarely quite visible. It has its good moments and its bad moments, but to the United States it symbolizes, if nothing else at all, the integrity of continuity and wholeness." This Senate was an institution where, when a man was sworn in, he assumed a mantle of dignity and honor. It was honor enough for any man to be in this body.

When the *Citadel* came out, Senator J. William Fulbright noticed that for a few days some of his colleagues attempted to play senator, walking the halls of Congress as if they were wearing togas. On January 15, 1957, Lyndon B. Johnson had a luncheon for the six new Democratic senators. He gave the six freshmen autographed copies of *Citadel* and he told them that they should think of the book as a kind of McGuffey's *Reader*.

Johnson knew that White's Senate was not his, but he may have found a certain comfort in that mythical body. To White, the Senate was a great conservative body, the naysayer and watchman of democracy. But what gave the Senate its greatness were individual senators with individual ideas. They worked in the body of Congress to transform their ideas into legislation that would affect the nation. When Johnson had come to Washington, George Norris of Nebraska was still in the Senate. For years Norris had studied how to protect the land and the people. He had prepared his bill for the Tennessee Valley Authority, and he had defended it as if it were a part of his very being, which in a sense it was. Robert Wagner of New York was in the Senate too. For years he worked on the great legislation of the New Deal, including the labor bill that bears his name. Bob LaFollette and Robert Taft were also in the Senate in those years. What these senators had in common was an organic relationship between what they believed, the people they served, and what they did and said to achieve their ends.

When Robert Byrd entered the Senate, he accepted the life of the Senate as the central reality of his being. "Over the years he has cloaked himself in what he perceives to be senatorial dignity and aura," said one of Byrd's former aides, "but even when he arrived, there really was very little dignity left and the aura was gone."

Byrd allied himself with Lyndon Johnson of Texas and more closely yet with Richard Russell of Georgia. Those who watched Byrd often thought him great only in petty things. But to a man who revered the Senate as much as Byrd, there were no petty duties. In 1960, during an all-night civil rights filibuster, Byrd talked for a record twenty-one hours. Five years later in another filibuster, he talked for fifteen hours. Byrd was always ready to volunteer for the KP duty of legislative life. The Senate was based on rules and precedents. And Robert Byrd, alone of his generation, was willing to learn the rules and the precedents. He studied them until he knew them as did no one else and then he studied them some more.

Byrd performed duties, great and small, for senators of every persuasion, north and south, Democrat and Republican. He helped colleagues whenever he could. When he had helped, he sent them notes saying that he had been glad to be of service. These he filed away. In

1967 he was elected Secretary of the Democratic Conference, the number-three position in the Senate Democratic leadership. Four years later he defeated Ted Kennedy and became senate whip, the number-two position in the Senate Democratic leadership.

As a Senate leader, Byrd worked even harder. He knew the Bible, the book of Senate rules and the book of precedents, and these were just about the only books he figured he would ever have to know. He had read the 900-page collection of precedents cover to cover, two times, and late at night at home he was reading it for the third. When the Senate was planning to go into closed session on matters of national security, he would go over Rule 35 once again. When there was going to be a vote on cloture, he would read the rule on cloture. Byrd knew the rules and he knew the precedents and could make them turn upside down and dance on their heads. It was *his* Senate now, and he left the floor rarely.

The Washington monument splits the window of his vast inner office in the Capitol. Senator Byrd speaks quietly, the twang of the hills in his voice: "The Senate is a forest. There are ninety-nine animals. They're all lions. There's a waterhole in the forest. I'm the waterhole. They all have to come to the waterhole. I don't have power but I have knowledge of the rules. I have knowledge of the precedents. I have knowledge of the schedule. So I'm in a position to do things for others.

"Now the majority leader is the dispatcher, the engineer, the fellow at the head of the engine who's looking out from the dark night at the headlight down the railway, pulling on the throttle a little harder, pushing on the throttle a little, or leveling off a little, moving it along. Or he determines to move over on this sidetrack or that sidetrack. This legislative organism, with its power, has to have direction. It has to have a leader, but he doesn't have the power. He's the umpire, the referee. He doesn't have any more of that raw power than any other senator has.

"The President, he has power. He's the chief executive of this country. The presidency of the United States should in reality seek the man. Someone said that. That's the way it ought to be. People ought not to be persuaded by a person's pretty teeth, by his smile, or by the way he cuts his hair — by his charisma. That's misleading. That's not to say that a person with pretty teeth and a pretty smile and a handsome build and charisma may not have the ability. But they don't necessarily go together either."

Talking about pretty teeth and a pretty smile and the cut of a man's hair, Robert Byrd could have been sketching a caricature of Edward Kennedy. Byrd and Kennedy were the two Janus faces of the Senate, Byrd often looking backward to a past that had never been, Kennedy looking forward to a future that might never arrive. They approached their work as differently as two men in the same profession possibly could. They also had different conceptions of power and how to use it.

Edward Moore Kennedy walked down the center aisle of the Senate to be sworn in as the junior senator from Massachusetts on January 9, 1963. He had the accent and bearing of the Kennedys, but was a big, brawny fellow with a rousing, friendly manner that suggested an Irish politician of a half century past. He was the scion of a family that seemed destined to dominate American political life in the last decades of the 20th century as had the Adams family in the first decades of the nation's history. . . .

Kennedy fit unobtrusively into the traditional role of the freshman senator. One morning he went around to see Senator James Eastland of Mississippi, chairman of the Judiciary Committee and champion of the old Senate. He drank bourbon with the senior senator and Eastland discovered that the Kennedys were not all alike. He went around to see Senator Richard Russell of Georgia, Robert Byrd's patron, and he went to the Senate prayer breakfast, too — once at least — and led his colleagues in prayer.

While Kennedy might act out such old-fashioned rituals of the Senate, he was still the most modern of freshmen. A decade later, James Macgregor Burns, a biographer of Kennedy, would call him a "presidential senator." Kennedy was a presidential senator not only in the sense that he had become the sole bearer of the Kennedy legacy and heir apparent to the White House. He was presidential in the way he went about being a Senator. He launched a frenetic, permanent presidential-like campaign within the very Senate.

In the favored analogy of his staff, Senator Kennedy stood at the center of a circle of aides who flowed in and around him. The Kennedys had always had a special talent for acquiring and using people whose talents met the needs of the moment. They attracted members of that natural aristocracy of the able and the ambitious. These aides were perhaps no more talented than those around other contenders for the ultimate prize in American politics. But in the livery of the Kennedys, they seemed to serve with extraordinary energy and devotion, and in the end they were, in one way or another, rewarded in kind.

One of those who was there when Kennedy entered the Senate was Milton Gwirtzman, now a Washington lawyer.

"From the beginning Kennedy knew how to use his staff," Gwirtzman observed. "Even in his first term he had that lineup outside his office. There were perhaps six professionals then and Kennedy used them as a multiplier." To a Borah or Taft or Wagner, the idea of a senatorial multiplier would have been absurd. It would, indeed, have been impossible, for until the Legislative Reorganization Act of 1946, most senators had only a clerk and a secretary.

Kennedy was one of the first senators to employ his staff so systematically that he helped create a new definition of "senator." Kennedy not only used the half dozen or so aides who were his natural due, but he subsidized two others. Gwirtzman, for one, left the staff in 1964 but for the next six years was paid $18,000 a year by the Park Agency, a Kennedy family conduit, for speeches and advice. Kennedy, moreover, had a press secretary. That itself was a relatively new position on the Hill: a media-savvy specialist who measured success in newsprint and television time, not merely in a product called legislation.

Kennedy understood how to develop his staff so that they would serve him. He did not want any one Super Aide around him who might become for him what Ted Sorensen had been for Jack. He did not want an alter ego. What he did want was a group of people who could work on their own, self-motivated young men ambitious for themselves and for him, men whose competitiveness with one another might sometimes spill over into jealousies, but whose energies and ideals could be channeled into furthering Senator Ted Kennedy and his career.

In those first years in office, Kennedy did not draw on his name. He did not use his power in ways that were memorable or important. He had a quotation from Machiavelli as his maxim: "Power not used is power saved." Machiavelli, however, was writing about power that had once been used. Kennedy was hoarding a commodity whose worth he could not know until he used it. He was acting as if even he accepted the common definition of himself as the last and the least of the Kennedys — the kid brother.

During the day Kennedy abided by all the rituals of egalitarianism: bantering with aides, employing the ersatz intimacy of first names. However, if an aide stepped over a certain line, visible only to Kennedy, that aide learned to regret it. By day they might be members of a team but not in the evening. It was simply understood that if you worked for Ted Kennedy you did not go to social gatherings that he attended. You learned to treat his family in a special way. An aide had taken a phone call from Rose Kennedy in Hyannis Port one day. "Your mother called," the aide said when Kennedy returned to the office. "You mean *you* talked to *my* mother?" Kennedy said. If politics was one world, and social life another, then the family was yet a third and the most exalted of Kennedy's worlds. Here the subordinates were not allowed to trespass, even for a moment.

On that November afternoon in 1963 when President John F. Kennedy was assassinated in Dallas, Ted Kennedy was performing that most thankless of tasks foisted on the freshman: presiding over a nearly empty Senate. When he learned of the shooting and he finally reached his brother on the telephone, Robert Kennedy told him, "You'd better call your mother and your sisters." In their division of the duties of mourning, it fell to Ted Kennedy to comfort the family.

By that next June, Kennedy had prepared his public face. His party back in Massachusetts was preparing to nominate him for his first full term in office. Kennedy, however, was still on the floor of the Senate waiting to vote on the civil rights bill. It was so typical of his life to have a dozen people, a dozen decisions, a dozen proposals backed up waiting for him.

Kennedy finally left Washington for Massachusetts by private plane, accompanied by Senator Birch Bayh of Indiana and his wife Marvella, and aide Ed Moss. It was no kind of weather to be flying in a private plane, but Kennedy lived in a world of days that were scheduled too tight, cars that were driven too fast, planes that were flown when they shouldn't have been. On the approach to the airpost outside Springfield, the plane crashed. The Bayhs were injured, the pilot was dead, Moss would die soon afterward, and Kennedy had cracked ribs, a punctured lung, and three damaged vertebrae.

Kennedy spent the next six months in bed. . . .

While still in the hospital, Kennedy won reelection in Massachusetts with 74.4 percent of the votes. In New York, his brother Bob defeated Kenneth Keating for a Senate seat by a much closer margin. Afterward his brother had come up to visit in the hospital. The two Kennedys had posed for the photographers. "Step back a little, you're casting a shadow on Ted," one of the photographers said to Bob Kennedy.

"It'll be the same in Washington," Ted Kennedy said laughing.

During the nearly four years that the two Kennedys served together in the Senate, Ted Kennedy largely deferred to his brother and to his leadership. In 1965 he took over the chairmanship of the Subcommittee on Refugees and Escapees. This was his first chairmanship, the natural legacy of the seniority system. It was a moribund subcommittee concerned largely with refugees who had fled Communist Europe. But it represented more staff and an area that he could now legitimately make his own.

Ted took the subcommittee and expanded its mandate to the refugees of Southeast Asia. He used it as his ticket of admission to the issue of Vietnam. He went to Vietnam and the papers were full of the poignant testimony of human suffering. . . .

It was not until after the murder of his brother Bob in 1968 that Ted Kennedy, the senator, began fully to emerge. In his time of mourning he had gone sailing for days on end, and drinking, and carousing. Then in August in Worcester he had given a speech important enough to be televised nationally. He told his audience that he had been at sea. But he said, "There is no safety in hiding. Not for me, not for any of us here today . . . like my brothers before me, I pick up a fallen standard." He went on to talk about the Vietnam War and all it had cost in money and blood. He proposed that the United States unconditionally end the bombing and negotiate a peace. . . .

The next office Kennedy did seek was one that his brothers would never have considered. In January he defeated Russell Long, that son of Louisiana, and son of oil, to become majority whip. The whip had a series of thankless bureaucratic duties such as rounding up senators and arranging schedules. He was, nonetheless, the number-two leader in the Senate. Kennedy set out to make the whip more than that. He brought in some of his own academic and other expert advisors to forge a cohesive policy for the Democrats. Senators, however, are a jealous and self-protective group. A hundred different policies were better than one, if the one came stamped with the mark of a particular senator. Worse yet, Kennedy simply did not perform the mundane, pesky tasks of the whip as they were supposed to be. Bored by them, he foisted such chores as he could onto his staff.

Kennedy was drinking heavily. At times his face had the florid look that showed him a full-blooded member of the race of Irish drinkers. Then in July on vacation he had gone over to Chappaquiddick Island to attend a party for some of Bobby Kennedy's "boiler-room girls." He had left with one of them, Mary Jo Kopechne, and the next morning the police had found her body in Kennedy's overturned Oldsmobile off a bridge on a dirt road on Chappaquiddick Island.

Kennedy, according to his own statement, had dived down to try to get her out and then he had left and gone back to his friends to get help. He had not contacted the police until the next morning. The Kennedys, whatever else one said about them, had always showed the grace under pressure that Hemingway had called the mark of courage, the mark of a man. The private Kennedy had failed that night, as those around him failed. "It was in part a failure of staffing," one of his aides said. "He had no one with him to tell him he was crazy."

Within hours Kennedy had left the island. He retreated into that flimsy story; he made a televised public statement prepared by Ted Sorensen, Gwirtzman, Richard Goodwin, and Burke Marshall and then backed into legal refuges, the power of wealth and position, and the sympathy that people of Massachusetts had for him and for his family. . . .

Until that night at Chappaquiddick, Kennedy had appeared an inevitable choice for the 1972 presidential nomination. But that was all over. When Kennedy returned to the Senate, Mike Mansfield, the majority leader, as goodhearted a man as was to be found in that body, noticed Kennedy pausing for a moment in the cloakroom. "Come here," Mansfield said encouragingly. "Come here, right back where you belong." To the last of the Kennedys, it was a phrase not without its ironies. . . .

O N NOVEMBER 2, 1948, RUS-
sell B. Long was elected to
the United States Senate to fill
the unexpired term of John H. Overton, who was Huey Long's handpicked candidate in 1932. Overton's
seat thus fittingly remained in the
hands of the Long organization. Huey
Long himself had had a short but
flamboyant career as a United States
senator, having been elected to the
Senate in 1930 while he was governor.
He retained both positions until 1932,
when he took the senatorial oath,
which required him under Louisiana
law to relinquish his governorship.
His son Russell's Senate "Class of
1948" included Hubert H. Humphrey
of Minnesota, Lyndon B. Johnson of
Texas, Robert Kerr of Oklahoma, and
Paul Douglas of Illinois, all of whom
became powerful members.

By 1964, Russell Long was the ranking member of the Senate Finance
Committee. He used his position of
power and prestige in the Senate to
launch a successful drive to become
majority whip in 1965. He became
chairman of the Finance Committee
in 1966. At that time, Long's personal
style, a combination of effective
wheeling and dealing and highly powerful oratory, was able to gain him
widespread Senate support. He was
not, however, nearly as flamboyant as
his father, and his quiet, reasonable,
and flexible maneuvering behind the
scenes was in line with Senate traditions.

After he became majority whip
Long's style changed. Robert Peabody

describes Long's post-1965 period as
follows:

> Throwing most of his energies into
> his prime love, the chairmanship of the
> Finance Committee, Long managed
> over the next three years to (1) incur
> the increasing displeasure of the Ma-
> jority Leader, (2) please few of his col-
> leagues with his performance as Major-
> ity Whip, (3) tie up the entire Senate for
> six weeks in an attempt to promote a
> presidential election campaign fund,
> (4) defend the unpopular cause of Sen-
> ator Thomas Dodd, (5) antagonize a
> number of liberals with rather heavy-
> handed and arbitrary floor maneuver-
> ing, (6) aggravate a drinking problem,
> and (7) neutralize the backing of sev-
> eral of the most important senior
> oligarchs in the Senate.[1]

Russell Long lost his position as whip
to Senator Edward Kennedy in 1969,
who in turn lost his position to Senator Robert C. Byrd in 1971. The defeats of Long and Kennedy were
mainly due to personal factors, and
resulting leadership styles that were
unacceptable to many Senate colleagues.

Although Long lost the post of majority whip in 1969, it was a close vote,
31 to 26. The defeat in no way affected
his position as chairman of the Finance Committee, which guaranteed
him a solid base for expansion of his
power if he wished. Losing the position of majority whip was only a temporary loss of power for Russell Long
in the Senate. He quickly retrenched,
and soon was able to renew the personal style that had led to his rise to
power. By the mid-1970s Long was
again a major force in the Senate.

[1] Robert L. Peabody, *Leadership in Congress* (Boston: Little, Brown, 1976), p. 366.

Under his chairmanship the Finance Committee became a power in determining tax legislation, and in the Ninety-fourth Congress (1976) he defeated a major attempt by Senator Edmund Muskie of Maine, chairman of the Senate Budget Committee, to force the Finance Committee to comply with the wishes of the Budget Committee.

Just as Long had maintained his independence within the Senate, he was determined not to be dominated by "the other body." The Finance Committee had operated for many years in the shadow of the House Ways and Means Committee, but under Long it was revitalized.

The major confrontations between the House and the Senate often come in conference committees, and Russell Long had become a master of conference committee technique. His skill in handling Senate-House negotiations often assured victory for the Senate side. The following selection is a case study of Russell Long's style and of his methods in making his personal imprint on legislation.

20 Aaron Latham
RUSSELL LONG

Richard Nixon probably spent too much time studying football. But Al Ullman (D., Ore.), the new chairman of the Ways and Means Committee, may have spent too little. If Ullman had known more about football strategy, he would never have committed the classic coach's blunder: publicly knocking the other team on the eve of the big game. That tends to get the other side riled up.

Ullman's indiscretion occurred on ABC's "Issues and Answers" show. The date was Sunday, March 23, the day before a House-Senate conference committee was scheduled to begin reconciling the differences between the House and Senate versions of the tax-cut bill. Since the two houses of Congress almost never pass exactly the same bill, such conference committees are necessary to work out a compromise. And in these conferences, Senate and House chauvinism often plays a role. In this case the trouble started when ABC's Bob Clark asked what would happen to the long list of amendments which the Senate had tacked onto the bill.

Ullman said, "We think many of the amendments added in the Senate cannot be justified. We think there is a real danger in being irresponsible here, and doing the things that might lead to an inflationary spiral. So, many of the Senate amendments will be cut back."

Clark asked for Ullman's assessment of a Senate amendment which would allow a tax credit of up to $2,000 to anyone who bought a new home.

Ullman said, "I personally think that that is not the right way to approach the housing problem."

The problem was that the housing credit was one of the amendments sponsored by Huey Long's son Russell, the leader of the Senate conferees, a paradigm of the Southern politician who hides his consummate legislative mastery in a good-ol'-boy verbal briar patch.

For years, when Senate and House conferees met to wrestle over money bills, Russell Long (D., La.), the chairman of the Senate Finance Committee, had been eclipsed by Wilbur Mills (D., Ark.), the long-reigning chairman of the House Ways and Means Committee. But now Mills was gone. Now Russell Long, the cagey veteran, would be up against Al Ullman, the new boy. Long looked forward to eclipsing Ullman the way Mills had eclipsed him.

And yet it wasn't working out quite that way. The media tended to treat Ullman as if he were Mills — and Long got left out. Ullman was always on the television news shows. And now, on the eve of the conference, here was Ullman, basking in the "Issues and Answers" limelight, saying Long's housing amendment would have to go.

This would be the first conference where Long and Ullman would be pitted head to head. Whoever won this one might just go on winning for the next decade, so Long was determined to prove he couldn't be run over.

Long's strategy was based in part on all those Senate amendments to which Ullman objected. Long was a horse trader and the amendments were his horses. If Ullman wanted any of them dropped, he would have to make concessions.

The total cost for all those amendments, if approved, would add billions to the tax-cut bill, which reminded Long of a story. He told reporters that when Clinton Anderson was on the Finance Committee, he had suggested that they install a gong which would be rung every time the committee gave away a billion dollars. He thought that such a gong would help provide some sense of reality. If the Senate Finance Committee had had a gong when it was tacking amendments onto the tax-cut bill, it would have rung as follows: *Bong . . . bong . . . bong . . . bong . . . bong . . . bong . . . bong . . . bong . . . bong . . . bong.* Ten times in ten hours.

The Senate had taken the $20-billion tax-cut bill voted by the House and added another $10 billion or so. That meant that, going into the conference committee, Russell Long had 10 billion chips to play with.

So, ask not for whom the gong bonged. The gong bonged for Al Ull-man.

The First Day

Russell B. Long, 56, who has been a senator since he was 30, moves with the inevitability of the Mississippi River. Sometimes he overflows with sentiment. Sometimes he simply drowns you in words. But he keeps on rolling. One of his colleagues says, "Long is the most colorful man in the Senate." Some reporters will tell you Long, whose ADA rating hovers under twenty, is their favorite senator, although they often disagree with him. Linda Wertheimer, who covers the Hill for National Public Radio, says, "In the Senate, you've got all these presidential hopefuls standing around saying presidential things, and then you've got Long, who knows how to get things done. It's often not passion but presidential passion guiding these other senators, but Long's passion seems real."

Long, like Mills, used to have a drinking problem. It almost seems to go with the job. The difference is that Long licked his with the help of his second wife, who often sits up in the gallery during late sessions as if to watch over him. Long still has something of a W. C. Fields nose and can be almost as funny, but he has been sober for years. He may look a little sleepy, but he isn't.

On the first day of the conference, a Monday, Russell Long got up at 5:30 in the morning. He was on Capitol Hill by 7 A.M. Before the conference started, Long caucused with the Senate's Democratic conferees in his office. The Senate was allowed ten members on the conference committee — six Democrats and four Republicans. If the six Senate Democrats did not get their way, they could simply stalemate the conference, provided they voted as a bloc.[1]

In the caucus, Long did just what a football coach would have done: he gave a pep talk in which he pointed out that the other side's coach had been mouthing off about the Senate team. He said that if the Senate Democrats did not stick together, the House would "run them right off Capitol Hill."

The Senate Democrats agreed to stick together. Moreover, they promised that, come what may, Al Ullman was going to accept the housing-credit amendment he had rejected on national TV.

[1] The Senate conferees were Long, Herman Talmadge (D., Ga.), Vance Hartke (D., Ind.), Abraham Ribicoff (D., Conn.), William Hathaway (D., Me.), Floyd Haskell (D., Colo.), Carl Curtis (R., Neb.), Paul Fannin (R., Ariz.), Clifford Hansen (R., Wyo.), Robert Dole (R., Kan.). The House conferees were Ullman, James Burke (D., Mass.), Dan Rostenkowski (D., Ill.), Phil Landrum (D., Ga.), Charles Vanik (D., Ohio), Herman Schneebeli (R., Pa.), Barber Conable Jr. (R., N.Y.).

The conference committee met that morning in H208, a small room just outside the House chamber. In years past, the door bore the name "Mr. Mills," and tourists posed next to it to have their pictures taken. Now the door bears the name "Mr. Ullman," and the tourists don't take pictures anymore.

The House and Senate, for the first time in history, had both held their markups on the tax-cut bill in public session, but when they went into conference, they closed the door, making a lot of reporters mad. As the conference was getting under way, the conferees could hear reporters grumbling through the louvered door. So they closed the louvers. Then there was no air; some reporters thought that was poetic justice.

Inside tiny H208, the conferees were incredibly cramped, with one lawmaker's knees jammed into another lawmaker's back. There was no oxygen. And, as one participant put it, "There was a lot of 'bad air,' as the French say." He meant there was a lot of hostility bordering on rudeness.

Russell Long kept needling Al Ullman about his appearance on "Issues and Answers." Long boasted that since he had not taken any positions on TV the day before, he could approach the conference with an open mind.

Only Long's mind really wasn't all that open. He had determined not to give in on anything that first day. Like any good coach, he knew that if you could stop your opponents cold in the first quarter, it might break their spirit.

One of the first issues taken up by the conference was relatively trivial but hotly contended. Al Ullman proposed that the conferees meet late into the evenings. Long objected. After all, he felt that time was on his side. With the whole Congress eager to take an Easter recess, the longer the conference, the greater would be the pressure to compromise. Long, who was prepared to outstall Ullman, definitely did not want to work late. He got his way.

The rest of the morning, the House side offered the Senate side compromises. And the Senate side stonewalled.

Just before lunch, Long complained that there was no air in the room and everyone was getting red in the face. He proposed that they meet in a larger room. For once, the Senate and House sides found themselves in agreement.

After lunch, the conferees reconvened in the Ways and Means hearing room in the Longworth Building. It is enormous. The move to the larger room seemed to open up the atmosphere. That afternoon, the House gave way on some minor points, but the Senate, although more amicable, refused to give on anything.

The Second Day

The conference's first major breakthrough came on the second day, when the House made a concession to Long. Russell Long, the son of a populist and a populist himself, had sponsored an amendment which he called the "work bonus" plan. He proposed to pay the working poor with dependent children a bonus amounting to 10 per cent (up to $400) of their income. The House conferees knew that Long had a substantial investment in this amendment, so they let him have it.

Long responded by giving up some amendments — ones he had not sponsored. He agreed to knock out an amendment providing a tax credit for people who installed insulation or solar heating in their homes. He agreed to throw out an amendment lifting the excise tax on trucks. He agreed to reduce the scope of an amendment which would have allowed all working parents to deduct the cost of child care as a regular business expense. (Under the old law, only working parents earning under $18,000 qualified for the full deduction. The conference committee simply agreed to raise this ceiling to $35,000.) And then Long agreed to give up the so-called "Chrysler bailout" amendment which would have allowed a company to write off current losses against profits way back in 1967, 1968, and 1969 — thereby qualifying for a refund of past taxes. So, in effect, Russell Long sacrificed a tax break for big corporations in order to assure one for the working poor. His old daddy would have been proud.

The Senate conferees also agreed to accept the House formula for a rebate to individual taxpayers. The Senate version called for a rebate of 12 per cent, but not more than $240, on 1974 taxes. The House version called for a rebate of 10 per cent, but not more than $200 — total cost $8.1 billion. *Bong . . . bong . . . bong . . . bong . . . bong . . . bong . . . bong . . . bong.*

The Senate and House conferees agreed to compromise on an investment tax credit for new machinery. This credit was raised from 7 to 10 per cent for the next two years, giving business slightly more than the House bill, slightly less than the Senate bill.

But tacked onto this provision was a major victory for Long. The senator from Louisiana calls it his "share the wealth" plan. This allows businesses an additional 1 per cent tax credit if they will invest that money in an employee stock-ownership plan. This idea originated with an economist named Louis Kelso, who persuaded Long to back it. For years, Long has crusaded for this idea with the fervor of a new convert. Long reels off statistics the way an evangelist reels off Scripture: "Three per cent of the people own 70 per cent of the country's net worth." The Aesop plan illustrates the power of an idea which has just one true believer pushing it. The other conferees let Long have his way. Long says, "The most significant thing in that bill is the Aesop plan." To him, the biggest tax cut in the history of the United States is eclipsed by his amendment.

The House-Senate conferees made good progress all morning, but after lunch they completely bogged down in an oil quagmire. The House of Representatives had given Al Ullman a mandate: put an end to the oil-depletion allowance. But Russell Long, who has invested in oil wells himself, whose family is in the oil business, and whose campaigns have been enriched with oil money, refused.

Actually, Long more than refused. He went into his act. He told stories. He philosophized. He filibustered. One person at the conference said, "Trying to pin Long down was like trying to grab 100 pounds of Jell-O."

For many years, oil companies were allowed to write off 22 per cent of their profits from their drilling operations. But the House had voted to shut off this allowance. When the House bill reached the Senate, it set off some Byzantine politics. On the Senate floor, Senator Ernest Hollings (D., S.C.) rose to move for an end of the oil-depletion allowance. Before he could make his motion, however, Senator Mike Gravel (D., Alaska) managed to offer an amendment which was itself amended by Senator Alan Cranston (D., Cal.). This amended amendment sought to preserve the oil-depletion allowance for independent producers. This was all an elaborate ruse worked out ahead of time, for the Senate rules stipulate that you cannot amend beyond the second degree, meaning that you can amend an amendment but you cannot amend an amendment of an amendment. So Hollings was shut out cold.

This trick made Hollings hopping mad. When the parliamentary dust had settled, this maneuver was ruled out of order. Eventually a compromise was worked out which was sponsored by Hollings, Cranston, and Edward Kennedy. This compromise ended the oil-depletion allowance for the majors but retained it in a limited form for independent oil producers, who were allowed to write off 22 per cent of their profits on 2,000 barrels a day. Since 28 states have independent oil companies, this provision passed the Senate.

It was this amendment which Russell Long carried into the conference committee. The oil-depletion allowance for the majors was dead, but he was determined to keep it alive for all the little independent "mom and pop millionaires" and "storefront barons."

In the conference, Long attempted to use Kennedy's sponsorship of the amendment to his advantage. At one point, Long accused Ullman of not understanding the Democratic caucus in the House. Long said, "Just go back and tell them that Kennedy is for it and they'll love it."

When that argument failed, Long retreated into storytelling. He talked so much and in so many circles that Ullman seemed disoriented, confused. Which was just what Long wanted. He rules by confusion. During the Finance Committee markups, several senators complained that they did not understand what they were being asked to vote on. Long replied, "If every man insists on knowing what he's voting for before he votes, we're not going to get a bill reported before Monday." In the land of the confused, the man who has some idea what is going on is king.

And now Russell Long had Al Ullman's head spinning. Ullman could simply never catch Long as he darted here and there in his briar patch.

Long told a story about a woman who went to the store to buy some eggs. She asked the storekeeper how he had the gall to sell eggs for 40 cents a dozen when the grocer down the street wanted only 30 cents a dozen. The storekeeper asked the woman why she didn't buy her eggs down the street. The woman said, "Because he's out of eggs." The storekeeper said, "Well, if I were out of eggs, I'd sell them for 10 cents a dozen." The moral of the story, according to Long, was that if you wanted something, like, for instance, oil, then you had to pay the price, and part of that price was oil depletion.

When the House conferees saw that they had no chance of ending the oil-depletion allowance forthwith, they proposed a compromise. Charles Vanik (D., Ohio) suggested that the allowance be phased out over twelve years.

Which reminded Long of another story. This one was about a sheik who caught a young courtier making love to his daughter. The sheik ordered the young man executed at dawn. They boy said, "If you'll give me three months, I'll teach an ass to talk." The sheik was intrigued by the idea, and so put him in a cell with an ass. One of the boy's friends came by the prison and asked why the boy had claimed he could teach the ass to talk. The boy said, "Because it got me three months. In that time, the sheik might die, or I might die, or I might just teach the ass to talk." The moral of the story, according to Long, was that it made no sense to phase out oil depletion over the years because you never could tell what was going to happen. You never knew what future Congresses or future presidents might want to do about the matter. (Listening to Long, some of the conferees felt that the young courtier had succeeded in his task.)

After hearing Long defend the oil-depletion allowance for hours, the House conferees finally backed down and proposed to continue the independents' depletion allowance but to phase it down over the years from 2,000 barrels a day to 500 barrels a day. Long seemed interested, but he said he would have to check with his people. The conference broke up for the day.

Russell Long went home to his apartment in the Watergate complex. That evening, Long called Senator Clifford Hansen (R., Wyo.), another member of the conference committee who also lives in the Watergate, and invited him to drop up for a visit. Long and Hansen belong to different parties but are allies on the oil-depletion question. They are also friends. Long sold Hansen his apartment. While the two senators were visiting, Long's telephone rang.

The president of the United States was calling. Gerald Ford wanted to discuss the tax-cut bill, but his tone was almost jocular. The president instructed Long more or less as follows: "If the tax-cut bill is over $25 billion, please make it as big as possible, because then it will be that much easier to veto."

Long told the president that Hansen was there. Ford, a gregarious president, asked to speak to Hansen and gave him a pep talk on reporting out a good bill.

After his chat with the president, Long never again took seriously all the White House threats to veto the tax cut. Long knew that the bill would come in well under 25 bongs.

The Third Day

On Wednesday morning, the conferees reported to the Ways and Means hearing room in an optimistic mood. They felt they were on the verge of wrapping up the tax cut. But before the conference got under way, Long and Ullman sat down together to talk. It was a private conversation, but their mikes were on. So the others knew that Long's answer was no. Gloom settled over the conferees once again.

The conference moved on to a discussion of Senator Vance Hartke's (D., Ind.) amendments to close loopholes which have saved multinational companies billions in taxes. Hartke's main points were dropped from the bill, but a few provisions were allowed to remain. The conference agreed to end both the tax break given money channeled through underdeveloped countries and the tax break on shipping income. And they restricted the size of the tax credit oil companies may take when they pay foreign taxes.

But then the conference seemed to bog down completely. Some conferees began to fear that the conference might fail to report out a bill at all.

Long and Ullman moved out into the seats where the audience would have been if the conference had not been closed. They bargained head to head, but still reached no compromise.

By noon, the conference seemed completely stalemated. It was a hung jury. Abraham Ribicoff (D., Conn.) chose this moment to speak. None of the senators except Long had said much during the conference, but Ribicoff had been especially quiet. Breaking his silence at last, Ribicoff observed that they seemed to have come to the end of the road.

As one last effort to avoid failure, he suggested that Long and Ullman go to lunch together and try to come back with some sort of compromise.

The conference voted unanimously in favor of Ribicoff's suggestion. One conferee offered to pay for the lunch.

Everyone left the room except Long, Ullman, and Laurence Woodworth, the brilliant chief of staff of the Joint Committee on Taxation. In a trivial sense, Long and Ullman double-crossed the others: they didn't go to lunch together. Instead, they stayed right there in the room and cut their compromise.

Sitting down together at the dais, they went to work. Long said that neither of them was going to convince the other, so, "Why don't we just split the difference?" And with Woodworth working as a catalyst, they did just that.

The Senate wanted to pay $100 to people on Social Security. The House didn't want to pay anything. So they settled on $50.

The Senate wanted to allow people who bought new homes in 1975 a 5 per cent tax credit up to $2,000 — estimated total cost: $1.1 billion. The House wanted no housing credit at all. So they settled on a housing credit for homes under construction by March 25 — estimated total cost: $600 million.

The Senate wanted to allow taxpayers to take a $200 tax credit rather than a $750 deduction if that made their taxes lower. Since the deduction is regressive, saving those in a lower bracket less than those in a higher bracket, this credit was supposed to help even out this inequity. Long and Ullman agreed to give every taxpayer a $30 credit on top of a deduction.

The Senate bill allowed independent oil producers a depletion allowance on 2,000 barrels a day. The House wanted to cut it out altogether. So they decided to phase down the depletion allowance from 2,000 barrels a day in 1975 to 1,000 barrels a day in 1980. They further agreed to phase down the percentage of income on these barrels which could be written off. This percentage would hold firm at the old 22 per cent until 1980, but between 1980 and 1984 it would phase down to 15 per cent.

Done and done.

After the lunch recess, the conference committee reconvened not in the Ways and Means hearing room but in S207 just off the Senate floor. This room is similar to H208, where the conference had started, but it is larger. Also, it is on the other side of the Capitol. This move seemed symbolic. In three days, the conference had migrated from the House side to the Senate side.

In its new digs, the conference committee immediately agreed to accept the oil-depletion compromise. Everyone felt like celebrating. It seemed to be all over but the easy items.

Then a house — or rather 400,000 houses — fell on them. The House conferees still would not accept the housing credit. It was all coming apart all over again.

Ribicoff spoke again. He made what bordered on a patriotic speech. He spoke of chaos in the economy. He spoke of a lack of leadership. He spoke of a need to take hold. He suggested that they vote all remaining provisions — the oil, Social Security, $30 credit, and housing — up or down as one complete package.

Then Phil Landrum (D., Ga.), a conservative Southerner who is in many ways Ribicoff's opposite, took the floor to make a speech much like Ribicoff's.

The liberal Northern senator and the conservative Southern representative carried the day. The conference committee voted to accept the whole Long-Ullman lunch-break package. The conference, which Ullman calls "one of the toughest I've ever been in," was over.

Ullman had managed to pare down the cost of the tax cut, but Long had retained all of the amendments about which he really cared. If you looked only at the price tag, then Ullman had won the conference. If you looked only at the provisions, then Long had won. So in a sense it was a compromise. However, Russell Long had never really expected, or even wanted, to get the full $30-billion Senate-approved tax cut. What he really wanted, he got. On Capitol Hill Russell Long was generally awarded the conference.

Mills is "dead" — long live Long.

In the hall, the reporters had organized a pool on the cost of the tax cut. The winners were Marya McLaughlin of CBS and Chuck Van Dyke of AP. Al Hunt, the *Wall Street Journal* reporter who acted as banker, threw the money at them. The tax-cut conference ended in a shower of dollar bills.

And what was the winning bet?

Bong, bong.

THOMAS P. ("TIP") O'NEILL IS THE epitome of the Massachusetts politician, which according to some political observers is a unique breed. O'Neill was born in 1912, into a second-generation Irish immigrant family. His father was a Cambridge politician, and by the time Tip O'Neill was in his teens, he was actively involved in political campaigns. He was elected to the Massachusetts Legislature in 1936, the same year he graduated from Boston College. He served in the state legislature until 1952, having been chosen minority leader in 1947 and 1948, and speaker of the House from 1948 until 1952. In 1952 he ran for John F. Kennedy's vacated House seat (Kennedy was running a successful senatorial campaign against Henry Cabot Lodge, Jr.), and after a close primary win he won the general election by a large majority, which was the case in all of his subsequent elections to the House.

Tip O'Neill advanced rapidly in the House, not only because of his own consummate skill as a politician, but because he was aided by another Massachusetts politician, John F. McCormack. In 1955, McCormack, who was majority leader, appointed O'Neill to the powerful House Rules Committee. When McCormack became speaker of the House in 1962, O'Neill served as an informal majority leader until the selection of Carl Albert. Tip O'Neill himself became majority leader in January 1971, after the untimely death of Majority Leader Hale Boggs of Louisiana, who was lost on a plane flight over Alaska. The backing of Boggs' people in the House helped to give O'Neill the majority leadership. O'Neill conducted the same kind of highly effective personal campaign for the House leadership that had always guaranteed him success with the regular electorate. Within the House, O'Neill's personal friendship with McCormack and his close working relationship with Carl Albert, both when Albert was majority leader and when he was Speaker, reflected O'Neill's effective personality and style. By the time the Democratic caucus met in January 1973 to choose its new majority leader, Tip O'Neill was unopposed. From the position of majority leader it was only one short step to the Speakership in 1977 after Albert retired. In the following selection we see why Tip O'Neill is truly a master politician; we are given a close look at his two major assets, his personality and style.

21 Jimmy Breslin
THE POLITICIAN

The hand that rocked the bureaucracy into motion was found, of a Saturday night in June 1974, wrapped around a glass.

"Will you drink a Manhattan?" Tip O'Neill asked a man joining the party.

The man thought about it.

"I asked you, will you drink a Manhattan?"

The man thought more about it. Agitation showed in O'Neill's face.

"The reason I'm asking you if you take a Manhattan is that there's no bar here and it takes them too long to bring us back a drink. So I ordered two Manhattans for myself and you can have one of them if you want."

This was in the early part of the evening, when more than forty people came into the private dining room of the Wayside Inn, at Chatham, on Cape Cod, the people gathering there in celebration and admiration of the thirty-third wedding anniversary of Tip and Milly O'Neill and simultaneously the sixtieth birthday of Milly O'Neill, that number being loudly announced to all by her husband.

O'Neill was standing in a circle of people, everybody talking, O'Neill talking back to everybody, when his son Tom — who was running, successfully it turned out, for Lieutenant Governor of Massachusetts — placed a hand on his father's elbow. "Dad, I just want to tell you this one thing."

O'Neill, looking straight ahead, the eyes taking in the entire room — politics is for backcourt men — said out of the corner of his mouth to his son, "Hey, I can listen to five conversations at once. Just keep telling me what you want me to know."

His father went back to the group. "Chuck, is the weather really that bad? I thought Bantry was part of Cork. Cork's not supposed to be that bad. Oh, it's in West Cork? Oh, they have bright spells. That's good. Bright spells. Dick, old pal, you look good. Mary, darling! How are you? What will you have to drink, dear? Are you playing any golf, Paul? Well, I played today. You know what happened the other day out there? I'm on the third hole and there's a ball on the fairway and I don't know where the hell it came from. And here coming through the woods from the other fairway is Jim St. Clair. I said to him, 'Hey, Jim, what are you doing over here?' He just gave me this shrug and I kept on going my way. Stop to talk to him? Oh, I wouldn't do that. It just so happens that we're both members of Eastward Ho. Do I know him? I'll tell you a story about Jim St. Clair. One day a long time ago I got a call on a Sunday morning from a man whose son was arrested for drunken driving the night before. The boy was a senior at West Point. He was taking a summer course at MIT. The boy had been out and he'd had a few and the officer arrested him in Central Square for drunk driving. Well, I get a call from the father. He said the son'll be thrown out of West Point. Could I help? Well, geez, a kid goes to his last year in the Academy. I'm not going to let him get into trouble over a few drinks. Of course, I'll try to help. I told him I'd get my brother Bill, who was alive then. Practicing law, you know. Well, Bill calls the guy and the father says there's ten thousand in it if you could get my son off. My brother says, no, one thousand will be the charge, and I *cahn't* guarantee you anything but a pretty good try. The father said, no, it has to be ten thousand. My brother Bill says, no, I'll charge you a thousand. So on a Sunday morning we all come to court. I take a seat and the clerk comes up to me and says the judge wants to see me in the back. So I go back there and the judge says, 'Tip, what are you doing in here?' So I tell him the story of this West Point lad. When I finish I go outside and by now the father and the boy are in court. And with them is Jim St. Clair. During the night, it seems the father had gotten nervous after he arranged to have my brother Bill. And the father asked for the name of the biggest lawyer in Boston and they told him Jim St. Clair. So Jim St. Clair sees Bill and I starting to leave and he says to the father, 'You know, I'm not as experienced in a city court like this one. I think you're better off with Bill O'Neill here.' So the father said all right, and Jim St. Clair went off to play golf and my brother handled the case. Well, it was in Cambridge, and you got to know Cambridge. The policeman got up on the stand and my brother asked him, 'Did you know that this boy was a senior at West Point and that he is taking summer courses at MIT in order to better prepare himself to defend his country, and that he just pulled off to the side of the road on Saturday night to sleep off the exhaustion?' And the cop said, 'No, I didn't. If I had known it, I never would have allowed the court clerk to issue the summons.' Now you see, in Cambridge at the time the cop did not issue the summons. The court clerk did. So now the cop decided not to press the matter any more. At the same time he himself didn't have to rip up any ticket or anything. It was up to the court clerk to revoke the summons. Which of course he did and the case was over. And now I'm going to show you where Jim St. Clair is so smart. Remember the father telling my brother Bill about ten thousand dollars for the case? Well, he gave Bill three hundred dollars on the first day. Now for the rest of the bill, seven hundred, it was pulling teeth to get it out of him. Anyway, Paul, old pal, you look marvelous. Hey, what about all this food? Come on now, let's eat." He began steering people toward the buffet table.

At the end of the night, on his way to the car, O'Neill led his wife into the crowded smoky taproom of the Wayside Inn. He waited until George McCue, who plays the piano, finished a song. Then he came through the tables and up onto the small bandstand. He wanted to do one thing before the evening was over.

"My name is Tip O'Neill and I fool around in politics. I just want to sing a song for my wife, Milly, on her thirty-third wedding anniversary. I want to sing the song they played on the day we were married. The name of the song is 'Apple Blossom Time.' "

George McCue began to play the song on the piano and O'Neill's barbershop voice boomed out the start of the song.

> I'll be with you in apple blossom time,
> I'll be with you
> To change your name to mine. . . .

He sang through the smoke to his wife, selling her a love song in front of strangers. You thought automatically of Nixon and his Haldeman and Ehrlichman, standing in the doorway of the amber light of the room, smirking and starting to leave, secure in the absolute belief that no such open, old-fashioned people could be dangerous. If O'Neill was Congress's idea of a leader, how could they be hurt? How could a man who sings to his wife in public ever qualify as an opponent? At the last note, O'Neill broke into a neighborhood cheer, his voice coming up from the sandlots:

"Milly Miller O'Neill! Yeah!"

The next day he went to Washington, taking with him in all his mannerisms and speech the loud, crowded life of the streets and of the frame houses of Cambridge and Boston, and the life as a politician that is much a part of the area. There is no way to understand what went on in Washington in the summer of 1974 unless you realize that what happened was because of politicians. Ask Peter Rodino what was the single most important thing he had to do to bring about the impeachment vote against Richard Nixon and watch the Constitutional scholars pack around to hear his answer:

"When I was able to hold Mann, Thornton, and Flowers, then I knew it could be done," Rodino tells you. "I had to have them. Once I had them I could start to put it together."

Put it together. A vote. The basics of clubhouse politics. He had to know that he had the votes of James Mann of South Carolina, Walter Flowers of Alabama, and Ray Thornton of Arkansas. With these Southerners for impeachment, the needed Republican votes would not be im-

possible to obtain. Let the scholars debate the narrow versus broad interpretations of the Constitution as the most meaningful thing to come
out of the impeachment. Peter Rodino knew it was the votes that did it.
The politics, not the scholarship of the matter.

And, from his position, Tip O'Neill knew it was the job of causing
the bureaucracy to move that enabled everything else to happen. He
knew this because he was a professional politician, and you might as
well know a little bit of what these people are and where they come
from.

For a little island, it has caused so much pain. In 1845, there was a
great potato famine in Ireland, people in remote areas trying to subsist
on yellow winter grass and, finally, crazed, entering the black torture of
cannibalism. Everywhere in the country there were children unable to
close their mouths, the lack of calcium in their bones preventing their
jaws from working. Three O'Neills — Pat, John, and Mike — left Cork
City for the terrible ocean crossing to Boston, and the promise of jobs
with the New England Brick Company. In Boston, the first money the
brothers gathered that was not needed for food went directly into the
Irish stock market — cemetery plots. The next money Pat O'Neill
had — in 1855 — was spent going home to Ireland and bringing back a
wife to America. A son from this marriage was Thomas P. O'Neill, Sr.
He was raised to be a bricklayer. In 1900, he won a seat on the Cambridge City Council. On the day his son was born — Thomas P.
O'Neill, Jr. — the father was picketing Harvard with people from the
bricklayers' union. The only thing better a man from Cambridge could
say about his father is that the father was elected President on the day
he was born. For Harvard, until it began to grow up in the last fifteen
years, always regarded the people outside its gates as leaves upon the
streets.

In 1914, Thomas P. O'Neill, Sr., received the highest mark in a Civil
Service test for the job of superintendent of sewers and sanitation for
Cambridge. There were 1700 men on the payroll, none of them Civil
Service, which meant that O'Neill was in charge of hiring and firing.
His hand immediately reached out to touch more jobs. He married the
executives of the Edison Cambridge Gaslight Company, a joining
together worth hundreds of jobs to O'Neill, Sr. In North Cambridge, he
became known as "The Governor." He ran the North Cambridge
Knights of Columbus baseball team, was President of St. John's Holy
Name Society and — strict Irish rather than dreaming Irish — head of
the St. Matthew's Temperance Society. Nobody in his house was allowed to wear anything that did not have a union label on it. No clothes
were ever thrown out — there always was a society for the needy. And
all the children in the household were brought up to regard the first

Tuesday after the first Monday in November as the most important day of the year. When Tip O'Neill was fifteen, he was out ringing doorbells to pull people out of their houses to vote for Al Smith for President and Charley Cavanaugh for Massachusetts State Representative. Tip O'Neill, in charge of half a precinct, reported at the end of the day that only four people in his area did not vote, and they were out of town.

Tip O'Neill hung out with a large crowd of kids at a place called Barry's Corner, and without anybody mentioning the fact, O'Neill was the leader. One of them, Red Fitzgerald, remembers his mother saying that Tip O'Neill was going to be a bishop. "He never pulled a dirty trick in his life, so how could he miss?" Red says. O'Neill always had a way to keep the crowd around him, and also to be useful to them. He had a job as a night watchman at a brickyard, and he fixed up the outdoor telephone pay station with a nail into the contact so that his nightly crowd of visitors had free phone service. It was in the middle of the Depression and nobody had the nickel for a call.

By 1931, O'Neill was out of high school and earning $21 a week as a truck driver for a brick company. November of that year was cold and work was slow. O'Neill took courses at Boston College High School at night, then entered Boston College. Neither the college nor the O'Neill family publicizes his scholastic achievements, although Boston College prints his picture on its literature and considers him as perhaps the school's most important alumnus. Meanwhile, if Boston College ever were to falter, Harvard would be more than happy to claim O'Neill as its own. The matter of academic brilliance was brought up over the summer in Washington, when Peter Rodino (who never went to college) and John Sirica (scholastic background at best vague) were busy showing the nation that honesty might be important.

"The night-school students are saving the country," Mary McGrory, the writer, was saying one day. "I don't think Sirica or Rodino spent a day in a regular undergraduate school. And I'm certain that Tip did not."

"Oh, no, he went to Boston College," she was told.

"Oh, yes, but thank God it wasn't serious," Mary McGrory said.

In his education O'Neill did himself and the country a favor by not following the traditional path of entering law school before going on to politics. During the early months of 1973, a Tip O'Neill, attorney at law, trained in the deviousness and tiny facts of the law, never would have come walking into Carl Albert's office saying that Richard Nixon was going to be impeached. That was too outrageous, and also too true, for a lawyer. Tip O'Neill, attorney, would have had instilled in him by professors the knowledge that he had not a scintilla of evidence upon which to base any judgment at all of Richard Nixon's status in February of 1973. O'Neill, not being a lawyer, did not know that he was using such terribly unsure methods as instinct, a little anger, and a boxcar full of common sense.

The fact that O'Neill is not a lawyer gives singularity to his success. It always has been extremely difficult for legitimate people to get into politics because the base of the American political system has been built on the needs of lawyers. They come out of offices that are one flight over a drugstore and have gold lettering on the windows that says "Attorney at Law," and they come into the political system because time and occupation make it the place to be. Lawyers are not lashed to a normal person's work schedule. Always, a lawyer can switch his schedule around so he may attend a City Council meeting at one-thirty on Thursday afternoon. Also, as the nation grew and started its sprawl at the turn of the century, the lawyers then in command drew up codes so intricate, so tangled that no citizen could ever do business with a government agency of any size, from town to federal, without the service of a lawyer. Particularly a lawyer involved in politics. Many of the rules and regulations adopted throughout the country, most still in effect today, carried with them the unwritten admonishment, "Bring Extra Money!" This, in envelopes, for sliding under the table. Corruption to benefit lawyers was built into the government structure as if it were notarized. Today in politics, at the place where most men must start, it seems to be almost solely a place for lawyers. Judges appoint referees, lawyers, for mock-auctions of foreclosed properties. The judges appoint lawyers known in the business, and politics is the business of judges. The items spiral upward to a point where you have foreclosure proceedings on multimillion-dollar mortgages and the judge appoints a referee, a monitor, again a clubhouse lawyer who receives as high as $30,000 on a million-dollar matter; receives the $30,000 for doing approximately nothing. How much of this does the lawyer keep for himself and how much does he hand back to the judge? That depends upon the bargaining ability of both. If they were to strike a poor deal, a quarrelsome deal, somebody might hear of it and a district attorney would consider the subject a prime opportunity for career advancement. Other matters between lawyer and judge can be settled in ways that almost can be traced; the judge has a son and daughter who attend expensive colleges, all bills paid from a sort of scholarship set up by a lawyer.

Because there is money to be made from the system, lawyers get into politics as a business necessity. The reasoning is that lawyers are necessary in government because government makes and deals with laws, and lawyers are best equipped for this. But laws are things to be understood and obeyed by everybody, so why should the making of laws be left to a small inbred system? The major reason for the presence of so many lawyers in government is, of course, the economics. Less than 5 per cent of the lawyers in the nation ever stand on their feet in a courtroom. That is too unsure a life. A public payroll, however, is very sure. Representing a contractor who does business with government agencies — where the lawyer knows many people through his political life — also can be considered a certainty. And then the financial structure of public life makes office-holding a dream for a lawyer. Most local and state and many federal elective posts allow a person to practice law on the side. Senator Jacob Javits has a law firm on Park Avenue in New York City. State Representative Michael LoPresti has a law practice in Boston. The rewards produced by the situation cannot be counted. Therefore, at the start of a career, it bothers not a politician to have to live in the state capital for four or five months a year, at a salary of perhaps less than $15,000, because his law office in his home district is producing a living for him. But for a college teacher with ideas, or a steamfitter with ideas, it is financially impossible to serve in a state legislature. Some think or dream or even try. Always the result is the arithmetic of family bills makes politics impossible.

Left mainly to lawyers, then, the pursuit among most politicians on a local level is for the great prize: a judgeship. Judges receive excellent money, serve lengthy terms, and have short working hours and long vacations. In New York, higher courts pay up to $49,000 for terms of fourteen years. Foraging rights appear to be limitless. The scramble for a judicial vacancy becomes so intense that the entire political structure of a county can be frozen while councilmen and assemblymen and leaders push and swirl and bargain — often openly passing money about — for the judgeship.

Tip O'Neill represents the ones who came another way. If you see the system work on a local basis, you wonder how anybody worth while ever lasts through it and gets anyplace. But for O'Neill, there was no way he could not be a lifetime politician. Clearly, the viral containers in his genes held, who knows, a couple of thousand years of the ability to control, to calm others, to decide without being abrasive, to be affable while the insides boil. For good politicians, real politicians, are not created in law school or in bank vaults. They are born, as their fathers were born, and the father of the father before them, and then back through the ages, with this viral container of public life in the genes. Just as the ability to play a piano in concert or to write a lasting novel is present at birth.

As a senior at Boston College he ran for Cambridge City Council. His father did virtually nothing to help him, and he lost the election by a hundred and fifty votes. The arithmetic still is fresh. "I got four thousand votes," he says quickly, "and thirteen hundred of them were from North Cambridge. I should have gotten eighteen hundred votes there. That's if I pulled what I should have in wards seven, eight, nine, ten and eleven. What happened? My father said to me at the end of the election, 'You know, you never asked me for help.' The woman across the street said the same thing to me on election day. Her name was Mrs. Elizabeth O'Brien. She was an elocution teacher. She called over to me in the morning, 'Good luck, Thomas. I'm going to vote for you even though you didn't ask me.' I told her I'd known her all my life. 'Mrs. O'Brien, I used to run to the store for you. I didn't think I had to ask you.' And she said to me, 'Tom, people always like to be asked.' Well, you could of punched me right in the nose and I wouldn't of felt it."

The next time he ran he was working in a small insurance brokerage and real-estate office in Harvard Square. The insurance business can serve the same purpose as a law degree to a politician, but he never did very much with it. In the election this time, there was a candidate named Tierney who had to be beaten for a seat in the State Legislature. A few days before the election, an old pro named Foley said to O'Neill, "You've done well for a beginner. I don't want you to feel bad when you lose." O'Neill began to come continually late to street-corner rallies. He was too busy working the side streets and asking housewives to vote for him.

On election night, Tierney took a hotel room, had a few drinks, then slept for an hour. He showered and changed his clothes in order to look fresh and vibrant when acknowledging the cheers later on. Tierney came to his headquarters and, whistling softly, asked to see the results from his prime area, Ward 11, Precinct 3. Eleven-three contained St. John's School, its rectory and convent. Tip O'Neill had worked the area so thoroughly he owned it. The slip of paper for 11-3 was handed to Tierney. Tierney's soft whistle stopped, as did his heart. The results from 11-3 showed O'Neill with 712 votes and Tierney with 163. Rested, showered, Tierney went out in search of a pulmotor. And in his own headquarters, a rumpled, sweaty, flushed Tip O'Neill let out the first of what were to become a lifetime of election-night laughs.

Some years later, 11-3 was given a thorough campaigning by Congressional candidate John F. Kennedy. The area is changing now, with college students moving into houses that have been cut into small apartments; but if you walk into the kitchen of a house where lifelong residents live, the woman will point to a chair at the kitchen table and tell you, "He came in here and he sat right there. God rest his soul."

One day after the 1962 Congressional elections, Jack Kennedy saw O'Neill in the White House, and he said, "Say, Tip, how did you do in eleven-three?"

"You know, only thirty-four people voted against me," O'Neill said.

"And I'm sure you have the names and addresses of every one of them," Kennedy said.

In 1935 O'Neill was almost twenty-three when he won this first election. Also in that election, up in another section of Cambridge called

Greasy Village, Leo Edward Diehl, twenty-two, won a seat in the legislature. He won as much by his powers of observation as anything else. One morning, at the start of the campaign, Leo was out in the streets in time to see one Father John Geoghegan driving a woman named Peggy Dolan in the general direction of Peggy Dolan's job in Boston. You would have had to cut off Leo Diehl's head to make him forget this.

Some mornings later, Leo Diehl was on the same street at the same time and here was Father Geoghegan again driving Peggy Dolan to work. Leo grunted.

It then happened that in the core of the campaign, Leo Diehl heard that Father Geoghegan was going door to door on behalf of Leo's opponent, a man named Hillis. When this news was brought to Leo Diehl, the candidate showed no outrage. He simply asked for somebody to give him a lift. As the car pulled away, everybody on the sidewalk was surprised at the calmness with which Leo received the news, very bad news for his campaign because in Cambridge a priest's word had power second only to money.

The friend driving Leo Diehl said to him. "Where are we going?"

"I want to drop by and say hello to Peggy Dolan."

Peggy Dolan was shocked by Leo Diehl's accusations. "I do not go out with Father Geoghegan! I just let him drive me to work.

"Besides," she said, "Father Geoghegan goes steady with Theresa MacNamara."

Theresa MacNamara was a local dance instructress who had danced the parish to death. Leo immediately had his friend drive over to Theresa MacNamara's dance studio.

"We do not!" Theresa MacNamara squalled. "All we do is the Texas Tommy together."

Leo Diehl persisted. Soon, in tears, Theresa MacNamara said:

"He calls me Pussy Cat."

Later that night, grunting, grimacing, Leo Diehl pulled himself up the rectory steps and rang the doorbell. When Father Geoghegan appeared, Leo Diehl said, "I just wanted your permission for Theresa MacNamara to come around with me tonight and tell all the people that she's your best girl and that she wants them all to vote for me."

Father Geoghegan started to faint. He pulled himself together long enough to agree that he would make the rounds on behalf of Leo Diehl himself.

"Make sure you do," Leo said. "By the way, I don't know what's the matter with you. I'd rather jump on top of Peggy Dolan than Theresa MacNamara any day."

In January of 1936, O'Neill and Diehl entered the State House for the first time. It was the beginning of a relationship which is closer today than it ever was. And it also was the true beginning of a political career for Tip O'Neill.

There is in this country no place that could even be suggested as being anywhere near the Massachusetts State House for bone politics. Throughout the nation, the complaint with state legislatures is that they are part-time bodies. Not even that in many places. New York, supposedly so efficient, has a state legislature which meets in January and averages three days a week until the late spring. After which it is regarded as a criminal offense for the legislature not to be recessed well in advance of the closing days of the school year, thus giving legislators time to open summer houses, pack their kids' clothes for camp, and plan vacation trips. In Massachusetts, the legislators prefer to sit forever. They usually have to be driven out of the building, practically at gunpoint. If a Massachusetts legislator is removed from his game, his sport, his very life, then all that is left for him to do is return home to his wife and family, and in Massachusetts anybody can have a family but the true goal of life is to be a politician; or, true term, a Pol. It is not uncommon for the Massachusetts Pols to sit in the State House throughout the summer, arguing, spreading rumors, using the phones, and — true glory — plotting against each other.

But in this they are so right. For who would leave a building, and what possible reason could he give, where the life in its halls is dedicated to the memory of the actions of such as former Governor — among other things — James Michael Curley? Ask anybody in Boston about Curley and they will grope for a place to begin; there is so much to tell. Well, in 1933 new President Franklin D. Roosevelt offered Curley the post of United States Ambassador to Poland. From the State House there came a great cry, "He'll pave the Polish Corridor." And from James Michael Curley himself, in a face-to-face meeting with Roosevelt, there came, "If Poland is such a great place, why don't you resign and go there yourself?"

THE
COURTS

Chapter
Six

Character, personality, and style help to shape the judiciary at all levels. A true picture of the judicial process would not be complete without a personality profile of the actors that are involved, including judges, prosecuting attorneys, lawyers for the defense, plaintiffs and defendants, and, in some cases, jurors. At the trial level the drama of the courtroom is shaped by all of the personalities that are involved. The full-fledged and celebrated criminal trial is, however, a rarity, and personality usually affects the judicial process outside of public view.

The character of judges inevitably has a profound effect on the judicial process. At the trial court level their personalities determine the way in which they run their courts. At the appellate level, and particularly on the Supreme Court, their personalities and styles determine the effect they will have on colleagues. The character of judges has been molded long before they reach the bench. Certainly it would be profitable to apply James Barber's character classification of presidents to judges. An active-positive judge would deal with cases quite differently than would an active-negative judge. The value system of the former would be better developed and more likely to affect opinions without at the same time being rigid. An active-negative judge would be opportunistic on the bench, and particularly below the Supreme Court, would always be keeping an eye out for the possibility of higher judicial or political office. The character of some judges will cause them to seek the emulation of colleagues, and others will exhibit a strongly independent and iconoclastic streak. Some judges will attempt to control everything that goes on in their courts and will seek efficiency before justice. Others will go out of their way to protect the rights of defendants who they feel deserve a break. The character of every courtroom will reflect the personality and style of the presiding judge.

The Supreme Court is unique, not only because its decisions are far-reaching, but also because it is affected more by group dynamics

271

among the justices than other courts are. Coalitions are formed, and pressures are used to change minds. The effectiveness of the chief justice and the influence of other justices largely depend on their personalities. A strong and persuasive personality can often change colleagues' minds. The chief justice is potentially an important leader. He presides over the weekly, secret conferences of the justices, gives his opinion first, and votes last. When he votes with the majority he determines which majority justice will write the opinion. A forceful chief justice can bring unity to a divided Court, and in some cases bring about unanimity on politically crucial decisions, such as the desegregation decision in *Brown* v *Board of Education*, decided in 1954. At that time, Chief Justice Earl Warren, who assumed office in October 1953 after the Brown case had been taken up by the Court, used his considerable powers of persuasion and his highly personal leadership style to bring unanimity to a highly divided Court.[1]

Judicial decision-making, at both Supreme Court and lower levels, is a far more fluid process than is commonly known. In commenting on Supreme Court decisions in the decade that ended with the *Brown* decision, one scholar concludes on the basis of reviewing the private papers of Supreme Court justices that "hardly any major decision in this decade was free of significant alteration of vote and language before announcement to the public."[2] Justices often change their minds regardless of their seeming ideological commitment. Group pressure has its effects on Supreme Court justices as on ordinary human beings. The "freshman effect" causes instability in voting patterns among new justices to the Supreme Court.[3] Freshman justices may follow rather than lead their colleagues during their initial period of assimilation onto the Court, although this certainly was not true of Chief Justice Earl Warren, who was a pivotal justice from the time he was appointed in 1953.

Most Supreme Court justices have had little or no prior judicial experience before joining the Court and almost without exception those justices ranked as great or near-great have been more "political" than "judicial" in their styles.[4] Many of the most effective justices from John

[1] See S.. Sidney Ulmer, "Earl Warren and the Brown Decision," *Journal of Politics* 33 (1971):689–702.

[2] J. Woodford Howard, Jr., "On the Fluidity of Judicial Choice," *The American Political Science Review* 52 (March 1968):43–56, at p. 44.

[3] Ibid., p. 45.

[4] An interesting rating of Supreme Court justices by law school deans and professors of law, history, and political science, undertaken in 1970, may be found in

Marshall to Earl Warren held elected or appointed political offices, and often were highly partisan politicians. This political experience helped to shape their style of operation once on the Court. The Court was viewed as a political arena, in which pressure and persuasion could be used to change the minds of colleagues on cases that had far-reaching political ramifications.

Although the Supreme Court is somewhat more cloistered than the other branches of the government, the justices do not remain in isolation from each other or from Congress, the president, and administrative officials. Conflicts between the Court and other branches is often smoothed through personal contacts. While the New Deal Court was turning down much of Roosevelt's New Deal legislation, Justice Harlan F. Stone, at an informal party, gave Frances Perkins, FDR's secretary of labor, the idea to use the taxing and spending authority of Article I to support the Social Security Act.[5] The Court is not supposed to give advisory opinions, but nothing prevents a justice from informally communicating his ideas to the president or a member of his administration. Justice Felix Frankfurter remained a close personal friend of Franklin Roosevelt after he was appointed to the Court, and Abe Fortas was a constant political adviser to President Lyndon B. Johnson. Hugo Black, who wrote the majority opinion in the 1952 *Steel Seizure* case, which held that President Truman did not have independent constitutional authority to seize the steel mills, invited President Truman to dinner to help keep the president and the Court on good terms with each other. Justice William O. Douglas was present, and he described the incident in his autobiography as follows:

> Hugo loved company and long conversations. His spacious garden in his exquisite Alexandria home was ideal for that purpose during spring and summer. He loved to entertain there; and when, during the Korean War, the Court held on June 2, 1952, that Truman's seizure of the steel mills was unconstitutional, Hugo asked me what I thought of his idea of inviting Truman to his home for an evening after the decision came down. I thought it a capital idea. So in two weeks Hugo extended the invitation and Truman accepted. It was stag dinner, and only Truman and members of the Court were present. Truman was gracious though a bit testy at the beginning of the evening. But after the bourbon and canapes were passed, he turned to Hugo and said, "Hugo, I don't much care for

Henry J. Abraham, *Justices and Presidents* (New York: Oxford University Press, 1974), pp. 289–90. Holmes and Cardozo were notable exceptions to the usual lack of prior judicial experience among justices ranked as great.

[5] Frances Perkins, *The Roosevelt I Knew* (New York: Viking, 1946), p. 286.

your law, but, by golly, this bourbon is good." The evening was a great step forward in human relations, and to Hugo Black, good human relations were the secret of successful government.[6]

As this anecdote has shown, the personalities and styles of the justices affect external as well as internal relationships.

[6] William O. Douglas, *Go East Young Man* (New York: Random House, 1974), p. 450.

NOWHERE IN GOVERNMENT is the impact of character and personality more important than on the Supreme Court. Each week while the court is in session, the justices meet secretly in conference to deliberate their decisions on cases involving some of the most important issues that confront our government, such as discrimination, freedom of speech and press, the death penalty, the busing of school children, executive privilege, the separation of church and state, and abortion. The decisions of the Court take precedence over those of the president, the Congress, and the state legislatures, and the actions of the Court are unreviewable.

The scales of justice are supposed to be balanced through a rational, deliberative process that carefully and objectively ascertains the facts of individual cases and applies the law. However, the law is not readily defined objectively but requires interpretation to give it meaning. The process of judicial interpretation necessarily involves a highly subjective element. It is the subjectivity of the law that permits and even encourages judges to apply their own values and prejudices in making decisions. And, on the Supreme Court, where the justices must work in close contact with their colleagues, interpersonal relationships among "The Brethren" may influence the outcome of a case as much as the ideological orientation of the justices.

The private world of the Supreme Court, like that of the other branches of the government, is characterized by maneuvering among the justices to gain internal power and status. The highly personal and political dimension of Supreme Court decision making has generally been overlooked in the study of constitutional law. The following selection gives a behind-the-scenes view of the role of personalities in the historic Supreme Court decision that held that women have a constitutional right to obtain abortions.

22 Bob Woodward and Scott Armstrong
THE BRETHREN AND THE ABORTION DECISION

Douglas had long wanted the Court to face the abortion issue head on. The laws in effect in most states, prohibiting or severely restricting the availability of abortions, were infringements of a woman's personal liberty. The broad constitutional guarantee of "liberty," he felt, included the right of a woman to control her body.

Douglas realized, however, that a majority of his colleagues were not likely to give such a sweeping reading to the Constitution on this increasingly volatile issue. He knew also that the two cases now before the Court — challenging restrictive abortion laws in Georgia and Texas (*Doe v. Bolton* and *Roe v. Wade*) — did not signal any sudden willingness on the part of the Court to grapple with the broad question of abortions. They had been taken only to determine whether to expand a series of recent rulings limiting the intervention of federal courts in state court proceedings. Could women and doctors who felt that state prosecutions for abortions violated their constitutional rights, go into federal courts to stop the state? And could they go directly into federal courts even before going through all possible appeals in the state court system? Douglas knew the Chief wanted to say no to both these jurisdiction questions. He knew the Chief hoped to use these two cases to reduce the number of federal court cases brought by activist attorneys. The two abortion cases were not to be argued primarily about abortion rights, but about jurisdiction. Douglas was doubly discouraged, believing that his side was also going to lose on the jurisdiction issue.

These are difficult cases, the Chief said. No one could really tell how they would come out until the final drafting was done. . . .

Brennan and Marshall counted the vote 5 to 2 — Douglas, Brennan, Marshall, Stewart and Blackmun for striking the laws; the Chief and White dissenting.

Douglas, however, thought there were only four votes to strike the laws. Blackmun's vote was far from certain. He could not be counted on to split with the Chief on such an important issue.

For his part, Blackmun was for some kind of limited ruling against portions of the laws, but he had not decided what to do. . . .

. . . The puzzle was Blackmun.

The Chief's assignment sheet circulated the following afternoon. Each case was listed on the left side in order of the oral argument, the name of the Justice assigned to write each decision on the right.

It took Douglas several moments to grasp the pattern of the assignments, and then he was flabbergasted. [Flouting Court procedure] the Chief had assigned four cases in which Douglas was sure the Chief was not a member of the majority. These included the two abortion cases, which the Chief had assigned to Blackmun. He could barely control his rage as he ran down the list. Was there some mistake? He asked a clerk to check his notes from the conference. Douglas kept a docket book in which he recorded his tabulation of the votes. It was as he suspected. . . .

Never, in Douglas's thirty-three years on the court, had any Chief Justice tried to assign from the minority in such fashion. For two terms now there had been incidents when the Chief had pleaded ignorance, had claimed he hadn't voted, had changed his vote. Until now they had been isolated instances.

On Saturday, December 18, Douglas drafted a scathing memo to Burger, with copies to the other Justices. He, not the Chief, should have assigned the opinions in four of the cases. And, Douglas added, he would assign the opinions as he saw fit.

The Chief's response was back in a day. He conceded error in two of the cases, but insisted that the voting in the two abortion cases was too complicated. "There were . . . literally not enough columns to mark up an accurate reflection of the voting," Burger wrote. "I therefore marked down no votes and said this was a case that would have to stand or fall on the writing, when it was done.

"That is still my view of how to handle these two sensitive cases, which, I might add, are quite probable candidates for reargument."

Douglas ascribed to Burger the most blatant political motives. Nixon favored restrictive abortion laws. Faced with the possibility that the Court might strike abortion laws down in a presidential-election year, the Chief wanted to stall the opinion, Douglas concluded.

Blackmun was by far the slowest writer on the Court. The year was nearly half over and he had yet to produce a first circulation in a simple business case that had been argued the first week . . . It was the kind of case in which Douglas produced drafts within one week of conference. But in the abortion cases, Douglas had a deeper worry. The Chief was trying to manipulate the outcome.

Blackmun might circulate a draft striking portions of the restrictive abortion laws. But as a judicial craftsman, his work was crude. A poor draft would be likely to scare off Stewart, who was already queasy, and leave only four votes. Or if Blackmun himself were to desert the position — a distinct possibility — precious time would be lost. Either defection would leave only a four-man majority. It would be difficult to argue that such a major decision should be handed down on a 4-to-3 vote. There would be increasing pressure to put the cases over for the sort of case that Nixon had in mind when he chose Powell and Rehnquist.

Blackmun was both pleased and frightened by the assignment. It was a no-win propostion. No matter what he wrote, the opinion would be controversial. Abortion was too emotional, the split in society too great. Either way, he would be hated and vilified.

But from Blackmun's point of view, the Chief had had little choice but to select him. Burger could not afford to take on such a controversial case himself, particularly from the minority. Douglas was the Court's mischievous liberal, the rebel, and couldn't be the author. Any abortion opinion Douglas wrote would be widely questioned outside the Court, and his extreme views might split rather than unify the existing majority. Lastly, Blackmun had noticed a deterioration in the quality of Douglas's opinions; they had become increasingly superficial.

Brennan was certainly as firm a vote for striking down the state abortion laws as there was on the Court. But Brennan was the Court's only Catholic. As such, Blackmun reasoned, he could not be expected to be willing to take the heat from Catholic anti-abortion groups. Marshall could not be the author for similar reasons: an opinion by the Court's only black could be unfairly perceived as specifically designed for blacks: That left only Stewart. Blackmun believed that Stewart would certainly relish the assignment, but he clearly had trouble going very far.

Blackmun was convinced that he alone had the medical background and sufficient patience to sift through the voluminous record for the scientific data on which to base a decision. He was deeply disturbed by Douglas's assumption that the Chief had some malicious intent in assigning the abortion cases to him. He was *not* a Minnesota Twin.

True, Blackmun had known the Chief since they were small children and had gone to Sunday school together. They had lived four or five blocks apart in the blue-collar Daytons Bluff section of St. Paul. Neither family had much money during the Depression. The two boys had kept in touch until Blackmun went to a technical high school.

Blackmun's seven years at Harvard, however, put the two men worlds apart. Burger had finished local college and night law school in six years and was already practicing law when Blackmun came back to clerk for a judge on the Court of Appeals. Blackmun was best man at Burger's wedding, but the two drifted apart again as they established very different law practices.

Blackmun tried to tell his story every chance he got. His hands in his pockets, jingling change uncomfortably, he would explain how he had practiced in Minneapolis, where large law firms concentrated on serving major American corporations. Burger had practiced in St. Paul, across the river, in the political, wheeler-dealer atmosphere of a state capital.

"A Minneapolis firm," Blackmun would say, "will never practice in St. Paul or vice versa." Left unsaid was the disdain so obvious in the Minneapolis legal community for St. Paul lawyers.

But Blackmun was a hesitant and reserved storyteller, and he was never sure that the others got the message. Douglas, however, should have realized by now that Harry Blackmun was no Warren Burger twin.

Blackmun had long thought Burger an uncontrollable, blustery braggart. Now, once again in close contact with him, he was at once put off and amused by the Chief's exaggerated pomposity, his callous disregard for the feelings of his colleagues, his self-aggrandizing style. "He's been doing that since he was four," he once told Stewart.

Blackmun was just as aware as Douglas was of the Chief's attempts to use his position to manipulate the Court. Douglas was correct to despise that sort of thing. But this time, Blackmun felt, Douglas was wrong. When he arrived at Court, Blackmun had assumed the Chief's job as scrivener for the conference. Burger had finally given up trying to keep track of all the votes and positions taken in conference, and had asked Blackmun to keep notes and stay behind to brief the Clerk of the Court. Even then the Chief sometimes misstated the results. Blackmun would deftly field the Chief's hesitations, filling in when he faltered. When Burger misinformed the Clerk of the Court, Blackmun's cough would cue him.

"Do you recall what happened there, Harry?" the Chief would then say. "My notes seem to be a bit sporadic."

Blackmun would fill in the correct information as if Burger had initiated the request.

Part of the problem was that the Chief spread himself too thin. He accepted too many social, speaking and ceremonial engagements, and exhibited too little affection for the monastic, scholarly side of the Court's life. As a result, Burger was often unprepared for orals or conference. Too often, he had to wait and listen in order to figure out which issues were crucial to the outcome. His grasp of the cases came from the summaries, usually a page or less, of the cert memos his clerks prepared. The Chief rarely read the briefs or the record before oral argument.

The problem was compounded by Burger's willingness to change his position in conference, or his unwillingness to commit himself before he had figured out which side had a majority. Then, joining the majority, he could control the assignment. Burger had strained his relationship with everyone at the table to the breaking point. It was as offensive to Blackmun as it was to the others. But one had to understand the Chief. For all his faults, here was a self-made man who had come up the ladder rung by rung. Blackmun did not begrudge him his attempts at leadership.

The abortion assignment really amounted to nothing more than a request that Blackmun take first crack at organizing the issues. It was one of those times when the conference had floundered, when the briefs and oral arguments had been inadequate, when the seemingly decisive issue in the case, jurisdiction, had evaporated. The Court had been left holding the bull by the tail.

Blackmun was not so naïve as to think that the Chief had given him the abortion cases with the intention of having him find a broad constitutional right to abortion. But he was distressed by Douglas's implicit suggestion that he was unfit for the assignment or was somehow involved in a deception.

Blackmun also knew that he, after all, had a unique appreciation of the problems and strengths of the medical profession. At Mayo, he had watched as Doctors Edward C. Kendall and Philip S. Hench won the

Nobel Prize for research in arthritis. He rejoiced with other doctors after their first successful heart-bypass operation, then suffered with them after they lost their next four patients. He sat up late nights with the surgical staff to review hospital deaths in biweekly meetings, and recalled them in detail. He grew to respect what dedicated physicians could accomplish. These had been terribly exciting years for Blackmun. He called them the best ten years of his life.

If a state licensed a physician to practice medicine, it was entrusting him with the right to make medical decisions. State laws restricting abortions interfered with those medical judgments. Physicians were always somewhat unsure about the possible legal ramifications of their judgments. To completely restrict an operation like abortion, normally no more dangerous than minor surgery, or to permit it only with the approval of a hospital committee or the concurrence of other doctors, was a needless infringement of the discretion of the medical profession.

Blackmun would do anything he could to reduce the anxiety of his colleagues except to spurn the assignment. The case was not so much a legal task as an opportunity for the Court to ratify the best possible medical opinion. He would take the first crack at the abortion case. At the least, he could prepare a memo to clarify the issues.

As was his custom, Douglas rushed through a first draft on the cases five days after conference. He decided not to circulate it, but to sit back and wait for Blackmun. He was still bitter toward Burger, whom he had taken to calling "this Chief," reserving "The Chief" as an accolade fitting only for retired Chief Justice Earl Warren. But Douglas broke his usual rule against lobbying and paid a visit to Blackmun. Though he would have much preferred that Brennan write the draft, he told Blackmun, "Harry, I would have assigned the opinion to you anyway."

Reassured, Blackmun withdrew to his regular hideaway, the Justices' second-floor library, where he worked through the winter and spring, initially without even a law clerk to help with research.

Brennan, too, had little choice but to wait for Blackmun's draft. But in the interval, he spotted a case that he felt might help Blackmun develop a constitutional grounding for a right to abortion. Brennan was writing a majority opinion overturning birth-control activist Bill Baird's conviction for distributing birth-control devices without a license (*Eisenstadt v. Baird*). He wanted to use the case to extend to individuals the right to privacy that was given to married couples by the 1965 Connecticut birth-control case.

Brennan was aware that he was unlikely to get agreement on such a sweeping extension. He circulated his opinion with a carefully worded paragraph at the end. "If the right to privacy means anything, it is the right of the individual, married or single, to be free from unwarranted governmental intrusion into matters so fundamentally affecting a person as the decision whether to bear or beget a child."

That case dealt only with contraception — the decision to "beget" a child. He included the reference to the decision to "bear" a child with the abortion case in mind. Brennan hoped the language would help establish a constitutional basis, under the right to privacy, for a woman's right to abortion.

Since the last paragraph was not the basis for the decision, Stewart could join it without renouncing his dissent in the 1965 case. Brennan got Stewart's vote.

But Blackmun was holding back. The Chief was lobbying Blackmun not to join Brennan's draft. Brennan's clerks urged their boss to lobby Blackmun.

Brennan refused. Blackmun reminded him, he said, of former Justice Charles E. Whittaker, who had been paralyzed by indecisiveness. Whittaker's indecision had ended in a nervous breakdown and his resignation. Former Justice Felix Frankfurter had misunderstood Whittaker's indecision and had spent hours lobbying him. Instead of influencing him, Frankfurther had drawn Whittaker's resentment. No, Brennan said, he would not lobby Blackmun.

Blackmun finally decided not to join Brennan's opinion, but simply to concur in the result. That worried Brennen. Without adopting some logic similar to that provided in the contraception case, Blackmun would have difficulty establishing a right to abortion on grounds of privacy.

With the official arrival of Powell and Rehnquist, the Chief scheduled a January conference to discuss which cases should be put over for reargument before the new nine-man Court. Burger suggested that cases with a 4-to-3 vote should be reargued. His list included the abortion cases, . . .

Blackmun spent his time — apart from oral argument, conferences and a bare minimum of office routine — in the Justices' library. Awesome quantities of medical, as well as legal, books were regularly carried in. But all indications pointed toward no circulation of a first draft until much later in the spring. . . .

Blackmun began each day by breakfasting with his clerks in the Court's public cafeteria, and clerks from the other chambers had a standing invitation to join them. Blackmun would often spot a clerk from another chamber eating alone and invite him over. He seemed, at first, the most open, unassuming and gracious of the Justices.

Breakfast-table conversation generally began with sports, usually baseball, and then moved on to the morning's headlines. There was an unspoken rule that any discussion of cases was off limits. Where other Justices might openly debate cases with the clerks, Blackmun awkwardly side-stepped each attempt. The law in general was similarly out of bounds. Blackmun turned the most philosophical of discussions about law around to his own experience, or to the clerk's family, or the performance of a younger sibling in school.

The clerks in his own chambers saw a different side of Blackmun which betrayed more of the pressure that he felt. The stories were petty. An office window left open all night might set him off on a tirade. It was not the security that worried Blackmun, but the broken social contract — all clerks were supposed to close all windows each night. Number-two pencils, needle-sharp, neatly displayed in the pencil holder, need include only one number three or a cracked point to elicit a harsh word. If Blackmun wanted a document photocopied, and somehow the wrong one came back, he might simply fling it aside. An interruption, even for some important question, might be repulsed testily.

The mystery of the Blackmun personality deepened. His outbursts varied in intensity and usually passed quickly. "Impatient moods," his secretary called them. But they made life more difficult; they added an extra tension.

Yet none of his Court family — clerks, secretaries, or his messenger — judged Blackmun harshly. They all knew well enough the extraordinary pressures, real and imagined, that he worked under.

From his first day at the Court, Blackmun had felt unworthy, unqualified, unable to perform up to standard. He felt he could equal the Chief and Marshall, but not the others. He became increasingly withdrawn and professorial. He did not enjoy charting new paths for the law. He was still learning. The issues were too grave, the information too sparse. Each new question was barely answered, even tentatively, when two more questions appeared on the horizon. Blackmun knew that his colleagues were concerned about what they perceived as his indecisiveness. But what others saw as an inability to make decisions, he felt to be a deliberate withholding of final judgment until all the facts were in, all the arguments marshaled, analyzed, documented.

It was a horribly lonely task. Blackmun worked by himself, beginning with a long memo from one of his clerks, reading each of the major briefs, carefully digesting each of the major opinions that circulated, laboriously drafting his own opinions, checking each citation himself, refining his work through a dozen drafts to take into account each Justice's observations. He was unwilling, moreover, to debate the basic issues in a case, even in chambers with his own clerks. He preferred that they write him memos.

Wearing a gray or blue cardigan sweater, Blackmun hid away in the recesses of the Justices' library, and his office had instructions not to disturb him there. The phone did not ring there, and not even the Chief violated his solitude. Working at a long mahogany table lined on the opposite edge with a double row of books, Blackmun took meticulous notes. He spent most of his time sorting facts and fitting them to the law in a desperate attempt to discover inevitable conclusions. He tried to reduce his risks by mastering every detail, as if the case were some huge math problem. Blackmun felt that if all the steps were taken, there could be only one answer.

These abortion cases were his greatest challenge since he came to the Court. Beyond the normal desire to produce an opinion that would win the respect of his peers in the legal community, Blackmun also wanted an opinion that the medical community would accept, one that would free physicians to exercise their professional judgment.

As general counsel at the Mayo Clinic, Blackmun had advised the staff on the legality of abortions the hospital had performed. Many of them would not have qualified under the Texas and Georgia laws now in question.

Blackmun plowed through both common law and the history of English and American law on the subject. He was surprised to find that abortion had been commonly accepted for thousands of years, and that only in the nineteenth century had it become a crime in the United States. At that time, abortion had been a very risky operation, often fatal. The criminal laws had been enacted largely to protect pregnant women.

The use of antiseptics and the availability of antibiotics now made abortion relatively safe, particularly in the first few months of pregnancy. The mortality rates of women undergoing early abortions were presently lower than the mortality rates for women with normal childbirths. That medical reality was central for Blackmun. It was itself a strong medical justification for permitting early abortions.

A decision to abort was one that Blackmun hoped he would never face in his own family. He presumed that his three daughters felt that early abortions should be allowed. He claimed to be unsure of his wife Dottie's position. But she told one of his clerks, who favored lifting the restrictions, that she was doing everything she could to encourage her husband in that direction. "You and I are working on the same thing," she said. "Me at home and you at work."

By mid-May, after five months of work, Blackmun was still laboring over his memorandum. Finally, he let one of his clerks look over a draft. As usual, he made it clear that he did not want any editing. The clerk was astonished. It was crudely written and poorly organized. It did not settle on any analytical framework, nor did it explain on what basis

Blackmun had arrived at the apparent conclusion that women had a right to privacy, and thus a right to abortion. Blackmun had avoided extending the right of privacy, or stating that the right to abortion stemmed from that right. He seemed to be saying that a woman could get an abortion in the early period of pregnancy. The reason, however, was lost in a convoluted discussion of the "viability of the fetus," the point at which the fetus could live outside the womb. Blackmun had added the general notion that as the length of the pregnancy increased, the states' interest in regulating and prohibiting abortions also increased. But there was no real guidance from which conclusions could be drawn. Blackmun had simply asserted that the Texas law was vague and thus unconstitutional.

The clerk realized that the opinion could not settle any constitutional question. It did not assert, or even imply, that abortion restrictions in the early months of pregnancy were unconstitutional. The result of this opinion would be that restrictive laws, if properly defined by the states, could be constitutional.

The draft seemed to fly in the face of Blackmun's statements to his clerks. "We want to definitely solve this," he had told them. But he seemed to be avoiding a solution.

In the Georgia case, he had found that the law infringed on a doctor's professional judgment, his right to give advice to his patients. Blackmun proceeded from the doctor's point of view; a woman's right to seek and receive medical advice did not seem an issue.

Blackmun's clerk, who favored an opinion that would establish a woman's constitutional right to abortion, began the laborious task of trying to rehabilitate the draft. But Blackmun resisted any modification of his basic reasoning or his conclusions. He circulated the memo to all chambers with few changes.

Stewart was disturbed by the draft. Aside from its inelegant construction and language, it seemed to create a *new* affirmative constitutional right to abortion that was not rooted in any part of the Constitution. Stewart had been expecting a majority opinion. Blackmun's memo did not even have the tone of an opinion, merely of a tentative discussion.

Stewart decided to write his own concurrence, specifying that family-planning decisions, including early abortions, were among the rights encompassed by the Ninth Amendment, which says that all rights not specifically given to the federal or state governments are left to the people. Rather than identify the rights that women or doctors have, Stewart preferred to say that states could not properly interfere in individuals' decisions to have early abortions. He circulated his memo two weeks after Blackmun's but immediately joined Blackmun's original.

Douglas saw no shortage of problems with the Blackmun draft, but Blackmun had come a long way. At least it was a step in the right direction. Though Douglas was still holding on to his concurrence, he did not circulate it. Instead, he joined Blackmun.

At the time, the Court was considering an antitrust case against a utility company, the Otter Tail Power Company, which operated in Minnesota. Douglas saw an opportunity to flatter Blackmun. "Harry, you're not a Minnesota Twin with the Chief," he told him. "I am the real Minnesota Twin. . . . We were both born in Minnesota and you were not."

Blackmun appreciated the point.

"Furthermore, Harry, I belong to the Otter Tail County regulars. You can't belong, because you weren't born there."

Douglas regaled Blackmun with stories of his father's life as an itinerant preacher in Otter Tail County, and he praised Blackmun's abortion draft. It was one of the finest presentations of an issue he had ever seen, he said.

Blackmun was ecstatic. Douglas, the greatest living jurist, had freed him of the stigma of being Burger's double. Soon, Blackmun had five votes — his own and those of Douglas, Brennan, Marshall and Stewart. It was one more than he needed; it would have been a majority even if Powell and Rehnquist had participated.

For White the term had its ups and downs like any other year at the Court. He had been a fierce competitor all his life. He loved to take control of a case, pick out the weaknesses in the other Justices' positions, and then watch them react to his own twists and turns as he pushed his own point of view. When he could not, which was often, he took his frustrations to the third-floor gym to play in the clerks' regular full-court basketball game.

Muscling out men thirty years his junior under the boards, White delighted in playing a more competitive game than they did. He dominated the games by alternating savage and effective drives to the basket with accurate two-hand push shots from twenty feet. White consistently pushed off the clerk trying to cover him, calling every conceivable foul against the hapless clerk, while bitching about every foul called against himself. He regularly took the impermissible third step before shooting. The game was serious business for White. Each man was on his own. Teamwork was valuable in order to win, not for its own sake.

One Friday afternoon White was out of position for a rebound, but he went up throwing a hip. A clerk pulled in the ball and White came crashing down off balance and injured his ankle.

The Justice came to the office on crutches the next Monday: he would be off the basketball court for the rest of the season. He asked the clerks to keep the reason for his injury secret. The clerks bought him a Fuss-ball game, a modern version of the ancient game of skittles. It was competition, so White enjoyed it, but it lacked for him the thrill of a contact sport like basketball — or law.

On Friday, May 26, Byron White read a draft dissent to Blackmun's abortion decision that one of his clerks had prepared. He then remolded it to his liking. The structure of Blackmun's opinion was juvenile; striking the Texas law for vagueness was simply stupid. The law might have several defects, but vagueness was not among them. The law could not be more specific in delineating the circumstance when abortion was available — it was only to protect the life of the mother.

Blackmun was disturbed by White's attack, but whether it made sense or not, it showed him that he had more work to do. The more he studied and agonized over his own memo, the less pleased he was. He needed more information, more facts, more insight. What was the history of the proscription in the Hippocratic oath which forbade doctors from performing abortions? What was the medical state of the art of sustaining a fetus outside the womb? When did life really begin? When was a fetus fully viable? What were the positions of the American Medical Association, the American Psychiatric Association, the American Public Health Association?

These and dozens of other questions plagued Blackmun. His opinion needed to be stronger. It needed more votes, which could mean wider public acceptance. A nine-man court was essential to bring down such a controversial opinion. "I think we can get Powell," he told his clerks.

One Saturday toward the end of May, the Chief paid Blackmun a visit, leaving his armed chauffeur-bodyguard in the outer office. Blackmun's clerks waited anxiously for hours to find out what case the Chief was lobbying. The Chief finally left, but Blackmun also departed without a word to his clerks. The next week, the Chief shifted sides to provide the crucial fifth vote for Blackmun's majority in an antitrust case against professional baseball (*Flood v. Kuhn*).

The following Saturday, June 3, Blackmun drafted a memorandum withdrawing his abortion opinion. It was already late in the term, he wrote. Such a sensitive case required more research, more consideration. It would take him some time both to accommodate the suggestions of those in the majority, and to respond to the dissenters. Perhaps it would be best if the cases were reargued in the fall. He asked that all copies of his draft memo be returned.

Douglas was once again enraged. The end of the year always involved a crunch. Of course, there was tremendous pressure to put out major opinions without the time to fully refine them. That was the nature of their work. The pressure affected them all. It was typical that

Blackmun could not make up his mind and let his opinion go. Douglas had heard that the Chief had been lobbying Blackmun. This time, Burger had gone too far. The opinion had five firm votes. It ought to come down. It was not like cases with only four votes that might change when Powell's and Rehnquist's votes were added. Douglas also did not want to give the Chief the summer to sway Blackmun.

Burger was taking the position that there were now five votes to put the case over to the next term — Blackmun, White, Powell, Rehnquist, and himself. Douglas couldn't believe it. Burger and White were in the minority; they should have no say in what the majority did. And Powell and Rehnquist had not taken part; obviously they could not vote on whether the case should be put over.

The looming confrontation worried Blackmun. There were no written rules on such questions, and Douglas's apparent willingness to push to a showdown would further inflame the issue. Finally, Blackmun turned to Brennan, who was sympathetic. Obviously the opinion could not come down if its author did not want it to come down. But Brennan also wanted it out as soon as possible.

Blackmun said he understood that Douglas did not trust him, but insisted that he was firm for striking down the abortion laws. The vote would go the same way the next year. They might even pick up Powell. That would make the result more acceptable to the public. He would be able to draft a better opinion over the summer.

Brennan was not so certain of Blackmun's firmness. At the same time, he did not want to alienate him. He agreed to tell Douglas that he, too, was going to vote to put the case over for reargument. He was fairly certain Marshall and Stewart would join. That would leave Douglas protesting alone.

Douglas was not pleased by the news of Brennan's defection. But the battle was not yet over. He dashed off a memo, rushed it to the secretaries for typing and to the printers for a first draft. This time, Douglas threatened to play his ace. If the conference insisted on putting the cases over for reargument, he would dissent from such an order, and he would publish the full text of his dissent. Douglas reiterated the protest he had made in December about the Chief's assigning the case to Blackmun, Burger's response and his subsequent intransigence. The senior member of the majority should have assigned the case, Douglas said, . . .

Douglas knew a fifth Nixon appointment was a real possibility on a Court with a seventy-four-year-old man with a pacemaker; with Marshall, who was chronically ill; and with Brennan, who occasionally threatened to quit. . . .

Borrowing a line from a speech he had given in September in Portland, Douglas then made it clear that, despite what he had said earlier, he did in fact view the Chief and Blackmun as Nixon's Minnesota Twins. "Russia once gave its Chief Justice two votes; but that was too strong even for the Russians. . . .

"I dissent with the deepest regret that we are allowing the consensus of the Court to be frustrated."

Douglas refined his draft three times, circulated it, and left for Goose Prairie.

The Court erupted in debate over whether Douglas was bluffing or was really willing to publish the document. Though sympathetic to his views, Brennan, Marshall and Stewart could not believe that Douglas would go through with it. No one in the history of the Court had published such a dissent. The Chief might be a scoundrel, but making public the Court's inner machinations was a form of treason. And the reference to the Russian Chief Justice with two votes was particularly rough. They pleaded with Douglas to reconsider. His dissent would undermine the Court's credibility, the principal source of its power. Its strength derived from the public belief that the Court was trustworthy, a nonpolitical deliberative body. Did he intend to undermine all that?

Douglas insisted. He would publish what he felt like publishing. And he would publish this if the request to put over the abortion decision was not withdrawn.

But, the others argued, what good would it do to drag their internal problems into public view?

It would have a sobering influence on Blackmun, Douglas retorted. It would make it harder for him to change his mind over the summer.

Brennan's impatience with Douglas turned to anger. Douglas had become an intellectually lazy, petulant, prodigal child. He was not providing leadership. Douglas was never around when he was needed. His departure for Goose Prairie was typical. He was not even, for that matter, pulling his share of the load, though he certainly contributed more than his share to the tension. The ultimate source of conflict was the Chief. But Douglas too was at fault.

Finally, Brennan gave up arguing.

Blackmun then took it up, pleading with Douglas to reconsider. He insisted that he was committed to his opinion. He would bring it down the same way the next term; more research would perhaps pick up another vote.

Douglas was unconvinced. He needed time to think it over. His clerks would remain instructed to publish the opinion if the cases were put over for reargument.

But Blackmun had made his point. Douglas finally decided that he couldn't publish. It would endanger next term's vote on the abortion cases.

No longer speaking to his own clerks, whom he blamed for slow mail delivery to Goose Prairie, Douglas called Brennan and told him to have his dissent held. A memo came around to the Justices from Douglas's chamber asking for all the copies back.

The conference agreed to put over the abortion cases, but they would not announce their decision until the final day of the term. . . .

Harry Blackmun returned to Rochester, Minnesota, for the summer of 1972 and immersed himself in research at the huge Mayo Clinic medical library. Rochester and the clinic were home to Blackmun, a safe harbor after a stormy term. He worked in a corner of the assistant librarian's office for two weeks without saying a word to anyone on the Mayo staff about the nature of his inquiry.

In his summer office in a Rochester high-rise, Blackmum began to organize the research that would bolster his abortion opinion. He talked by phone nearly every day with one of his clerks who had agreed to stay in Washington for the summer. . . .

The clerk who was working on the opinion began to worry that one of the other clerks, strongly opposed to abortions, might try to change their boss's mind. He took no chances. Each night he carefully locked up the work he had been doing for Blackmun. At the end of the summer, he carefully sealed the latest draft in an envelope, put his initials across the tape, and had it locked in Blackmun's desk. Only Blackmun's personal secretary knew where it was.

Powell also made abortion his summer research project. As a young lawyer in Richmond in the 1930s, Powell had heard tales of girls who would "go away" to Switzerland and New York, where safe abortions were available. If someone were willing to pay for it, it was possible to have an abortion.

Powell understood how doctors viewed abortion. His father-in-law had been a leading obstetrician in Richmond, and his two brothers-in-law were obstetricians. Powell had heard all the horrifying stories of unsanitary butchers and coat-hanger abortions.

Nevertheless, Powell came quickly to the conclusion that the Constitution did not provide meaningful guidance. The right to privacy was tenuous; at best it was implied. If there was no way to find an answer in the Constitution, Powell felt he would just have to vote his "gut." He had been critical of Justices for doing exactly that; but in abortion, there seemed no choice.

When he returned to Washington, he took one of his law clerks to lunch at the Monocle Restaurant on Capitol Hill. The abortion laws, Powell confided, were "atrocious." His would be a strong and unshakable vote to strike them. He needed only a rationale for his vote.

In a recent lower court case, a federal judge had struck down the Connecticut abortion law. This opinion impressed Powell. The judge had said that moral positions on abortion "about which each side was so sure must remain a personal judgment, one that [people] may follow in their personal lives and seek to persuade others to follow, but a judgment they may not impose upon others by force of law." That was all the rationale Powell needed.

Brennan and Douglas worried that votes might have shifted since the previous spring. Blackmun remained a question mark, Stewart might defect, and they were not sure what Powell would do.

At conference on October 12, Blackmun made a long, eloquent and strongly emotional case for striking down the laws. Stewart too seemed ready to join. But the big surprise was Powell. He made it 6 to 3.

Immediately after conference, Douglas called Blackmun to tell him that his presentation had been the finest he had heard at conference in more than thirty years. He hoped the call would sustain Blackmun for the duration.

Before the end of October, Blackmun's new draft in the abortion case was circulated to the various chambers. . . .

The clerks in most chambers were surprised to see the Justices, particularly Blackmun, so openly brokering their decision like a group of legislators. There was a certain reasonableness to the draft, some of them thought, but it derived more from medical and social policy than from constitutional law. There was something embarrassing and dishonest about this whole process. It left the Court claiming that the Constitution drew certain lines at trimesters and viability. The Court was going to make a medical policy and force it on the states. As a practical matter, it was not a bad solution. As a constitutional matter, it was absurd. The draft was referred to by some clerks as "Harry's abortion." . . .

By early December, Blackmun's final draft had circulated. Stewart's and Douglas's concurrences were finished, and White's and Rehnquist's dissents were ready. There was still nothing from Burger. . . .

Stewart and Brennan thought he was stalling. The Chief was scheduled to swear in Richard Nixon for his second term as President on January 20. It would undoubtedly be embarrassing for Burger to stand there, swearing in the man who had appointed him, having just supported a sweeping and politically volatile opinion that repudiated that man's views.

At the Friday, January 19, conference, the Chief said that his schedule had been busy, and he still had not gotten to the abortion decision. Stewart figured that, having manipulated a delay until after the Inaugural, Burger would acquiesce. The others wanted a Monday, January 22, announcement, three days later, and Burger said that he would have something.

Over the weekend, he wrote a three-paragraph concurrence. Ignoring the sweep of the opinion he was joining, Burger said that one law (Texas) was being struck because it did not permit abortions in instances of rape or incest, and he implied that the other law was being struck because of the "complex" steps that required hospital board certification of an abortion. He did not believe that the opinion would have the "consequences" predicted by dissenters White and Rehnquist, and he was sure that states could still control abortions. "Plainly," he concluded, "the Court today rejects any claim that the Constitution requires abortion on demand."

The day of the scheduled abortion decision the Chief sat in his chambers reading the latest edition of *Time* magazine. "Last week TIME learned that the Supreme Court has decided to strike down nearly every anti-abortion law in the land," an article said. The abortion decision had been leaked.

Burger drafted an "Eyes Only" letter to the other Justices. He wanted each Justice to question his law clerks. The responsible person must be found and fired. Burger intended to call in the F.B.I. to administer lie-detector tests if necessary.

Dutifully, Rehnquist brought up the matter with his clerks. It was harmless in this case, he said. But in a business case, a leak could affect the stock market and allow someone to make millions of dollars. None of Rehnquist's clerks knew anything about the leak, but they asked him if it were true that the Chief was thinking of lie-detector tests. "It is still up in the air," Rehnquist said. "But yes, the Chief is insisting."

Rehnquist's clerks were concerned. Such a witch-hunt would be met with resistance. Certainly, some clerks would refuse to take such a test and would probably have to resign. The Chief is mercurial, Rehnquist explained. "The rest of us will prevail on him."

Brennan summoned his clerks and read them the Chief's letter. It was another example, he said, of the Chief usurping the authority each Justice had over his own clerks. "No one will question my law clerks but me," Brennan said. Then in a softer voice, he added, "And I have no questions." The real outrage for Brennan was not the leak but the delay. If the Chief had not been intent on saving himself and Nixon some embarrassment on Inauguration day, there probably would have been no damaging leak.

Marshall asked what his clerks knew about the incident. When he was assured that they knew nothing, he told them to forget it.

Douglas treated the letter as he had treated a request from the Chief the previous term that all clerks be instructed to wear coats in the hallways. He ignored it.

Powell was out of town, so one of his clerks opened the Chief's letter. The clerk had talked to the *Time* reporter, David Beckwith, trying to give him some guidance so he could write an intelligent story when the decision came down. But the delay in announcing the decision had apparently left *Time* with a scoop, if only for half a day.

The clerk called Powell and told him about the Chief's letter and his own terrible mistake in talking to Beckwith. He volunteered to resign.

That would not be necessary, Powell said. But a personal explanation would have to be given to the Chief.

Powell called Burger and explained that one of his clerks, a brilliant and talented young lawyer, was responsible. The clerk realized his mistake and had learned his lesson. The clerk went to see the Chief.

Burger was sympathetic. Reporters were dishonest and played tricks, he said. It was a lesson everyone had to learn.

Apparently never expecting to learn so much about the little deceptions of both reporters and sources, Burger pressed for all the details. It took nearly forty-five minutes to satisfy his curiosity.

The clerk concluded that Burger understood, that he was being a saint about the matter. Burger wanted a memo detailing exactly what happened. The clerk would not have to resign.

Later, the Chief met with top editors of *Time* in an off-the-record session. He labeled Beckwith's efforts to get inside information at the Court improper, the moral equivalent of wiretapping.

Blackmun suggested to his wife, Dottie, that she come to Court to hear case announcements on Monday, January 22. He did not tell her why. As Blackmun announced the decisions, Powell sent a note of encouragement to Blackmun's wife. Powell suspected they were about to witness a public outcry, the magnitude of which he and Blackmun had not seen in their short time on the Court.

"I'm very proud of the decision you made," Dottie later told her husband.

After the abortion decision was announced, Blackmun took congratulatory calls through most of the afternoon. But former President Lyndon Johnson died that same day, and the news of his death dominated the next morning's newspapers.

Blackmun was unhappy that the abortion decision did not get more attention. Many women, especially the poor and black, would not learn of their new rights. But the outcry quickly began, led by the Catholic Church. "How many millions of children prior to their birth will never live to see the light of day because of the shocking action of the majority of the United States Supreme Court today?" demanded New York's Terence Cardinal Cooke.

John Joseph Cardinal Krol, of Philadelphia, the president of the National Conference of Catholic Bishops, said, "It is hard to think of any decision in the two hundred years of our history which has had more disastrous implications for our stability as a civilized society."

Thousands of letters poured into the Court. The guards had to set up a special sorting area in the basement with a huge box for each Justice.

The most mail came to Blackmun, the decision's author, and to Brennan, the Court's only Catholic. Some letters compared the Justices to the Butchers of Dachau, child killers, immoral beasts, and Communists. A special ring of hell would be reserved for the Justices. Whole classes from Catholic schools wrote to denounce the Justices as murderers. "I really don't want to write this letter but my teacher made me," one child said.

Minnesota Lutherans zeroed in on Blackmun. New Jersey Catholics called for Brennan's excommunication. Southern Baptists and other groups sent over a thousand bitter letters to Hugo Black, who had died sixteen months earlier. Some letters and calls were death threats.

Blackmun went through the mail piece by piece. The sisters of Saint Mary's hospital, the backbone of the Mayo Clinic, wrote outraged letters week after week. He was tormented. The medical community and even his friends at Mayo were divided. Blackmun encountered picketing for the first time in his life when he gave a speech in Iowa. He understood the position of the antiabortion advocates, but he was deeply hurt by the personal attacks. He felt compelled to point out that there had been six other votes for the decision, besides his, that the Justices had tried to enunciate a constitutional principle, not a moral one. Law and morality overlapped but were not congruent, he insisted. Moral training should come not from the Court but from the Church, the family, the schools.

The letters continued to pour in. Every time a clergyman mentioned the decision in his sermon, the letters trickled in for a month from members of the congregation. The attack gradually wore Blackmun down. At breakfast with his clerks, when the discussion turned to the decision, Blackmun picked up his water glass reflectively, turning it slightly on edge and staring into it in silence.

The criticism also drew Blackmun and Brennan closer. Blackmun wrote Brennan a warm thank-you note: "I know it is tough for you, and I thank you for the manner in which you made your suggestions."

Brennan tried to cheer up Blackmun. Doing the right thing was not often easy, he said. The one thing in the world Brennan did not want known was his role in molding the opinion.[1]

Blackmun did not cheer up easily. The hysteria on each side of the issue convinced him that any decision would have been unpopular.

---

[1] When the clerks later put together bound volumes of the opinions Brennan had written that term, they included the abortion opinions, and on page 156 they wrote, "These cases are included with Justice Brennan's opinions for the October term 1972 because the opinions for the Court were substantially revised in response to suggestions made by Justice Brennan."

However, the deepest cut came when the state of Texas filed a petition for rehearing that compared Blackmun's conclusion, which held that a fetus was not a person, to the Court's infamous 1857 decision that said that Dred Scott, a slave, was not a citizen or person under the Constitution. Blackmun thought that comparing his opinion with the Court's darkest day of racism was terribly unfair. And, after all, it had been Stewart who had insisted on that part of the opinion.

Months later, Blackmun gave a speech at Emory Law School in Atlanta. He was chatting with students and faculty when a petite young woman with black curly hair ran up the steps to the stage. She squeezed through the group, threw her arms around Blackmun and burst into tears. "I'll never be able to thank you for what you have done. I'll say no more. Thank you."

The woman turned and ran from the room.

Blackmun was shaken. He suspected that the woman was probably someone who had been able to obtain an abortion after the Court's decision. He did not know that "Mary Doe," the woman who had filed one of the original suits in Texas under a pseudonym, had just embraced him.

EARL WARREN PRESIDED OVER the Supreme Court during its most active and controversial period. Named as Chief Justice by President Eisenhower in 1953, Earl Warren served until 1969. The decisions of the Court during this time caused major changes in constitutional law, and eventually, they resulted in the desegregation of public education in the South, the reapportionment of state and congressional legislative districts, and the widening of most of the protections of the Bill of Rights to limit state action. Before becoming Chief Justice, Earl Warren had an extensive career in public office. He was attorney general of California from 1939–43 and was elected governor in 1943, a position he held until he was appointed to the Court in 1953. He was one of the most popular governors in the history of California and received widespread support from both parties. He brought a political approach to his job as Chief Justice, and as the following selection reveals, his political background, style, and personality had a strong effect on the direction the Court took while he was Chief Justice.

Although Warren was to become one of the most forceful chief justices in the history of the Supreme Court, he did not come to the Court with firm goals in mind. "The day of my induction as Chief Justice of the United States Supreme Court was for me at once the most awesome and the loneliest day of my public career," wrote Warren. "I approached the high office with a reverential regard," he continued, "and with a profound recognition of my unpreparedness to assume its obligations in such an abrupt manner." Warren was unacquainted with Washington, knew only a few members of the Supreme Court personally, and had long been absent from the courtroom. "Since becoming Governor," Warren said, "I had not been engaged in handling legal matters except to study contracts of the state with other parties to see that they were consistent with my policies and to study all bills passed by the legislature to determine, among other things, if they conformed to the state and federal constitutions."[1] Although Warren's experience in dealing with the more technical aspects of state and federal court procedure was limited, his experience as governor in judging the constitutionality of legislation was, he felt, a valuable background for his future career on the Supreme Court.

The following selection is a personal account by Warren of his role on the Supreme Court as it faced a number of difficult issues, including the desegregation cases of 1954.

---

[1] Earl Warren, *The Memoirs of Earl Warren* (Garden City, New York: Doubleday and Co., 1977), pp. 275–276.

23

Earl Warren
A CASE OF EMOTIONAL IMPACT

The home of the Supreme Court of the United States, facing Capitol Plaza, has often been called the most beautiful building in Washington, D.C. It is indeed an awesome sight as one stands before its Grecian serenity and reads the words chiseled in white marble above the main entrance. Like the building itself, the words are inspiring. They say: "Equal Justice Under Law."

As one enters through the massive bronze doors and passes down a lofty hallway to the courtroom around which the building was designed, a feeling of solemnity and a sense of history build until the visitor arrives at the Supreme Court room itself. Inside, the stately side columns of Italian marble, the polished mahogany furnishings and the red velour hangings induce a self-imposed, respectful silence. This silence invariably prevails in deference to the cause of justice whether the Court is in session or not. Thousands of visitors come each month; on some individual days as many as twenty thousand. Yet one almost never hears a discordant sound. In the entire sixteen years that I presided as Chief Justice of the Supreme Court, I never heard an unauthorized voice raised during a session.

Rarely, in fact, did there appear to be even an air of tension in the courtroom, regardless of the importance of the case being argued or reported.

It was very different, however, on May 17, 1954.

That was the day when the historic school segregation case of *Brown* v. *Board of Education* was reported to an expectant American public. Seventeen of our states, by their own laws, had racially segregated public schools. A number of others had *de facto* segregation because of the rapid growth of ghettos which concentrated minority groups in the larger cities. The *Brown* case, when it came before the Supreme Court, challenged such discrimination in public schools as being unconstitutional.

For weeks before the announcement of our decision, the courtroom had been jammed with people; anticipation had been mounting and political writers had been hazarding all kinds of guesses as to why the opinion had been delayed from December 8, 1953, when the case had been argued, until this momentous day in May of the following year.

Contrary to speculations in the press, there had *not* been a division of opinion expressed on the Court at any time. At the weekly conference after arguments in the case, the members, conscious of its gravity and far-reaching effects, decided not to put the case to a vote until we had thoroughly explored the implications of any decision. As a result, we discussed all sides dispassionately week after week, testing arguments of counsel, suggesting various approaches, and at times acting as "devil's advocates" in certain phases of the case, but not stating our final decision until February of 1954.

At that time we voted unanimously among ourselves to declare racially segregated public schools to be unconstitutional.

Although the Chief Justice always assigns opinions when he is with the majority, I neither assigned nor pre-empted the writing of this one. Some of the senior members of the Court voluntarily suggested that I write it. The others agreeing, I did so. The opinion was submitted to the Court in conference, and, after suggestions were incorporated into it, it was officially reported, as I have noted, on May 17.

I write this at some length to emphasize that there was no dissension within the Court in connection with the *Brown* case. There was not even vigorous argument. Our decision represented the judgment of every Justice independently arrived at in the finest collegiate tradition. In my entire public career, I have never seen a group of men more conscious of the seriousness of a situation, more intent upon resolving it with as little disruption as possible, or with a greater desire for unanimity. To show how desirous we all were to present a united front, Justice Robert Jackson, who had been in the hospital for a month or so as the result of a heart attack, surprised us all by insisting on dressing and coming to the Court for the announcement. I showed concern about the danger of his overdoing, but he insisted that the case was of such importance as to call for a full Court, and he prevailed.

The lawyers and the public knew in advance that the decision must soon be reported because the usual date for adjournment of the term was not far distant.

As we Justices marched into the courtroom on that day, there was a tenseness that I have not seen equaled before or since. When I announced that I was about to report the judgment and opinion of the Court in *Brown* v. *Board of Education of Topeka, Kansas,* there was a general shifting of positions in the crowded room and a rapt attention to my words. It was not a long opinion, for I had written it so it could be published in the daily press throughout the nation without taking too much space. This enabled the public to have our entire reasoning instead of a few excerpts from a lengthier document.

In the middle of the opinion, I read:

> "We come then to the question presented: Does segregation of children in public schools solely on the basis of race, even though the physi-

cal facilities and other tangible factors may be equal, deprive the children of the minority group of equal educational opportunities? We unanimously believe that it does."

When the word "unanimously" was spoken, a wave of emotion swept the room; no words or intentional movement, yet a distinct emotional manifestation that defies description. Some of it undoubtedly was occasioned by relief that the case was decided in such a manner; some of it because of disagreement with the result; but I am sure that much of it stemmed from the word "unanimously," which flew in the face of previous news stories about dissension on the Court with regard to this case. I assume this because for weeks thereafter people would phone the Clerk's Office and demand to see the dissenting opinion. When informed that the decision was unanimous and, therefore, there could be no dissenting opinion, they would demand to know, "By what right is the dissenting opinion withheld?" or "Who outlawed dissenting opinions?"

Much has been said and written concerning this unanimity. I have been praised by many who favor the opinion for bringing it about, and I have been condemned by others who object to it. But I am entitled to neither approbation nor condemnation. The real credit for achieving unanimity, in my opinion, should go to the three Justices who were born and reared in that part of the nation where segregation was a way of life and where everyone knew the greatest emotional opposition to the decision would be forthcoming. They were Justices Hugo L. Black of Alabama, Stanley F. Reed of Kentucky, and Tom C. Clark of Texas. The others of us, while enthusiastic in our adherence to the decision and fervent in our desire for unanimity, were not in danger of being faced with animosity and harassment in our home states because of centuries-old patterns of life.

Incidentally, this was the genesis of the phrase "The Warren Court." It was coined not as a symbol of achievement or endearment, but as an indication of scorn by those who resented the decision. Since that time, it has been used in various senses. I say this advisedly because, shortly after *Brown*, Southern congressmen signed and introduced into the Congressional Record the so-called "Southern Manifesto," pledging that they would use every means at their command to overcome the *Brown* decision. Several of them told me personally that I had "stabbed them in the back." I know of no reason why they should have thought me ever to have been in favor of segregation in the first place. As far as I am aware, there was nothing in my career that would convey such an impression. I had been born and reared in California where there was no accepted policy of school segregation. I had attended public schools and the University of California, and had sat in classrooms with blacks and members of almost every minority group. I never gave it a second thought.*

As the wartime governor of California, I had integrated the National Guard shortly after its return from the War. In fact, I was one of the first, if not the first, governor to do so. I appointed some Negroes as judges. Walter Gordon, a Negro who later distinguished himself as governor of the Virgin Islands and as a United States district judge, was appointed by me to the important position of chairman of the California Adult Authority, which fixed the sentences and determined the paroles of all the prisoners in our state penitentiaries. I saw to it that Negroes and all minority groups shared in the employment benefits of our Civil Service of sixty thousand employees. All of this could hardly have been reasonably interpreted as a bias in favor of segregation.

But people do misinterpret a public figure's instincts and motivations, and I have often encountered this in my career. It has been written that there was nothing in my background to presage my so-called "liberal" decisions on the Supreme Court. This notion has always been something of a mystery to me. Of course, I could well have some prejudice, as most of us do, in favor of my own consistency, but my actions have been exposed to the public constantly for more than half a century, and I feel that my views and actions in later years are but an outgrowth of the earlier ones.

Many people believe that my views on crime are radically different from those of my district attorney and attorney general days. I have been accused of being "soft on crime" and "in favor of permissiveness." Senator Joseph McCarthy once said on the floor of the Senate, "I will not say that Earl Warren is a Communist, but I will say he is the best friend of Communism in the United States."

I have also had the experience of having two presidential candidates, George Wallace and Richard Nixon, work against me and the Court over which I presided by conveying the impression that we were a menace to the internal security of the nation and pledging themselves to undo our work of sixteen years. Even the fatherly President Dwight Eisenhower was widely quoted as having said that his appointment of me as Chief Justice "was the biggest damn fool thing I ever did."

I knew he had some such opinion because we once discussed his view of the opinions of the Court which I either wrote or joined. On this occasion, President Johnson had appointed me to head the United States delegation to the funeral service of Sir Winston Churchill in London. He assigned his *Air Force One* plane for the use of the delegation,

*Ed. note in *The Memoirs of Earl Warren*: In the preceding the author uses the more modern and socially aware term "black," but elsewhere interchanges it with "Negro." For him, the latter was never a pejorative word; it was simply the usage of his time and in his mind carried recognition of class dignity and due respect.

and former President Eisenhower accompanied us. Eisenhower was not a member of the delegation, but he was invited by the Churchill family to the ceremony. I do not recall how the conversation started, but Eisenhower said he had been disappointed in Justice Brennan and me; that he had mistakenly thought we were "moderate" when he appointed us, but eventually had concluded otherwise. I replied that I had always considered myself a moderate, and asked him what decisions he was referring to.

He said, "Oh, those Communist cases."

"What Communist cases?"

"All of them."

I pursued the discussion, and asked if he had read the opinions. He said he had not, but he knew what was in them. I then suggested that he must have some particular case in mind, and he said, "The Communists in California." I knew he probably meant the *Yates* case, which involved some garden variety Communists of no great importance. Ironically, he had just praised Justice Harlan, whom he had also appointed, for his moderation, so I said with some satisfaction, "John Harlan wrote that one." He responded that it didn't make any difference who wrote it. I tried to explain that in the judging process we were obliged to judge Communists by the same rules that we applied to all others. He refused to accept this statement, and I asked him:

"What would you do with Communists in America?"

"I would kill the S.O.B.s," he said.

I was sure this remark was merely petulant rather than definitive, so I replied, "Perhaps that could be done in the Army, but it could not be done through civilian courts."

It being dinnertime, the conversation ended. It was not a pleasant session. However, I was glad that it occurred, not only because I was always fond of the general and appreciated his having given me the opportunity to serve on the Supreme Court, but also because it afforded me the first opportunity I had had in years to explain to him my views on the difference between moderation in the political process and in the judicial processes. Through politics, which has been defined as the art of the possible, progress could be made and most often was made by compromising and taking half a loaf where a whole loaf could not be obtained. The opposite is true so far as the judicial process was concerned. Through it, and particularly in the Supreme Court, the basic ingredient of decision is principle, and it should not be compromised and parceled out a little in one case, little more in another, until eventually someone receives the full benefit. If the principle is sound and constitutional, it is the birthright of every American, not to be accorded begrudgingly or piecemeal or to special groups only, but to everyone in its entirety whenever it is brought into play. I think of this principle often because many people have said to me concerning our civil rights decisions, "I agree that everyone should have equal rights, but don't you think we are going too fast?" This is but another way of saying that moderation calls for doling out rights only a little at a time to the minority groups, the poor, the uneducated, and the otherwise underprivileged. It was this misunderstanding that was responsible for the outburst of emotion in some quarters when *Brown* v. *Board of Education* was decided.

In my more than fifty years of public service, I have been exposed to both processes, the political and the judicial, and to the interrelationship between the two, until I have what I believe is a clear concept of each in the administration of justice. In those official positions I have held, I have tried to carry this distinction in mind, and to honor both sides as essential ingredients of our governmental system. One is not born with such a concept, nor is it acquired overnight. It is an evolving thing that stems from one's experiences in life and from interpretations he or she gives them, particularly when the paths of the two processes cross.

My years on the Court were crowded with cases involving segregation, voting rights, and other civil rights, malapportionment of representative bodies, incursions on the Bill of Rights, and so forth — all of which had an emotional impact on large segments of the nation. Such cases would provoke controversy regardless of the way they might be decided. I, of course, understood that it was in the nature of the judicial process to evoke criticism because no judge can satisfy both sides, particularly in emotion-charged cases. Therefore, I never took objection to the criticism leveled at me or the Court, and made no attempt to justify publicly any of our decisions. On the other hand, I did want General Eisenhower, who had appointed me to the Court, to know from me that I had not changed my spots; that I was acting from conscience in accordance with my view of the judicial process, even though doing so resulted in unpopularity in some circles.

THE BUREAUCRACY

Chapter Seven

The bureaucracy is usually thought of as consisting of hordes of civil servants whose greatest interest is in job security, and who spend their lives in eight-hour days engaged in routine matters, never taking a chance, hoping to reach retirement safely. Whatever ripples bureaucrats are supposed to cause on the political scene are generally thought to go no further than the invention of ingenious ways of increasing red tape and regulations that irritate the public. Bureaucrats are seldom pictured in the grandiose terms that are used to describe presidents, members of Congress, Supreme Court justices, and the leaders of parties and pressure groups. The bureaucracy and the people that serve within it may not seem as dynamic and forceful as the charismatic leaders that populate the political scene elsewhere, but the personalities and styles of bureaucratic leaders have had a profound effect on the political system and public policy over the years.

The great size and diversity of the bureaucracy, and the many functions it performs, allows many kinds of personalities to be effective. There is greater movement into and out of the bureaucracy from the private sector than is the case with other governmental branches. The infusion of new personalities into the bureaucracy may cause changes in methods of operation and may cause different policies to be adopted or emphasized. There is a constant struggle in the administrative branch between defenders of the status quo and incoming or even permanent members of the bureaucracy who wish to innovate. The personality of bureaucrats goes a long way toward explaining such conflicts.

Contrasting personalities and styles are readily observable throughout the bureaucracy. There is the cautious bureau chief, who over the years has developed careful relations with the chairmen of the congressional committees that have jurisdiction over his agency. He will not make a move without consulting them and may have developed close personal friendships with them. Other administrative officials may pay only token attention to Congress, going to Capitol Hill only when it is absolutely necessary. Some officials may try to cultivate power relationships within the bureaucracy, whereas others may seek public acclaim and outside support. Some officials, when dissatisfied with policies that they see being implemented by the White House or by their agency, may resign in protest, making their dissatisfaction known to the press and the public. Other bureaucrats in the same position will try to change the policy from within, and if they resign will keep their discontent to themselves, knowing that in some agencies a public attack on the bureaucratic establishment will close the doors to future employment there. Differing bureaucratic personalities will result in a wide variety of styles, including playing it safe, playing an external or internal power game, becoming a bureaucratic politician, and seeking power and status through expertise. The positive and negative character attributes of administrators at all levels of the bureaucracy greatly affect government.

CERTAINLY NO ONE WOULD have predicted, when J. Edgar Hoover was born in 1895 in Washington to a family of undistinguished civil servants, that he would become one of the most powerful men in the federal bureaucracy, using the Federal Bureau of Investigation as his power base. The Bureau of Investigation within the Justice Department was created in 1906 and expanded during World War I; it was taken over by J. Edgar Hoover in 1924 when he was appointed its acting director by Attorney General Harlan Fiske Stone, who was shortly to join the Supreme Court.

Hoover had been working as a lawyer in the Justice Department, when he became an assistant in 1918 to the director of a newly created General Intelligence Division, which had been assigned the task of compiling information on alleged radicals. During this period, A. Mitchell Palmer, the attorney general, used the Bureau to carry out the infamous "Palmer Raids" on radicals throughout the country. Thousands of people, particularly new immigrants, were arrested without warrants, and thrown into seamy jail cells. Most were eventually released, although some noncitizen anarchists were deported. The raids brought the Bureau of Investigation into disrespect in many quarters of the country. When President Warren G. Harding assumed office, a new director of the Bureau was appointed, William J. Burns, who had once been head of the Secret Service, and had established the William J. Burns Na-

tional Detective Agency in 1909 after his retirement. As a private detective he had been convicted of a misdemeanor charge after illegally entering a New York law office. Sanford J. Ungar notes, however, that to the Harding administration the conviction

> seemed to be taken as a qualification rather than as a blot on his record, and it became widely known that Bureau men, under Burns's leadership, randomly wiretapped, broke into offices, and shuffled through personal files, and kept tabs on people's private lives. The most likely targets were "enemies" — persons who criticized [Attorney General] Daugherty, the Department of Justice, and the Bureau of Investigation; Senators who asked too many questions; and other competing government departments.[1]

The Bureau continued to be deeply involved in political activities under the directorship of Burns, and attacks were launched on alleged radicals within and without government. When Democratic Senator Burton J. Wheeler of Montana attacked corruption in the Justice Department after his election in 1922, the Bureau used every device possible to discredit him, including supplying information to the Republican National Committee on the Senator's alleged radicalism, spying on his Washington home, and attempting to lure him into a compromising situation with a woman. But the Bureau was not to stop there; it even aided the Justice Department in securing an indictment against Wheeler from a federal grand jury in Montana for influence peddling. The

[1] Sanford J. Ungar, *F.B.I.* (Atlantic–Little Brown, 1975), p. 45.

attempt by the Bureau to frame Wheeler failed, and the Senator was acquitted.

When Calvin Coolidge assumed the presidency after the death of Harding, he replaced Attorney General Daugherty, who had been implicated in the Teapot Dome scandals, with Harlan Fiske Stone. Burns was forced to resign. It was Stone who chose Hoover to clean up the Bureau. When Stone called Hoover into his office in May of 1924 to offer him the job, the following exchange took place:

> Hoover said, "I'll take the job, Mr. Stone, on certain conditions."
> "What are they?" the Attorney General asked.
> "The Bureau must be divorced from politics and not be a catch-all for political hacks. Appointments must be based on merit. Second, promotions will be made on proved ability and the Bureau will be responsible only to the Attorney General," Hoover replied brashly.
> As this account has it, Stone was delighted with the terms and said, "I wouldn't give it to you under any other conditions. That's all. Good day." [2]

With that, J. Edgar Hoover became director of the Bureau of Investigation, and was to turn the FBI into one of the most politically oriented agencies of government under the guise of maintaining political neutrality at all costs, and operating solely as a highly efficient federal police force.

Hoover proceeded cautiously after taking over the Bureau of Investigation, but soon he was to involve it in extensive public relations to fortify its image. Both he and the Bureau were to become invincible in the minds of both the public and Congress. The agency was always treated with extreme favoritism by most senators and congressmen. Within the Bureau, Hoover tried to rule over every detail, and he was to develop a cult of personality that has never been seen in the bureaucracy before or since. In the end, J. Edgar Hoover became more powerful in many ways than the presidents he served. During the Nixon years, he single-handedly vetoed a White House-sponsored plan to establish extensive domestic political surveillance, using the FBI, because he felt that it would not serve his purposes, but the president's. Hoover had for many years used the FBI for political surveillance.

In the following selection, we see how complete Hoover's domination was. For many years the FBI was run on the basis of Hoover's supposed strengths. In this selection Ungar shows that Bureau operations equally reflected Hoover's many weaknesses.

[2] Ibid., p. 48.

24

Sanford J. Ungar
THE KING:
J. EDGAR HOOVER

FBI Director Clarence M. Kelley came to the office of Senator James O. Eastland (D-Mississippi), chairman of the Senate Judiciary Committee, one day in June 1974 for a little ceremony in which Eastland presented Kelley with the first copy of a handsome black volume in memory of J. Edgar Hoover, containing *Memorial Tributes in the Congress of the United States and Various Articles and Editorials Relating to His Life and Work.* The following exchange occurred, as Kelley sought to turn a rather stiff and formal occasion into a relaxed and social one:

KELLEY: "Senator, there's an awful lot about J. Edgar Hoover in this book."

EASTLAND: "Chief Kelley, there's an awful lot about J. Edgar Hoover that ain't in this book."

There is a treasury of jokes about J. Edgar Hoover in FBI folklore, stories that agents tell each other during long, uneventful surveillances while they wait for things to happen and that assistant directors use to cheer each other up in moments of exasperation. In one, the Director is at the beach with his constant companion, Clyde Tolson. Tolson agitatedly scans the shoreline back and forth and finally says with a sigh of relief, "Okay, Boss. The coast is clear. Now you can practice walking on the water." Another tale has it that Hoover and Tolson, as they became older, decided to check into the cost and availability of cemetery plots. When Tolson reported back to him on the high price, Hoover, a notorious cheapskate, was outraged. "Never mind, Clyde," he declared. "You buy yours. But I'll just rent a crypt. I don't plan to be there for more than a few days anyway." Yet another related that whenever Tolson became depressed or dispirited, which was apparently often, the Director would seek to cheer him up by saying, "Clyde, why don't you transfer somebody?" If that didn't do the trick, Hoover would escalate the suggestion: "Go ahead, fire someone." And if Tolson still complained that this didn't help, the Director would add, "Fire him with prejudice" — a device that made it nearly impossible for the victim to find another job. Only then, went the story, did Tolson feel better.

Such bizarre fantasies conjure up the image of a man who regarded himself as infallible and godlike and who exercised arbitrary and sometimes inexplicable control over thousands of lives. J. Edgar Hoover had a degree of authority and prerogative seldom seen in democratic governments. The longer he stayed in power, the greater these prerogatives became and the more inconceivable it became that he might ever be removed; the phenomenon seemed at times to grow out of the medieval notion of the divine right of kings. Indeed, some suggested that, in times of trouble, the elevation of Hoover was just what the country needed, and his friend, Senator Joseph McCarthy of Wisconsin, tried more than once in the 1950s to launch Hoover-for-President boomlets.

But Hoover disavowed any such ambition. He was content to stay where he was, ruling over a limited but significant realm — an agency that he had salvaged from the depths of scandal and raised to the heights of honor and influence. The Director turned away other job offers — to become national baseball commissioner or head of the Thoroughbred Racing Association. Hoover put his own distinct imprint on the FBI and then turned himself into an institution. It became a tradition — and a necessity for those who sought to advance through the ranks — to say what the Director wanted to hear. By definition, it was right. It also became a tradition, as one FBI official put it, "that you do what the Director says without really agreeing with him." Hoover's words and acts were converted into legends, and some of them came out sounding as stiff and unreal or as difficult to believe as those of such other authoritarian leaders as Chairman Mao Tse-tung of the Chinese Communist party. If an attorney general or a President made him angry, the Director could just threaten to resign, and that was usually enough to bring the offender back into line. No President could afford to lose him.

Reflecting on the reverence that came to be accorded Hoover, Clarence Kelley, his successor, says, "His most casual remark [to a member of the FBI leadership] would be turned into a point of philosophy. They would even go out and document it and build it up, so it could aid them at a future time."

This treatment could be taken to laughable extremes. Once asked how he got along so well with the Director, Sam Noisette, Hoover's black retainer who was an "honorary agent," replied, "It's easy. . . . If it's snowing and blowing outside and the Director comes in and says it's a beautiful, sunny day, it's a beautiful, sunny day. That's all there is to it."

John Edgar Hoover — he abbreviated his name when he learned of a namesake who had large debts — was born the third child of an obscure family of civil servants in Washington on the first day of 1895. His father, like his father before him, worked for the Coast and Geodetic Survey, and his brother, Dickerson N. Hoover, Jr., became inspector general of the Steamboat Inspection Service in the Department of Commerce. In high school Hoover distinguished himself as a good student, a debater (overcoming an early childhood stutter and arguing, on occasion, in favor of American annexation of Cuba and against women's suffrage), and a member of the cadet corps. He had to work for anything he obtained after his high school graduation in 1913, and while studying law at night at George Washington University he had a daytime job, for thirty dollars a month, as an indexer at the Library of Congress.

After obtaining two degrees, a bachelor's and a master's of law, and passing the District of Columbia bar exam, he went to work in 1917 as a law clerk in the Justice Department. As Jack Alexander noted in a unique and intimate 1937 profile of Hoover in *The New Yorker*, from his earliest days in the Department,

> certain things marked Hoover apart from scores of other young law clerks. He dressed better than most, and a bit on the dandyish side. He had an exceptional capacity for detail work, and he handled small chores with enthusiasm and thoroughness. He constantly sought new responsibilities to shoulder and welcomed chances to work overtime. When he was in conference with an official of his department, his manner was that of a young man who confidently expected to rise. His superiors were duly impressed, and so important did they consider his services that they persuaded him to spend the period of the [First] World War at his desk.

Rise he did. By 1919, at the age of twenty-four, Hoover became a special assistant attorney general in charge of the General Intelligence Division of the Bureau of Investigation. In that position, he was responsible for assessing the threat to the United States from communists and other revolutionaries, and the information he developed became essential background for the "Red raids" conducted by Attorney General A. Mitchell Palmer in 1920. Few of the ten thousand persons arrested and detained in the raids were ever convicted under the wartime Sedition Act, but Hoover was successful in his personal efforts before a Labor Department tribunal to have at least three well-known figures deported: radicals Emma Goldman and Alexander Berkman as well as Ludwig Martens, the unofficial representative in the United States of the new Soviet government. Hoover became an assistant director of the Bureau of Investigation under Director William J. Burns during the presidency of Warren G. Harding; but his patience and freedom from association with the Harding scandals were rewarded when after his exchange with Coolidge's new attorney general, Harlan Stone, about the need to keep politics out of the Bureau, Stone named Hoover its Acting Director at age twenty-nine.

Before and after he took over the troubled Bureau of Investigation in 1924, Hoover was something of a mystery man in Washington. He kept very much to himself, living in the house where he was born and caring for his mother, the descendant of Swiss mercenary soldiers and a strong disciplinarian, until her death in 1938. But although he remained close to her, Hoover apparently shunned the rest of his family. His sister Lillian fell upon hard times, but got no help from him. "J.E. was always accessible if we wanted to see him, but he didn't initiate contacts with his family," said Margaret Fennell, his niece, to interviewer Ovid Demaris. Indeed, even Hoover's most persistent admirers and defenders within the FBI complained occasionally that the absence of any family devotion on his own part contributed to his lack of compassion toward or understanding of strong family men who worked for him. "Hoover couldn't have a family-type feeling toward anyone," observed one agent long stationed in New York; "a man who has never been a father cannot think like a father." The wife of a former assistant director of the FBI said that "the man just had no feeling at all for families." There was a certain paradox to this attitude, as Hoover expected his married agents to be loyal family men.

Hoover's coldness to his own family could not be readily explained by a busy schedule of other commitments and associations. For a time, especially in the 1930s, he was seen frequently with well-known writers and other friends on the New York nightclub circuit; and sometimes he went with bachelor friends to baseball games and other sports events (he was occasionally joined on excursions to watch the Washington Senators in the 1950s by then Vice-President Richard M. Nixon); but Hoover generally turned away all other social engagements, unless they involved official business at the Justice Department. There was little socializing in the top ranks of the Bureau itself, and relations between Hoover and his associates were intentionally kept on a businesslike level. The only woman in the Director's life, it was often said, was Shirley Temple, his favorite actress and then a child. His most frequent and celebrated diversion, especially as he became older, was horse races, where he generally placed small, losing bets and sometimes presented trophies in the winner's circle.

The replacement for family, and eventually for everyone else, in Hoover's celibate life was Clyde A. Tolson, a native of Missouri who came to Washington at the age of eighteen to work as a clerk in the War Department. He eventually became confidential secretary to Secretary of War Newton D. Baker and two successors, but after getting a law degree in night school at George Washington University, he joined the Bureau in 1928. He originally planned to move on to practice law in Cedar Rapids, Iowa, where he once attended business college for a year. But for reasons that were never entirely clear, Tolson rose quickly and was soon working at the Director's side. Hoover and Tolson became so close that, as Don Whitehead put it in his history, "They have even reached the point where they think alike." They also came to spend a great deal of time together, including, on most days, lunch at a restaurant and dinner at one or another's home. When Hoover appeared at an official function, Tolson was invariably a few steps behind and to the right of him, almost like a courtier carrying a king's cloak. As associate director, a title Hoover finally gave him in 1947, Tolson was in effect the Director's chief of staff and his mouthpiece. He chaired the Bureau's executive conference of assistant directors. Many of Hoover's attitudes and opinions, his wrath or his satisfaction, were transmitted through Tolson, who, as the years went on, seemed to do very little thinking or acting on his own. Tolson would invariably write his comments on a memorandum in pencil rather than pen, so that he could change them to conform with the Director's point of view if necessary. If the executive conference voted unanimously on a matter but Hoover was later found to disagree,[1] Tolson would take it upon himself to solicit unanimity for the "correct" position, and he usually got it. Long-time Bureau officials, asked to list Tolson's contributions and innovations to the service, are generally unable to come up with any. And even to those who worked for years near his office, he remained an enigma. Efforts to fraternize with him were turned away abruptly, and any other Bureau executive presumptuous enough to try to join him and the Director for their ritual daily lunch at Harvey's Restaurant or the Mayflower Hotel risked disciplinary action or some more subtle punishment.

Tolson's only known diversion was to dream up obscure inventions, and he actually obtained patents on a few, including a mechanism to open and close windows automatically. Hoover usually agreed to try out Tolson's inventions, either in the Bureau or at home.

According to the persistent gossip in Washington for decades, Hoover and Tolson were homosexuals; and — according to this interpretation — their attempt to repress and conceal their relationship helped explain the Bureau's vigilant, even hysterical bias against men of that sexual orientation. In fact, any such relationship between the two was never acknowledged or discovered. As one former ranking official put it, "If it was true, they were never caught. And you know how we feel in the Bureau: you are innocent until proven guilty." Another debunked the rumors about their relationship on the basis of the fact that Hoover "liked to crack jokes about sex."

Tolson was always the more sickly of the two men, and whenever he fell ill, he would move into Hoover's home to be nursed back to health by the Director's servants. When Hoover died suddenly in May 1972 Tolson was grief-stricken, and after going through the formality of being acting director of the FBI for about twenty-four hours, he announced his retirement. But for a few token items and sums of money

---

[1] The Director's famous euphemism was to say, "I approve the minority view."

willed to others, Hoover left all of his worldly possessions — an estate valued at half a million dollars — to Clyde Tolson. Tolson, increasingly ill, closed himself up in Hoover's home and declined to talk with anyone, even most of his former Bureau colleagues. He died on April 14, 1975, at the age of seventy-four, passing most of the fortune on to other loyal Bureau folk.

From all accounts, of those who knew Hoover and those who studied him, the Director was a cold and self-indulgent man. His expressions of warmth were few and far between and private — friendship with neighborhood youths whom he invited into his house; a gift of a beagle pup to replace one that died which had belonged to his neighbors in the 1950s, Senator and Mrs. Lyndon B. Johnson; offers to pay a hospital bill for one of the children of Assistant Director Cartha D. DeLoach. But according to one official who was sometimes the beneficiary of such largess from Hoover, "He extracted a pound of flesh for every ounce of generosity," especially from those who worked for him. From them he expected repayment in the form of intensified loyalty and utter obeisance. From someone like Johnson he wanted political capital; from other neighbors he seemed to require only respect and deference. Seldom did his gestures seem to be motivated simply by unselfishness or humanitarian concern toward others.

Hoover moved only once in his life — after his mother's death in 1938, from the family home in Seward Square on Capitol Hill to a large red-brick house that he bought on 30th Place in Northwest Washington, near Rock Creek Park. There he built a huge collection of antiques, art objects, and pictures, mostly of himself with other famous people. According to his neighbors, the position of each item, once settled upon, remained the same year after year. Each time a new President was elected, Hoover would move a photograph of himself with that President into a place of particular prominence in the entrance hall. Some of the art objects were fine and valuable, but others, it was discovered when they were auctioned after his death, were peculiar items like an eight-sided basket made of Popsicle sticks; a wooden stork from the old Stork Club, one of the Director's favorite New York nightclubs; a salt shaker with a nude woman on the side; and other assorted bric-a-brac. Hoover's house was impeccably well kept (he had a fear of insects and germs and kept an ultraviolet light in the bathroom) and his Kentucky bluegrass front lawn was the pride of the neighborhood until it was replaced with artificial Astro Turf shortly before his death.

He was a man of habit, leaving the house and returning at precisely the same hour every day. He always ate cottage cheese and grapefruit for lunch. If he ever had serious health problems, beyond an ulcer condition, they were a carefully guarded secret; and he did not even like it to be known that in his later years he took a nap in the office for about two hours each afternoon. Hoover did not smoke, and he took only an occasional drink of bourbon, preferably Jack Daniels, with water.

His life was the FBI and there were few diversions from it. The Director did have pretenses of being a religious man. (As a high school student he sang in a Presbyterian church choir and taught a Sunday school class, and at one point, according to his biographers, he considered becoming a minister.) But one man who worked closely with Hoover for many years claimed in an interview that the Bible on his desk was really just "a prop" and that the Director exploited organized religion and famous preachers and evangelists for his own and the FBI's selfish purposes. Despite his extraordinary power and exposure, in the eyes of most of his associates Hoover seemed to remain a man of small dimensions who never became sophisticated or graceful. He was prejudiced and narrow-minded, overtly biased against black people ("As long as I am Director, there will never be a Negro special agent of the FBI," he was often heard to say in the years before Attorney General Robert F. Kennedy exerted pressure on him to change that policy), distrustful of other minority groups, and intolerant of women in any but subservient positions. Always somewhat defensive and insecure about his own education, Hoover had a notorious distrust of people who had gone to Harvard and other Ivy League universities; he claimed that they had little knowledge of the real world. He was embarrassingly susceptible to manipulation through flattery or fulsome praise and sometimes hopelessly out of touch with the realities of changing times. He was, above all, a lonely man.

When Hoover first took over the Bureau, he was little known and seldom noticed. When he was appointed to the job, *Time* magazine remarked only that he was distinguished by "an unusually accurate and comprehensive memory," but most of the press merely ignored him. It was almost five years, in fact, before he ever achieved a distinction symbolic to Washington bureaucrats, mention in the *Congressional Record*. A Democratic congressman from Texas, Thomas L. Blanton, took the floor of the House of Representatives in early 1929 to compliment Hoover for "the high character of the splendid work they are doing" at the Bureau. Four years later, during a budget debate, Congressman John McCormack (D-Massachusetts) — later Speaker of the House and always one of Hoover's staunchest supporters — praised the Bureau as "a credit to the Federal Government" and the Director as "a brilliant young man . . . one of the finest public officials in the service of the Federal Government."

But before long, once he had consolidated power and genuinely improved the agency, Hoover determined to go public, to build a reputation for the Bureau and to construct what came to be a cult around himself. This took the form initially of an anticrime "crusade," a zealous effort to awaken the citizenry to the threat and the consequences of lawlessness and to the need to cooperate with the authorities. The wisdom and invincibility of the "G-men" (a name that gangster George "Machine-Gun" Kelly allegedly gave the Bureau agents, who had previously been known mostly as "the Feds") were trumpeted in comic strips; children wore G-man pajamas to bed and took G-man machine guns out to play. Alongside the easy, mass-appeal aspects of the crusade, however, there was also a loftier pitch for the federal police efforts, the development of a philosophy that gave the Bureau coherence and lasting importance. The Director came to have the image of an expert, a sage, almost of a saint come to deliver the nation from the forces of evil — even if he had never been out on the street working a case.

Hoover was hardly a scholar, nor was he a particularly literate man. He had made an early effort to "understand" the radical forces in the country, holding long arguments in his Justice Department office, for example, with Emma Goldman and others he had deported during the Palmer Raid era. But he soon abandoned any such dialogue and effort to understand and turned to the attack. Apart from the most important reports crossing his desk, he was said to read very little, and one of the best stories about the Director was that not only had he not written the books published under his name, but he hadn't even bothered to read them. His letters often bordered on incoherence, especially in his last years, and sometimes what semblance of logic and rationality they had came from "corrections" mercifully made by close aides like Louis Nichols and Cartha DeLoach or Hoover's lifelong secretary, Helen Gandy. The Director was notorious for his mispronunciation of words that he used often, such as communist ("cominist") and pseudo ("swaydo"), a term he generally put in front of "intellectual" or "liberal" as an expression of contempt; but it was taboo for anyone who intended to have a bright future in the Bureau to correct him on such matters.

Most of Hoover's vocabulary was graphic and quotable, and some of it was crude. Criminals were generally "rats" of one form or another and those who failed to keep them in jail were "yammerheads." One of the greatest threats to the nation came from "venal politicians." Those who criticized him might be diagnosed, as columnist Westbook Pegler was, as suffering from "mental halitosis." The press, for that matter, was full of "jackals." In a speech before the Washington, D.C., chapter of the Society of Former Special Agents of the FBI in 1971, he attacked the "few journalistic prostitutes" who could not appreciate the FBI; in that same appearance, one of his last major public addresses, he insisted that the FBI had no intention of compromising its standards "to accommodate kooks, misfits, drunks and slobs." "It is time we stopped coddling the hoodlums and the hippies who are causing so much serious trouble these days," he declared; "let us treat them like the vicious enemies of society that they really are regardless of their age."

Whatever the level of the discourse, Hoover found respectable forums and outlets for his ghostwritten elegies on law and order. He appeared regularly, for example, in the *Syracuse Law Review*. His treatise there on juvenile delinquency in 1953, replete with footnotes, advised the reader:

> Of primary importance in the child's early environment is a wholesome family life. A happy home which glows with morality provides a healthy atmosphere for the growing child. During the years of accelerated character development, the child quickly learns from observing his parents. As the language of his parents becomes his language, so the cleanliness of body and soul displayed by them exerts early influence on him. The child who is confronted with parental strife, immorality, and unhappiness in the home must look beyond the family circle if he is to develop orderly, wholesome ideals. Too often the child does not find proper guidance when it is not provided in the home.

The same article advised that it was a bad idea for both parents in a family to be employed, that poolrooms and other "hangouts" bred juvenile delinquency, and warned that "law enforcement agencies in various parts of the United States are required to adhere to restrictions which hamper policy efficiency. . . . the tendency to discount juvenile crime and to assume an overly protective attitude toward the juvenile offender is dangerous." And there were generally a few words on behalf of the old virtues:

> Truthfulness is one of the strongest characteristics of good citizenship. All criminals are liars; their lives are patterned after the deceit which they reflect in both word and deed. Certainly each parent must insist of his children that they be truthful in their every word. A child should be disciplined more severely when he attempts to hide his misconduct behind a lie than when he is guilty of misconduct alone. That truthfulness can best be learned in the everyday association between the child and his parent is self-evident. Likewise the father who is caught in a lie hardly can demand the truth from his child.

Eleven years later, he was back in the same law review on the same subject, with some rather strident warnings:

> There is a growing possibility that Nikita Khrushchev will never be forced to make good his boast of burying us — we may save him the trouble by doing it ourselves through the dissipation of the youth of our country. . . . The moral deterioration in our people is another basic cause for the large juvenile involvement in criminal activity. . . . Either we solve the problem or we may well go down!

In his prime, Hoover gave frequent speeches, and he had something to say about nearly everything:

Corruption. "One of the worst degenerative forces in American life during the past fifty years has been corruption in public office. Corrupt politicians make venal politics, and right-thinking citizens know there is but one answer and one remedy. Corruption must be eradicated. . . . Few communities in the land are free from contamination of the syndicated leeches who masquerade behind the flattering term — 'politician.' " (National Fifty Years in Business Club, Nashville, May 20, 1939.)

American home life. "When the home totters, a nation weakens. Every day it is my task to review the histories of scores who obey only the laws of their own choosing. Always the one thing that stands out is a lack of moral responsibility and any feeling of religious conviction. . . . While we fight for religious freedom, we must also fight the license sought by the atheist and those who ridicule, scoff and belittle others who would seek spiritual strength." (Commencement exercises, St. John's University Law School, Brooklyn, June 11, 1942.)

Loyalty. "In our vaunted tolerance for all peoples the Communist has found our 'Achilles' heel.' The American Legion represents a force which holds within its power the ability to expose the hypocrisy and ruthlessness of this foreign 'ism' which has crept into our national life — an 'ism' built and supported by dishonor, deceit, tyranny and a deliberate policy of falsehood. . . . We are rapidly reaching the time when loyal Americans must be willing to stand up and be counted. The American Communist Party . . . has for its purpose the shackling of America and its conversion to the Godless, Communist way of life." (Annual convention of the American Legion, San Francisco, September 30, 1946.)

Hoover was even sought out by *Parents' Magazine* in 1940 for remarks on "The Man I Want My Son to Be." His answer:

> I would want him to be intelligent, not necessarily possessed of learning derived from reading, but equipped to face the world with a self-reliant resourcefulness that would enable him to solve, in the majority of instances, the problems of human existence. . . . I would want him to realize that nothing in life can be truly gained without paying the equivalent price and that hard, intensive work is necessary.

There were subjects, perhaps, that Hoover, with his accumulation of influence and credibility, could have profitably addressed himself to, but did not. For example, he never wrote or spoke about the need to control the distribution of handguns. Instead, in sensationalized accounts written for *American Magazine* under his byline by Courtney Ryley Cooper, with titles like "Gun-Crazy," he seemed to lend some romanticism to such groups as the "Brady gang," "the gun-craziest gang of desperadoes ever to fall to the lot of the Federal Bureau of Investigation to blast into extinction."

The Director did not hesitate to pronounce his views on other issues of national controversy. He bitterly opposed the visit to this country of Nikita Khrushchev in 1959 (although he would later endorse President Nixon's voyages to Moscow and Peking). He frequently spoke out against the parole system, which he felt was administered by "sob sisters" with irresponsible leniency. "It is time that we approached the parole problem with a little more common sense," Hoover proclaimed in 1939; "it is time that sound practical businesslike methods supersede the whims of the gushing, well-wishing, mawkish sentimentalist. . . . The guiding principle, the basic requirement, the sole consideration in judging each and every individual case in which parole may be administered, should be the protection of the public."

Hoover often made decisions about people and chose his friends on the basis of their conformity with his own ideological attitudes. He was delighted, for example, when federal Judge Irving Kaufman in New York gave death sentences to Julius and Ethel Rosenberg, who were convicted of espionage in his courtroom for the alleged leak of U.S. atomic secrets to the Soviet Union. Kaufman and Hoover became fast friends. Whenever the judge went to visit his son at college in Oklahoma, he was chauffeured by agents from the Oklahoma City Field Office; and even into the 1970s, after Hoover was gone, the FBI did special favors for Kaufman, by then chief judge of the U.S. Court of Appeals for the Second Circuit. Just a phone call from the judge to the New York Field Office, complaining about a group that was demonstrating outside his courthouse, was enough to launch a preliminary Bureau investigation of the group.

With the help of his publicity-conscious lieutenants, Hoover cultivated his own image as the fearless enemy of every criminal, so effective in his job as to be loathed by them all. The Director always behaved as if there were an imminent danger to his life. He would put his hat on one side of the rear-window ledge in his chauffeured limousine and then sink down in the corner of the other side, on the assumption that any would-be assassin would fire at the hat first. He and Tolson always sat against the wall in a restaurant so they could see anyone approaching them. And whenever Hoover traveled out of town, he invariably had a large retinue of agents from the nearest field office on duty to protect him. On one occasion, Hoover became alarmed over the origin of suspicious stains that appeared on the floor of his limousine. He ordered the FBI Lab to do tests on the carpet. The conclusion: the stains came from a package of bones that he had taken home from a banquet for his dog. As former agent Joseph L. Schott has reported in his light-hearted memoir of life in the Bureau, *No Left Turns,* after an incident in California during which Hoover was jostled uncomfortably during a left-hand turn of his car, he issued a strict order of procedure: there would henceforth be no left turns. His drivers would have to learn to chart their routes accordingly.

Occasionally the Director was criticized — for example, by Senator Kenneth McKellar of Tennessee in 1936 — for having little, if any, experience himself in the investigation and detection of crime and for never having made an arrest. As one sympathetic Hoover biographer, Ralph de Toledano, puts it, after McKellar's criticism "Hoover was boiling mad. He felt that his manhood had been impugned." In response, he staged a dramatic trip to New Orleans and supposedly led the raiding party to capture a member of the "Barker gang," Alvin Karpis. Later, thanks to arrangements made by his friend, columnist Walter Winchell, he repeated the performance in New York for the capture of rackets boss Louis "Lepke" Buchalter. Such gestures grabbed headlines and calmed his critics. It was only years later that it became known that Hoover strolled into both situations after all danger was past and that he played a purely symbolic role.

Many of those who worked closely with the Director privately re-sented his comfortable daily schedule. While he took an interest in all the important matters before the Bureau, says one longtime aide, he "never lost sleep" — neither from working around the clock nor from worrying about the progress on cases. While his agents logged the required "voluntary overtime," he usually left the office on schedule at 4:45 P.M. There was a standing order not to call him at home after 9 P.M. He handled Bureau affairs in a routine and businesslike manner, apparently leaving most of the stresses and strains to others. Nonetheless, Hoover showed unusual leadership abilities and maintained the undying loyalty of almost everyone in the FBI for nearly half a century. He managed to persuade underlings that he cared deeply about their careers, and there are thousands of people still in the FBI who, like Special-Agent-in-Charge Arnold C. Larson of Los Angeles, attribute their success in life to such inspirational personal advice from Hoover as "Set your goals high. Go to college. Better yourself. Don't remain a clerk forever." Anyone in the Bureau who ever had a personal audience with the Director remembers it in intimate detail, even if it consisted merely, as it often did, of listening to a Hoover monologue on the evils of communism or the misdeeds of politicians. There was competition among some people to the very end to offer proof of their closeness to the Director; one ex-Bureau official, John P. Mohr, asserts that he was the first to be notified of Hoover's death, and John J. Rooney, the New

York congressman who supervised the FBI budget for many years, boasted that he was the only member of Congress at the gravesite after Hoover's funeral.

Hoover was often arbitrary and unreasonable, especially with those jockeying for his favor, but they seldom resisted his way of doing things. "There was a constant desire on your part to please him," explained one man who worked at it for some thirty years. "You wanted to obtain that praise from him, that letter of commendation, that incentive award. When you did, you had a great sense of pride in it. It gave you a feeling of exhilaration; you had accomplished something. He had an ability to keep you at arm's length, yet make you want to work your guts out for him. . . . I rebelled at the idea of working through fear, but I did it anyway. This was my niche. I have always wondered whether the fear was necessary, whether it might have been better to rule on the basis of mutual respect. But it is hard to fight success."

Working for the FBI and for Hoover meant, above all, submitting to discipline and regimentation that sometimes exceeded the military in its severity and lack of compassion. During the Prohibition era, taking a single alcoholic drink was grounds for being fired, if it were discovered. Hoover assumed the right to set standards for his agents' personal lives, and the sexual taboos, for example, were absolute. Not only would young unmarried male and female clerks be dismissed if it were learned that they had had illicit sexual relations, but the same punishment would be dealt to a fellow clerk who knew about any such indiscretion and failed to report it. The rules persisted, at least for agents, well after Hoover's death, and as late as mid-1974 Director Clarence Kelley approved the transfer and demotion to street-agent status for the special-agent-in-charge of the Salt Lake City Field Office because of his alleged amorous adventures.

Cars had to be kept bright and shiny, and agents were to wear conservative suits and white shirts — even though such uniform characteristics often gave them away and made them less effective at their work. Coffee-drinking on the job was forbidden, especially at FBI headquarters, and some veterans still tell of "Black Friday," in the 1950s, when a large number of agents were caught drinking coffee in the Justice Department cafeteria after the deadline hour of 9 A.M. and severely punished. The official justification for such harsh standards was that Hoover wanted all his men to have "an unblemished reputation." As one official explained it, "The FBI name was to be so good that whenever an agent went before a jury, he would be believed."

Sometimes Hoover was simply mean; when he discovered that one agent's wife had an alcohol problem and his son was in trouble with drugs, he exiled the family to a small resident agency far away, apparently out of concern that the Bureau would be embarrassed if the agent remained where he was stationed. The Director was so angered when he heard that another agent had indiscreetly said he was willing to serve "anywhere but New York or Detroit" that he made a personal effort to guarantee that the man's entire career was spent in those two cities. The no-mistake concept that Hoover constantly preached caused the Bureau to lose some valuable people to other agencies. William V. Broe, for example, was an up-and-coming supervisor when one minor error in a report that came to the Director's attention brought him a cut in pay and a transfer. Broe decided he could not afford to accept the punishment and instead resigned and went to the Central Intelligence Agency, where he rose to one of its top positions.

One of the most-publicized disciplinary excesses involved agent Jack Shaw of the New York Field Office, who was taking graduate courses at the John Jay College of Criminal Justice under FBI auspices. Shaw wrote a letter to one of his professors, in part defending the Bureau but also criticizing Hoover for concentrating on "dime-a-dozen" bank robbers and neglecting organized crime, and for a "sledgehammer" approach to public relations, among other matters; foolishly, Shaw had the letter typed in the office secretarial pool and its contents became widely known. Hoover, when the matter reached him, sent Shaw a telegram accusing him of "atrocious judgment" and transferring him to the Butte, Montana, Field Office, despite the fact that his wife was dying of cancer. When Hoover learned that the Shaw letter had been stimulated in the first place by remarks critical of the Bureau by one of Shaw's professors, he also ordered that no more agents were to attend the John Jay College or any other educational institution where the FBI was not held in appropriate esteem. Shaw sued for reinstatement, and on behalf of agents' freedom of speech, but ultimately dropped his efforts to return to the Bureau and settled for damages of $13,000. He eventually came back into the Justice Department after Hoover died, first working for the Office of National Narcotics Intelligence, then the Drug Enforcement Administration, and eventually the department's Office of Management and Finance.[2]

Hoover had some extraordinary fetishes. His dislike for sweaty or moist palms was rumored to be so extreme that some desperate agents with hands that tended to perspire were nearly driven to seek medical or psychiatric assistance in advance of an occasion when they were expected to shake hands with the Director. Jay Robert Nash, in *Citizen Hoover*, tells of an incident in which Hoover, meeting with a new agents class, stared repeatedly at one man in the group who had a

---

[2] The Bureau can bear a long grudge on its late Director's behalf, however. When it issued passes in 1975 authorizing access to the new FBI building for certain Justice Department personnel, it excluded Shaw.

sallow complexion. The reason was that the man had been wounded in the face during wartime combat, and plastic surgery had been only partially successful; but Hoover didn't like his men to look that way, and so the prospective new agent, who had previously done well during the training course, was told that he had failed a critical examination. The Director also instituted a stringent "weight-control program" which followed a life insurance company chart and went well beyond the actual restrictions within which men would be able to perform their jobs effectively. But resourceful individuals sometimes found their way around the rules, and on occasion the nation's number one G-man was easily fooled. Kenneth Whittaker, for example, later special-agent-in-charge of the Miami Field Office, once found himself overweight in advance of a scheduled interview with Hoover. He solved the problem by buying a suit and shirt that were too big for him — to create the impression that he had lost weight, rather than gained it — and personally thanked the Director for "saving my life" with the weight requirements. In another instance a man slated to be assigned to one of the Bureau's overseas offices was hesitant to keep an appointment with the Director because he had gone bald since their last meeting and Hoover did not like to promote bald men. Thinking ahead, and with the help of some clever colleagues, the man wrote to Hoover saying he felt that it would be selfish and unfair to take up the Director's precious time just before his annual appearance before the House Appropriations Committee. Hoover agreed and appreciated the man's sacrifice. When the agent later had to visit Hoover on his return from the overseas post, he brought the Director a gift large enough to distract his attention from his offensive hairless scalp.

Gifts to Hoover — and sometimes to Tolson — were the clue to many dramatic promotions and rapid advances within the FBI ranks. One up-and-coming man had especially good luck after giving the Director a custom-made Persian rug with the initials JEH woven into the center. After a time, major gifts to Hoover from the top leadership were, in effect, informally required on such occasions as his birthday and the yearly anniversary of his appointment as Director. Each time his choice, usually things for the home, would be communicated through Tolson, and then the assistant directors would chip in the appropriate amount of money to try to find the item wholesale through Bureau contacts. On Hoover's last Bureau anniversay before his death, his forty-seventh on May 10, 1971, his aides spent almost two hundred dollars on a trash compacter obtained through an FBI friend at the RCA Whirlpool Corporation. Sometimes, if Hoover was not particularly fond of a gift, he would not hesitate to give it to someone else in the Bureau, even though the recipient might have seen it the first time around. It saved him money. On one occasion, office assistant Sam Noisette was surprised and pleased to receive an expensive pair of cuff links from his boss; then he discovered that they were engraved with JEH on the back.

In order to believe that he looked good himself, the Director often needed to hear that others looked bad. Some of his men played up to that need. In an FBI memorandum that became available to Justice Department officials during a court case in the 1960s, an assistant director, James H. Gale, described to Hoover a meeting with the attorney general, in this case Nicholas deB. Katzenbach — Gale wrote that the attorney general "squirmed" in his chair and "turned pale" during the discussion; when they later shook hands, the assistant director said, the attorney general's hand was "cold and clammy." On another occasion, Hoover returned from a meeting at the White House with President Truman and was furious — the Director had quoted a passage from the Bible and Truman had insisted he was misquoting and had corrected him. Back at the Bureau, Hoover wanted the matter researched. As it turned out, the Director was wrong; but his aides twisted the context and presented their findings to Hoover so that it was the President who seemed foolish.

Others found different routes to favor with the Director. One, Robert Kunkel, spent years as a clerk under the tutelage of Hoover's influential secretary Helen Gandy; she was generally considered to be responsible for his becoming an agent and, eventually, a special-agent-in-charge (although he also gained some leverage by giving good stock market tips to the Director). John F. Malone, long the special-agent-in-charge in Los Angeles and later the assistant-director-in-charge in New York, is another Bureau executive who became close to Hoover, in part because of the friendship he developed with bandleader Lawrence Welk, whose television program was one of the Director's favorites.

Even those who admired Hoover's style and tolerated some of his excesses had difficulty with his more irrational and extreme acts. He tended, for example, to go overboard in trying to correct abuses or avoid controversy. After the Central Intelligence Agency was exposed in the late 1960s for having funded the National Student Association and other university groups, the Director for a time withdrew authorization for anyone in the FBI to contact anyone on any campus, a ruling that made it difficult for agents to handle some routine inquiries. Eventually he relented. When Hoover declared in 1969 that agents were forbidden to fly on Trans World Airlines, because a TWA pilot had criticized the FBI's handling of a hijacking crisis, agents simply ignored the order because, as aides had tried to point out to Hoover, there were some air routes covered only by TWA. (In connection with the same incident, Hoover wrote to the president of the airline and, apparently drawing upon confidential files, told of the pilot's earlier "difficulties in the Air Force.") When Hoover was dissatisfied with the cooperation of the Xerox Corporation in the investigation that followed the theft and distribution of documents from the Bureau's Media, Pennsylvania, Resident Agency, he sought to have all Xerox photocopying machines removed from all FBI offices and replaced with another brand; that plan was canceled only when assistant directors persuaded him that the change would be cumbersome, time-consuming, and expensive.

It required considerable Bureau resources to build and nourish the desired public interest in Hoover. A "correspondence section" handled the replies to incoming mail that sought personal information about the Director, ranging from his favorite recipe for apple turnovers to how he ate his steak and what color neckties he preferred. Sometimes the correspondence was handled in a laughable, almost cynical way. Once, for example, a two-page letter was drafted explaining why Hoover's favorite hymn was "When the Roll Is Called up Yonder." When the Director saw the draft, he changed his mind and ordered up a new one giving his choice as "Rock of Ages." The correspondence section merely substituted the name of one hymn for the other and sent the letter out, with the explanation for the choice left the same.

One of the major occasions for pronouncements of wisdom from the Director was his annual trip to Capitol Hill to justify the Bureau's budget request before the House Appropriations Committee. (He testified only occasionally before the parallel Senate committee.) The transcripts of these sessions read smoothly and show Hoover first giving an eloquent statement and then responding with impressive clarity to every question posed by his congressional interrogators. Bureau officials familiar with the closed-door committee meetings, however, say that quite a lot of work went into sprucing up the public version of the transcripts; one told it this way: "There would be serious mistakes every time he appeared, especially before the House committee. The Director would recite the facts concerning particular cases, and he might have them all wrong, even providing false information about individuals. Sometimes he would be completely off base, especially when he attempted to answer the congressmen's questions. . . . So we would always get the record back the next day, and we would work almost around the clock for three or four days to straighten it out. The job was controlled by John Mohr in the Administrative Division. We would take out the garrulous crap and replace it with perfect language and grammar. When the record came out [publicly], it would be beautiful; it had to be, because Hoover would issue it to everyone on the FBI mailing list. . . . The congressmen were proud to be part of it all, and most of them probably didn't even notice the difference."

But some of the Hoover statements were impossible to take out or doctor up, especially if some of the legislators had immediately latched on to them for their own purposes. The story is told of the occasion in the late 1940s when the Director was asked how much crime cost the country each year and he answered, off the top of his head, twenty-two billion dollars. Back at headquarters later, in trying to justify the figure, the best anyone could come up with was eleven billion. But the public record was left to stand, of course, since Hoover's word was assumed to be gospel. That figure was used blindly for years until finally someone wrote in and asked why, in light of the increase in crime, its cost to the nation never changed. From that time on, the Bureau began raising the estimate slightly each year.

These slips and quirks were not publicly known, however, and even had they been revealed, they would have posed no serious threat to Hoover's position. He had himself locked securely in place and employed foolproof techniques for keeping himself there. One was to let it be widely known, or at least believed, that his men in the field were collecting juicy tidbits about political figures, unrelated to pending cases but submitted for Hoover's personal interest and, if necessary, his use. Francis Biddle, one of President Franklin Roosevelt's attorneys general with whom Hoover got along well, wrote in his memoirs that the Director, in private sessions with him, displayed an "extraordinarily broad knowledge of the intimate details of what my associates in the Cabinet did and said, of their likes, their weaknesses and their associations." Such information was stored in special locked file cabinets in Hoover's inner office. Access was permitted to only about ten Hoover lieutenants through Miss Gandy. The Director's personal files included some political dynamite — allegations about the extramarital affairs of President Roosevelt and his wife Eleanor, the inside story about an undersecretary of state believed to be a homosexual and his alleged attempt to seduce a porter during a train ride to Tennessee, incidents from Richard Nixon's years as Vice-President, and the early escapades of John F. Kennedy. The files grew thicker and more significant all the time, because whenever someone entered the running for President, Hoover would have any records on him in the Bureau's general files pulled out, updated, and transferred to his office. What use Hoover made of any particular file is a matter of speculation; but what is now clear is that the implicit threat to use them was always there. It was one way of instilling in politicians a special kind of loyalty toward the FBI: fear of what Hoover might have on them and could choose to reveal. What became of each of Hoover's controversial private files after his death is still a subject of some mystery and concern. Miss Gandy and Tolson are each believed to have taken some with them when they left the Bureau, and others were moved into the office of W. Mark Felt, who became acting associate director under Acting Director L. Patrick Gray III, and were later inherited by Associate Director Nicholas Callahan. Many of the files are unaccounted for and were probably shredded before Hoover died or shortly after.

Attorney General Edward H. Levi, testifying before the House Judiciary Subcommittee on Civil Rights and Constitutional Rights on February 27, 1975, announced an inventory of the 164 files that had been made available to him from the associate director's office. Classified as Official and Confidential material or marked OC, they included "many routine, mundane and totally innocuous materials," Levi said; but he also acknowledged that at least forty-eight of the folders contained "derogatory information concerning individuals," including members of Congress. It seemed clear that some of the most important OC files were missing — and that there was probably another entire set of delicate Hoover files, perhaps labeled Personal and Confidential, that were missing and were never made available to the attorney general at all. Miss Gandy later admitted destroying the "personal" files.

Another of Hoover's successful techniques was to calculate carefully his relationships with those in power. As one former associate noted, the Director had "many of the attributes of a genius. He could identify people's foibles and weaknesses and play upon them cleverly." He was not particularly fond of the Kennedy brothers, but the brother he liked least was Robert, who sought to assert unprecedented control over the FBI when he became his brother's attorney general. (One irritant, according to those in the Justice Department in the early 1960s, was Kennedy's personal comportment; Hoover felt that he desecrated the hallowed halls of the Justice Department by strolling around in his shirtsleeves and by bringing his dog to the office.) Hoover knew of, and exploited, Lyndon Johnson's distrust of Robert Kennedy, and immediately after John Kennedy's assassination the Director virtually suspended communication with the attorney general. He replaced a Kennedy intimate, Courtney Evans, as White House liaison with a Johnson favorite, Cartha D. DeLoach. Hoover's antennae were excellent and helped him move quickly to keep up with any realignment of power.

Whatever the complaints about Hoover, most observers generally praised him for keeping the Bureau honest and above the temptation of corruption to which so many other law enforcement agencies succumbed. But it has become clear that the Director himself did not measure up to the rigorous standards of honesty and avoidance of conflict of interest that he set for others. In an agency where a man could be severely disciplined for taking an office car home overnight without special permission, it was a little difficult to reconcile and justify the fact that the Director had five bulletproof limousines, each worth about $30,000, at his service — two in Washington and one each in Los Angeles, New York, and Miami — and that he regularly used them for personal business, like trips to the racetrack or on his vacations with Tolson. The vacations, in Florida or southern California, were never officially called vacations but "inspection trips" — meaning that Hoover would drop in at a field office or two each time and shake hands. That was enough for him to charge the whole trip to the government.

In Miami Hoover stayed free at a hotel owned by Meyer Schine, who admitted in congressional testimony that he also had ties with big-name bookmakers. (Schine's son, G. David, was counsel to Senator Joseph McCarthy's investigating subcommittee, along with Roy Cohn.) In La Jolla, California, his stays at the Hotel Del Charro were at no cost, courtesy of the owners, millionaire Texas businessmen Clint Murchison and Sid Richardson. Sometimes they had elaborate parties in La Jolla in Hoover's honor, flying in specially prepared chili from Texas for the occasion; the bills that were never presented to Hoover and Tolson ran into the thousands of dollars. Murchison and Richardson gained control of a nearby racetrack that Hoover frequented; some of the profits from it were supposed to be channeled to a newly established charitable foundation, but prominent members of the foundation board soon quit when they found that this was not happening. Both of these Hoover friends came under investigation in the mid-1950s in connection with a controversial proxy fight to win control of the New York Central Railroad, and it was learned years later that Richardson, who had extensive oil holdings, made payments to Robert Anderson while Anderson was serving as President Eisenhower's secretary of the treasury and was in a position to influence national oil policy. By means that were never publicly known, Hoover himself amassed substantial oil, gas, and mineral leases in Texas and Louisiana — they were valued at $125,000 at the time of his death — alongside his other valuable investments. All the while the Director was growing rich, he never hesitated to accept free accommodations wherever he traveled.

His annual visit to the West Coast became one of the most important events on Hoover's calendar. If the invitation to stay at the Del Charro did not arrive on schedule, the SAC in San Diego was asked to nudge it along. One year the field office there was sent into a frenzy because it had neglected to stock the hotel's freezer with the Director's favorite ice cream. When he asked for it upon arrival, the SAC had to call the ice cream manufacturer to open his plant at night in order to satisfy Hoover's needs. A stenographer from the field office was then dressed up as a waitress and dispatched to the Del Charro to serve the ice cream to Hoover and Tolson.

The Director eagerly used the extensive and sometimes expert facilities of the Bureau for his own personal whim and benefit. He was reluctant, ostensibly for security reasons, to permit outside workmen in or near his home, so it was the FBI Laboratory that performed such duties as building a porch or installing new appliances. The Lab was sent in on one occasion because Hoover was impatient with how long it took his television set to start up. The problem was solved by rigging the unit so that it was always on; he just had to turn it up to get the picture. Unknown to Hoover, this just meant that the tubes burned out and had to be changed often — at government expense. Sometimes the Lab's assignments nearly resulted in disaster, as on the occasion Hoover decided that he wanted a new toilet installed. But the Director did not like the new one, because it was too low, and he demanded the old one back. Fortunately, the technicians were able to reclaim it from a junk heap after a search.

In his earliest days at the Bureau, Hoover had steadfastly and emphatically declined to profit from the G-man boom, turning back the honoraria when he gave speeches and declining to endorse cigarettes or other commercial products. But as time passed he became avaricious. When the Freedoms Foundation, a conservative organization based in Valley Forge, Pennyslvania, twice gave him its gold medal and five-thousand-dollar award, it called ahead to the Director's aides, pointing out that it was customary for the recipient of the award to donate the money back to the foundation. Both times Hoover refused and said he intended to keep the money for himself. Perhaps the most profitable transactions, however, involved the books published under Hoover's name, especially the enormously successful *Masters of Deceit,* subtitled *The Story of Communism in America and How to Fight It.* The book was written primarily by agent Fern Stukenbroeker, a Bureau researcher on subversive groups, but the substantial royalties were divided five ways — one-fifth each to Hoover; Tolson; Assistant-to-the-Director Louis B. Nichols; William I. Nichols (no relation to Louis), editor and publisher of *This Week* magazine, who helped to market the book; and the FBI Recreation Association — which permitted the Director to contend that the profits were going to the hard-working FBI personnel. Hoover aides urged that Stukenbroeker be rewarded for his efforts with an incentive award. Hoover balked, but agreed after a dispute; however, he knocked the amount down from five hundred dollars to two hundred and fifty. Later, when Warner Brothers wanted to launch a television series about the FBI, Hoover's condition was that the film studio purchase the movie rights to *Masters of Deceit.* His price was seventy-five thousand dollars. As the deal was being closed, the Director suddenly got cold feet and worried whether he would be subjecting himself to criticism. He sent Cartha DeLoach to President Johnson to discuss the situation, and Johnson gave his confidential approval. The television series, with Efrem Zimbalist, Jr., as the star, got off to a successful start. Hoover pocketed the money and later left it to Clyde Tolson.

When J. Edgar Hoover died suddenly on May 2, 1972, the news was initially kept from the agents for about three hours; the day began like any other in the Bureau, early and busily. When the word finally came out, it was greeted with a combination of shock and relief. Some felt comfort, for Hoover's sake, that he had died painlessly and in the job rather than suffering the indignity of replacement after forty-eight years; others looked ahead to the opportunity, at last, for a review and reconsideration of the FBI and its roles. Many were oblivious to the turmoil Hoover was leaving behind, and few sensed the trouble ahead.

That night, hundreds of agents and former agents, some traveling from far away, gathered at a funeral home in Washington to pay their respects to the Director. One who came from out of town later recalled the scene this way: "They had washed his hair, and all the dye had come out. His eyebrows, too. He looked like a wispy, gray-haired, tired little man. There, in the coffin, all the front, all the power and the color had been taken away."

The next day his body lay in state in the rotunda of the United States Capitol and Hoover was eulogized by Chief Justice Warren E. Burger as "a man who epitomized the American dream of patriotism, dedication to duty and successful attainment." A day later, in the National Presbyterian Church, President Nixon added his own tribute: "He was one of those individuals who, by all odds, was the best man for a vitally important job. His powerful leadership by example helped to keep steel in America's backbone and the flame of freedom in America's soul." He was buried not at Arlington National Cemetery but, in accordance with his instructions, at the Congressional Cemetery in the Capitol Hill section of Washington, with members of his family.

On the first anniversary of Hoover's death — a day that one can imagine Hoover would have wanted to be elaborately noted — there was no ceremony because the FBI was in disarray. On the second anniversary, Director Clarence M. Kelley led the assistant directors in a solemn, private wreath-laying ceremony at the Director's grave. For the faithful, that made things seem a little better again.

FBI DIRECTOR J. EDGAR HOOver became a legend in his own time. He was the paradigm of the bureaucratic politician, building an empire that transcended and circumvented the formal lines of authority that placed the FBI under the attorney general. Presidents did not attempt to fire Hoover, as some of them would have liked, nor did powerful members of Congress call for the director's resignation. They did not love Hoover, but feared him and respected his power.

The bureaucracy is highly political at every level, but especially at the top. Those who make the bureaucracy a life-long career must play a particularly astute political game if they want to maintain and expand the power they have attained. Civil Service laws protect the lowly bureaucrat, but not the ambitious one who has achieved a policymaking position by moving up from within the bureaucracy.

Outside political appointees, such as cabinet secretaries, must also be skilled in making their voices heard at the White House, on Capitol Hill, and within their own departments. Unlike their bureau chiefs and many of their principal aides, however, cabinet secretaries usually have a firm base outside of the bureaucracy to which they happily return if trouble overwhelms them. When President Jimmy Carter fired Joseph Califano, his secretary of Health, Education and Welfare, Califano simply returned to his prosperous Washington law practice where he reportedly makes $1.5 million a year, a sharp contrast to his $60,000 per year salary as secretary. There are others like Califano, such as Caspar Weinberger, Reagan's defense secretary, and John Connally, former Texas governor and treasury secretary under Nixon, who move in and out of government with ease, all of the time maintaining their reputations for power.

By contrast with the Califanos of the political world, those who have chosen to make the bureaucracy a permanent career must construct barriers against the winds of political change, or learn to bend with them. Those who stay in power often use their entrepreneurial talents to build empires that are immune from outside attack. Others learn to serve, or appear to serve, their master of the moment. The entrepreneurs, such as J. Edgar Hoover and Admiral Hyman Rickover, often become public figures because of their ability to cultivate and manipulate the press. But there are largely invisible bureaucrats as well who eschew publicity and remain in power by making themselves indispensable to their chiefs.

The following selection depicts both the entrepreneurial, often flamboyant holders of bureaucratic power, and those that quietly stay at the top by effectively adjusting to constant political change.

25 Jonathan Alter
THE POWERS THAT STAY

What's hard, at the political level [of the bureaucracy], is *staying* in — figuring out how to avoid those four-year dry spells when all you can do is write op-ed pieces, agonize over lunch dates, and decide which boring law firm or think tank to bide your time in while waiting for a chance to get back to the action. The real survivors don't have to worry that they're not so terrific at picking *which* obscure former governor will win the Iowa caucuses. Why sweat it? They're still in.

How does this group of high-wire performers do it? Well, most of the survivors themselves aren't of much help beyond a grunt or two and the startling revelations that they "worked hard" or "just outlived 'em." Like other great con men, they can't ever admit their secrets, for if they do — confessing to "gambits" and "techniques" — it's a good bet they've just taken the first step toward permanent retirement. That's because success in this slippery game is determined by whether they have come to believe their own cons, and whether they've so adroitly melded their personalities, instincts, and accomplishments that they fool everybody, even themselves.

But taking that as a given, there are basically two ways of surviving in the government: call them "ring kissing" and "empire building." Ring kissing is based on the model practiced by low-level civil servants and other prostrate subordinates throughout American society, but at the high levels we're talking about, it must be perfected to an art form. This requires that the aspiring survivor perform all sorts of tasks that convince his superiors (and potential future superiors) that he is indispensable. By making the boss look good, or by simply doing the boss's bidding, the imaginative ring kisser can collect a government check practically forever.

Empire building, by contrast, doesn't require the help of superiors at all. In fact, the best empire builders have prevailed over active opposition from presidents, cabinet secretaries, and others who would prefer they hang up their spikes. They survive by carving out independent power bases that are stronger than normal lines of authority, and by developing constituencies on Capitol Hill and in the press that help them to pursue their own goals. Because these goals are their own and not simply a divining of what the boss wants, the empires often take

Reprinted with permission from *The Washington Monthly*, March 1982, pages 10–18. Copyright 1982 by The Washington Monthly Co., 2712 Ontario Road, N.W., Washington, D.C. 20009.

on a momentum that translates into longevity for the people who build them.

Ring kissers, you may have guessed, are by far the more common breed. In fact, most government officials planning a career in survival are only dimly aware that another model exists. This is their loss, for the very greatest of Washington players — the sultans of survival — have rejected supplication as a technique. The career of Hyman Rickover certainly testifies to that. He served in the navy for more than sixty years, at least half of them under chiefs of naval operations who would have preferred he stay submerged for good after one of his sea trials. Or consider J. Edgar Hoover. Almost every president and attorney general he served under during his forty-eight-year career as director of the FBI disliked him, but when he left the bureau, it was on his back. These masters may have been exceptions, but the skills they plied contain some useful lessons about how to complete lengthy service in the U.S. government — and how to do it without acting like a toady.

Shanghai Log Cabins

To get a sense of the real difference between the two kinds of survival, let's look at a few examples of people who fall into the ring-kissing category, who fit the conventional image of how a "Washington survivor" is supposed to behave.

The man believed by himself and some others to be Washington's "ultimate survivor" is Joseph Laitin, a public affairs officer who survived at a high level from Kennedy to Johnson to Nixon to Ford to Carter. Laitin's aim was to serve his "client," as he put it, the point being that clients tend to appreciate good service and respond with job security. His biggest client was Lyndon Johnson, and his idea of serving him — in fact the principal Joe Laitin accomplishment of the years he spent as deputy White House press secretary — was to feed the president gossip. When LBJ went to the ranch, he'd call Laitin frequently at about 11 to hear scuttlebutt on reporters traveling to Texas. Johnson felt particularly unfriendly toward one reporter for the old *New York Herald Tribune*, and Laitin was only too happy to regale the boss with tales of the reporter's after-hours activities. "At first I told true stories about him," Laitin has proudly recounted on several occasions, "but then I began making them up. I think the president knew I was making them up, but he loved it just the same."

That story, pathetic as it is, has been trotted out for years as testimony to Laitin's uncanny ability to survive. Of course, "serving the client" can also take the form of genuinely helping the boss, and Laitin was good at that, too. So good, in fact, that the Ford and Carter White Houses got angry at him because he made his clients, James Schlesinger under Ford and Michael Blumenthal under Carter, look good in the press at the expense of the president.

Take the time Treasury Secretary Blumenthal flew out to the Far East for meetings. As assistant secretary for public affairs, Laitin went too, fulfilling the classic survivalist dictum that you should always travel with the boss. (The logic, now a bit dated, being that if you and the chief happen upon certain naughty diversions, it makes it hard for him ever to fire you.) Anyway, Laitin, employing his gift, suddenly insisted that Blumenthal visit Shanghai, where the new treasury secretary had lived as a boy after escaping Nazism. "That's your log cabin," Laitin told him. Blumenthal made the trip and came away with enormous publicity, not to mention respect for Laitin. Was Laitin providing good information to the public about economic issues? That didn't matter to Blumenthal. Was the large section of the department for which he was responsible well run? That didn't matter either.

So Laitin, like countless other ring kissers, could hardly be blamed for sensing that all that really matters in surviving is pleasing those above you. As for subordinates, according to this model of survival they aren't especially relevant. That explains why reporters tend to like Laitin as a person and as a professional (in part because he leaked a lot), while a number of former subordinates show a decided lack of enthusiasm on the subject of their old chief. If Laitin was known around press haunts as a guy who never forgot the name of an important reporter or government official, at Treasury he spent so much time on the phone and out to lunch that he is said not to have known even the names of two of the secretaries in his own office. A few years earlier, while at the FAA, he walked into the office of one of his top staffers one day and the secretaries remarked that they had never even *seen* him before. But why should they have? Laitin wasn't building an empire; he was building a reputation — for service to superiors.

As you can imagine, such reputations don't often depend heavily on a person's beliefs. Like most public affairs officers — indeed, like most ring kissers who bounce from agency to agency — Laitin was not much of a policy man. To come across as one is considered bad form for survivors choosing this mode, the obvious reason being that the more closely associated you are with a particular policy, the worse off you'll be when administrations change. (The new guard can usually tell the difference between those who make policy and those who just mouth it.) On the other hand, if you don't identify with the administration at least partially, you could be out *before* the next election. So there's a balance to be struck.

A man who has spent the better part of a lifetime striking that balance is Dwight Ink, who for thirty years was a top manager at a half-dozen different agencies. Ink was a competent manager as managers go, but his greatest skill, according to several people who worked with him, was appearing neither too partisan nor too facelessly neutral. The latter is the way most career civil servants play it, and that's why few rise to be superbureaucrats at a political level. Ink was different. Whether he was at the AEC, or HUD, or OMB he could subtly — and without really saying anything — convey a sympathy with the prevailing political ideology, then just as effortlessly shed those few calculated ounces of conviction when bosses or administrations changed.

"If he knew what the secretary wanted, he'd help you get it," recalls Charles Haar, a Harvard law professor who was an assistant secretary of HUD in the late 1960s when Ink was assistant secretary for administration. "But he'd never move anything too fast; the instinct was for more paper, more copies, more dotted i's and crossed t's rather than for getting something done." The reason for that, as Haar and others have noted, is that getting something done too fast might have put him in a vulnerable position, and that kind of vulnerability is what the ring kissing survivalist fears most.

Like many other administrators who endure for years, Ink is smart, hard working, and competent; that's his reputation, and it's one reason he gets tapped so frequently. The problem with the definition lies with that word "competence." More often than not, the word has come to mean a peculiarly calibrated type of bureaucratic performance that doesn't have much to do with commitment to goals. While sometimes sharing and acting upon the boss's goals, subordinates too often substitute for genuine aims the kind of "managerial" efficiencies that so many administrators mistakenly believe can be separated from issues of policy.

Thus, just as Joe Laitin never cared much about the politics of his clients as long as they sold briskly and reflected well on the salesman, so Dwight Ink never cared much about the prevailing philosophy of government as long as it allowed him to "do the job," whatever that meant. Given that, it was no big surprise when Ink accepted Reagan's offer last year to come out of retirement and coordinate the dismantling of the Community Services Administration, snuffing out some of the very same programs he once helped create while working at HUD. It wasn't that Ink had decided on long reflection that the programs didn't work. He simply did what good ring kissers believe they are supposed to do. He did what he was told.

Wind Sniffing

Now, in some ways it's a little unfair to single out Laitin and Ink. After all, they simply responded to the same ground rules for survival that most other upper-level bureaucrats, including many still in the government, subscribe to. Take William Heffelfinger of the Department of Energy. Reagan is planning to put DOE out of its misery, and Heffelfinger, as assistant secretary for management and administration, will do the bulk of the honors (the secretary, James Edwards, is a deferential sort of tooth puller). The fact that Heffelfinger held a similar job under Carter when the department was *created* passes in Washington without notice. After all, the standard response goes, these are bureaucrats we're talking about, and they're supposed to be "professionals."

Heffelfinger's hard-nosed — many call it brutal — style of management is said to be the only reason he survives at all. A congressional subcommittee learned in 1978 that during his many earlier government incarnations he had falsified his resume by adding degrees and awards he never received, and had destroyed public documents, among other vices. When a man can undergo a full-scale congressional investigation and still get reappointed — and the reason he can get the new job is that he has a reputation for cracking the whip and otherwise pleasing whoever is boss — the legend of this route to survival grows stronger. This is true despite the fact that Heffelfinger does not appear to act like a timid ring kisser. He yells and screams and tries to be a "tough" manager who gets things done. Depending on whom you talk to, that may even be true. The point, though, is that he furthers the impression that the best strategy for getting ahead in the government is to do others' bidding rather than your own. Heffelfinger may have missed out on other survivalist secrets — a clean nose, for instance — but he remembered the one about sniffing the wind to catch the drift of one's superiors.

The current master of that art is Frank Carlucci, a hard-working, bright, former foreign service officer, ambassador, deputy director of the Office of Economic Opportunity, deputy director of OMB, deputy CIA director, and now deputy secretary of defense. Carlucci's legendary budget-cutting abilities, like those of his current boss, Cap (nee "the Knife") Weinberger, were dulled considerably once it became clear what *Weinberger's* boss — the president — really thought about defense spending. The quickness of Carlucci's response to Reagan's concerns about leaks testifies to this uncanny meteorological ability that is so often believed to be essential for ring-kissing survival. Carlucci embraced and implemented the order that lie detector tests be administered to senior defense officials. And like the good soldier he is, went first.

Ultimately, the lie detectors may prove far more destructive to Reagan than the leaks. As high-ranking Carter administration officials can attest, nothing so quickly breaks down basic loyalty to a president as this particular brand of faith in one's trustworthiness. But more to the point, the lie detectors prove once and for all that Carlucci belongs among the ring kissers. He apparently considers it a productive day's work to have humiliated colleagues and subordinates in order to keep the boss happy.

Persuasion by Polar Water

Of course in his heart of hearts, Frank Carlucci probably doesn't like ring kissing very much. In his line of work, ambition is not easily sublimated, and people who know him say that his will to survive is developing into a will to conquer. What Carlucci may be learning is that conquering can assure surviving, and that it makes some sense to develop empire-building skills, which in Washington means contacts in the press and on the Hill. These contacts are not meant to make your boss look good (the survival technique of a Laitin) but to make *you* look good, and to hell with your boss.

The greatest empire builder of recent years is Admiral Hyman G. Rickover, who as a captain after World War II came up with an idea — nuclear submarines — and in the next thirty-five years proceeded to shape almost every aspect of the U.S. navy: training, technology, surface ships, and so forth. The way he did it is a fascinating story, but equally interesting is the way he got away with it without losing his job.

It was in 1952 that Rickover first realized the classic ring-kissing route wouldn't work for him. He had already beaten the odds and made great progress on the development of the first nuclear submarine (it was eventually finished many years ahead of schedule), but that year a navy selection board passed him over for promotion from captain to rear admiral for the second time. Whether it was because of his Jewish background or simply that he already nettled navy brass, his career appeared over. Up to then, two rejections meant automatic retirement.

But Rickover was smart enough to know that if he could create enough interest outside the navy, he might have a fighting chance after all. In part because he had a sexy project (though it really wasn't much more newsworthy that year than a lot of what goes on in government today), he caught the attention of the press, particularly a young Pentagon correspondent for *Time* named Clay Blair. Blair knew a good story when he saw one, and Rickover knew how to be cooperative — he even lent the use of his office and his wife's editing skills for the book Blair eventually wrote about him. In later years, once safely ensconced, Rickover shunned reporters. But when it counted he played them masterfully, especially those journalists like Edward R. Murrow whom he knew could endow him with some of their own respectability.

Meanwhile, he wasted no time meeting the right people on the Hill. The year before the promotion controversy he happened to have been seated on an airplane next to a young politician named Henry Jackson. They became friends, and along with Rep. Sidney Yates, Jackson led the charge that forced the navy to make Rickover a rear admiral, notwithstanding the selection board's decision. Rickover reached the mandatory retirement age for all navy personnel in 1963, but until last year (when at age eighty-one he almost sank a submarine while at the controls) he continually had been granted special two-year extensions, a biennial event that caused untold teeth gnashing among his superiors.

Why did Congress admire Rickover so much? Part was clever flattery. He took members on submarine rides, wrote them hundreds of handwritten notes while on historic sea trials (who wouldn't save a letter with the dateline, "At Sea, Submerged"?), and brought back "polar water" as gifts for their offices. But most important, according to his recent biographers, Norman Polmar and Thomas B. Allen, was a peculiar "chemistry" he developed with many congressmen that made them believe they actually were involved with the building of the world's first nuclear-powered submarine and, later, with the creation of a nuclear navy. That chemistry — a critical element in any kind of empire building — is really just the reflection of an ability to accomplish goals.

The fact that Congress and the press respond best to tangible achievement — as opposed to loyal ring kissing — has not always been a positive thing for the country. Just because reporters and congressmen can see it, touch it, and report it back home, doesn't mean the rest of us need it, as Rickover's success in winning support for a poorly conceived weapon like the Trident submarine suggests. But if this kind of congressional behavior can bring us bad weapons and wasteful pork barrel projects, it can also bring out the best in government employees — the desire to create and produce, and the understanding that if you do a good enough job in those areas, forces outside the bureaucracy will help you survive.

Rickover should be particularly inspirational to budding empire builders because he proves that rank plays no role in such survival. He was a *fourth-echelon* officer (as deputy commander for nuclear propulsion, Naval Ships System Command, he reported to the chief of naval materiel, who reported to the chief of naval operations, who reported to the president). That's not to say he didn't use what position he did have, but in Rickover's case this meant an additional position *outside* of the navy, at the Atomic Energy Commission (and later at the Department of Energy).

Many powerful survivors have donned two hats before — Richard J. Daley was both mayor of Chicago and chairman of the powerful party committee that slated candidates for mayor of Chicago — but Rickover elevated it into an art form. Admiral Elmo Zumwalt, who despised Rickover for upstaging him when Zumwalt was chief of naval operations, recalls that when a navy request irked Rickover, his standard practice was to reply on AEC stationery, which allowed him to distribute copies of his position to congressional friends without going through the navy chain of command.

It was that chain of command that drove Rickover to distraction. Acting solicitous toward Congress and the press was one thing, the point being that it helped you accrue more autonomy for yourself. But performing like that every day for your boss was quite another (although Rickover expected it of *his* much-abused staff). "What was fatal to [General Wilhelm] Keitel [chief of Hitler's combined general staff] was not his weaknesses," Rickover lectured a congressional committee during one of his more than 150 formal appearances on the Hill, "but his virtues — the virtues of a subordinate." Among such regrettable virtues, Rickover believed, was a conception of the chain of command as something that entitled a bureaucrat to someday win perquisites. As far as he was concerned, such niceties had nothing at all to do with power and survival.

So where Frank Carlucci tends to want the best office space available, Rickover worked for thirty years out of a converted ladies room with no rug and flaking yellow plasterboard; where William Heffelfinger dines most afternoons at the likes of Le Provencal, Rickover had canned soup, cottage cheese, and skimmed milk at his desk; and where Joe Laitin, while assistant secretary of defense, bragged that he sat ahead of the generals in a motorcade, Rickover rarely wore a uniform and was indifferent to the idea of a fourth star. After all, he reasoned, what did organization charts have to do with building and keeping an empire?

Passport to Perpetuation

Now, not everybody in the government can, or should, think like Hyman Rickover. If they did, we'd have a country of anarchists and ulcers. But the fact remains that in almost any realm — military or civilian — chain of command tends to impede action. The best empire builders recognize this and risk angering others in the hierarchy who believe individual initiative is a threat. Their power *and* their survival depend on a base outside the normal line of authority.

The greatest practitioner of this art was J. Edgar Hoover. When Hoover took over the FBI in 1924, it was a weak, corrupt, politicized, highly ineffective agency. When he died in 1972, the same thing might have been said. But in between, the FBI was, in the words of Victor Navasky, editor of the *Nation* and hardly a Hoover admirer, the "least corruptible, most sophisticated investigative agency in the world." Hoover revolutionized the science of crime detection — *legitimate* crime detection — by sponsoring innovation in lab work and training and by creating a high standard of performance for his agents.

The point is not to absolve this racist redbaiter of his crimes — against Martin Luther King, Jean Seberg, and the Constitution in general —

but simply to make it clear that Hoover could not rely solely on his survivalist wits. If his cagey bureaucratic abilities had not been underlain by a strong conviction on the part of outsiders that he was doing something good, he wouldn't have made it.

But accomplishment, as any government official should know, takes you only so far. Like Rickover, Hoover undertook a major effort to cultivate the press, particularly columnist Walter Winchell, and the Congress, particularly Rep. John J. Rooney, who for twenty-five years oversaw the FBI's budget. Equally important, he cultivated a public image, by using gimmicks like the Ten Most Wanted List and a long-running television series. Efrem Zimbalist, Jr., may be reluctant to star in the TV version of "The FDA" (co-starring special agent James Beard?), but that doesn't mean heads of government agencies less dramatic than the FBI cannot borrow some of the imagination Hoover used to create a public constituency for his programs.

You don't have to be as famous as Rickover or Hoover in order to use such skills. Consider the case of a woman named Frances Knight, who ran the passport office at the state department for more than twenty years, largely over the objections of most of the secretaries of state she saw come and go. These men resented her fiefdom but were essentially powerless to do anything about it. (Finally, in 1977, the state department succeeded in turning the passport office into what the career people always wanted — a place to let foreign service officers punch their tickets while waiting for another overseas assignment.)

Knight was controversial, but she realized that controversy, because it keeps the press interested, can be the stuff of survival, even for those in seemingly modest positions. She also understood that the press and Congress respond best if they are fed and cared for. When Drew Pearson called one Christmas Eve to say he needed fifteen passports right away, she hustled down to the office. When a congressman had a problem with a constituent's passport, she took care of it within hours, an ability that members of Congress still recall with awe.

These survival skills, applied on the Hill and in the press, should not necessarily make us feel more cynical about the way the government works. As it happens, Knight often would extend the same service to anyone (airline clerks at international terminals across the country had her home phone number). But even if she hadn't, such cultivation of outside sources of power isn't objectionable in itself. What is objectionable is the use of such networks solely for the purpose of surviving. When the aim instead is survival as a way of accomplishing admirable goals — even if the goal is simply running an efficient passport office — well, then even the most dubious survival techniques can be put to good use.

To demonstrate the point, let's look at the most base and contemptible of those techniques, namely Hoover's use of blackmail. The conversation with a congressman usually went something like this:

"Hello, congressman. Edgar Hoover here. Terribly sorry to hear about this unfortunate matter."

"What do you mean?"

"Well, we've had some reports that have come into our field office in your district. Frankly, I personally find them very difficult to believe. The whole thing just doesn't sound like you. But I just wanted to alert you to the fact that some reports have indeed been filtering into the Bureau."

"What reports?

"Believe me, congressman, this matter will be kept in strictest confidence between us. I've instructed the field office to route all the details of your case straight to the Director."

Whatever the congressman's little embarrassment — a drunken visit to a whorehouse, a son who happened to be a homosexual — Hoover knew how to use it to his advantage. The strategy, which didn't have to be employed too often to be effective, worked equally well with presidents. Hoover's reappointment was John Kennedy's first order of business after his election, and even after a feud broke out between Hoover and his nominal boss, Robert Kennedy (during which the director instructed tour guides at the FBI building to point out that he had become head of the bureau the year before the attorney general was born), JFK never even considered his removal. How could he? Hoover knew certain, uh, *details* about Kennedy's personal life. If William Sullivan, longtime number three man at the bureau, is to be believed, Hoover used this strategy even on Nixon of all people, after he and Bebe Rebozo were spotted in the company of a particular Chinese woman during trips to Hong Kong in the mid-1960s. By the early 1970s, Nixon, once a big Hoover booster, wanted him fired too, but like other presidents, he subscribed to Lyndon Johnson's memorable judgment that given the permeability of the administration's tent, it made more sense to have Hoover inside pissing out.

Honorable Blackmail

It doesn't require a deep sensitivity to fine moral distinctions to see that Hoover's form of persuasion constitutes the most reprehensible form of survivalism imaginable. But if you think about it a moment, you might realize that Hoover's blackmail, *sans* the prurient details, can be surprisingly instructive, especially to people who, unbelievable as it sounds, want to do good with their government service.

Suppose you hope to improve your program or agency, and that such improvement demands a certain level of performance from your boss. To the extent that you let the boss know that you are cognizant of what is wrong in this program or agency, and to the extent that he knows you care enough to do something about it, you have created in him a dependency not unlike that felt by presidents toward Hoover. This assumes, of course, that the boss is aware that you have attended to the fundamental empire-building duties of making contacts on the Hill and in the press that might allow you to make good on the implied threat of revelation, and it assumes that you have the guts to use those contacts. If the boss believes that you really are willing and able to go public, then he's more likely to want you inside his tent. That means you now have a powerful ability to pursue your own vision of how your agency or program should be run. Your boss, respecting this new power, will provide you more autonomy, which, assuming you maintain those essential outside contacts, could be the beginning of your own empire.

But what's remarkable is that even if you have no designs on an empire — even if you like your boss so much that you might be characterized as a ring kisser — you still can play a form of this game. In fact, the most effective user of constructive blackmail is the person who admires his superior, who wants to believe the best about him, who hopes that the boss soon realizes that his subordinates and all of the people who believe in his program will be disappointed if he doesn't shape up. What this really involves is a genuine, sincere version of what Hoover was disingenuously saying on the telephone to that congressman. It is an unconscious, unspoken way of playing not on the boss's fear of being exposed, but on his sense of guilt — guilt that he will disillusion those who share his goals.

Naturally, the only way the ring kisser can inspire that very positive form of guilt is if he does indeed share those goals. And if he does share them, he might not be such an objectionable ring kisser after all. Harry Hopkins (FDR's aide) and D. B. Hardeman (Sam Rayburn's aide) are examples of this better breed. Because they believed in what their bosses were trying to do, they shared in their bosses' accomplishments. Conversely, when ring kissers do not believe in what their superiors are trying to do — when they are simply determined to outlast them — then they do not share in their major accomplishments, except in the sense that they feel a little battered for having endured the long ride. Joe Laitin showed a keen sensitivity to this point when he admitted to the *Los Angeles Times* last year after his luck finally ran out that "I can't point to one thing I've accomplished, but my blood is all over this town for fighting for what I believe is right." What was "right," of course, was simply survival itself.

So the determining factor is not which strategy you choose to employ, but what you want to employ those survivalist techniques *for*. If survival is an end in itself, then none of the gambits are worthy of our respect. On the other hand, if survival is used as the means to genuine accomplishment, then ring kissing, currying favor with Congress and the press, even blackmail have their place when done constructively. That doesn't make all survival techniques equal in morality or even in plain tastefulness, but it can hook them to some larger purpose. The best survivors — the ones we all should learn something from — have made this essential connection.